APOCALYPSE SECRETS

Reviews

Apocalypse Secrets is a unique perspective on the Book of Revelation as a history of monotheistic Faiths since 96 AD...the primitive faith of Abraham, Judaism, Zoroastrianism, Buddhism, Hinduism, Christianity and Islam....Very interesting reading

—Prof. Jon Paulien, Dean of Religion, Loma Linda University

Your adaptation and application of Revelation is ingenious....I am impressed by the sheer weight of references to particular events

—Richard Woods, Professor of Theology, Dominican University

Dr Able has written an interesting provocative commentary on the Book of Revelation. He has set aside historical-critical methodology and its preterist approach in favor of a historicist approach....His commentary is well-written and clear

—Prof. Phil Muñoa, Hope College, Author of *Jesus and the Gospels*

You write stylishly and readably, and you develop intelligently your thesis that the Book of Revelation extends beyond its strictly Christic origin....More readable, better organized and more cogently argued than other treatments of the Middle Eastern context of the Book of Revelation. I came away respecting the quality of your work

—Dr Ralph Townsend, Headmaster, Winchester College, UK

Dr John Able brings a probing mind and penetrating understanding to the great religious mysteries. His book is the culmination of years of research and analysis. It is sure to be an engaging, enlightening, and thought-provoking read

—Rabbi Shmuley Boteach

Very Midrashic while etymologically interesting. I have not seen previous use of such exegesis

—Dr Harold Landa, Yeshiva University

This book is an interesting historical perspective of the Book of Revelation. It provides a new interpretation of many important passages....With colorful photographs and illustrations...imagery that adds to the understanding of the historical. The use of different type face is very effective in producing a different feeling when reading sacred text

—Mrs Marguerite Sears, Desert Rose Institute, Eloy

I admire your devotion to your goal....Your writing is colorful and alive suiting your colorful personality

—Dr Hushidar Motlagh, Author of *I Shall Come Again*

APOCALYPSE SECRETS

Baha'i Interpretation of the Book of Revelation

John Able MD

John Able Books Ltd
McLean
http://www.JohnAbleBooks.com

ISBN 9780970284785
Revised 2013/06/21
B&W softcover version (60 illustrations)
Library of Congress Control Number 2009930682

Dr John Able is a retired intensive-care physician who trained and taught at the Cambridge, University College London, Hebrew University, and Baylor Medical Schools, and practiced medicine in the UK, Israel, and USA

Apocalypse Secrets appears in the following versions, each with the same text and illustrations in B&W or color:

- This B&W softcover version ISBN 9780970284785
- A color softcover version ISBN 9780970284761
- A color hardcover version ISBN 9780970284778
- A color PDF ebook version ISBN 9780970284754
- A color EPUB ebook version ISBN 9780970284730

You can savor the spirit of *Apocalypse Secrets* and buy it at

- Amazon via http://tinyurl.com/66a3t06
- GoogleBooks via http://tinyurl.com/6xnwzy4
- Amazon Kindle ebook via http://tinyurl.com/ahs6z6m
- Your local bookstore
- Web sources of ebooks

♾The paper used in this publication meets the minimum requirements of the American National Standard for Information Services—Permanence of Paper for Printed Library Materials, ANSI Z39.48–1992

(For a very brief initial trial period, *Apocalypse Secrets* went by the now passé title *Beyond Malignant Materialism: Revelations of a Glorious New Apocalypse*)

Let your vision be world embracing. The earth is but one country and mankind its citizens

—The Messenger of the Book of Revelation[1]

To my grandchildren

May you gain inclusive vision.
Yet may a little doubt always tickle your hearts
and stop your minds falling prey to absolute truths

To all the daughters of Jerusalem

May you discover your lover

To the Messenger of the Book of Revelation

Thank you for having revealed Apocalypse secrets
and for having brought a message of
hope to the heart and
peace to the soul
in our troubled times

Apocalypse Secrets diligently honors the Integrity Formula of the Book of Revelation

The Book of Revelation ends with an integrity formula issued by its main Messenger, who warns:

> ***I myself swear to all the hearers of the Words of the prophecy in this same short scroll. If anybody add to them, God shall add to him or her the afflictions recorded in this same short scroll! If anybody take away from the Words in the short scroll of this same prophecy, God shall take away from his or her share in the Tree of Life and the Holy City recorded in this same short scroll!***[A]

In other words, nobody should dare to change the text of the Apocalypse, on pain of punishment. At the same time, the formula has always permitted translation of the original Greek into other languages like English and the insertion of modern punctuation, capitals, and chapter and verse numbers into the text.

[A] Rev. 22.18–19 on page 277

TABLE OF CONTENTS

TABLE OF ILLUSTRATIONS AND CREDITS

Art Director: Warwick Knowles, http://www.pagemarks.co.uk

Disclaimer

I have made every effort to find and contact copyright owners. However, for some illustrations, I could not trace the copyright owners or identify the photographers. Should you recognize work that is yours, please email me at *johnablebooks@gmail.com*, and I shall be glad to acknowledge it in future revisions.

Forewords

The following four forewords come from

- Dr Robert Stockman, a highly regarded member of the US Baha'i community and author of *Baha'i Faith in America*
- Rabbi Suzanne Carter, a charismatic South Florida rabbi
- Robert Riggs, author of a prior Baha'i-based interpretation of the Book of Revelation called *Apocalypse Unsealed*
- Professor David Aune, a world-renowned authority on Revelation Greek and author of *Word Biblical Commentary 52: Revelation*.

Dr Robert Stockman

I have always been skeptical about efforts to interpret prophecies. Such interpretations are attempts to discern the intent of God and are ultimately unprovable. It is rather like looking at a cloud in the sky and seeing in its ever-shifting shapes a horse, a person, or an angel. Who is to say God did not choose to make the cloud look like an angel when someone was looking at it? Who is to say the resulting (approximate) correlation of shapes was due to mere chance? How can one determine which is the case?

John Able is up against this challenge in his book *Apocalypse Secrets*. His study is the culmination of a remarkable decade-long quest. Able has carefully surveyed the Baha'i authoritative writings not only for interpretations of the Book of Revelation, but of the Bible in general and of relevant related subjects such as history, politics, and economics. He has collected every known interpretation of the Book of Revelation that 'Abdu'l-Baha and Shoghi Effendi offered to pilgrims. He has also read just about everything Bahá'ís have ever written about the subject, a level of literature research rarely seen in scholarship by Bahá'ís. To understand the text itself, he has taught himself Koine Greek, the language in which the Book of Revelation was written, and has corresponded with prominent New Testament scholars to revise his translation. He has traveled to visit some of the actual places mentioned in the Book of Revelation, to acquire a geographical feel for them. Taking all these inputs, Able decided to produce a comprehensive word-by-word, verse-by-verse commentary on the Book of Revelation followed by a detailed explanatory apparatus.

While the results are, by definition, unprovable, they are intriguing and, in some sense, testable: Is the interpretation of the Book of Revelation comprehensive? How deeply does it go? How wide ranging was the effort to collect the inputs needed to produce the result?

How many threads of the prophetic text have been woven together, and how many are left over? Is the resulting interpretation internally and rationally consistent?

On these criteria, John Able's *Apocalypse Secrets* is by far the most careful, thorough, and holistic work yet produced in the genre of Bahá'í interpretation of biblical prophecy. It leaves no narrative threads unexplained and in assembling its detailed interpretation, no stones were left unturned. Remarkably, this interpretation of the Book of Revelation based on the Baha'i Writings has been produced by someone who is not a member of the Bahá'í community. Future students of the meaning of biblical prophecies who wish to build on the insights in the Bahá'í authoritative texts will find *Apocalypse Secrets* a tour de force and an essential foundational work for their investigations.

Dr Robert H. Stockman
Instructor of Religious Studies
DePaul University, Chicago

Rabbi Suzanne Carter

Apocalypse Secrets is a unique parallel interpretation of the Book of Revelation that transcends religious dogma, bridges religious faiths, and explains nineteen hundred years of troubled events in Christianity and Islam with clarity and amazing prescience in providing a template for understanding and peace.

In the 1990s, Able discussed with me what are now main topics in his book, especially economic issues. Back then, few people in the prosperous United States or the West saw any economic reckoning coming. No one expected that such a collapse could happen. The economic system seemed just too well adjusted.

Even now, March 2009, people still do not understand—if Able is right—that the present recession is set to shrivel down into a universal paralysis "creeping over the minds and souls of men". Sadly, a global depression worse than the one that our forebears went through in the 1930s seems to be needed to open the door for spiritual economics to do its work and revive human nature.

Rabbi Suzanne Carter
Delray Beach

Author Robert Riggs

In the mid-1970s, I was at West Point attending a conference of some of America's leading military leaders and engineers. Finding a Gideon Bible in my motel room, I thought it ironic to see this symbol of peace this close to elite West Point that was training the top soldiers of one of the world's two superpowers. So I took a look at the Apocalypse in case I could discern anything pertinent to the terror of history that I was helping to perpetuate. Surprisingly some of its meanings were immediately clear to me—because I understood them within the context of the sacred Writings of the Baha'i Faith, a worldwide movement of which I was already a member.

My "Apocalyptic" success set me on an adventure of the mind to discover other meanings in this exceedingly complex book that might lie hidden under the dross of twenty centuries. My journey lasted about five years and took me into ancient lands, ancient science, and ancient minds. I discovered that every word of the Apocalypse has multiple meanings, and it would be impossible for any one person to fully end them all. Being a history buff, I was able to correlate the events of the Apocalypse with the unfolding of the spiritual history of the seven major religions of Asia from the early days of Christianity up to the present day, and even with a hint of what lies ahead for us. The result was my own *Apocalypse Unsealed.*

Now I am blinded by John Able's profound and astonishing work in biblical exegesis and the beauty of his rhetoric. It is a wonder. His amazing work is beautifully crafted and researched. One strength of his approach is that it greatly enhances the readability of the text; another is that it does not discourage the efforts of future scholars. I sincerely hope and pray that his book will reach a large readership.

This Aquarian Age is the one in which the Apocalypse and other prophetic works of antiquity are being unsealed. The treasure of priceless gems lying within this bottomless trove of wisdom and knowledge may never be exhausted.

Robert Riggs
Author of *Apocalypse Unsealed*
Charlottesville

Professor David Aune

The Revelation of John is without doubt the most puzzling of all the books in the Bible. As a New Testament scholar, I have spent much of my professional life trying to understand this enigmatical Greek text. Dr John Able has produced an accurate, idiomatic, and insightful translation of this peculiar and difficult text that is often very, very good, and includes a huge amount of research on religious history.

Though our approaches to the Revelation of John are quite different, over the last ten years or so, Dr Able and I have frequently had occasion to discuss some of the many problems associated with translating this first century text written in Koine Greek into modern English. With regard to ancient Greek, his autodidactic approach has both advantages and limitations. Important advantages in approaching a difficult text like that of the Revelation of John are the fresh perspective and enthusiasm that he brings to this peculiar Greek text. His translation, which has gone through many drafts, is couched in idiomatic English and is intended to capture nuances in the Greek original that are often unintentionally masked by standard English translations of the Revelation of John. Mitigating the limitations of his approach has been my role in our many discussions over the years of some of the many semantic and syntactic problems presented by this text. Much of our discussion has been carried on through e-mail, though we've met in various venues on three continents too.

Dr Able has produced a strikingly lively translation that sticks to the intention of the Greek original and provides an authoritative base for his distinctive interpretive approach to the text. Impressive.

David E. Aune PhD
Professor of New Testament and Christian Origins
The University of Notre Dame

Preface

In the 1950–60s, the not-so-Cold War between the Communist East and the Capitalist West was giving the world as hard a time as the war between Muslim Militarism and Malignant Materialism is giving the globe today. At the blink of an eye, Russia and America were ready to spark the smallest political clash into the nuclear holocaust of an apocalyptic *Battle of Armageddon* flashing the world white-hot.

Back then, the looming nuclear holocaust would evaporate the small English market town of Oundle where I attended boarding school. Just two miles away the military airfield of Polebrook packed the explosive power of 450 Hiroshima bombs. In World War II, the US Air Force had posted a certain Clark Gable to Polebrook. Now in the Cold War, Polebrook was hosting three *Thor* ballistic nuclear missiles as well as planes. The Thors made Polebrook a prime target for Russian nuclear strikes to evaporate, along with Oundle too. Not only had Polebrook gone up **in** the world but would soon go up **with** it.

The UK had allowed its US ally to park sixty Thors on its territory, most in East Anglia. They were valeted out in threes like eggs in each of twenty UK airfield-baskets like Polebrook. Each Thor, painted with an RAF roundel, was tipped with a 2-megaton nuclear warhead packing the explosive power of 150 Hiroshima bombs. On some Sunday afternoons, my friends and I would furtively peek through the barb-wire fence of the airfield and see a Thor lying flat out of its bunker or standing already proudly erect on its launch pad like some huge white thorn pricking up from the green countryside. Its 1,750-mile range would let it evaporate cities like Moscow, Leningrad, or Kiev, but not Stalingrad—or so we lads reckoned.

A *Thor* nuclear missile cruising through a village in East Anglia

A *Thor* nuclear missile at Polebrook Airfield 1960

Oundle bordered the strategic UK coastland closest to Russia. This flat terrain of East Anglia was dotted with scores of military airfields, which formed, as it were, the flight deck of *US-BATTLESHIP-UK*. Since World War II, the RAF and USAF had run these UK airfields jointly. They took their names from nearby picturesque villages like Polebrook, which sported cute thatched cottages, quaint family pubs, and manicured village greens smelling of new-mown grass, and echoed the clicks and calls of bucolic Saturday afternoon cricket matches and the voices of lonesome English lasses pursuing US pilots.

In World War II, the Allies had moored *US-BATTLESHIP-UK* off Europe as a key launch pad for their bombers to destroy an enemy called Nazi Germany, mere flight hours away. Now in the Cold War, the West was mooring this battleship off Europe as a key launch pad for its nuclear rockets to erase an enemy called Communist Russia, mere rocket-minutes away. While posing as a face of the West's cutely called "nuclear shield", East Anglia was really shaping the sheath of its sharp nuclear sword.

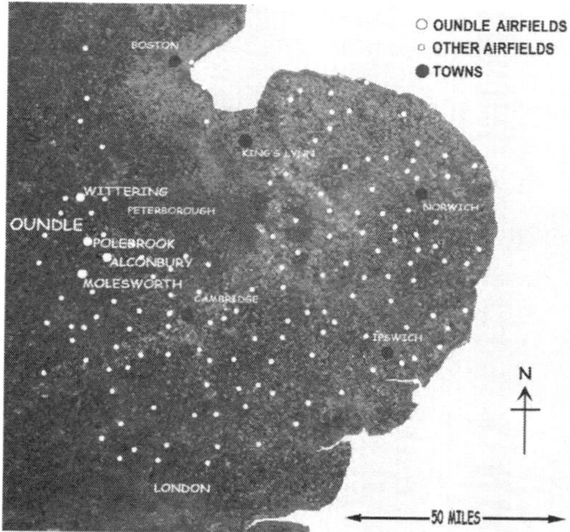

Map locating East Anglia's
RAF/USAF Cold War airfields

Oundle's productive gravel-pits had fed the acres of runway concrete of Polebrook and other airfields nearby. Alconbury, twelve miles southeast, hosted the planet's biggest-ever arsenal of nuclear bombs, with plans, planes, and pilots to deliver them. Years later, one of its retired pilots told me that his payload would have let him nuke his USSR target but would have left his fuel short for the full journey back. Wittering, sixteen miles north, bristled with a battery of rockets smaller than Thors, standing on launch pads in a field in full view right next to the main London-to-Edinburgh A1 highway. From international crisis to international crisis, their eastward tilt would visibly change even—if only to warn or disinform Russia via its UK spies. Molesworth, six miles southeast, was a dark impenetrable mystery, to be later revealed as a notorious cruise-missile base. Back then, missiles trucked to it could not even cruise through Oundle, solved by converting the town's railway line into a bypass road.

In those **MAD** days of **M**utually **A**ssured **D**estruction, East Anglia's RAF/USAF airfields were set to nuke key sites in the USSR at a nod, each airfield with its own specific agenda of destruction.. Likewise, the USSR was ready to nuke key UK and USA sites at the drop of a pin. But for us living at ground-zero, it mattered little who struck first. Either way, we would simply flash to ash, at least spared any **BANG**. Rehearsing "duck and cover" under tables like our American cousins on TV was pointless. And anyway, they too would die, but far more miserably, frozen slowly to death by nuclear winter.

Thus, our would-be halcyon schooldays had us eating and drinking the numbing bill of fare of the looming nuclear holocaust of Armageddon. At first, we breathed and slept its heavy agenda quietly with little discussion. Later on, we opened our minds, hearts, and mouths, and debated the grave prospect seriously. Soon, many of us joined the **CND C**ampaign for **N**uclear **D**isarmament and went marching to "ban the Bomb", demonstrating with others in broadening battalions.

Yet meanwhile, Oundle School was an island of peace set within the nuclear sea. Here Apocalypse images less threatening than Armageddon filled our hearts and etched our minds. We sang Apocalypse Hallelujahs in Handel's Messiah, praised its Lamb (really *Ram*) in Verdi's Requiem, and reverberated its Holy City in Blake's *Jerusalem* in our end-of-term assemblies. Our daily chitchat tripped out its buzzwords like *Millennium* and *666*. Our divinity classes emanated the essence of its incenses and the stench of its sacrifices, and explained what its Angels, Tree of Life, and New Jerusalem meant. Our Anglican Sunday chapel services set us under the gaze of the Apocalypse's *Lion, Ox, Human-Face,* and *Eagle* painted on now wooden, non-nuclear, shields hanging high on the chapel wall.

Back then, these four Living-Beings portrayed the top four Jewish Prophets Isaiah, Zechariah, Daniel, and Ezekiel, and also the four Christian Evangelists Matthew, Mark, Luke, and John. Now the same four Living-Beings portray the four Primary-Figures of the new Baha'i Faith too.

Such Book of Revelation themes hugged our young minds just as they grip the collective consciousness of the West generally via books like *Armageddon, Appointment with Destiny, End of the Age,* and *Coming Judgment of the Nations*; in movies like *Seventh Seal, Four Horsemen of the Apocalypse,* and *Pale Rider*; and as motifs for stained-glass windows in churches and in cathedrals like Chartres.

The four Living-Beings of Revelation painted on shields

Just as Old Testament Books take their very first word as their title, so the Book of Revelation takes *Apocalypse* as its title. This first word means literally *An Unveiling*—hence *A Revelation*. From here on, the name *Revelation* or *Apocalypse*[A] will be used interchangeably to refer to the Book of Revelation.

Regardless of theory or theology, practically I wanted to know **when** the looming nuclear holocaust of the Battle of Armageddon would start, naively hoping that I might escape from East Anglia in time! It was the scary word *Armageddon* that led me to read the Book of Revelation that had spawned it. Revelation mention *Armageddon* just once, in v. 16.16, between a *war of this Great Day of Almighty God*—clearly nuclear war—and a barrage of catastrophes ended by *heavy hail*—clearly nuclear missiles! Yet despite offering coded timings for other important events, the Apocalypse offered no timings for when Armageddon would begin.

[A] Orthodox and Catholic Christians tend to prefer the title *Apocalypse*. Protestants tend to prefer the title *Revelation*. The oft-heard titles *Book of Revelation**s*** or *Revelation**s*** are incorrect, however nicely they may project the Book's many visions

So, next, I tried another way to discover when our Armageddon would happen. I tried to trace the Apocalypse's predicted train of events occurring before its v. 16.16 *Armageddon*. But no unified interpretation of the Apocalypse was to be found, despite its reputation as being the Bible's most literarily unified Book. Available interpretations, mainly Christian-based, proved profoundly piecemeal, and were peppered with paradox. They explained just a verse here, a dragon there, or a number elsewhere. They failed to join the dots. They showed many Revelation trees but no Apocalypse forest. They offered many Revelation treatments but no Apocalypse cure. Even the title *Unveiling* was a divine joke, for the last thing that the Apocalypse wanted to do was to unveil anything. The pages of the Ages of its vast spans of prophetic time simply mocked the pitifully short time that my friends and I had left to live in the shadow of those Thors. Any possible Armageddon date for was simply a needle lost in the Apocalypse haystack.

Frustrated at my efforts to discover the timing of Armageddon being snubbed, breathless and irked, I abandoned my search. But at the same time, I swore angrily that I would, one day, indeed discover what the Apocalypse and its Armageddon were all about.

Just then, a sudden happy realization soothed my fears. It was so obvious, so simple, that I had missed it. After Chapter 16 and its Armageddon, the Apocalypse ran on for another six Chapters 17–22—predicting an economic collapse, a glorious Millennium, and a New Jerusalem. I read this to mean that Armageddon could **not** be global nuclear holocaust wiping humankind off the planet! Finally I felt assured that human life, including mine, would continue. Re assured, I relaxed, and did not even bother to watch the Cuba crisis wax and wane in 1962. Instead, I focused my energies and time on graduating from medical school and specializing in intensive care.

Over the next decades the fog of East-West tensions steadily cleared, the Cold War thawed, and warmer political air blew across the face of the planet. Most of East Anglia's airfields were decommissioned. Polebrook returned to farmland plus a new industrial estate. Alconbury became a base for high-altitude USAF U-2 SR-71 spy planes, then a container storage site. Molesworth turned into NATO's Joint Analysis Center for Europe. Only Wittering continues to operate as an RAF airfield.

Yet in spite of my first futile foray with prophecy, I continued to feel the power of it to reveal higher realities and to *foretell new things before they sprout.*[2-J] Appreciating the power of prophecy has helped me make sense of the human lot and of the sufferings of my patients.

The voice of one set of Old Testament prophecies rang especially loud. These prophecies predicted that the People of Israel would return to their homeland from all corners of the earth. And lo and behold, within my own lifetime in 1948, the Jews had just established the State of Israel. Having survived tenaciously as a nation without a state for nineteen centuries, they were now fulfilling these prophecies. Recent history fulfilling prophecy so pertinently held me in great awe. It led me to visit Israel, learn Hebrew, marry a native, and to live, raise a family, and practice medicine there.

Now writing *Apocalypse Secrets* in retirement has switched me from intensively managing medical minutes that save lives to intensively analyzing prophetic millennia that save souls. Only toward the end of writing *Apocalypse Secrets* did I recall my angry teenage oath to figure out the Apocalypse. This oath must have subliminally driven my keystrokes from the start. In the process, I have learnt that prophecy is less a matter of proactive prediction and more a matter of retrospective proof. In other words, prophetic hindsight validates prophetic foresight.

Again, it was the word *Armageddon* that the Apocalypse into me got and me into the Apocalypse. Its Hebrew source *HAR–MAGIDO***N** (with an opening *H*) means *Mount Magidon*, or *Mountain* of *Magidon Valley*. The Old Testament mentions *Magidon* as a *Valley*[A] just once.[3] But it does mention *Magido* (with no final *N*) as the capital of this valley many more times.[4] The strategically located city of Magido controlled the pass from the lower coast to the Galilee's Magidon Valley where battles would occur; had two water sources to withstand sieges, and stabled warhorses and chariots. Both the Magidon Valley and Magido fit the biblical bill of Armageddon warfare well.

The city of Magido is now just an archeological mound called and spelt *Tel Megiddo*.[B] Routinely, coach-loads of visitors, tour guides, and even biblical scholars identify Tel Megiddo as *Armageddon*. Yet how can this meager mound—a mere 200–225 feet in height and a paltry 10–15 acres in area—pass as a mountain (*HAR*)! It cannot! Instead, the Valley of Magidon has only one real HAR that can be called a mountain. It stands in full view, dominating the valley, flanking it as its south-west escarpment. This mountain of **Mount Carmel is *Armageddon*.**

[A] Now the Magidon Valley is called the Jezreel Valley

[B] The city of Magido was abandoned in 332 BC, well before John's Apocalypse vision

Tel Megiddo simply serves as a pointer to Mount Carmel as the mountain of the Magidon Valley. Nestling at the base of Mount Carmel, Tel Megiddo has for centuries neighed as a Trojan horse with hidden cargo. Now, at last, it presents its hitherto hidden cargo of the true mountain in full sight.

Mount Carmel fits the biblical bills of the *sacred mountain of God* in Isaiah and of the *large and lofty mountain* in Revelation.[5-JR] The extended meaning of *HAR-MAGIDON* fits Mount Carmel further. In addition to *HAR-* as *mountain*, *-MAGIDON* means *preaching*. Therefore, *Armageddon* means, and really interprets as, *Mountain of Preaching*. (Alternatively, without its final *-N*, *HAR-MAGID-O* may mean also *Mountain-Preacher-His* or *Mountain of God's Preacher*).

As a *Mountain of Preaching*, Mount Carmel fits a scriptural bill for Preachers of God. Prior Mount Carmel Preachers of God were Elijah and Elisha. Today's Mount Carmel Preachers of God are the twin Baha'i Prophets called *the Bab* (*the Door*) and *Baha'u'llah* (*Glory of God*). Thus, Mount Carmel echoes yesteryear's twentieth century worldwide warfare, delivers today's new Prophets of God, and announces tomorrow's divine civilization of New Jerusalem.

The true Armageddon mountain of Mount Carmel viewed from Tel Megiddo

The would-be Armageddon "mountain" of Tel Megiddo, once capital of the Magidon (Jezreel) Valley, viewed close-up

The would-be Armageddon "mountain" of Tel Megiddo, once capital of the Magidon (Jezreel) Valley, viewed from above

Acknowledgments

I thank the many first-class folk who have played roles in creating *Apocalypse Secrets* in approximate chronological order as follows:

My early teachers Bert Raine, Dick Knight, Frank Spragg, and Hugh Williams inspired me with love of language: Ioan Thomas and Gordon Lindsay-Jones inspired me with love of science.

Marie Edwards was the first to show me Baha'i Writings that interpreted the Apocalypse. Susan Kreider gave me keys to it (she knows what I mean). Christine Rayner shared her Baha'i library.

Dr Rob Stockman gave unstinting support from the very conception of *Apocalypse Secrets*, providing prompt, resilient, ongoing input come rain or shine. From that same seminal moment, Rabbi Suzanne Carter shared her own intuitive insights and computer expertise.

Peter Terry and Thellie Lovejoy opened up their invaluable Pilgrim Notes archives. Professor Mahmoud Farshchian (http://www.farshchianart.com) provided slides of his beautiful *Morning Star* painting. Hushidar Motlagh (http://www.globalperspective.org) let me use his list of Millennialist Writings. Fahmi Ibrahimi presented his jizya tattoo and Arnold Segal photographed it in his taxi. Val Chesser spotted all 24 New Jerusalem gemstones. Rina Vardy displayed the original Dead Sea Scrolls one hypoglycemic afternoon. Badi Daemi (*Catifs Badi*) translated Persian sources. Richard Peritz (http://www.rcptv.com) applied entrepreneurial expertise. Roger Dahl and other Baha'i Archive researchers diligently answered questions.

Prof. David Aune debated and supplied penetrating translation insights into the odd Greek of Revelation ever so patiently. Dr Harold Landa made Midrashic research and told more-than-Midrashic jokes. Profs. Arthur Eidelman and Peter Vardy, Rabbis Chaim Richman and Shmuley Boteach, translated tricky Hebrew words. Bishop Jacob Barclay translated tricky Greek and Aramaic words. Dr David Instone-Brewer and the Cambridge Tyndale Library (http://www.tyndalehouse.com) located Jewish and Christian texts and debated different Hebrew ovines. St John's College Cambridge Library (http://www.joh.cam.ac.uk/library) sent pictures of pages from *Oedipus Aegyptiacus*.

Professor Peter Winnington (http://www.peakestudies.com) supplied his spy picture of a Thor rocket, extensively edited, and promptly answered my many questions. Llewellyn Drong (http://www.chainandcross.blogspot.com) supplied analyses of many Revelation symbols. Dr Rob Stockman, Simon Hewat, Dr Mike Joffe, Val Chesser, and Craig and Alison Karr helped coin titles and subtitles. The dear late Geoff Evans edited, insisted on paragraph spacing, and called spades "spades" ever so plainly. Peter Terry found many useful Baha'i sources for *Apocalypse Secrets*, edited its structure extensively, and spotted its long-term potential from the start.

Rev. Jeremy Swayne, Michael Downes, Dr Ralph Townsend, David McMurray, David Piff, David Lawrence, Marguerite Sears, Dr Albert Cheung, Gloria Ahmadjian, Tim Quilter, Drs. Mia and Jeremy Marcus, Dr Martin Evans, Bryn and Sherna Deamer, Sharon Emmons, Clare Allcard, Denise and Neil Davidson, and Vanessa Spence reviewed drafts, commented, edited, and proposed changes. Bill, Jaden, Aileen Maggie, and Gene offered many morsels of useful advice.

Bob Riggs (http://bahai-library.org/books/apocalypse) offered useful interpretive input and general support. John and Gloria Ben-Daniel (http://www.newtorah.org) shared their insightful Revelation structure, spotted its Yom Kippur events, and debated fervently. Leora Skolkin-Smith (http://www.leora skolkinsmith.com), James Barrington (http://www.james barrington.com), Morris Rosenthal (http://www.fonerbooks .com), Colin Ringrose, and James Fraser gave layout, printing, and publishing input. Robin Williams (*Non-Designer's Design Book*) gave free design advice and recommended Old Claude small caps font for old texts. Marcia Gorner took a picture of a picture of the four Living-Beings.

Art Director Warwick Knowles illustrated skillfully and taught patiently with endless empathy (http://www.pagemarks.co.uk). Designer Dani Battat solved many layout problems. Indexer Nigel d'Auvergne explained indexing and built the Index (http: //www.nigeldauvergne.co.uk). Roy Kellerman, Peyman Sazedj, Yael Reinhardt-Matsliach, and Jason Gorner designed various websites. Dr Instone-Brewer and Ehud Tokatly provided useful computer input.

Finally, in the great tradition of keeping the best to last, I thank angelic Joan profusely for her loyal and steadfast support throughout the long production of *Apocalypse Secrets*, and for letting me slip her shy-self into two-and-a-half illustrations! I further thank all others deserving of my thanks whom I have left out inadvertently.

INTRODUCTION

As a person who keeps formal religion at arm's length, I have written *Apocalypse Secrets* for readers from any religious background or none. Yet why–now—yet another interpretation of the Book of Revelation?

My reason is that *Apocalypse Secrets* is a timely fresh interpretation that brings cogent insights into the mess that the world is now in. These insights reveal root historical causes for the serious military and economic global events that are exploding so fast and furious across the screens of our TVs and the front pages of our newspapers. One way and another, most of these explosions are resounding from an apocalyptic World War III waging between the resurging *Muslim Militarism* from the Middle East and the driving *Malignant Materialism* of Christian West and now the whole globe. These two forces are as set on finishing each other off as Russian Communism and American Capitalism were in the Cold War. In the wake of this war the economic world is spiraling into the Greatest Depression that the Book of Revelation predicts as the *fall of Babylon*. These present difficult years of ours fit the "end-times"[A] that monotheistic Faiths foretell.

Yet viewed through the kaleidoscope of the latest Baha'i Faith, these predicted end-times of ours double as beginning-times. For the horrific military, political, and financial events now sweeping so swiftly over the peoples of the planet, Baha'i-based interpretations of Revelation offer a unified explanation and also augur the happy times of the *New Jerusalem* Millennium of Revelation. With pressing immediacy they explain modern times: the mess the world is in, how it got into it, and how it will get out of it.

Spurred on by the global events now unfolding so rapidly, *Apocalypse Secrets* hastens to share these interpretations of Revelation. In setting the Apocalypse to the end of its New Testament, Christianity kept the best to last as the final reservoir of prophecy of the Bible combining prophecies that span the whole Old Testament. The Apocalypse is the *I-Ching* of the West, a far more important Book than most people realize, including Christians. Its moving tale throbs with forceful meaning and rings out compelling truth. The prophetic thrust it packs reaches far beyond its own mere 2% of the Bible. Its meager 10,000 words fill barely seven pages of the New York Times[6] yet prophesy events spanning three millennia —two in the past and one in the future.

[A] These *end-times* are also known as *the end of times*, *end of the world*, *last days*, or *final days*

The past nineteen centuries have seen interpreters, including ones of the caliber of Isaac Newton,[7-C] savoring the Apocalypse's rich literary nectar. Chapter by chapter, century by century, Apocalypse interpreters have telescoped out a steadily growing train of historical events. In time, each interpreter centers on his own century. In space, each interpreter centers on his own homeland. *Apocalypse Secrets* follows suit. In space it centers on the Middle East home of the Apocalypse author John. In time it centers on the last half of the 1800s.

Recent decades have seen interpretations of Revelation mushroom to deck long walls of shelves from floor to ceiling in top theological libraries like the Pitts in Atlanta and the Tyndale in Cambridge.[8-C] These interpretations take three recognized tacks:

- ***Historicist*** interpretations read Revelation prophecies as telling tales describing past, present, and future events centered on the century of the interpreter (and subdivided further into preterist, pre-millennial, and post-millennial prophecies).
- ***Spiritual*** interpretations hear Revelation prophecies teaching spiritual messages.
- ***Revealed*** interpretations savor Revelation prophecies revealed by new divine Messengers, as Jesus once revealed Jewish prophecies, and as Buddha once revealed Hindu prophecies.

The Baha'i sources that interpret Revelation and guide *Apocalypse Secrets* take all three tacks. They read Revelation's tale narrating serial events centered on the Middle East and in the late 1800s. They hear its coded story teaching eternal spiritual messages. They savor its fragrant perfumes as revealed by Baha'i Messengers.

The Baha'i sources that interpret Revelation can be trusted. Their hindsight into the past events predicted by Chapters 1–16 validates them provably. So their prophetic foresight into the future events predicted by Chapters 18–22 are credible too. In particular, Revelation's **time-prophecies** supply important litmus tests validating Baha'i-based interpretations by interpreting exact years for key events. Today, sadly, Baha'i-based interpretations emit the hovering stench of an awful economic depression. But for the future, happily, they shine the beckoning light of an awesome glorious Millennium.

Accordingly, the 22-chapter stage Revelation plays out scenes of past, present, and future historical. Its Chapters 1–16 cover past events. Its Chapter 17 covers modern times. Its Chapters 18–22 cover future events:

- **Chapters 1–16** narrate events in the past that played out up to the 1800–1900s. Chapter 16's own seven afflictions have already played out in the world of the Middle East, are the last past events. The first three afflictions played out in the Persia of the 1800s. The next three afflictions played out across the Persian and Ottoman Middle East of the 1800s. The last seventh affliction of Armageddon has been playing out as the past century of worldwide warfare stressing and distressing the planet ever since 1914, but now almost over.
- **Chapter 17** fits modern times. By wonderful coincidence, Revelation's main Messenger reappears in this special Chapter 17 to teach us how to interpret symbols. The chapter's useful examples of symbols depict key players on the ancient and modern world stage. Its *mountains, heads,* and *waters* depict ancient Empires and peoples. Its *beast* growls as today's Muslim Militarism. Its *horns* lunge as modern fanatic rogue regimes and terrorist organizations. Its *whore of Babylon* incarnates today's global system of Malignant Materialism and its greed.
- **Chapters 18–22** augur the future millennium, the Millennium, and more. Chapter 18 narrates the fall of the Babylon of Malignant Materialism, fuelling, sparking, stoking, burning, and blazing its whore of greed into the ash of a Greatest Depression. As Malignant Materialism and Muslim Militarism go for good, Chapter 19 throws a spiritual and economic banquet to welcome to the globe the worthy prosperity engendered by spiritual economics. Chapter 20 opens a glorious Millennium for our great-grandchildren to savor. Chapter 21 launches the divine civilization of New Jerusalem for their great-grandchildren to relish. Chapter 22 surges the Baha'i Faith's river of new knowledge of the One Religion of God filling the world.

MM is the Latin number of the millennial year AD 2000. Aptly, these ***MM*** initials stand for also God's **M**anifestation **M**essengers (and for **M**uslim **M**ilitarism and **M**alignant **M**aterialism as their nemeses too). His last three of these Manifestation Messengers came in a *new name...rising again* over *three Days* of religious Eras to *rebuild the Temple* of His One Religion. Now the teachings of His last two, the Bab and Baha'u'llah, have begun to turn our trying end-times into the buoyant beginning-times of a *world to come.*[9-C]

The writer of the Apocalypse calling himself "John" was almost certainly John the Apostle. He was the beloved disciple of Jesus, the son of Zebedee and younger brother of James, a secular fisherman and a spiritual fisher of men. Early Church fathers like Justin Martyr (Ephesus, AD 132–35) and Irenaeus (Smyrna, AD 140) name John the Apostle as the author of the Apocalypse. The very canonization of the Apocalypse fits it as the work of an Apostle like him. In support, the Orthodox Church celebrated the Apocalypse's 1995 nineteenth centennial on the September 26 date of death of John the Apostle. The modern Catholic Church and many Protestant Churches agree that John the Apostle authored the Apocalypse. Yet often Protestants feel otherwise. They believe that another John called *John the Elder* wrote the odd Greek of Revelation. Yet no early Church writings mention any such *John the Elder*, and John the Apostle himself took the title *Elder* anyway.[10-C]

Regardless, why does John's Revelation Greek sound so odd—flawed at worst, cutely quaint at best? After all, in his Gospel and Epistles, the same John did manage to write normal Koine Greek. Must we simply excuse him as a high-ranking Apostle seeing a vision as he wilted from age?[A] Not at all! Instead, the following various credible explanations exist for his odd Revelation Greek:

- John probably heard the Apocalypse in his native religious Hebrew (possibly Aramaic), reporting it in Hebrew too to his Greek Jewish disciple Prochorus. But even though Prochorus could speak and understand Hebrew, he could **only write it fast enough in his mother tongue of Greek**. The resulting *Greek text written with a Hebrew accent*[11-C] married the oral Hebrew of John with the written Greek of Prochorus.
- Many Old Testament Hebrew prophecies pepper John's Revelation cocktail in acclaiming his mastery as *a unique prophet with more in common with Old Testament prophecy than with early Christian prophetic traditions.*[12-C] In any case, the many references to the Jewish Temple in the Apocalypse also called for distinctive Hebraized Greek.[13-C]
- Hebraized Greek targeted specifically Jewish readers living back home in Judea and Galilee. In contrast, the Common (*Koine*) Greek of the rest of the New Testament, including John's own Gospel and Epistles, targeted generally gentile and Jewish Greek readers living across the wider Mediterranean world.
- The genre of the Apocalypse is that of a punctilious real-time report that spells out the fast-flashing sights, sounds, feelings, scents, and tastes of a vision. In contrast, the genre of John's Gospel is that of a stylish story that tells the life, teachings, and miracles of Jesus.

[A] All mentions of John as the Apocalypse author include his scribe Prochorus implicitly

- The personal situation of John had worsened between writing the Gospel and Apocalypse. His Gospel he wrote comfortably as the young spiritual leader of Ephesus writing for himself at home. His Apocalypse he dictated in his late eighties as an exile with fading eyesight camping in a cave.
- In any case—overall—the Hebraized Apocalypse Greek of John is so very bizarre, so extensively flawed, and so consistently odd, that it **must surely be deliberate**. Yes, John and Prochorus did code many hidden meanings into the Hebraized Greek of their text. We shall soon see just how many there are.

John was born in the Galilee around AD 10. As a devout Jew, he was steeped in the Scriptures that would came to imbue his vision. His father Zebedee, his brother James, and he, John, ran the family business of *Cohen and Sons, Fishmongers*, fishing the Sea of Galilee. Their best client seems to have been the distant Jerusalem Temple. As Cohens, these men were hereditary Temple-Priests, and even close kin of the High Priest. So John, *being a Priest, wore the sacerdotal plate,*[14-C] indicating that he could have well taken an active turn to serve as a Temple Priest. He would have known the Temple first-hand, along with its sacred objects and services—not least the 12 breastplate gemstones of the High Priest that in his vision would shine big as New Jerusalem's foundation-gemstones.

Christians hold John in high regard, celebrating him by his birthday. as they do for Jesus and Mary (rather than his death-day as for other saints). John was the disciple that Jesus loved most. The dying Jesus asked John to care for his mother Mary, whom he took to Ephesus, the main port and commercial hub of Turkey, known then as the Roman province of *Asia,* whose Christian community he came to lead. Then came Rome's AD 64–96 persecution of Jews and Christians, when Roman Emperor Domitian, in *the fourteenth year of his reign,*[15-C] namely AD 94, banished John from Ephesus and sent him sixty miles across the sea to the island of Patmos. There, John and his disciple Prochorus made home in a cave facing northeast to Ephesus.

No one can know exactly how the Apocalypse vision flashed, but perhaps as follows. Late one AD 95 winter Friday afternoon, John and Prochorus see a storm gathering over Patmos. At sunset, they light Sabbath candles, sing in the Sabbath as a Bride, break bread, sip sanctified retsina Patmos wine, sup a modest dinner, and close with prayer. Then they sit at the mouth of their cave beside a fire of crackling resinous Patmos pine, watching its flickering flames dancing their shadows on the cave-wall, and reminiscing.

The cave of John and Prochorus on Patmos
where John saw his vision, now a chapel

Suddenly, the storm breaks and shatters their peace. Lightning flashes the scenes of a vision and thunder peals its voices off the backdrop of the cave-wall. The heavenly Messenger of the vision immediately tells John to start recording. So John tells Prochorus:

Prochorus, write what I say! Right now!

Prochorus scrambles for papyrus and quill and begins to record the nineteen-to-the-dozen didactic dictation of John verbatim as a single swift script seamlessly sewing scores of staccato sayings snapping the speed of the storm and shining its scenes. Their cave-wall displays sights of their beloved late Temple just destroyed in AD 70. Their cave turned-Temple thunders its trumpet-warnings. Their cave-floor quakes its calamities. Their cave-wall reverberates its priestly rites and its levitical psalms. Their fire at the cave-mouth gusts up the aromas of its glowing incenses and burning flesh. Their herb-garden outside the cave is beaten flat by the hailstones of its tough spiritual lessons. Then, right at the end, the Temple vanishes in a puff of spiritual smoke, and up puffs the vast magical mushroom of begemmed New Jerusalem instead.

The storm and vision abate as fast as they began. Relieved, Prochorus exclaims:

Master, let's edit what I wrote!

But John flashes back:

No way, Prochorus! Leave it just as it is!
Just as I heard and saw it in Hebrew.
Just as you wrote it in Greek!

In AD 96, Domitian is assassinated. His successor Nerva lets the two exiles sail back to Ephesus. En route their boat capsizes. But they and the Apocalypse scroll survive. John had been a fisherman and still swims well, helped by a handy corkboard too. Back in Ephesus, he leads the Christian Church for ten more years and dies naturally as the only Apostle of Jesus not to be martyred.[16-C]

Alas, no original Apocalypse scroll has ever been found. Just a few fragments of its earliest copies have been found. Full texts appeared only as late as the AD 300s–400s, in the first Bible Books called *Codices*, specifically the *Codex Sinaiticus*[A] and *Codex Alexandrinus*.[17-C] The first Apocalypse page in the Codex Sinaiticus looks like this:

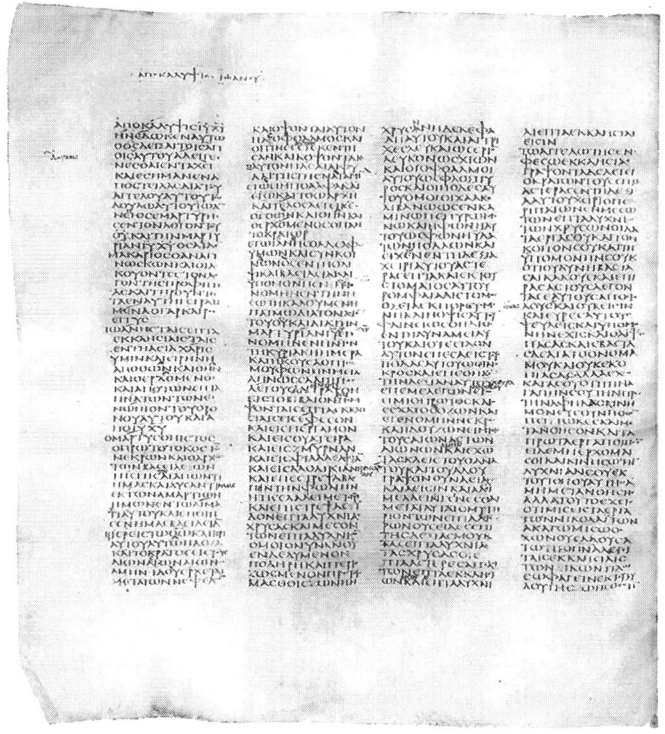

The first *Codex Sinaiticus* page
of the *Apocalypse* of John
©The British Library

[A] Discovered, notably, in the special year of 1844

Immediately, we see that the Apocalypse's original

CONTINUOUSBLOCKLETTERTEXTSETINCOLUMNSWITHOUTANYPUNCTUATIONORCHAPTERORVERSENUMBERINGSORSPACESBETWEENWORDSMAKINGITQUITEILLELEGIBLE

would read far more readily as

CONTINUOUS BLOCK LETTER TEXT SET IN COLUMNS WITHOUT ANY PUNCTUATION CHAPTER OR VERSE NUMBERINGS **BUT WITH** SPACES BETWEEN WORDS MAKING IT QUITE **LEGIBLE**

Clearly, by modern standards, the Greek language of the first century was quite crude. It had no spaces between words, punctuation marks, capitals, or chapter and verse numberings.[A] Such nuances, which we now take for granted, took centuries to evolve. Lack of spaces between words, in particular, permits ambiguous meanings. For example, *GODISNOWHERE* can mean both *GOD IS NOW HERE* or *GOD IS NOWHERE*! Similarly, the two Greek letters *OI* may act as a plural ending for a noun, or as *THE* before a plural noun, or—and here's the rub!—as **both** possibilities concurrently.

The Hebraized Greek of John seems deceptively transparent while using linguistic devices coding for hidden meanings. The places he hid his spiritual gems appear to be as "obvious" as once bookshelves and fridges were as hiding places for physical gems in homes. The devices of John spin layers for the veil of his Apocalypse bride, which has concealed her slim silhouette and let it slip safely past translators and interpreters for nineteen centuries. He steadily **unveils** this bride of his Apocalypse under their noses, from its *sealed* status in Chapter 5 to its *unsealed* status in Chapters 21–22, to **reveal** her as the Sabbath-Bride of New Jerusalem's divine civilization.[18]

The linguistic devices of John veiled the Temple from both Romans and Church, neither of whom liked the Temple. For Rome, a vision reviving the Temple as a physical memory might anger censors, inflame zealous Jews, and get the Apocalypse banned and John more than just banished. For the Church, reviving the Temple as just a symbol in a vision could anger Church leaders, for the advent of Jesus had made the Temple passé. For that matter, the Church would run hot and cold over the Apocalypse for many centuries anyway.[B]

[A] Although useful, chapter and verse numberings do hamper the flow of the Revelation text, especially at Chapter cusps 6/7, 8/9, 10/11, 11/12, and 12/13

[B] Finally, Western Churches locked the nut of canonization onto the Apocalypse bolt in AD 397, and Eastern Churches in the AD 600–700s

Furthermore, John's veiling stopped interpreters from interpreting prophecies too well. He prevented a critical mass of readers from interpreting any prophecy accurately enough to hamper it happening—for better or worse—especially serious prophecies like the fall of Babylon.

John's Hebraized Greek is guided by three important literary concepts:

- **Artful ambiguity** (from *NLP* **n**euro-**l**inguistic **p**rogramming) is deliberate ambiguity arising from choice, not chance. Shakespeare wrote it into his plays. Mozart composed it into his symphonies. Dali painted it into his pictures. Escher sketched it into his graphic works. Yet well before AD 95, John had weaved artful ambiguity as yarn into his Apocalypse tapestry and had fed it as grist into his Revelation mill. Artful ambiguity fills his whole Apocalypse text, whose ambiguities are so many that they have to be artful.
- **Inclusive thinking** projects a *win/win* open approach in embracing several meanings concurrently and using combining **con**junctions like "both" and "and". In contrast, exclusive thinking pursues a single direction with tunnel vision and uses oppositional **dis**junctions like "either" and "or". For example, in *they shall prophesy for 1,260 days,* ***dressed in sackcloth,*** *these men are the two olive trees,*[19] the bold *dressed in sackcloth* is a floating-term that is doubly valid in qualifying both the prior term *they shall prophesy for 1,260 days* and the ensuing term *these men are the two olive trees.*
- **Semantic codes** are special numbers or words in the holy languages of Hebrew, Greek, and Arabic. Number-codes form the warp and woof of Jewish *gematria*, Christian *numerology*, and Muslim *abjad*. Word-codes include the Hebrew ones of Drosnin's *Bible Code*;[20-J] Greek ones like the ***FISH*** acronym ***IXTHUS*** for ***I****esous* ***X****ristos* ***TH****eou* ***U****ios,* ***S****oter* meaning ***J****esus* ***Ch****rist* ***S****on of* ***G****od,* ***S****avior*; and Arabic ones in the Quran. In a similar vein, less-than-holy lingoes like Afro-talk, Irish-speak, and Cockney rhyming slang also use semantic codes, these designed to keep secrets from overlords.

The fleet of linguistic devices plied by John across the ocean of his Apocalypse knowledge are loaded with artful ambiguity, inclusive thinking, and semantic codes. His linguistic devices link Apocalypse verses as snakes and ladders connect the squares of the board game. They join its chapters as wormholes connect galaxies in space and as branes connect eras in time. They echo various versions of its original Greek sources. They fill its text with teasing riddles, subtle word orders, cute subtext comments, intriguing feedback-loops, confusing cross-references, tantalizing contrasts, staged interludes, shrewd allusions, and scattered praises. They mesh its mystic matrix with a mishmash of Midrashic meanings all jostling together in *Alice through the Looking-Glass* style.

John's five main linguistic devices are his number-codes, floating-terms, verbal-thematic links, hidden-titles, and cover-names:

Number-codes are interpreted by three kinds of people:

- People who can count, and
- People who cannot count!

Joking aside, number-codes tag Messengers or their Faiths or foes. As one example, ***12*** codes for Faiths; for their qualities as *12 tribes*; for their founders as *12 stars, Angels*, or *pearls*; for their ways of loving wisdom as *12 gates*; for their strong teachings as *12 gemstone foundations*; and for the hard work by their many followers as *12 thousand furlongs*.

Floating-terms concurrently and inclusively qualify the term just before and the term just after them, in referring both backwards and forwards as *dressed in sackcloth* just did. Again, in *I myself John...came to be on the island called Patmos* ***due to this Word of God and to this testimony of Jesus Christ*** *I was soaring in spirit* (Rev. 1.9–10), the bold floating-term qualifies both the prior and the ensuing terms.

Verbal-thematic links are key-phrases or trigger-words found in certain biblical verses that connect these verses. For example, the trigger-words *lion, root*, and *rainbow* trace the main Revelation Messenger slipping from role to role. Similarly, the key-phrase *in his hand* tracks him moving from chapter to chapter. Impromptu pursuit of such wonderful word trails has carried me soaring into many late nights on the magic carpet of my word processor on rewarding treasure hunts over the fertile linguistic wonderland of the Apocalypse as fascinated and exhilarated as *Alice in Wonderland*.

Hidden-titles are words that do double duty as also titles for Messenger Angels. Even ***WORD*** itself, in its original block-letter form, can mean just ***word*** or ***Word*** as a title. John uses ***Word*** as a title in his Gospel for Jesus as a *Divine Speaker*, and in his Apocalypse for the two Baha'i Prophets as *Divine Speakers*.[21-BR]

Cover-names are Revelation words that look like Proper-Names but simply bear literal meanings. Each such "Proper-Name" is a cantering Trojan horse bearing hidden cargo as its literal meaning. Each cover-name's literal meaning makes far more sense than its apparent "Proper-Name". Thus, *ABBADON* works far better as *destruction* than as *Abbadon*. For example, *DAVID* sounds far better as *beloved one* than it does as *David* a king.

More examples of John's coded linguistic devices appear later. They prepare us on pages 130–2 for the subsequent Parallel Interpretation Section. Then the fullest listing of them appears in the final Translation Section on pages 311–28.

What did the Apocalypse Unveil?

What prophetic news did the Apocalypse first veil and then unveil? Today, topically, it announces the war that is now waging between Muslim Militarism and Malignant Materialism, along with the looming Greatest Depression that it has triggered coincidentally. Longer term, it proclaims the news of the Baha'i (*Glory*) Faith.

I write *Apocalypse Secrets* as an interpretation of the Book of Revelation based on sources in canonical Baha'i Writings as my own best good-faith interpretation as a friend of the Baha'i Faith. Otherwise, I disclaim representing the Baha'i Faith or its agencies in any official way. Some time ago, a Baha'i conference invited me to be a guest lecturer presenting an early draft of *Apocalypse Secrets*. My primarily Baha'i audience—many converts from Christian backgrounds—were happily surprised to learn just how many Baha'i Writings do indeed interpret Revelation. Given the fame and importance of the Book of Revelation, these Baha'i-based interpretations of it deserve to be widely read.

The Baha'i Faith is

> *the most recent of the world's religions and the second most widespread religion after Christianity. Its founder Baha'u'llah brought an essential message of unity, teaching that there is only one God, one human race, and that all the world's religions have been progressive stages in the revelation of God's will and purpose for humanity. Baha'u'llah declared that humanity's long-awaited stage of maturity is at hand, an age when the oneness of humankind will be recognized and established. He laid down principles, laws and institutions for a world civilization, including: abandonment of all forms of prejudice, full equality between the sexes, recognition of the common source and essential oneness of the world's great religions, elimination of the extremes of poverty and wealth, universal compulsory education, right and responsibility of each person to search independently for truth, establishment of a world federal system, recognition that faith must be consistent with reason and that science and religion should be in harmony. The Baha'i Faith has no clergy and its affairs are administered through a system of elected councils at the local, national and international levels. There are currently over 180*

> *national councils and more than 12,000 local councils around the world. The international governing body, known as the Universal House of Justice, functions from its seat at the Baha'i World Centre in Haifa. All the costs associated with the activities of the Baha'i World Centre are covered by voluntary contributions from Baha'is around the world. No donations are accepted from other sources.*[22]

The still young Baha'i Faith has, by 2013, historically developed to where Christianity, say, had reached by AD 170. Like the monotheistic Faiths of Sabaeanism, Judaism, Zoroastrianism, Hinduism, Buddhism, Christianity, and Islam, the Baha'i Faith is a fully-fledged monotheistic Faith too. Just as Judaism followed the teachings of Adam, Noah, and Abraham; as Christianity validated the Judaism of Moses; as Islam expanded the Christianity of Jesus; and as Buddhism fulfilled the Hinduism of Krishna; so the Baha'i Faith has followed, validated, expanded, and fulfilled

> *the first and everlasting principles that animate and underlie the religions that have preceded it. The God-given authority, vested in each one of them, it admits and establishes as its firmest and ultimate basis...as different stages in the eternal history and constant evolution of one religion, Divine and indivisible, of which it itself forms but an integral part....Its unalterable purpose is to widen their basis, to restate their fundamentals, to reconcile their aims, to reinvigorate their life, to demonstrate their oneness, to restore the pristine purity of their teachings, to coordinate their functions and to assist in the realization of their highest aspirations. These divinely-revealed religions...are doomed not to die, but to be reborn....Does not the child succumb in the youth and the youth in the man; yet neither child nor youth perishes?'*[23-S]

Queen Marie of Romania, a niece of Queen Victoria, became a Baha'i. She described her new Faith as

> *a wide embrace, gathering together all those who have searched for words of hope. It accepts all great Prophets gone before, it destroys no other creeds and leaves all doors open....Baha'i teaching brings peace to the soul and hope to the heart. To those in search of assurance, the words of the Father are as a fountain in the desert after long wandering....It is a wondrous message that Baha'u'llah and His son 'Abdu'l-Baha have given us. They have not set it up aggressively, knowing that the germ of eternal truth which lies at its core cannot but take root and spread....It is Christ's Message taken up anew....If ever the name of Baha'u'llah or 'Abdu'l-Baha comes to your attention, do not put their writings from you. Search out their books, and let their glorious, peace-bringing, love-creating words and lessons sink into your hearts as they have into mine.*[24-S]

Apocalypse Secrets follows an established mainstream trend of Baha'i-based interpretations of the Book of Revelation. The trend began with Ruth Moffett's zealous *New Keys to the Book of Revelation*. There followed *Apocalypse Unsealed* by space-scientist Robert Riggs followed, which delved into diligent detail and shared cryptic astronomical, astrological, and numerological insights. Later *Chaining of the Dragon* by Schreiber focused on the histories of Christianity and Islam. *Book of Revelation: One Bahá'í's Concept* by Beach listed many Baha'i sources. *Understanding the Revelation to Saint John* by Clark explored Faiths from Sabaeanism to Islam. *Logic of the Revelation of St. John* by Beebe reasoned its own cogent case. Other Baha'i-based books interpret much of Revelation too, such as Motlagh's *I shall Come Again*, Sears' *Missing Millennium*, Sours' *Understanding Biblical Prophecy*, the Maudes' *The Servant, The General and Armageddon*, and Tai-Seale's *Thy Kingdom Come*.

Baha'i Writings extol prophecy generally. They teach that *the allusions made in the Scriptures have been unfolded...for this wondrous Day* and *produce wonderful effects in the minds and thoughts of men and cause their hearts to be attracted*. Specifically, Baha'i Writings extol the prophecies in the Apocalypse, stating:

- *What truth can be greater than that announced by the Revelation of St. John the divine*
- *Reflect upon the words of John*
- *There are many meanings in each word of the Apocalypse*
- *Revelation is allusively very rich and offers abundant material for study*
- It is *a very important book in teaching the Baha'i interpretations of certain biblical passages to devout Christians*
- *The Revelations of St. John are not to be taken literally, but spiritually as the mysteries of God, since it is not the reading of the words that profits you; it is the understanding of their meanings.*[25-AS]

In this vein, the Apocalypse has

> *intimated to the souls of men, through veiled allusions and hidden symbols, the glad-tidings of the One Who was to come after Him, saying 'His eyes were as a flame of fire', and 'brass-like were His feet', and 'out of His mouth goeth a two-edged sword'....Shouldst thou reflect upon these statements, thou wouldst find them to be of such surpassing eloquence and clarity as to mark the loftiest heights of utterance and the epitome of wisdom.*[26-B]

(For official translations of many early Baha'i Writings, including the citation above, this "Olde English" of the King James Bible was chosen purposefully to capture and emulate their original rich and elevated Persian and Arabic prose. Please bear with it!)

Yet Baha'i Writings do not interpret Revelation *from beginning to end*, any more than, say, the New Testament reveals any Old Testament Book from start to finish. Rather, Baha'i Writings reveal choice parts of Revelation, in the way that they reveal choice parts of the biblical Books of Daniel and Isaiah and other Scriptures too.[27-AC]

Still, interpreting a particular verse often unlocks meanings in other verses. For example, decoding *1,260 days* in verse 11.3 explains it in also verse 12.6. Similarly, interpreting *Trumpet-Blast* in verse 11.14 expounds it in also verses 8.13, 9.1, 12, 12.12, 18.10, 16, & 19. Likewise, Isaac Newton noted that

> *comparing Scripture with Scripture establishes the meaning of a symbol, which then holds true for the entire Bible.*[28-AC]

Further, Baha'i teaching acknowledges that

> *the individual is free to accept, or refute...what scholars...say....By discussion of...statements by scholars, the truth will ultimately be found, but at no time should their decision be considered as final.*[29-S]

In addition, Baha'i teaching encourages believers to interpret gaps in Revelation for themselves, in order that they may

> *unaided, comprehend these inner meanings* and *expound at full length every single word* and, thus, *a spring of wisdom will well up, and jet forth even as a fountain that leapeth from its own original source.*[30-A]

Moreover, Baha'i-based interpretations of the Apocalypse go far to explain some of its odd wordings. For example, it simply

- Views its four Living-Beings oddly positioned *at the center of the Throne and around the Throne* (v. 4.6) as two Living-Beings seated on the Throne and as two Living-Beings standing beside and guarding the Throne
- Accepting its two oddly singular *Trumpet-Blasts* ***is*** *still coming* (v. 9.12) as a duo of concurrent Prophets (like, say, Moses and Jesus living at the same time)
- Hearing its oddly accusative-case direct object *His servants the prophets* of *joyfully proclaimed* (v. 10.7) as the proclamation itself (thus dismissing as a **mis**translation the usual non-existent dative-case ***to*** *His servants the prophets*).

Baha'i Writings transmit their own inherent authority that is lucid and powerful. So they speak most authentically for themselves. Accordingly, *Apocalypse Secrets* cites most Baha'i Writings directly. Trying to paraphrase them would sap their thrust too much.

TERMINOLOGY

Capital Letters head **N**ames and **T**itles for God and Messenger Angels, for important entities like **F**aiths, **E**ras, and **C**ycles; and for the Temple and entities in it like its **A**ltar, **A**rk, **D**oor, **M**enorah, **R**am, and **T**hrone.

Citations take usual form of ***Author, Work, 345***, where ***345*** indicates a page number. Some take extended form as ***Author, Work, 12.345***, where ***12*** (when present) indicates a section, chapter, or paragraph number. Different editions of Baha'i Writings do their best to keep page numbers constant. Yet inevitably, slippage of a page or two forward or backward sometimes occurs. (In future, citing by paragraph number will obviate this problem.) For page-numbers, the main reference standard was the 2006–2007 *Ocean Library of Baha'i Writings*. Baha'i citations can be readily confirmed by Google searches for websites citing Baha'i Writings.

Endnote and Footnote Marks assemble each paragraph's citations at its end, so as to cut clutter as much as possible. These grouped citations appear listed under their ***opening words*** in bold their footnote or endnote in the *References* section. Many endnote marks carry superscript source-suffixes shown here in bold as follows: Revelation[1-R], Jewish[2-J], Christian[3-C], Muslim[4-M], Baha'u'llah[5-B], 'Abdu'l-Baha[6-A], and Shoghi Effendi.[7-S]

Internet Links were last successfully accessed on January 27, 2009.

Numbers commonly appear as digits in order to underscore their frequent function as codes.

"Revelation", capitalized, may mean either "the Book of Revelation", or a Religion/Faith specifically, or religion/faith generally. For each occurrence of "Revelation", its context clarifies its meaning.

Sequences of Messenger Names and Faiths routinely follow rough chronological order from Abraham, Moses, Zoroaster, Krishna, Buddha, Jesus, Muhammad, to the Bab and Baha'u'llah, and from Sabaean, Jewish, Zoroastrian, Hindu, Buddhist, Christian, Islam, to the Babi and Baha'i Faiths.

Spelling and Style is American, except for citations of works originally written in British English.

Transliteration has been kept as simple and accent-free as possible. Yet a long ē has been retained for the Greek letter *eta*; a long ō for the Greek letter *omega*; and a single generic " ' " for the opening Greek h-sound, the Hebrew glottal-stop *alef*, and the Hebrew guttural *ayin*.

Year-Dates follow various calendar formats, depending on context, including the ***Common Era*** **CE**, the Christian ***Anno Domini*** **AD**, the Jewish ***Anno Moshe*** **AM**, the Muslim ***Anno Hijrae*** **AH**, and the ***Baha'i Era*** **BE** formats. The **AD/BC** format tends to be favored because it comports with the historically Christian origin of the Book of Revelation. The **AM** and **CE/BCE** formats appear for Jewish contexts and the **AH/BH** format appears for Muslim contexts. Note too that year-dates must inevitably slip part of year forward or backward between different calendars. For example, the Christian year AD 2000 overlapped part of Jewish year AM 5760 (2000/01/01–2000/09/29) and part of Jewish year AM 5761 (2000/09/30–2000/12/31). As a result, citing years in two formats inevitably involves slippage across the years involved, as for example here, the year AD 2000 is both AM 5760 and AM 5761.

Middle East Faiths and Empires

For our end-times that double as beginning-times, *Apocalypse Secrets* unfurls two sets of seven flags across the stage of John's Middle East. The first set of flags welcomes the seven serial Eras of Asia's Sabaean, Jewish, Zoroastrian, Hindu, Buddhist, Christian, and Muslim Faiths that have launched the one Religion of God from their Cycle of Prophecy. The second set of flags laments the seven serial Eras of the same Cycle's Egyptian, Median, Assyrian, Persian, Greek, Roman, and Byzantine Empires that have pursued millennia of militarism and materialism until today. These seven Faiths and seven Empires have danced a tango of progress per the following

Chronological list of Middle East Faiths and Empires

Date	Faiths and Empires
BCE 3761/AM 1	Adam's creation starts AM Jewish calendar
BCE 3228	Krishna
BCE 3100–1070	Egyptian Empire
BCE ~1900	Abraham
BCE ~1400	Moses
BCE ~1300	Exodus of the People of Israel from Egypt
BCE 1900–722	Assyrian Empire
BCE ~1000	Zoroaster (Zarathustra)
BCE 710	Assyria conquers and disperses Israel
BCE 968–928	Solomon builds the Jewish Temple
BCE 722–540	Median/Late Babylonian Empire
BCE 557–331	Persian Empire
BCE 586	Nebuchadnezzar destroys the Temple
BCE 586–457	Persian Empire holds the People of Israel captive
BCE 500–148	Greek Empire
BCE ~563–483	Buddha
BCE 457	Decree of Artaxerxes restarts Temple services
BCE 168	Greece desecrates the Temple
BCE 264–CE 476	Roman Empire
CE 1 (trad.)	Jesus's birth starts AD Christian calendar
CE ~30	Jesus proclaims
CE ~33	Jesus crucified
CE 64–96	Rome's 1st persecution of Jews and Christians
CE 95	**John's sees his Patmos vision**

DATE	FAITHS AND EMPIRES
CE 70	Rome destroys the Temple and disperses the Jews
CE 100	John dies at Ephesus
CE 110–238	Rome's 2nd persecution of Jews and Christians
CE 249–311	Rome's 3rd persecution of Jews and Christians
CE 313	Constantine makes Christianity a state religion
CE 325	Constantine summons the Council of Nicea
CE 330–1461	Byzantine Empire (Constantinople)
CE 401	Barbarians invade the Western Roman Empire
CE 410	Barbarians capture Rome
CE 570	Muhammad born
CE 613/BH 10	Muhammad sees his Mt. Hira vision
CE 613/BH 10	Muhammad proclaims
CE 622/AH 1	Muhammad's flight starts AH Muslim calendar
CE 628	Muhammad signs Hudaybiyyah peace treaty
CE 632	Muhammad dies
CE 632–61	Rashidun Caliphate (Abu-Bakr, Umar, Uthman, Ali)
CE 633–778	150 years of Muslim *Locust and Scorpion* forces
CE 638	Rashidun Caliph Umar captures Jerusalem
CE 656–61	First Shi'a Imam (4th Sunni Rashidun Caliph) Ali
CE 656–873	Shi'a Imamate
CE 661	Ali is assassinated
CE 666	Mu'awiya proclaims as First Umayyad Caliph
CE 666–749	Umayyad Caliphate (Damascus)
CE 749	Abbasids seize most of the Umayyad Empire
CE 750–1258	Abbasid Caliphate (Baghdad)
CE 756–1031	Spanish Umayyad Caliphate (Cordoba)
CE 873	Imamate ends historically
CE 1299–1918	Ottoman Empire (Istanbul)
CE 1453	Ottoman Empire captures Constantinople
CE 1492	Christians expel Spain's Jews and Muslims
CE 1796–1924	Persian Qajar dynasty starts
CE 1817	Baha'u'llah is born
CE 1819	The Bab is born
CE 1844/BE 1	The Bab's proclamation starts BE Baha'i calendar
CE 1844/BE 1	Edicts of Toleration take effect in Palestine
CE 1850	The Bab is executed by firing squad
CE 1852	Baha'u'llah sees his Black Pit vision
CE 1863/BE 19	Baha'u'llah proclaims
CE 1892	Baha'u'llah dies
CE 1914–18	World War I opens Armageddon century of war

DATE	FAITHS AND EMPIRES
CE 1921	'Abdu'l-Baha dies
CE 1935–45	Nazi Germany persecutes Jews for 10 years
CE 1939–45	World War II
CE 1948	State of Israel is founded
CE 1957	Shoghi Effendi dies
CE 1963/BE 119	Baha'i Universal House of Justice is founded
CE 1995	Nineteenth Centennial of the Apocalypse
CE 2000–3000	Christian AD Third Millennium
CE 2014	Armageddon Century of war hopefully ends
CE 2240–3240	Jewish Seventh AM 6000–7000 Millennium

Since the dawn of history, the tango danced by Faiths and Empires has brought humanity long-term material and spiritual progress. In other words, over millennia, the progress has taken an upward course on average. Ideally the course of the progress should have happily meandered steadily upwards along the graph's gently undulating learn-as-you-go yellow brick road. But alas, all too often, especially recently, the progress has jerked humanity sharply up and down on the graph's scary bipolar boom-to-bust red roller-coaster route. *Apocalypse Secrets* will explain how and why and offer its own spiritual lithium as a remedy.

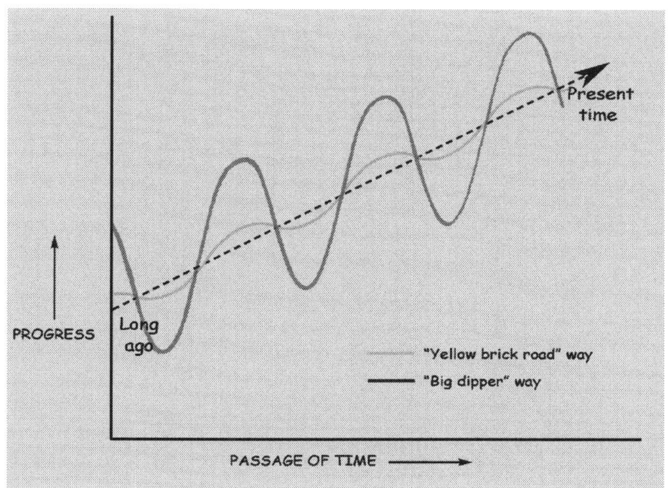

Two different curves of human progress—
gently undulating, or boom-to-bust bipolar

The Apocalypse is a Book of Codes

The Apocalypse is a game of *Snakes and Ladders* sliding up from verse and slipping down to another verse. It is a crossword puzzle filled with anagram-clues. It is a web of discovery whose gossamer radials interpreters scale to the center. It is a Gordian knot whose strings they cut with swords of spiritual truth. It is a forest whose scented trails they race as literary hounds. It is a grade-4 maze whose chapter and verse paths, forks, rotaries, and bridges they crisscross anywhere and everywhere. It is a jigsaw puzzle whose edge-piece verses flash imperial and religious history, and whose panoramic chapters dawn sky-blue truth, project forest-green ideals, and blaze fiery-red warfare.

However, best of all, the Apocalypse is a beautiful palace whose doors open to Baha'i keys, whose foundation symbols Baha'u'llah reveals, whose wall chapters and pillar verses 'Abdu'l-Baha interprets, and whose mosaic floor meanings Shoghi Effendi explains.

At the Chapter–1 Apocalypse Door, Baha'u'llah welcomes us. He leads us into its lamp-lit Chapters–2/3 Foyer to address the surviving seven monotheistic Faiths. He guides us into its Chapter–4 Throne-Room and introduces the four Primary-Figures led by him. In its Chapter 4/5 Library, he introduces us to its librarian Bab. In its Chapters–6/7/8/9 East-Wing, he narrates histories for Christianity and Islam. In its Chapter–10 Reception-Room, he tells us about God's hidden intent. In its central Chapter–11 Great Hall, he opens up its One Religion of God to us—including Muhammad, the martyred Bab, and himself. In its Chapters–12–16 West-Wing, he makes us run the gauntlet amid brutal Muslim regimes and afflictions.

Now we have reached the Chapter–17 Operations-Room of Apocalypse palace. Here Baha'u'llah teaches us how to interpret prophetic symbols. Afterwards, he takes us out into Chapters–18–22 palace gardens. In its Chapter–18 Winter-Garden, we feel a Greatest Depression crashing and crushing its shady shaky shed of Malignant Materialism. In its Chapter–19 Spring-Garden, we watch spiritual economics bring to the world material recovery and worthy prosperity. In its Chapters–20–22 Summer-Garden, we hear the One Religion of God broadcast across the globe, smell the perfume of its blossoming Millennium, and savor the fruit of its divine global civilization.

Prophetic words and symbols act as vehicles bearing meanings. The story of a flash flood submerging a small Texas city illustrates the concept neatly. Its Mayor's Order goes out to leave town. But one man, a true believer named Bob, flatly refuses, saying:

God shall save me!

Fast-flowing waters gush through the city streets. Next drives up a Police truck to take Bob to safety. Again, Bob refuses to get in, calling out:

God shall save me!

The rushing waters surge higher and Bob goes upstairs. Now a Coastguard launch zooms in to rescue him. Again, Bob refuses to get on board, calling out:

God shall save me!

In full-spate, the swelling waters rise yet higher. Bob climbs onto the roof. Then an Air Force helicopter whirls down to save him. Yet again, Bob still flatly refuses to climb in, calling out:

God shall save me!

At last, the heaving flood washes Bob away—and he drowns.

At the pearly gates of heaven, an angry Bob confronts God:

God, I trusted you! Why didn't You save me?

God, upset too, replies:

> *But Bob, I did everything I could! First, I broadcast* ***My Mayor's Order*** *to tell you to leave town! Next, I drove up* ***My Police Truck*** *to take you away! Then, I zoomed in* ***My Coastguard Launch*** *to rescue you! Finally, I whirled down* ***My Air Force Helicopter*** *to save you! But each and every time, you snubbed them all and downright refused to be saved!*

Just as the divine Order, Truck, Launch, and Helicopter sent by God tried to save Bob, so His divine Chariots of Prophetic Words and Symbols try to save souls.

Prophetic words transmit evocative power more than literary meaning or plausibility. The many apparently absurd statements in Revelation make the point crystal-clear. A man holds seven stars! A star falls upon rivers and receives a key! A reed speaks! The land opens up its mouth and swallows a river! An angel stands in the sun! And so on.[31-R]

Statements like these make sense only **symbolically**. Otherwise, how could the Revelation statement that its main Angel's

> *'eyes were as a flame of fire', and 'brass-like were His feet', and 'out of His mouth goeth a two-edged sword'...be literally interpreted? Were anyone to appear with all these signs, he would assuredly not be human?*[32-B]

John makes the same point with internal interpretations that identify the following Revelation symbols:

Stars as *Angels*
Menorah-Lamps as *churches*
Seven stars as *seven Spirits of God*
Torches of fire as *God's seven Spirits*
Horns and eyes as *God's seven Spirits*
Incenses as *prayers*
Mystery of God as *His own servants the Prophets*
Ancient serpent as *lying-evil* and *hate*
You heavens *as those manifesting God's Presence*
Beast as *a human-being*
Confused Babylon as *Mother of the Whores and the vile things in the world*
Heads as *mountains*
Horns as *rulers*
Waters as *peoples, populations, nations, and language-groups*
Woman as *the great city*
Fine-linen as *righteous deeds*
Bride as *New Jerusalem.*[33]

These internal interpretations of John are freebie loss-leaders that he uses as bait to hook readers into the spiritual ocean of Revelation and deeper down into its profound meanings. His internal interpretations appear in 11% (43 of 404) of its verses, with four of them stressed further as *mysteries* too.[34]

Accordingly, it is clear that

> *divine Words are not to be taken according to their outer sense. They are symbolical and contain realities of spiritual meaning. For instance, in the book of Solomon's songs you will read about the bride and bridegroom. It is evident that the physical bride and bridegroom are not intended. Obviously, these are symbols conveying a hidden and inner significance ....**The teachings of all religions are expressed largely by parables and metaphors and not in the plain language of the people**, **for divine things are too deep to be expressed by common words**. **The heavenly teachings are expressed in parable in order to be understood and preserved for ages to come*** [my emphasis]. *When the spiritually minded dive deeply into the ocean of their meaning they bring to the surface the pearls of their inner significance. There is no greater pleasure than to study God's Word with a spiritual mind.*[35-AC]

To symbolize aspects of spiritual reality, prophetic sky symbols are especially important, since

> *the heavens and the earth...the sun and the moon, all have been created to the end that His* [God's] *servants may have unswerving faith in His presence.*[36-B]

The prime image of the sky or heaven signifies the One Religion of God or one of its Messengers or Faiths, for

> *'heaven' denoteth loftiness and exaltation as the seat of the revelation of those Manifestations...descended from the heaven of the will of God. Though they be dwelling on this earth, yet their true habitations are the retreats of glory in the realms above. Whilst walking amongst mortals, they soar in the heaven of the divine presence.*[37-B]

Individual prophetic sky-images like *sun, moon, stars, lightnings, thunders, hail,* and *clouds* symbolize aspects of spiritual reality. Each image appears in the left-column text of the Parallel Interpretation, and its interpretation appears opposite in the matching right-column text.

Sky-images put a material face on spiritual reality. The material reality that we see, hear, feel, smell, and taste reflects, echoes, and emanates an infinite reality that is farther past our ken than the Big Dipper star-constellation is past the electron dotting about the nucleus of a hydrogen atom. Or seen another way, the entire material *world* is *worth as much as the black in the eye of a dead ant.*[38-B]

Above the ocean of truth, *Reality*'s titanic iceberg displays its small tip of *material-reality*; under this ocean, it hides its huge chunk of *spiritual-reality*. Its iceberg's small visible tip of material-reality serves as simply a beacon for its huge hidden chunk of spiritual-reality. Yet folk generally believe that material reality is the reality there is. In the diagram, the small face of humanity persists in seeing itself at the center of the show, remaining oblivious to the spiritual gold circle of Godhead as the true center of Reality.

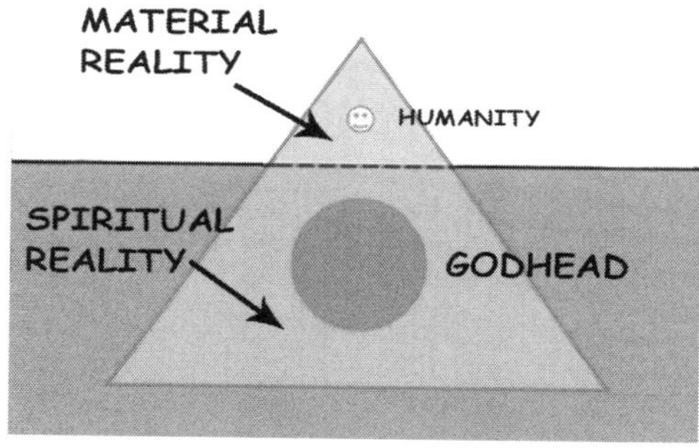

The *Reality* iceberg

PROPHECIES FOR THE YEAR 1844

Prophecy addresses reality in space and time. As a spiritual as well as a scientific man, Albert Einstein connected space and time with thought-experiments. In one experiment, he sits on a beam of light, watches physical reality stretch through endless space, senses spiritual reality extend through infinite time, hears centuries shoot by as days, feels millennia flash by as months, and asks God:

God, how long is a million years?

God replies:

For Me, Albert, it's a Minute.

Then Einstein asks:

God, how much is a million dollars?

God replies:

For Me, Albert, it's a Cent.

So Einstein asks:

Please God, give me a Cent.

God replies:

OK, Albert. In a Minute!

While sky-images help prophecy to address reality in space, so time-prophecies help prophecy to address reality in time. All Faiths' Scriptures contain coded time-prophecies that predict year-dates for special events. To decode these time-prophecies, the Old Testament states that *each day corresponds to a year* stressed in one case as *one year for each of the 40 days*.[39-JAR] This is the tried, tested, and true *a-day-for-a-year* formula.

The Apocalypse indirectly refines the a-day-for-a-year formula further. Its *five-month* time-prophecy evokes a prior five-month Old Testament period defined as exactly 150 days.[40-RJ] So each prophetic *month* equals 30 prophetic *days*. Fixed 30–day months accord with the Bible's first Chaldean calendar, each of whose solar years had twelve 30-day months, plus another 5–6 leap-days that keep its year with the sun.

The refined a-day-for-a-year formula thus defines a prophetic *day* as one real year, a prophetic *month* as 30 real years, and a prophetic *year* as 360 real years.[A] The following pages 36–40 will use the formula to decode a whole range of scriptural time-prophecies that predict the year 1844.

[A] In addition, a less-used *a-day-for-a-thousand-years* formula is discussed separately on page 89

1844 in the Book of Revelation

The a-day-for-a-year formula lets two Revelation time-prophecies decode for 1844, one on the Christian calendar, the other on the Muslim calendar. Muslim years began in AD 622 with ***Anno Hijrae*** calendar year **AH** 1. It has lunar years of 354 days with 12 alternating months of 29 and 30 days, along with a leap-day every three years to keep its months with the moon. These two time-prophecies are:

- ***A day plus a month plus a year*** signifying *391 days* (= 1 + 30 + 360) of Christian years from AD 1453 when Christian Constantinople fell to Islam, up to AD 1844 (1453 + 391 = 1844).[41]
- ***1,260 days, 42 months,*** and ***3½ days/seasons*** as three versions of a single time-prophecy whose

  three days and a half signify three years and a half, and three years and a half are forty and two months, and forty and two months twelve hundred and sixty days....As each day by the text of the Holy Book signifies one year, the meaning is...twelve hundred and sixty years.[42-A]

  These 1,260 *days* are the years of the AH 1–1260 (AD 622 to 1844) Muslim Era. Read as *1260 days* of years, they promote joy over two Witnesses and a pregnant woman. Heard as *42 months* of 42 × 30 *days* of years, they mourn Jerusalem trampled by a beast. Felt as *3½ days/seasons* of 3½ × 360 *days* of years, they support two Witnesses, their teachings, and the survival of the woman.[43-A]

Three lesser Revelation time-prophecies of ***ten days*** (v. 2.10), ***about half-an-hour*** (v. 8.1), and ***five months*** (v. 9.5) are decoded separately in their verses' respective *Comments* on pages 149, 189, and 194.

The Christian year AD 1844 coincided with the Muslim year AH 1260 as the year that acted as the spiritual fulcrum tipping the old Cycle of Prophecy into the new Cycle of Fulfillment.[44] For this year,

> *the prophecies correspond to one another. In the Apocalypse, the appearance of the Promised One is appointed after forty-two months, and Daniel expresses it as three times and a half, which is also forty-two months, which are twelve hundred and sixty days....Nothing could be clearer than this agreement of the prophecies with one another....For him who is just, the agreement of the times indicated by the tongues of the Great Ones is the most conclusive proof.*[45-A]

The special year AD 1844 launched four tough end-time centuries, near whose middle we now live, close to their nadir moment when they begin to double as beginning-times for the golden Millennium starting in AD 2140.

1844 in Judaism

Judaism predicts 1844 with the following prophecies:

- God *shall smite you* [Israel] *sevenfold*.[46-J] This decodes tightly as 2,520 years (7 × 360 *days*) of the People of Israel[A] suffering from Assyria conquering Israel in 677 BC up to 1844 (677 + 1844 – 1 = 2520, where "–1" corrects for no "year 0"). *Sevenfold* may also decode broadly for (1) Assyria, (2) Media, (3) Greece, (4) Rome, (5) the Crusaders, (6) the Inquisition, and (7) the Holocaust serially smiting the People of Israel severely seven times
- *The daily sacrifice forsaken due to sin, the sanctuary surrendered, the army trampled...for 2,300 days*. These *2,300 days* decode as 2,300 years from the 457 BC Artaxerxes decree that let Ezra restart services in the rebuilt Jerusalem Temple up to 1844 (457 + 1844 – 1 = 2300). This decree fulfilled similar prior 536 BC and 519 BC decrees by Cyrus and Darius.[47-J]
- *The kingdom of a beast that would change times and law for three-and-a-half seasons*.[48-J] The *3½ seasons* decode as the 1260 years (*3½ years* × 360 *days* of years) of the AH 1–1260 or AD 622–1844 brutal Era of Islam.
- *In the year 600 of the sixth millennium, the gates of Wisdom of above and the fountains of Wisdom below shall be opened and the world shall be prepared to enter the Seventh Millennium*.[49-J] This short-form *year 600* decodes as Jewish year AM 5600 (AD 1840, almost 1844) that opened our four end-time centuries up to the start of the Jewish Seventh Millennium due to begin in AM 6000/AD 2240
- The Messiah will come after *Christianity and Mohammedanism ...universally extend their sway*. As for timing, *the key to the mystery* is *Ba'laam's statement, Num. 23.23...'WHAT HAS GOD WROUGHT'*.[50-J] These were the exact words that Samuel Morse chose to wire as his first code message from Washington to Baltimore on May 24 1844, one day after the proclamation of the Bab.

1844 in Zoroastrianism

Zoroastrianism predicts the advents of its *Hushidar* or *Door of Wisdom* and another Prophet, both timed in terms of the *religion of the Arabian*—but a thousand years **before** the advent of Islam:

- *When 1,260 years have elapsed from the religion of the Arabian ....Hushidar will appear* and *the Iranians will kill him*.[51] The *1,260 years* decode as the AH 1–1260 (AD 622–1844) Muslim Era. The title *Door of Wisdom* fits the Bab as a spiritual Door.

[A] The term *People of Israel* refers to the remnant of the 12 tribes of Israel, primarily today's Jews, but potentially also some or all of today's Palestinians

- *A thousand two hundred and some years...from the inception of the religion of the Arabian and the overthrow of the kingdom of Iran and the degradation of the followers of My religion, a descendent* [sic] *of the Iranian kings will be raised up as a Prophet.*[52] The *1200 and some years* decode as 1250 Muslim years from AD 650 (AH 30) when Muslim forces defeated Persia's last Zoroastrian King Yazdigird, up to the proclamation of his descendant Baha'u'llah as in AD 1863 (AH 1280).
- *In three separate Dispensations, the sun must...be brought to a standstill. In the first Dispensation...for ten days; in the second for twice that time; in the third for no less than one whole month. For the Muhammadan Dispensation...each day is reckoned as one century...from the setting of the Star of the Imamate to...the Báb.* In this triple time-prophecy, the
  - *Ten days* decodes as ten centuries from the end of the Imamate in AH 260 (AD 873) up to AH 1260 (AD 1844)
  - *Twice that time* decodes as twenty *days* of years for the Era *inaugurated by the Báb...in the year 1260 A. H.* (AD 1844) coming *to a close in the year 1280 A. H.* (AD 1863)
  - *Not less than one whole month* decodes as a stellar 2147-year *Month* of the Age of Aquarius (see pages 40, 56, and 102).[53-AS]

1844 in Hinduism

Hinduism predicts the appearance of its Kalki Tenth Avatar:

When the practices taught by the Vedas and the institutes of law shall nearly have ceased, and the close of the Kali age shall be nigh, a portion of that divine being...shall descend upon the earth...born as Kalki in the family of an eminent brahmin...then reestablish righteousness upon earth....The minds of those who *live at the end of the Kali age shall be awakened, and shall be as pellucid as crystal. The men who are thus changed by virtue of that peculiar time...shall give birth to a race who shall follow the laws of the Krita age.*[54]

In 1844, the 4,800-year Kali Budding Era of Hinduism, which closed its Long Cycle, tipped into its Krita Golden Era, which opened its Truth Cycle.[55]

1844 in Buddhism

Buddhism predicts the coming of its Maitreiya Fifth Buddha:

Before this same auspicious aeon runs to the end of its years ...there will be Maitreiya.

Since Buddhism shares the Hindu calendar, this *auspicious aeon* means the Hindu Kali Era. *Maitreiya* means *kindness,* as does *Husayn*, Baha'u'llah's given name as *a Messenger...full of kindness.*[56-M]

1844 in Christianity

The two aforementioned Apocalypse time-prophecies predict the return of Jesus, whose statement that *Jerusalem shall be trampled by the gentiles until the times of the gentiles are fulfilled*[57] had itself augured how v. 11.2's *1260-day* prophecy involves gentiles.

In the mid-1800s, Christian Millennialists accurately decoded the 2,300-day time-prophecy of Daniel for the 1844 return of Jesus. They knew that AD 1844 was also the same as the Muslim year AH 1260. But they blithely chose to disregard the perfect fit between their AD 1844 and the Islam's AH 1260, in spite of it matching the 1260-day time-prophecy in both the Books of Daniel and Revelation. They refused to accept that the Muslim calendar could predict, specify, or endorse any year for the return of Jesus. By ignoring the perfect timing, the blind Millennialists missed the good news. For them, 1844 came and went as a non-event they called the *Great Disappointment*. Disheartened, Millennialists fell from the fold or became Jehovah's Witnesses, Seventh-Day Adventists, or Branch Davidians.

However, ironically, Millennialists did accept that Revelation could predict Islam as **bad** news. Thus, in Chapter 9, they did see militant Islam's Umayyad *Locust* cavalries swarming out of Arabia, heard its *Scorpion* archers' arrows whistling over the Middle East, and smelled its Ottoman cannon smoke enveloping Constantinople.[58]

ZOAR 1844 engraved on a Welsh church.
ZOAR (better, *ZOHAR*) is Hebrew for *GLORY*

1844 in Islam

Shi'i Islam expects the return of its Qaim Twelfth Imam:

- *The Qa'im...to be made manifest...in the year 'sixty'...his cause shall be revealed and his name noised abroad.*[59-MS] This short-form *year 'sixty'* decodes as AH 12**60** (AD 1844)
- *Everything will ascend to Him on a Day that will measure a thousand years.*[60-M] These *thousand years* (Muslim years) date from the Imamate ending in AH 260 (AD 873) up to the advent of the Bab as the Twelfth Imam in AH 1260 (AD 1844; see page 123)[61]
- *In the year 'GHARS' the earth shall be illumined by his light.*[62-MS] By Abjad numerology, *GHARS = 1260*, again for AH 1260 (AD 1844)
- *The year of his Revelation is identical with half of that number which is divisible by nine.*[63-MS] The number 2520 is the lowest to be divisible cleanly by all nine digits. Half of 2520 is 1260. So this prophecy decodes as AH 1260 (AD 1844) too.

1844 in the Baha'i Faith

The Baha'i Faith identifies 1844 retrospectively as *the ninth year* dated from the 1852 vision of Baha'u'llah:

- *In the year nine this Most Great Revelation arose and shone forth brightly*, decoded as AH 1268 (1260 + 8, or AD 1852)
- *The Báb announced that the greater manifestation would take place...in the ninth year*, decoded as AH 1268 (AD 1852)
- *His Cause will be made known after 'HIN'*. By Abjad numerology, this short-form *HIN = 68* decoded as AH 12**68** (AD 1852).[64-ABS]

Therefore, simple arithmetic lets the prophetic Scriptures of all main monotheistic Faiths predict 1844.[A] Complex calculations or odd notions like *rapture* or *tribulation*[65] are not needed. As the Muslim year AH 1260, the pivotal year of 1844 rang out the Cycle of Prophecy's last Muslim Era. As the Baha'i year BE 1, the same pivotal year of 1844 rang in the Cycle of Fulfillment's first Baha'i Era. So the Baha'i calendar began in AD 1844 with **B**aha'i **E**ra year BE 1. This Baha'i calendar runs on solar years, each with 19 months of 19 days, plus 4–5 leap-days that keep its years with the sun.

The year 1844 dawned also the Age of Aquarius, which launched a fleet of magnificent inventions across the ocean of its new knowledge, unleashed a torrent of utopian universal messianic religions, and laced many rivers of learning with divine power.

[A] In addition, a Toltec Indian prophecy predicts that *a Savior will dawn from the East...in the 13th Era* (AD 1844–1896), where each Toltec *Era* is 52 years (Kahn 8 cited by Motlagh 357–8)

1844 in the Ottoman Edicts of Toleration

Starting in 1839, to try to revive its crumbling Empire, the Ottoman Sultanate enacted *Tanzimat* reforms whose *Edicts of Toleration* played a key part in reversing centuries of legal discrimination against the Empire's non-Muslims as second-class citizens and giving them legal equality. Especially in Palestine, the Edicts would benefit its Jews and Christians who had been habitually

> *barred from offices* and *had to humble and to humiliate themselves in diverse ways, wear clothes and badges that set them apart. Their places of worship were desecrated, damaged, or destroyed....Like their Christian fellow subjects, the Jews were inferior citizens in the Muslim-Ottoman state which was based on the principle of Muslim superiority.... Their testimony was not accepted in the courts of justice, and in cases of the murder of a Jew or Christian by a Muslim, the latter was usually not condemned to death. In addition, Jews as well as Christians were normally not acceptable for appointments to the highest administrative posts; they were forbidden to carry arms (thus, to serve in the army), to ride horses in towns or to wear Muslim dress. They were also not usually allowed to build or repair places of worship and were often subjected to oppression, extortion and violence by both the local authorities and the Muslim population.*[66]

Even in just the street, Jews and Christians had to walk on the left side, making them easy targets for Muslim stones. Worst of all, Muslims who converted to Christianity were executed.

Prior to the Edicts, the Empire had given its *People of the Book* (non-Muslims of other Faiths) legal status as *zimmis* (*protected*), for which they had to pay the *jizya* poll-tax as a form of protection money. Even the process of paying the jizya was turned into

> *a sign of their inferior status*, with the *object in levying the tax the subjection of infidels to humiliation. During the process of payment, the zimmi is seized by the collar and vigorously shaken and pulled about in order to show him his degradation.*

After all, the Quran told Muslims to *fight those of the People of the Book...until they pay the jizyah.* The Umayyad Caliphate and later the Ottoman Sultanate compounded the cruelty. They enforced payment of the jizya tax by obliging zimmis to take a tattoo on the forehead (a later similar tattoo on the hand/wrist would enforce a *kharaj* property-tax on landowners).

Yet Muhammad had begun the jizya sensibly enough as a 5% income tax exempting zimmis from serving in the Muslim army or from paying the 2.5% *zakat* income-tax as a *pillar of Islam* obligatory on Muslims.[67-M]

In Palestine, particularly, Muslim discrimination against Jews and Christians was rife, especially in Jerusalem amid holy sites where they rubbed shoulders with Muslims daily. In Jerusalem Jews had already suffered discrimination for two millennia from the Roman, Christian, Persian, and Muslim rulers of Palestine. For example, Christian Patriarch Sofronius had conditioned his peaceful AD 638 surrender of Jerusalem upon Muslim conqueror Caliph Umar agreeing to ban Jews from the city (he did). Therefore in Palestine, not surprisingly, it took five more years for the 1839 Edicts of Toleration to take effect and benefit Jews and Christians there. Two precedents helped. In the 1830s, Egyptian invaders had proposed similar reforms for Palestine; in 1840, the new Edicts had prevented a massacre of Jews in nearby Damascus.[68]

Finally, in 1844, a signal legal case let the new Edicts bite in Palestine. A Muslim court ignoring the new Edicts and had condemned a Muslim convert to Christianity to death.[69-M] European governments cried foul, and invoked the Edicts with Istanbul. The Ottoman Government (*Sublime Porte*) responded favorably and forbade the *putting to death of the Christian who is an apostate.* In concert, the Sultan promised that *henceforward neither shall Christianity be insulted in my dominions, nor shall Christians be in any way persecuted for their religion.*[70-M]

The date of these Ottoman decrees was March 21 (Nissan 1) 1844. On that exact same Nissan 1 date 2,300 years before, Ezra had left Persia to restart Jerusalem's Temple services, authorized by the 457 BC decree of Artaxerxes, to fulfill to the day the 2,300-day prophecy of Daniel—from Nissan 1, 457 BC to Nissan 1/March 21, AD 1844.[A]

For Palestinian Jews, the main thrust of the Edicts was to let them own property and land there legally at last. After 1844, Jews began to buy both, much in Jerusalem,[71-J] where they became the majority by the end of the 1850s. In 1844, the Palestine Council of Agriculture opened up its membership to Jews for the first time. In 1844, George Bush, a Professor of Hebrew at New York University called and an ancestor of two American Presidents, published a proto-Zionist book called *The Dry Bones of Israel Revived* that promoted the restoration of the People of Israel to the Holy Land.[72-J]

Accordingly, the prophetic year 1844 ended *the breaking of the power of the holy people.*[73-J] This seminal year of conception of the State of Israel seeded its embryonic burst of land-purchase, led to its fetal century of Jewish ingathering, and bore it painfully as a state in 1948.

[A] Back then, the main Jewish New Year began on Nissan 1

TWIN MESSIAHS

The Bab as The *Door*

The year 1844 began the Baha'i Era of God's lesser and greater Messiahs. In 1844, the Bab proclaimed himself as the lesser Messiah of God predicted by the Scriptures of all main monotheistic Faiths as

- Judaism's *Messiah Ben Yosef* or *Return of Elijah*
- Zoroastrianism's *Hushidar Door of Wisdom*
- Hinduism's *Kalki Tenth Avatar*
- Buddhism's *Fourth Buddha*
- Christianity's *Second Coming* or *Jesus Returned*
- Sunni Islam's *Guided Mahdi*, and
- His own Shi'a Islam's *Raised Qa'im*.[74-S]

The Bab, a title meaning *The Door*, was born in Shiraz, Persia in AD 1819. He worked as a merchant and lived an exemplary personal life. He taught new spiritual truths and severely condemned the many injustices promulgated by Persia's Qajar regime and Shi'a clergy. His claims and teachings led to his arrest. In prison, he wrote his central scripture, the *Bayan* (*Exposition*), whose main purpose was to herald the advent of a greater Twin Messiah of God to follow him imminently.

In 1850, the Bab was sentenced to die by firing squad in Tabriz. Over 10,000 people watched his execution, including reporters from Europe. The 750-man squad fired. Yet after the smoke cleared, no body was visible. Instead, the Bab was found alive, unscathed, back in his cell, closing a final dictation that had been rudely cut short before. The firing squad deserted. Hours later a new squad was marshaled; this squad did kill the Bab.[75] His followers hid his remains for fifty years, the brought them to Haifa in 1899–1900, to be buried on Mount Carmel as the mountain of the first Elijah on March 21, 1909.

The Jewish *Zohar* predicted these events:

> *The king of Persia will...kill...Messiah Son of Joseph* who *will remain dead until...he will gather life from the higher hill* and *in the year 66 appear in the land of Galilee....A star from the east will swallow up seven stars*.[76]

The *king of Persia* was Shah Nasir-i-Din. The *Messiah Son of Joseph* was the Bab. The *higher hill* was Mount Carmel. The short-form *year 66* was Jewish year AM 56**66**, namely AD 1906 (almost 1909). The *star from the east* was the Bab. And the *seven stars* were God's prior seven Messengers.

The Bab was a lot like Jesus:

- He was raised a devout Muslim as Jesus had been raised a devout Jew
- He worked as a merchant as Jesus had worked as a carpenter

- He proclaimed himself aged only 24 as Jesus had proclaimed himself aged only 30
- He taught for only six years (1844–1850) as Jesus had taught for only three years (~AD 30–33)
- His teachings enraged Persia's Qajar regime and imams as Jesus's teachings had enraged Israel's Roman regime and rabbis
- He was executed aged 30 as Jesus had been executed aged 33
- He was held before his execution at a military barracks in Tabriz as Jesus had been held before his execution at a military barracks in Jerusalem
- He was pierced by firing squad bullets as Jesus had been pierced by crucifixion nails
- His disciples were all martyred as all of Jesus's Apostles had all been martyred (except for John).

The Bab was a full Manifestation of God in his own right, with his own Babi Era. However, the Bab was also a lesser Messiah heralding a greater Messiah akin to *John the Baptist...another time* whose book

> *the Bayan deriveth all its glory from Him Whom God shall make manifest....All that hath been revealed in the Bayan is but a ring upon My hand, and I Myself am, verily, but a ring upon the hand of Him....Were He to appear this very moment, I would be the first to adore Him, and the first to bow down before Him.*[77-S]

Concurring, Baha'u'llah explains that

> *the sole object of whatsoever My Previous Manifestation* [the Bab] *hath revealed hath been My Revelation* as his *Latter Manifestation...whereof He hath made mention in His Tablets, and in His Books, and in His Scriptures.*[78-B]

The AD 1844–1863 (BE 1–19) Babi Era of the Bab was indeed short for a Messenger of God, lasting just 19 years, not the usual thousand. This meant that the Baha'i Era of Baha'u'llah's was

> *at hand in less than the twinkling of an eye....That so brief an interval separated this most mighty and wondrous Revelation from Mine* [Baha'u'llah's] *is...a mystery such as no mind can fathom...its duration...foreordained.*[79]

The Babi Era flowed smoothly into the Baha'i Era, to be subsumed by it inexorably. In time, the Bab augured Baha'u'llah. Yet in spirit, Baha'u'llah raised the Bab. By 1848, the Bab and his followers had already begun to recognize the leadership of Baha'u'llah. As an example, they readily adopted new titles that Baha'u'llah assigned to the first 18 disciples of the Bab (the *Letters of the Living*).[80-S] He and the Bab exchanged letters, but the two Prophets never met in person.

Baha'u'llah as the *Glory of God*

In 1863, Baha'u'llah rang himself in as the *Most Mighty Bell,*[81-B] to proclaim as the greater Messiah of God predicted by the Scriptures of all main monotheistic Faiths as

- Judaism's *Ancient of Days* or *Messiah Ben David*
- Zoroastrianism's *Saoshyant Bearer of Benefit* or *Shah Bahram*
- Hinduism's *Vishnu Yasha Avatar*, *Kalki Tenth Avatar*, or *Reincarnation of Krishna*
- Buddhism's *Maitreiya Fifth Buddha* or *Amitabha of Limitless Light*
- Christianity's *Appearance of the Father*
- Sunni Islam's *Muhdi Guider*
- His own Shi'a Islam's *Qayyum Raiser*, and
- His own Babi Faith's *One Whom God shall make manifest.*[82-S]

In other words, Baha'u'llah was

> *to Israel...neither more nor less than the incarnation of the 'Everlasting Father,' the 'Lord of Hosts' come down 'with ten thousands of saints'; to Christendom Christ returned 'in the glory of the Father'; to Shí'ah* [sic] *Islám the return of the Imam Husayn; to Sunni Islám the descent of the 'Spirit of God' (Jesus Christ); to the Zoroastrians the promised Shah-Bahram; to the Hindus the reincarnation of Krishna; to the Buddhists the fifth Buddha.*[83-S]

Baha'u'llah is a title meaning *Glory of God.* He was a nobleman born in Teheran, Persia, in AD 1817. Like the Bab, Baha'u'llah lived an exemplary personal life. Baha'u'llah taught spiritual truths for over forty years, expanded the teachings of the Bab, condemning injustices in Persia, the Middle East, and the world, and decrying war.

The lineage of Baha'u'llah was both noble and prophetic. He was a

> *descendant of Abraham through both Katurah and Sarah ...(through a son of his other than Isaac and Ishmael, from his wife Katurah*). Isaiah's words that *there shall come forth a rod out of the stem of Jesse, and a Branch shall grow out of his roots...apply word for word to Baha'u'llah* as the *Pre-Existent Root....Jesse, son of Sarah* [the line of Judah] *was the father of David and the ancestor of Baha'u'llah.* Baha'u'llah's *connection with the Faith of Judaism...is a tremendous and fascinating theme...which possesses great interest to Jew and Christian alike.* Furthermore, Baha'u'llah *derived his descent...from Zoroaster, as well as from the last Sasaniyan king Yazdigird.*[84-AS]

During Persia's persecution of Babis in 1852, Baha'u'llah was arrested on false charges, chained and incarcerated in Teheran's notorious *Black Pit* dungeon. Here a vision of a *Maiden symbolizing the Most Great Spirit* announced his mission and promised:[85-S]

We shall render Thee victorious by Thyself and by Thy Pen. Grieve Thou not for that which hath befallen Thee, neither be Thou afraid, for Thou art in safety. Erelong will God raise up the treasures of the earth—men who will aid Thee through Thyself and through Thy Name.[86-B]

After four months, Baha'u'llah was declared innocent and released. Regardless, the Persian government feared his influence, stripped him of titles and wealth, and exiled him and his family to Baghdad in Iraq, which its ally Ottoman Turkey ruled. In Baghdad, he spent ten years (including two alone in the wilds of Kurdistan), and his fame grew. In 1863, Turkey summoned him to Istanbul, partly to discover who he was, partly pressed by Persia to take him farther from Iran.

On his way out of Baghdad in 1863 Baha'u'llah proclaimed himself and his mission. In Turkey, he was first held in Istanbul, then in Adrianople. Finally, in 1868 he was shipped to perpetual imprisonment in the notorious Ottoman prison colony of Acco (Acre, Akko) in Palestine. He was a prisoner until he died aged 75 in 1892, under steadily easing conditions, teaching and writing continually.

Baha'u'llah's Passport

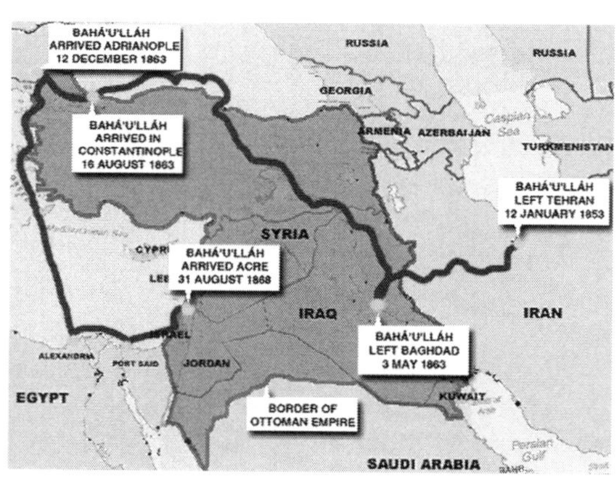

Map showing Baha'u'llah's route to the Holy Land

The 1863 proclamation year of Baha'u'llah is as important as the 1844 proclamation year of the Bab. In 1863 (AH 1280), the prophetic *'thousand two hundred and ninety days', fixed by Daniel...elapsed.* These *1290 days* decode as Muslim years from the 10 BH (AD 613) *proclamation of the prophethood of Muhammad* up to Baha'u'llah's AH 1280 (AD 1863) proclamation (10 + 1280 = 1290).[87-SA]

Further, the 1963 centennial of 1863

brought into fulfillment Daniel's great prophecy of...1335 days. What could be more wonderful than taking part in the fulfillment of religious prophecy! This *blissful consummation (1335 days) announced by Daniel...had commenced* after *a century...elapsed* from the *dawn of the Sun of Truth,* and with *the Teachings of God...firmly established upon the earth,* and *the spread of the Faith over the face of the earth.*[88-SA]

These *1335 days* decode *as solar and not lunar years* that date from the AD 628 signing of the Hudaybiyyah peace treaty that "gelled" Islam up to the 1963 establishment of the Baha'i House of Justice (628 + 1335 = 1963) that "gelled" the Baha'i Faith.[89-AS]

The Tombs of Baha'u'llah and the Bab

The tombs of Baha'u'llah and the Bab are the Baha'i Faith's holiest shrines. Its most holy shrine is the modest tomb of Baha'u'llah within the magnificent Bahji Gardens just outside Acco.

Tomb of Baha'u'llah near Acco

But for the Bab's tomb, Baha'u'llah instructed that it should have a grand design at a prominent site in Haifa

on the wonderful efflorescence of Mount Carmel

where it would always be seen widely as the

Queen of Carmel enthroned on God's Mountain crowned in glowing gold, robed in shimmering white, girdled in emerald green, enchanting every eye from air, sea, plain and hill.[90-S]

This celebrated shrine of the Bab is located at

> *THE CENTER OF NINE CONCENTRIC CIRCLES* around which *the realities of the Prophets and Messengers revolve....The outermost* [9th] *circle in this vast system, the visible counterpart of the pivotal position conferred on the Herald of our Faith, is...the... planet. Within the heart of this planet lies the* [8th circle] *'Most Holy Land', acclaimed by 'Abdu'l-Baha as the 'Nest of the Prophets'...the center of the world and the Qiblih of the nations. Within this Most Holy Land rises the* [7th circle] *Mountain of God the Vineyard of the Lord* [*Carm-El*], *the Retreat of Elijah, Whose return the Báb Himself symbolizes. Reposing on the breast of this holy mountain are the extensive...precincts of the Báb's* [6th circle] *holy Sepulcher. In the midst...is the* [5th circle] *most holy court comprising gardens and terraces which at once embellish, and lend a peculiar charm to, these sacred precincts. Embosomed in these lovely and verdant surroundings stands in all its exquisite beauty the* [4th circle] *mausoleum of the Báb... tomb of the Martyr-Herald of our Faith. Within this shell is enshrined that Pearl of Great Price...the* [3rd circle] *tomb itself. Within the heart of this holy of holies is the* [2nd circle] *tabernacle, the vault wherein reposes the most holy casket...the* [1st circle] *alabaster sarcophagus in which is deposited that inestimable jewel, the Báb's holy dust.*[91-S]

Tomb of the Bab on Mount Carmel

Mount Carmel

Mount Carmel is the *sacred mountain of God* in the Book of Isaiah and the *large and lofty mountain* and the *Armageddon* or *Mountain of Preaching* in the Book of Revelation. Baha'u'llah visited Mount Carmel in 1890. As he walked on it, the mountain *cried out, trembling as if shaken by the breezes of the Lord.*[92-BS] Here he delivered his *Tablet of Carmel* addressing the mountain for God, saying:

> *This Day...the countenance of the Ancient of Days hath turned towards His holy seat....Carmel...the light of the countenance of God...hath been lifted upon thee....Rejoice, for God hath in this Day established upon thee His throne, hath made thee the dawning-place of His signs....Well is it with him...that proclaimeth the revelation of thy glory, and recounteth that which the bounty of the Lord thy God hath showered upon thee....He, verily, loveth the spot which hath been made the seat of His throne, which His footsteps have trodden....Call out to Zion, O Carmel, and announce the joyful tidings: He that was hidden from mortal eyes is come! His all-conquering sovereignty is manifest; His all-encompassing splendour is revealed....The City of God...hath descended from heaven....Say unto the cities of Judah: 'Behold your God!'....This Day all the signs have appeared....Carmel...the Hill of God....Here...the Tabernacle of Glory hath been raised....The splendor of Carmel...shall see the glory of the Lord, and the splendor of our God. These passages stand in need of no commentary. They are shining and manifest as the sun, and glowing and luminous as light itself. Every fair-minded person is led, by the fragrance of these words, unto the garden of understanding.*[93-B]

Mount Carmel,

> *this Spot, this scene of transcendent splendour...enshrines the heart of the Faith itself, its Cradle...and its most sacred and historic sites* where the Baha'i Faith's *three Central Figures...are buried.* Mount Carmel is *not only the centre of Baha'i pilgrimages from all over the world but also the permanent seat of our Administrative Order...attracting widespread interest, not only on the part of the Baha'is, but of the public of the State of Israel as well....Mount Carmel expresses the oneness of the Faith's being. In contrast to the circumstances of other world religions, the spiritual and administrative centres...are inseparably bound together in this same spot on earth, its guiding institutions centered on the Shrine of its martyred Prophet....The harmony...in the variegated flowers, trees and shrubs of the surrounding gardens seems to proclaim the ideal of* ***unity in diversity*** [my emphasis].[94-S]

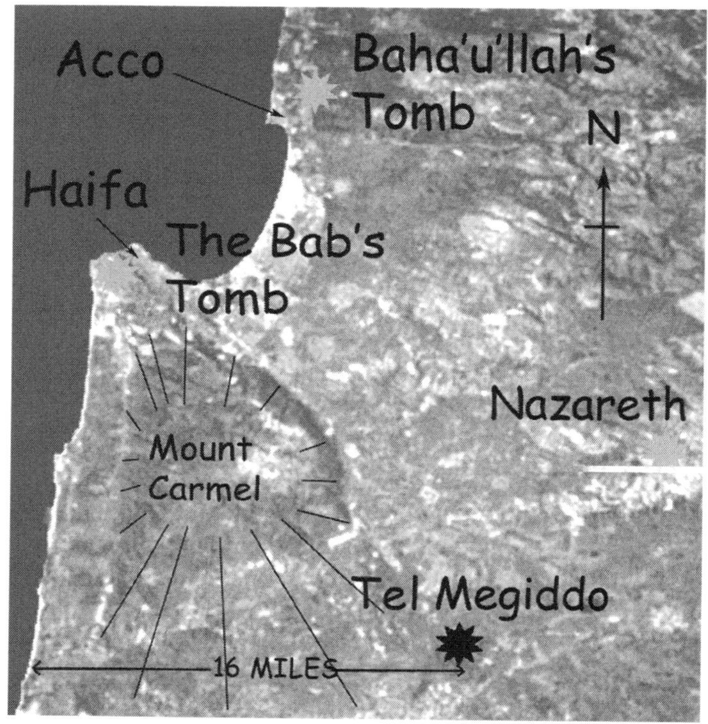

Map showing Baha'i Holy Sites near the triangle of Mount Carmel

Furthermore, Baha'u'llah's

> *Tablet of Carmel* called *into being the metropolis of the Kingdom of God on Earth...so linked with the city of 'Akká that a single grand metropolis will be formed to enshrine the spiritual as well as the administrative seats of the future Baha'i Commonwealth....From Mount Carmel will stream forth rivers of laws and ordinances...with all-conquering power and awe-inspiring majesty, the like of which past ages have never seen.*[95-S]

RELIGIOUS REVELATION IS PROGRESSIVE

For its first million years or so, humanity wandered, and gathered and hunted its food.[96] In contrast, for the past ten thousand years, humanity has been steadily settling, farming fields, foddering flocks for food; creating written records; and bonding and banding into bigger and bigger tribes, villages, towns, counties, countries, and now the globe. During humanity's settled period, divine Messengers were serially *sent down through the operation of the Divine Will*[97-B] and each reincarnated the spirit of

> *all the Prophets and Messengers of God as one soul and one body, as one light and one spirit...united in their message.*[98-BA]

As the same planet Venus as the *Evening-Star* ends an old day and as the *Dawn-Star* begins the new day, so spiritually each divine Messenger ends the Day of an old Era and begins the Day of a new Era. These Messengers come down from the heaven of the same limitless past and immeasurable future and teach the same things in order to

> ***liberate...men from the darkness of ignorance...ensure the peace and tranquillity of mankind, and provide all the means*** [my emphasis] *by which they can be established ....Prophets of God have ever appeared in the ages of the past and will continue to appear throughout the ages of the future. Where was Adam when God was exercising his divinity? Where was this petty infinitesimal world of ours when God was bestowing his bounties upon this infinite universe?* ***If we limit the number of his appearances through his prophets, it is equal to limiting God himself*** [my emphasis].[99-BA]

As God has many names, so do His Messengers as *Avatars, Delegates, Enthroned-Ones, Founders, Luminaries, Manifestations, Presences, Prophets, Revelators, Revealers, Spirits, Teachers, Words,* and especially,

> *inasmuch as these holy beings have sanctified themselves from every human limitation, have become endowed with the attributes of the spiritual, and have been adorned with the noble traits of the blessed, they therefore have been designated as 'angels'.*[100-B]

Angel means *Messenger*. Both *Angel* and *Messenger* are good translations of the Old Testament Hebrew *Malach* and of the New Testament Greek *Angelos*. The Parallel Interpretation balances their presence by using *Angel* in its left-side translation and *Messenger* in its right-side interpretation.

Revelation's *Seven-Churches of Asia* portray the seven monotheistic Faiths of Abraham, Moses, Zoroaster, Krishna, Buddha, Jesus, and Muhammad, whose separate Faiths have successfully survived to span time across six millennia and space across Asia.

The Seven Faiths from Asia

Asia's Fertile-Crescent was home to the serial Messengers Adam, Noah, Abraham, Moses, Jesus, and Muhammad. Adam's teachings[101] were a nucleus for Noah's teachings. Noah's teachings seeded the **Sabaeanism** of Abraham. Sabaeanism's teachings jump-started the **Judaism** of Moses. Judaism's teachings catalyzed the **Christianity** of Jesus. Christianity's teachings inspired the **Islam** of Muhammad. Each time, a later Messenger's teachings entrained a prior Messenger's teachings.

Asia's Indian-Subcontinent was home to the serial Avatars Matsya (*Fish*), Kurma (*Tortoise*), Varaha (*Boar*), Nrisinha (*Man-Lion*), Vamana (*Dwarf*), Parasurama (*Axe*), Rama, Krishna, and Buddha. The teachings of Matsya, Kurma, Varaha, Nrisinha, Vamana, and Parasurama peppered the teachings of Rama. Rama's teachings spiced the **Hinduism** of Krishna. Hinduism's teachings laced the **Buddhism** of Buddha.[102] Now just Hinduism and Buddhism survive today as separate Faiths in this line.

Asia's Persia, between the Fertile-Crescent and the Indian-Subcontinent, was home to *many...Prophets...prior to the Dispensation of Zoroaster*.[103] The teachings of those Prophets zapped zest into the **Zoroastrianism** of Zoroaster. Today, just this line's last Faith of Zoroastrianism survives.

Messengers of God

Messengers are the divine champions running the spiritual relay of the One Religion of God. Each Messenger has advanced the One Religion by his own millennial stride of an Era. He has taken up the torch of truth from the Messenger before him, blazed it for a thousand years, and passed it on to the Messenger after him.

Revelation itself runs its own prophetic relay too. First, it burns as a Jewish Apocalypse. Next, it flames for Christianity and Islam. Now it blazes for their successor Baha'i Faith. Just as the last Old Testament Book of Malachi (*My Messenger*) ended the Jewish Era and began the Christian Era, so the last New Testament Book of Revelation ended the Christian Era and began the Baha'i Era. Just as Christians see the Messenger of Malachi as Jesus, so Baha'is see the Messenger of Revelation as Baha'u'llah.

A *chain of successive Revelations...linked the Manifestation of Adam with that of the Báb,*[104-AB] with each Manifestation serially unfurling

the standard of divine guidance, so that each *fulfilled the promise of the One Who came before Him and...announced the One Who would follow....Abraham foretold the coming of Moses, and Moses embodied the Abrahamic statement. Moses prophesied the Messianic cycle, and Christ fulfilled the law of Moses.*[105-B]

Divine Messengers have guided humankind through the growing pains of its babyhood, infancy, early childhood, late childhood, puberty, and adolescence, each cutting a step on a spiritual path matching the developmental level of his own Era:

The position of Adam...was in the embryonic condition....In the time of Christ, the divine teachings were given in accordance with the infancy of the human race....The teachings of Baha'u'llah have the same basic principles, but are according to the stage of the maturity of the world and the requirements of this illumined age.[106-A]

Adam[A] nursed humankind through its helpless babyhood, taught the existence of God, promoted family and work, and condemned murder and theft. Noah guided it through its narcissistic infancy, prohibited idolatry, blasphemy, murder, theft, cruelty to animals, and sexual immorality, and began courts of law. Abraham reared humankind through its early childhood, taught social laws, and banned idol-worship.[B] Moses raised it through its boisterous late childhood and dictated 613 commandments. Jesus has guided humankind through its insecure puberty and stressed brotherly love. Muhammad has disciplined through its stormy adolescence, refined Jewish and Christian laws, and stressed social love. Now the Bab and Baha'u'llah are guiding humankind through its early adulthood and are urging the planet's burgeoning seven billion folk to unite and launch a prosperous Millennium based on a divine global civilization.

Each of these Messengers has been

charged to act in a manner that would best meet the requirements of the age in which He appeared....Because of this difference in their station and mission...the words and utterances flowing from these Well-springs of divine knowledge appear to diverge and differ....Like the sun...in different seasons they ascend from different rising points on the horizon....The sun of today is the sun of yesterday....The sun of truth rises in each season from a different point of the horizon—to-day it is here, yesterday it was there, and to-morrow it will appear from

[A] The name ***Adam*** shares its triconsonantal A/D/M root with the Hebrew words ***adam*** for *human-being*, **adom** for *red* (a human skin color), and ***adam**ah* for *earth*

[B] One night, Abraham smashed all his father's idols except the biggest, whom he accused mockingly the next morning of having destroyed all the others during the night!

> *another direction. Why do you keep your eyes eternally fixed on the same point? Why do you call yourselves Christians, Buddhists, Mohammedans, Bahais? You must learn to distinguish the sun of truth from whichever point of the horizon it is shining!*[107-BA]

On the one hand, each divine Messenger has shown

> *a distinct individuality, a definitely prescribed mission, a predestined Revelation, and specially designated limitations. Each...is known by a different name, is characterized by a special attribute, fulfills a definite Mission, and is entrusted with a particular Revelation.*

At the same time, divine Messengers share a *station of essential unity* with *no distinction...between any of them,*[108-B] since they all have

> *brought the message of love. None has ever thought that war and hate are good. Everyone agrees in saying that love and kindness are best.* Each as a *manifestation of the Messiah was synonymous with universal mercy. His providence was universal and his teachings were for all. His lights were not restricted to a few....The light of Christ is evident. The candle of Buddha is shining. The star of Moses is sparkling. The flame ignited by Zoroaster is still burning.*[109-A]

Each prior Messenger shone as a single spiritual sun lighting an Era in the Cycle of Prophecy. But now **two** Messengers blaze brightly as a **binary** sun system opening the grand new Cycle of Fulfillment.

> *All the peoples of the world are awaiting two Manifestations who must be contemporaneous....In the Bible the Jews have the promise of the Lord of Hosts and the Messiah; in the Gospel the return of Christ and Elijah is promised. In the religion of Muhammad there is the promise of the Mihdi and the Messiah, and it is the same with the Zoroastrian and the other religions ....The essential fact is that all are promised two Manifestations ...one following on the other.*[110-A]

For Baha'is, these binary suns are the Bab and Baha'u'llah, Twin Messiahs who must by definition, appear together (as if Moses and Jesus had notionally appeared in one generation in one country). The Bab and Baha'u'llah fit twin prophetic bills of all Faiths as

- Judaism's *Ancient of Days* and *Return of Elijah*, its *King of Glory* and *Holy One of Israel*, or its *Messiah son of Joseph* and *Messiah son of David* who are born together from a *womb... encompassing two chambers...to give birth...to two Messiahs*[A] *...Messiah...son of Joseph* and *Messiah son of David*[111]

[A] Double-womb (*uterus didephys*) may indeed carry a twin in each cavity (see *Mich. woman with 2 wombs delivers twins,* http://www.msnbc.msn.com/id/29446416)

- Zoroastrianism's *Hushidar Door of Wisdom* and *Shah Bahram /Saoshyant*
- Hinduism's two last *Avatars*, with Baha'u'llah as its *Tenth Kalki Vishnu Yasha Avatar* or *Reincarnation of Krishna*
- Buddhism's *Fourth Buddha* and *Maitreiya Fifth Buddha*
- Christianity's *Jesus Returned* and *Appearance of the Father*
- Sunni Islam's *Mahdi* and *Muhdi* or as its *Return of Christ* and *Messiah*, and
- Shi'a Islam's *Qa'im Twelfth Imam* and *Qayyum Raiser*.[112]

Nine Faiths Survive

Nine monotheistic Faiths survive, with the number nine

> *symbolic of the perfection of the Bahá'í Revelation as the ninth... of...nine great world religions....The eighth is the religion of the Bab, and the remaining seven are: Hinduism, Buddhism, Zoroastrianism, Judaism, Christianity, Islam, and the religion of the Sabeans* [sic]....***These religions are not the only true religions that have appeared in the world, but are the only ones still existing*** [my emphasis].[113-S]

The early monotheistic Faiths of Adam, Noah, the Persian Prophets before Zoroaster, and the seven Avatars before Krishna did not last as Faiths but were instead entrained into, and subsumed by, their respective successor Sabaean, Zoroastrian, and Hindu Faiths. Other Messengers, like the Quranic Prophets Hud and Salih, left no Faiths.

Nine mentions of God as *Almighty* appear in the Apocalypse[114-R] and nine is it number of symbols for Messengers (as Church Angels, Spirits, Menorah-Lamps, stars, torches of fire, seals, horns and eyes, trumpet Angels, and pitcher Angels—each seven times). Nine is the number of the united assembly of all His Messengers as a whiteness of nine spiritual swans soaring the sky of the One Religion of God. This whiteness of nine merges the seven Church Angels as a wedge of spiritual swans winging their way across Asia (as Abraham, Moses, Zoroaster, Krishna, Buddha, Jesus, and Muhammad), with the seven Trumpet/Pitcher Angels as a bevy of spiritual swans racing their route across the Middle East (as Abraham, Moses, Zoroaster, Jesus, Muhammad, the Bab, and Baha'u'llah).

For Baha'is, nine is numerologically *baha* (*glory*), and is the number of members in their spiritual assemblies, of sides to their Houses of Worship, and points of a symbolic star.

Long Cycles contain Short Eras

Cycles and Eras are used to measure the vast stream of prophetic time. Each long spiritual Cycle contains several shorter spiritual Eras.[A] The grouping of Eras is a concept neatly captured by the repeating literal Revelation phrase *into the Eras of the Eras.* Each Era covers a span of time

> *which a Manifestation of God hath lived,...characterized as God's appointed Day...to be distinguished from those that have preceded it...once in about a thousand years...renewed and re-adorned* as *none other than the Word of God revealed in every age and dispensation.*[115-B]

In contrast, Cycles last as long as it takes a piece of silk pulling once every hundred years to rub away a cubic mile of rock![116] For humanity, only the Cycles of Prophecy and Fulfillment are relevant.

The spiritual Era of Muhammad closed the Cycle of Prophecy, making him the *Seal of the Prophets*, so that through him *the Prophetic Cycle...verily, ended.* Now the new Baha'i Era has opened the new Cycle of Fulfillment. This first Baha'i Era shall *extend over a period of no less than one thousand years*, and may indeed last the whole 2,147-year Age of Aquarius, with

> *its duration...fixed for a period of one whole month* as *the maximum time taken by the sun to pass through a sign of the Zodiac.*[117-BAS]

In 1844, the Cycle of Prophecy switched to the Cycle of Fulfillment, signaling the

> *consummation of all the Dispensations within the Adamic Cycle, inaugurating...a cycle destined to last no less than five thousand centuries, signalizing the end of the Prophetic* [Cycle[B]] *and the beginning of the* [Cycle] *of Fulfillment.* The year 1844 marked *the confluence of two universal prophetic cycles, the Adamic* [Era] *stretching back as far as the first dawnings of the world's recorded religious history and the Baha'i* [Era] *destined to propel itself across the unborn reaches of time* as the *first stage in a series of Dispensations to be established by future Manifestations, all deriving their inspiration from the Author of the Baha'i Revelation.*[118-S]

Therefore, the Cycle of Prophecy has lasted "just" 6,000 years, while the Baha'i Cycle of Fulfillment shall last 500,000 years!

[A] In contrast, prehistory reverses the definitions; its longer *Eras* contain shorter *Ages*

[B] English translations of Baha'i Writings use terms like *Age*, *Epoch*, or *Eon*, In each case, the context makes clear if *Era* or *Cycle* is intended

IDENTIFYING THE 24 REVELATION ELDERS

The Bab and Baha'u'llah were the greater (big-*F*) **F**ounders of the Baha'i Faith. Then, as his successor, Baha'u'llah appointed his son 'Abdu'l-Baha. In turn, as his successor, 'Abdu'l-Baha appointed his grandson Shoghi Effendi as the

> *Guardian of the Cause of God, as well as the Universal House of Justice to be universally elected and established...both under the care and protection of the Abha Beauty* [Baha'u'llah] and *under the shelter and unerring guidance of the Exalted One* [the Bab].[119-A]

In addition, Baha'i Writings explicitly identify the Faith's (small-*f*) **f**ounders as the 24

> *'elders' mentioned in the Book of Revelation*, namely *the Bab, the 18 Letters of the Living* [first disciples of the Bab] *and five others who would be known in the future. So far we do not know who these five...are....In each cycle the guardians and holy souls have been twelve. So Jacob had twelve sons; in the time of Moses there were twelve heads or chiefs of the tribes; in the time of Christ there were twelve Apostles; and in the time of Muhammad there were twelve Imams....But in this glorious manifestation there are 24, double the number of all the others, for the greatness of this manifestation requires it.*[120-A]

Historically, later input came from the discovery of a

> *set of the Bab's Tablets to the 18 Letters of the Living* and from *two other tablets...one addressed to the 19th Letter who was Himself and the other to 'Him whom God will make manifest', i.e. Baha'u'llah.*[121-S]

The Bab's Tablets to the 18th, 19th, and 20th
Letters of the Living

Thus, Baha'i Writings identify the 19th and 20th Revelation elders as the Bab and Baha'u'llah.

In addition, through his

> *devoted services Haji Mirza Muhammad-Taqi brought victory and honour to the Cause of God.* Accordingly, *'Abdu'l-Bahá...designated him as one of the...'four and twenty elders which sat before God on their seats...in the Revelation of St John the Divine'.*[122-A]

Thus, 'Abdu'l-Baha identifies the 21st Revelation elder as Muhammad-Taqi. This cousin of the Bab performed noble deeds for the early Faith, including erecting its very first Temple in Ashkhabad. Importantly, 'Abdu'l-Baha assumed authority to identify him as a Revelation elder.

Here the trail fades. No known Baha'i Writings identify specific parties as the 22nd, 23rd, and 24th Revelation elders. Regardless, Baha'is generally presume that Baha'u'llah's devoted son 'Abdu'l-Baha, his faithful daughter Bahiyyih Khanum, and his dedicated great-grandson Shoghi Effendi were the last three Revelation elders.

At this point, Revelation—itself a spiritually inspired Scripture—helps to identify 'Abdu'l-Baha and Shoghi Effendi as two of the three last elders. The literal Greek of certain Revelation verses usefully reveals overlapping identities for the Enthroned-Ones, the Living-Beings, and the elders, as follows:

- 4.2: *A person seated upon the Throne* as the main Enthroned-One
- 4.6: *Four Living-Beings...at the center of the Throne, and around the Throne* as two Living-Beings seated on the Throne and as two more Living-Beings guarding alongside the Throne[123-C]
- 4.8: *Four Living-Beings...each...bearing aboard six wings* as four Living-Beings amid 24 elders
- 4.9: *The Enthroned Living-Being* as an Enthroned-One and Living-Being concurrently
- 5.5 & 7.13: *One of the elders* as the main elder
- 5.6: *A young Ram...at the center of the Throne and four Living -Beings, and at the center of the elders* as a second Enthroned-One, a Primary-Figure, and an elder concurrently
- 6.1 & 15.7: *One of the Living-Beings* as the main Living-Being
- 7.17: *The Ram up at the center aboard the Throne* as a second Enthroned-One seated concurrently tandem with the main Enthroned-One.

In other words, the main two elders play three roles as elders, as Living-Beings (*Lion* and *Ox*), and as Enthroned-Ones. The next two main elders play two roles as elders and as Living-Beings (the *Human-Being* and the *Eagle*). And the other twenty elders play just one role as elders. Comprehensively, the two Enthroned-Ones concurrently identify as also two of the four Living-Beings, and the four Living-Beings identify concurrently as also four of the 24 elders.

Symbolically, the Enthroned-Ones, the Living-Beings, and the elders pack together as a matryoshka doll with three shells. Her precious heart shell nests two Enthroned-Ones. Her middle shell encases four Living-Beings (including the two Enthroned-Ones within). Her outer shell contains 24 elders (including the four Living-Beings within). In all, there are just **24** parties (not 30). Baha'u'llah and the Bab concurrently identify as the two Enthroned-Ones, as the Lion and Ox Living-Beings, and as the 19th and 20th elders. 'Abdu'l-Baha and Shoghi Effendi concurrently identify as the Human-Being and Eagle Living-Beings and as two of the elders.

An all-inclusive matryoshka doll

In identifying Muhammad-Taqi as a Revelation elder, 'Abdu'l-Baha assumes authority implying that he too is an elder (the 22nd) at least. Shoghi Effendi making his personal emblem an eagle, like the one over his tomb, fits him as the *Eagle* Living-Being. Both 'Abdu'l-Baha and Shoghi Effendi were too modest to identify themselves openly as either elders or Living-Beings.

Tomb of Shoghi Effendi in London, with eagle

How Faiths rank their founders further helps to identify 'Abdu'l-Baha and Shoghi Effendi as elders. Traditionally, Faiths rank their founders in horizontal generations, like the 12 Sons of Israel and the 12 Apostles of Jesus, or in vertical family-lines, like the 12 Imams of Muhammad. But the new double Baha'i Faith ranks its 24 elder founders both ways:

- The Bab and his 18 founder Letters of the Living as a 19-person horizontal generation (a "gene-ration" of "nineteen-to-the-dozen" so to speak!)
- The Bab and his cousin Muhammad-Taqi as a short two-person horizontal generation
- Baha'u'llah, 'Abdu'l-Baha, Bahiyyih Khanum, and Shoghi Effendi as a putative four-person vertical family-line.

As for identifying the other Revelation elder, Baha'u'llah's daughter Bahiyyih Khanum fits this *station such as none other woman*.[124-B] Bahiyyih Khanum identifies best as 23rd of the 24 elders, since this a penultimate position for her will match that of the poetess Tahireh as penultimate 17th of the 18 Letters of the Living. In the male-dominated Qajar world of Shi'a Persia, even just two female elder founders honed a sharp edge for the emancipation wedge of the new Faith.

'Abdu'l-Baha, Bahiyyah-Khanum, and Shoghi Effendi as the 22nd, 23rd, and 24th Revelation elders

Accordingly, the 24 Revelation elders identify as follows:

- **The 1st–18th elders as the Bab's 18 Letters of the Living**
- **The 19th elder as the Bab**
- **The 20th elder as Baha'u'llah**
- **The 21st elder as Muhammad-Taqi**
- **The 22nd elder putatively as 'Abdu'l-Baha**
- **The 23rd elder putatively as Bahiyyih Khanum**
- **The 24th elder putatively as Shoghi Effendi**.

In addition to the 24 elders, other parties in Revelation interpretively portray groups of Baha'is. *Millions* and *roar of a huge crowd* echo the elation of modern Baha'is. *Hundreds of millions* and *loud roar of a huge crowd* shout the joy of more future Baha'is. The *souls of those slain* depict early Babi and Baha'i martyrs killed in Persia. *Brothers and sisters* portray fellow-Baha'is. The *144,000 persons stamped* endorse the Bab's many early followers progressively perfecting prior Faiths. *Those prevailing over the beast* represent Baha'i Primary-Figures and founders prevailing over the brutal Qajar dynasty of Persia.[125] Verbal-thematic links connect these groups together, using trigger-words like *Throne* or *censers* and key-phrases like *new song, singing praise, surging water,* and *sound of thunder*.

BAHA'I WRITINGS INTERPRET THE BOOK OF REVELATION

Baha'i Writings

Apocalypse Secrets uses the term *Baha'i Writings* for Scriptures written or dictated by the Bab, Baha'u'llah, 'Abdu'l-Baha, or Shoghi Effendi between 1844 and 1957. These Scriptures form the canon of the Baha'i Faith. Persian and Arabic were the languages in which the Bab, Baha'u'llah, and 'Abdu'l-Baha wrote and dictated, and Shoghi Effendi wrote and dictated in English. Their Writings are available in many languages on the web for free, and as books at cost.[126]

The Writings of Baha'u'llah in particular, surge as a *river of water of life* filling *more than one hundred volumes...the equivalent of all that has been sent down aforetime to the prophets.*[127-S] His most important *Most Holy Book* called the

> *Kitáb-i-Aqdas is of unique importance as the Charter of the future world civilization that Baha'u'llah has come to raise up. Its provisions rest squarely on the foundation established by past religions...brought to a new level of understanding, and the social laws, changed to suit the age now dawning, are designed to carry humanity forward into a world civilization the splendours of which can as yet be scarcely imagined.* It forms *the principal repository of that Law which the Prophet Isaiah had anticipated, and which the writer of the Apocalypse... described....This 'Most Holy Book,' whose provisions must remain inviolate for no less than a thousand years, and whose system will embrace the entire planet, may well be regarded as the brightest emanation of the mind of Bahá'u'lláh, as the Mother Book of His Dispensation, and the Charter of His New World Order...a Book from above whose horizon the day-star of* his *commandments shineth upon every observer and every observed one.*[128-BS]

Interpretively, the four Baha'i Primary-Figures play inherent Revelation roles—Baha'u'llah most, the Bab many, and 'Abdu'l-Baha and Shoghi Effendi some—to be discussed later. As important, Baha'u'llah, the Bab, 'Abdu'l-Baha, and Shoghi Effendi directly interpret Revelation verses and symbols in various ways as follows:[A]

- **Baha'u'llah** interprets specific Revelation symbols and verses in his *Gems of Divine Mysteries* Then his *Book of Certitude* expansively interprets many symbols found in Revelation, including

[A] For reading the Apocalypse, Baha'u'llah and 'Abdu'l-Baha used the Van Dyck Arabic version of the Bible, while Shoghi Effendi used the King James English Bible

Angel, Beginning and Ending, blood, bride, city, clothes, clouds, Dawn/Day-Star, door, earth/world, earthquake, eye, First and Last, gemstone, hand, divine Human-Being/Son of Man, judgment, King of kings, lamp, life and death, light, Lord of lords, moon, oil, ointment, oppression/hardship, prison, rain, resurrection, river, robe, rod, sea/ocean, smoke, sky/heaven, Spirit, star, sun, sword, Temple, Throne, tomb, tree, trumpet, warning, and *water*.

Altogether, Baha'u'llah explains symbols and verses that cover 52% (209 of 404) of Revelation's verses.

- **The Bab** addresses Revelation indirectly with his 20 letters to the Letters of the Living that help to identify the first 20 elders, and by interpreting *radiance of the sun* as Baha'u'llah.[129-S]
- **'Abdu'l-Baha and Shoghi Effendi** interpret many specific Revelation verses and symbols. 'Abdu'l-Baha's *Some Answered Questions* and *Selected Writings* address all of Revelation Chapter 11 and much of Chapters 12 and 21. Shoghi Effendi's *God Passes By* and *Promised Day is Come* expand the meanings of many verses. In all, 'Abdu'l-Baha and Shoghi Effendi explain verses and symbols covering 30% (121 of 404) of Revelation's verses.

Overall, Baha'i Writings fully or partly interpret some 64% (258 of 404) of Revelation's verses. Adding in verses that contain John's own internal interpretations of symbols raises the total to 72% (291 of 404) of Revelation's verses. Alas, just counting verses is a crude measure, for it ignores how much of each verse gets interpreted. Still, a crude measure is better than no measure at all.

Important Baha'i Writings relevant to the Apocalypse

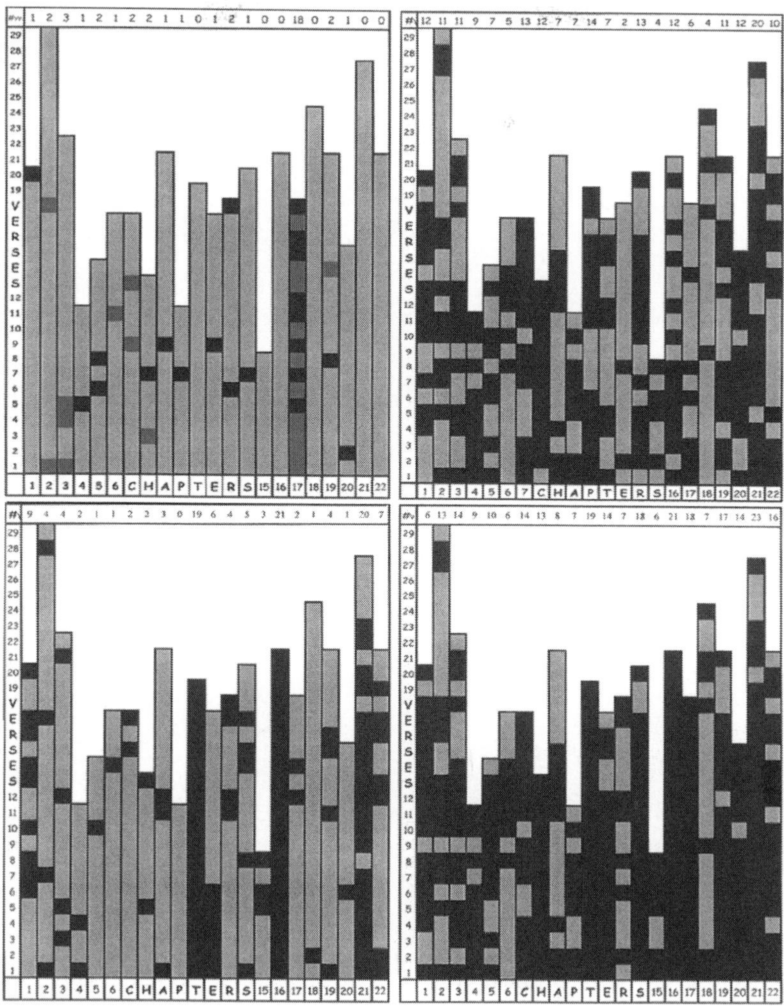

Bar-graphs of interpreted Revelation verses

Top Left: Verses with John's internal interpretations
Top Right: Verses with symbols that Baha'i Writings interpret
Bottom Left: Verses that Baha'i Writings interpret
Bottom Right: Verses with all three sets of interpretations

Black indicates verses interpreted directly
Dark grey indicates verses interpreted indirectly

Baha'i Pilgrim Notes

Unlike Baha'i Writings, Pilgrim Notes lack canonical authority. Pilgrim Notes report what early Baha'i pilgrims in the first century of the Faith heard Primary-Figures say—here about the Apocalypse. They circulated as sheets and pamphlets, in books, in a short-lived Baha'i newspaper called *Star of the West*, and a few in normal newspapers. Some Apocalypse-related Pilgrim Notes written by esteemed early Baha'is were endorsed by 'Abdu'l-Baha or Shoghi Effendi and as cited in various ways as follows:

- *The Dawn-Breakers, Nabil's Narrative of the Early Days of the Baha'i Revelation* translated, hence authorized, by Shoghi Effendi
- Isabel Brittingham reporting a letter written to her by 'Abdu'l-Baha interpreting Revelation Chapter 16, headed *Translated in Acco*
- Shahnaz Waite's *Lesson 10* of her *Twelve Lessons* detailing the 12 gemstone teachings of New Jerusalem, with a laudatory *Foreword* by Shoghi Effendi
- George Latimer's Preface to *The Light of the World* citing 'Abdu'l-Baha speaking publicly on the *Diamond Age*
- Esslemont's *Baha'u'llah and the New Era* and Corrine True's *Chicago North Shore Review* report in 1912 citing 'Abdu'l-Baha publicly predicting *Armageddon* as World War in 1914
- *The Diary of Juliet Thompson* citing 'Abdu'l-Baha speaking publicly about *Babylon* in Washington (1912/05/07)[130-AS]
- *The Star of the West* (*SW*) citing eight Apocalypse-relevant points by 'Abdu'l-Baha, three by Abu'l-Fadl, and one by Tudor-Pole
- Fourteen lesser statements by the authoritative Universal House of Justice also appear.

The Apocalypse Roles of Baha'u'llah

Baha'u'llah is as central to the Baha'i Faith as he is to the Apocalypse. He is its fleeting main master-of-ceremonies Messenger who opens Chapter 1, shape-shifts swiftly into *an apparition of a divine Human-Being* (*Son of Man*) amid various sets of seven, addresses the Seven-Churches in Chapters 2–3, then seemingly disappears. He later reappears in Chapter 17. Finally, in Chapter 22 he finally regains center-stage and closes the Apocalypse.

But where on earth or in heaven does this main Apocalypse Messenger go from Chapters 4 to 16?

The Riddle of St Ives takes us to the answer. The riddle runs:

As I was going to St Ives,
I met a man with seven wives.
Each wife had seven sacks.
Each sack had seven cats.
Each cat had seven kittens.
How many were going to St. Ives?

The number is simply "**one**", namely the lone "**I**" who poses the riddle in the first place! He or she is the only person **going to** St Ives! All the rest—the man and his telescoping-out sets of seven wives, cats, and kittens—are all **coming from** St Ives. The man and his sets of seven simply serve as red herrings to distract us from spotting the only person--the riddle's original opening lone fleeting "I"-who is **going to** St Ives.

In the same way, Revelation telescopes out similar sets of seven that also simply serve as red herrings to distract us from spotting its original lone fleeting opening Messenger during his eclipse from Chapter 4 to 16. But in reality his Chapter 4-16 hiatus sees him slip into a wardrobe of costumes, don a diversity of disguises, shine a series of faces, masquerade in many masks, and speak a series of voices as he plays many behind-the-scenes roles as Revelation's

> *Word of God, A and Z, divine Human-Being/Son of Man, First and Last, Spirit, the Holy One, the True One, holder of the key of a beloved David, Amen, Trustworthy and True Witness, Beginning of Creation, Enthroned-One, Living-Being like a Lion, one of the elders, Lion from the tribe of Judah, root of a beloved David, one of the four Living-Beings, Presence of God, gold Incense-Altar, third Trumpet-Blast, mighty Angel, seventh trumpet Angel, reed like a rod, Messiah, one of the four Living-Beings*, one of its *rulers from the rising-place of the sun, Glory of God, seventh Pitcher-Angel, one of the seven Angels*, one of *Jesus's Witnesses, one mighty Angel, rider on a white stallion, King of kings and Lord of lords, one Angel standing in the sun, "as God", Beginning and Ending, person speaking with me, root and shoot of a beloved David, Dawn-Star*, and *one witnessing to.*

Prophetic license lets the main Angel play these roles just as acting license once let the less-than-holy Peter Sellers play three roles in each of his two anti-war movies. *The Mouse that Roared* shows him playing Duchess Gloriana XII, Count Rupert Mountjoy, and Tully Bascomb. *Dr Strangelove or How I Learned to Stop Worrying and Love the Bomb* shows him playing Dr Strangelove, President Merkin Muffley, and Group-Captain Mandrake.

God, Religion, Law, and Afterlife

The Concept of Inclusive Unity

Modern theology needs inclusive unity as an essential concept, neatly captured by the ditty of *Seven Blind Men and the Elephant*:[131-M]

Seven men of Hindustan
To learning much inclined,
Went to see the Elephant
(Though all of them were blind),
That each by observation
Might satisfy his mind.

The First went to the Elephant,
And happening to fall
Against her broad and sturdy tum,
At once began to bawl:
God bless me, for the Elephant
Is very like a wall!

The Second reached out his eager hand,
And felt around her knee.
What most this wondrous beast is like
Is mighty plain, said he,
'Tis clear that this Elephant
Is very like a tree!

The Third no sooner had begun
About the beast to dare,
Then, sensing her breath so hot
Blowing down upon his hair,
I feel, said he, this Elephant
Is very like the air!

The Fourth had no sooner started
About the beast to grope,
Then seized upon her swinging tail
That fell within his scope,
I see, quoth he, *this Elephant*
Is very like a rope!

The Fifth, feeling of the tusk,
Cried, *Ho! what have we here*
So very round and smooth and sharp?
To me 'tis mighty clear
The wonder of this Elephant
Is very like a spear!

The Sixth approached the animal,
And happening to take
Her squirming trunk within his hands,
Thus boldly up and spake:
I see, said he, *this Elephant*
Is very like a snake!

The Seventh who chanced to touch her ear,
Said: *The blindest man*
Can tell what this resembles most;
Deny the fact who can,
The marvel of this Elephant
Is very like a fan!

So these blind men of Hindustan
Disputed loud and long,
Each in his own opinion
All so stiff and strong,
Though all were partly in the right,
And all were partly wrong!

MORAL

So oft in theologic wars,
The disputants, **I ween**,
Rail on in utter ignorance
Of what each other mean,
And prate on about an Elephant
Not one of them has seen!

Another version of the tale presents the elephant in a dark room for people to enter and discover what is in the room. Seven devout men take turns to enter the room. The Sabaean hears a rumbling belly. The Jew pats a warm leg. The Zoroastrian whiffs hot breath. The Hindu catches a long tail. The Buddhist feels a firm tusk. The Christian grasps a sturdy trunk. The Muslim caresses a broad ear.

Back outside, each man fervently tells the others what he had discovered in the room. The Sabaean recounts **the** loving tales narrated by **his** Abraham. The Jew waxes hot over **the** Sinai pillars of fire erected by **his** Moses. The Zoroastrian glows hot over **the** holy fire blazed by **his** Zoroaster. The Hindu praises **the** dharma directed by **his** Krishna. The Buddhist exalts **the** eightfold path laid out by **his** Buddha. The Christian preaches **the** loving way taught by **his** Jesus. The Muslim extols **the** Quran imparted by **his** Muhammad.

What each devout man says shocks the others. Each man reckons that the others are mistaken at best, liars at worst. They argue. Tempers flare. Words turn to blows. Blood starts to flow. They are all *blind though...on the bright ocean.*[132-M] Then happily, just in time, the owner of the elephant saves the day by bringing her out into the light. Now these devout men can see the whole elephant along with all her parts—including her belly, legs, mouth, tail, tusks, trunk, ears, and all. Finally, they realize that they *all were partly in the right and all were partly wrong* and stop fighting!

The owner portrays God, the elephant portrays His One Religion, and her parts portray His Faiths. Blind or in the dark, each man who feels the elephant, guided exclusively by his own Faith's "either/or logic", is "in it just for the Prophet" (pun intended!).

> *The followers of all the religions believe in a reality, the benefits of which are universal....The Jews call that reality Moses, the Christians Christ, the Mussulmans* [sic] *Mohammed, the Buddhists Buddha and the Zoroastrians Zoroaster....None of these religionists have ever seen the founders; they have only heard his name. Could they overlook these names they would at once realize that all believe in a perfect reality which is an intermediary....Should you speak to a Jew about the medium or channel between God and man, without referring to any particular name or person, he would say, 'Yes, this is right, but I say the name of this mediator is Moses.' If you give the exposition of the divine philosophy to the followers of each religion they will agree with you in the abstract, but they will stick to the names of their own prophets and arise in contention and strife over these names....Alas! The majority...attach themselves to the name of the mediator and lose sight of the real purport.*[133-A]

Each devout man living on the two-dimensional flatland of his own Faith can understand the three-dimensional spaceland of God's One Religion in just a limited way. He sees its elephant as just **a line passing through flatland over time**. First, she touches flatland as a dot. Next, she transects flatland as the line traced by her and extending steadily to full length. Then from her full width passing back out of flatland, she is the same line receding steadily back down and disappearing as a dot. Thus, the passage of time connects the flatland of each Faith with the spaceland of the One Religion of God.

Out in the light, each man now clearly sees the whole elephant of the One Religion of God with inclusive "both/and logic". Yet at the same time he remains free to continue worshiping God through the Faith of his own Messenger, now harboring no fear from nor hostility toward any other Faith or its adherents.

The Law of God

The Law of God is a divine recipe for human behavior, continually rehashed, revamped, revised, refined, and evolved by His Messengers, Era by Era. This *Law of God is divided into two parts. One is the fundamental basis which comprises all spiritual things....The second part...refers to the material world.*[134-A]

The material part of the Law of God

comprises fasting, prayer, forms of worship, marriage and divorce, the abolition of slavery, legal processes, transactions, indemnities for murder, violence, theft and injuries—this part of the Law of God...is modified and altered in each prophetic cycle in accordance with the necessities of the times.[135-A]

Each Messenger evolves and updates the material laws of the prior Faith. His new Faith starts a new calendar, festivals, and adjusts rules for items like marriage or food fitting for the times of the new Era. Thus, for example, Sabaeanism forbade brother-sister marriage, Judaism forbade aunt-nephew marriage, and Christianity frowns on first-cousin marriage.[A] Again, Judaism and Islam forbade eating pork, but not Christianity. And so on.

The spiritual part of the Law of God

is the fundamental basis which comprises all spiritual virtues and divine qualities; this does not change nor alter: it is the Holy of Holies… the essence of the Law of Adam, Noah, Abraham, Moses, Christ, Muhammad, the Báb, and Baha'u'llah...which lasts and is established in all the prophetic cycles. It will never be abrogated, for it is spiritual and not material truth; it is faith, knowledge, certitude, justice, piety, righteousness, trustworthiness, love of God, benevolence, purity, detachment, humility, meekness, patience and constancy. It shows mercy to the poor, defends the oppressed, gives to the wretched and uplifts the fallen. These divine qualities, these eternal commandments …remain established for ever and ever…renewed in each of the different cycles [Eras]; *for at the end of every* [Era] *the spiritual Law of God…disappears, and only the form subsists. Thus among the Jews... the Law of God disappeared…a form without spirit remaining. The Holy of Holies departed.…But the outer court...the expression for the form of the religion—fell into the hands of the Gentiles....The fundamental principles of the religion of Christ…have disappeared; and its form has remained in the hands of the clergy.…Likewise, the foundation of the religion of Muhammad has disappeared, but its form remains in the hands of the official 'ulamá.*[136-A]

[A] Apropos: Abraham had been made to marry his half-sister Sarah. Moses' parents were aunt and nephew, and Jewish law still lets uncles marry nieces

The Golden Rule

The Golden Rule is God's supreme yardstick that tells us humans how to behave by loving Him and treating other human-beings as we ourselves want to be treated. The Golden Rule is the bedrock of every material and spiritual Law of God. All the monotheistic Faiths teach the Golden Rule in their own following ways:

- **Judaism**: *Love your fellow as yourself. What is hateful to you, do not do to your neighbor. This is the whole Torah*
- **Zoroastrianism**: *Nature only is good when it shall not do to another whatever is not good for its own self. Whatever is disagreeable to yourself do not do unto others*
- **Hinduism**: *This is the sum of all true righteousness: Deal with others as you would yourself be dealt by. Do nothing to your neighbor that you would not have him do to you after. This is the essence of morality*
- **Buddhism**: *A clansman should treat his friends and familiars as he treats himself* and should be *as good as his word. Hurt not others in ways that you yourself would find hurtful*
- **Christianity**: *As you would that men should do to you, do also to them likewise. Do to others what you would have them do to you, for this sums up the Law and the Prophets*
- **Islam**: *Wish for others what you wish for yourself. None of you is a believer until he desires for his brother what he desires for himself. Hurt no one so that no one may hurt you*
- **Baha'i Faith**: *Choose thou for thy neighbour that which thou choosest for thyself. Wish not for others what you wish not for yourselves. Lay not on any soul a load which ye would not wish to be laid upon you. The seeker should not...promise that which he does not fulfill. He must not...speak that which he would not bear to hear spoken by another, nor yet desire for any soul that which he would not have desired for himself. Blessed is he who prefers his brother before himself.*[137-JCMB]

Furthermore, each Messenger also stressed a facet of God's Law especially relevant for his own Era and area:

- Abraham stressed idol-free worship of One God
- Moses stressed justice
- Zoroaster stressed good overcoming evil
- Krishna stressed God's Presence in all human-beings
- Buddha stressed enlightenment
- Jesus has stressed brotherly love
- Muhammad has stressed submitting to God and communal love
- Baha'u'llah and the Bab stress unity.

God is an Infinite Force

While we may *think religion is confined in an edifice, to be worshipped at an altar...in reality it is* ***an attitude toward divinity which is reflected through life***[138-A] [my emphasis], to connect us with the mysteries of the infinite, for even though

> *the reality of Divinity is sanctified and boundless, the aims and needs of the creatures* [humans] *are restricted. God's grace is like the rain...not bounded by the limitations of form....In a square pool, the water...becometh a square; in a six-sided pool it becometh a hexagon....The rain itself hath no geometry, no limits, no form, but it taketh on one form or another, according to the restrictions of its vessel. In the same way, the Holy Essence of the Lord God is boundless, immeasurable, but His graces and splendours become finite in the creatures, because of their limitations.*[139-A]

What we call "God" is the infinite all-pervasive Highest Force, transcending art, science, and language, that projects

> ***divine unity...sanctified above all concept of humanity. It cannot be comprehended or conceived because it is infinite reality and cannot become finite. Human minds are incapable of surrounding that reality because all thoughts and conceptions of it are finite, intellectual creations and not the reality of divine being which alone knows itself....The reality of divinity is sanctified above this degree of knowing and realization...hidden and secluded in its own holiness and sanctity above our comprehending. But although it transcends our realization, its lights, bestowals, traces and virtues have become manifest in the realities of the prophets, even as the sun becomes resplendent in various mirrors. These holy realities are as reflectors, and the reality of divinity is as the sun which although it is reflected from the mirrors, and its virtues and perfections become resplendent therein, does not stoop from its own station of majesty and glory and seek abode in the mirrors; it remains in its heaven of sanctity...Its lights become manifest and evident in its mirrors or manifestations....This is the unity of God...unity of divinity, holy above ascent or descent, embodiment, comprehension or idealization....The prophets are its mirrors; its lights are revealed through them; its virtues become resplendent in them*** [my emphasis].[140-A]

Inherently this Highest Force called "God" wants human-beings to know It, to obey Its rules, and to prosper. But because

> *there is no tie of direct intercourse to bind the true God with His creation...the transient and the Eternal, the contingent and the Absolute, He hath ordained that in every age and dispensation a pure and stainless Soul be made manifest.*[141]

Therefore, once in a while, Era by Era, the Highest Force shape-shifts into the form of a superb human Messenger whose spirit emanates Its Spirit. Each Messenger is a divine body incarnating Its Presence. He is a divine Temple presenting Its Law. He is a divine Word dictating Its Law. He is a divine Ark-Cabinet protecting Its teachings. He is a divine Throne broadcasting Its teachings. He is a divine lamp blazing Its love. He is a divine pot pouring the water of Its knowledge. He is a divine robe displaying Its virtue. He is a divine wine distilling Its fragrance. He is a divine perfume emanating Its bouquet. He is a divine baker breaking Its bread of life. He is a divine screen displaying Its hope. He is a celestial mirror reflecting Its *divine Essence.*[142-B] Through all Its Messengers, this Highest Force has connected with human-beings.

Again,

> *the essence of all the Prophets of God is one and the same....There is no distinction whatsoever....They all have but one purpose; their secret is the same secret. To prefer one in honor to another, to exalt certain ones above the rest, is in no wise to be permitted. Every true Prophet hath regarded His Message as fundamentally the same as the Revelation of every other Prophet gone before Him. At the same time, every one of them hath been the Bearer of a distinct Message...commissioned to reveal Himself through specific acts. It is for this reason that they appear to vary in their greatness. Their Revelation may be likened unto the light of the moon that sheddeth its radiance upon the earth. Though every time it appeareth, it revealeth a fresh measure of its brightness, yet its inherent splendor can never diminish, nor can its light suffer extinction....Any apparent variation in the intensity of their light is not inherent in the light itself, but...attributed to the varying receptivity of an ever-changing world. Through His Messengers, God, His name and His attributes, are made manifest in the world. They are all but Messengers of that ideal King...the Voice of divinity, the call of God Himself.*[143-B]

Life-after-Birth augurs Life-after-Death

Scientifically, we cannot prove if afterlife does or does not exist. Paradoxically, the uncertainty is comforting! If, indeed, life-after-death does exist, then the

> *world beyond is as different from this world as this world is different from that of the child while still in the womb of its mother.*[144-AB]

In other words, death marks the passage from our life-on-earth to our life-after-death as birth marks the passage from our life-before-birth to our life-after-birth! The valley of the shadow of our birth presages the valley of the shadow of our death. Birth switches our fetal life from the *embryonic world to the state of maturity,*[145-AB] while death switches our material body to the bodiless state of our spiritual soul.

In the physical realm, the substance called *H2O* switches state from cold solid ice, to tepid liquid water, to hot gaseous steam. The passage of ice melting into water presages the passage of water boiling into steam. While ice, water, and steam are poles apart, they all manifest simply different energy levels of the same substance called H2O. Likewise in the biological realm, the insect called *Monarch* switches state from caterpillar, to pupa, to butterfly. The passage of caterpillar spinning into pupa presages the passage of pupa popping out as butterfly. While caterpillar, pupa, and butterfly are poles apart, they too manifest simply different life-cycle stages of the same insect called Monarch.

In the human realm too, we switch state from fetus to body, then from body to soul. The passage of birth switches us from fetus to body, presaging the passage of death switching us from body to soul. Before our birth, we as fetuses live inside our mother, within our watery reality nourished and respired via our umbilical cord, tasting and swallowing our amniotic fluid, listening to the souffle of our placenta, feeling our limbs move, and sucking on our hands.

Suddenly, there is no more room in the womb! Birth kills us as fetuses. Yet birth is far from fatal. We simply switch state! Our life-after-birth has just begun. Now as babies free of the womb, we enjoy a new world, breath air, taste milk, feel clothes, and hear and see others. Yet even already as fetuses we have gotten glimpses, inklings, and hints of life-after-birth awaiting us. Medical studies report that as fetuses we receive signals from beyond. We see light to the front of our uterine home. We hear rumbles from our Mums' tums. We respond to outside noises (a test for fetal wellbeing). These signals from beyond during fetal life already tell us a bit about our coming life-after-birth beckoning from the space-time beyond our watery womb.

Bodily life ends too. Death kills us as bodies. Yet death too is far from fatal. We simply switch state! Our life-after-death has just begun. Now as souls shaken free from our mortal coils, we soar free and enjoy bodiless spiritual life. Yet even already as bodies, we have gotten glimpses, inklings, and hints of life-after-death calling us. Psychological studies report that, as bodies, we receive signals from beyond. We dream of other realms. We experience déjà-vu episodes. We notice meaningful coincidences. We even witness miracles, face out-of-body states, and undergo near-death experiences. These signals from beyond during bodily life tell us already a bit about our coming life-after-death beckoning from the space-time beyond our earthly tomb.

Prior Faiths *from the days of Adam until the days of Christ... spoke little of eternal life*. But the new Baha'i Faith says a lot, in teaching that even though

> *physical death...is a God-ordained and inescapable reality*, the *life of knowledge*, the *certitude of attaining unto the presence of God through the Manifestations of His Cause...is that blessed and everlasting life that perisheth not*, that *knoweth no death.... Through his ignorance man fears death, but the death he shrinks from is imaginary and absolutely unreal; it is only human imagination....For existence there is neither change nor transformation;* ***existence is ever existence*** [my emphasis], *it can never be translated into nonexistence. It is gradation; a degree below a higher degree is considered as nonexistence.... Absolute nonexistence is impossible; it is only relative....It is impossible for that world to become nonbeing, for it is the very genesis of God....It is a creational and not a subjective world, and the bounty descending upon it is continuous and permanent. Therefore, man, the highest creature of the phenomenal world, is endowed with that continuous bounty bestowed by divine generosity without cessation* just as *the rays of the sun are continuous....the bestowal of God is descending upon the world of humanity, never ceasing, continuous....The effulgences of existence are ever present and continuous.*[146-A]

Alas however (especially for atheists),

> *the conception of annihilation is a factor in human degradation, a cause of human debasement and lowliness, a source of human fear and abjection....conducive to the dispersion and weakening of human thought, whereas the realization of existence and continuity has upraised man to sublimity of ideals, established the foundations of human progress and stimulated the development of heavenly virtues. Therefore, it behooves man to abandon thoughts of nonexistence and death....He must turn*

> *away from ideas which degrade the human soul so that day by day and hour by hour he may advance upward and higher to spiritual perception of the continuity of the human reality. If he dwells upon the thought of nonexistence, he will become utterly incompetent; with weakened willpower his ambition for progress will be lessened.*[147-A]

Accordingly, Baha'u'llah reassures us:

> *I have made death a messenger of joy to thee. Wherefore dost thou grieve?...Thou art My dominion and My dominion perisheth not; wherefore fearest thou thy perishing? Thou art My light and My light shall never be extinguished....Why dost thou dread extinction? Thou art My glory and My glory fadeth not; thou art My robe and My robe shall never be outworn.*[148-B]

The Symbolic Meanings of the Jewish Temple

The smell of death emanated from many solemn sacrifices in the Jewish Temple, especially those on the Jewish year's holiest Day of Atonement, its Yom Kippur Sabbath of Sabbaths Day of "at-one-ment" when Jews fast, rest, and atone for their sins.[149-J]

Yom Kippur ran, sunset to sunset, its daily Dusk Perpetual *Tamid* Service, its daily Dawn Perpetual *Tamid* Service, and its Special Yom Kippur *Mosaf* Service. On the other 364 days of the year, the Dusk and Dawn Tamid Services continually sacrificed and continuously burned *keves* lambs on the Sacrificial-Altar.[150-J] But Yom Kippur's Tamid Services sacrifice *ayil* rams, not *keves* lambs.[151-J] On Yom Kippur, the High Priest conducts services, not the usual Cohen chosen by lot. On Yom Kippur, only gold, not silver, vessels are used. John's vision concurs. Its *arnion* ram replaces the *amnos* lamb[A] that skips elsewhere in the New Testament.[152-RC] Its main Messenger is dressed as a High Priest. Its vessels are gold. These and other distinguishing details fitting the three Yom Kippur Services appear in this

Table of Yom Kippur Events in the Apocalypse

Yom Kippur Dusk Service	**Pertinent Apocalypse verses**
The High Priest removes his usual golden garments, dons the white plain-linen garments of a regular Cohen's, and conducts the Dusk Service as he will conduct the Dawn-Service (shortly)	1.13, 14.14–15: *An apparition of a Human-Being clad in a long robe* 3.5, 18 & 4.4: *White garments* 7.14: *They have washed their robes and have bleached them*
He stays awake all night (to avert defiling any defiling emission)	7.15, etc: *day and night* mentioned many times
Yom Kippur Daily Dawn Service	**Pertinent Apocalypse verses**
Levites sight and welcome the planet Venus, shout *Barkai!* (*Dawn Star*), and open the Temple-Door loudly enough to be *heard as far as Jericho*[153-J]	2.28 & 22.17: *The Dawn-Star* 1.10 & 4.1: *A loud voice like a trumpet* 4.1: *A door open in the sky* 7.2 & 16.12: *The rising-place of the sun*

[A] *Ram* is AYIL in Hebrew, ARNION in Greek. *Lamb* is KEVES in Hebrew, AMNOS in Greek

The High Priest begins to conduct the Dawn Service, like the Dusk Service	1.13, 14.14–15: *AN APPARITION OF A HUMAN-BEING CLAD IN A LONG ROBE*
He trims, refuels, and rekindles the Menorah	1.12: *SEVEN GOLD MENORAH-LAMPS*
He sacrifices a ram (in the Dusk Service this happened **after** the burning of the incense)	5.6: *A YOUNG RAM STANDING AS IF SLAIN*
He collects its blood in a pitcher and dashes it on the Sacrificial-Altar	7.14, 12.11, also 5.9: *THE BLOOD* OF *THE RAM*
He takes incense and embers from the Sacrificial-Altar, and burns the incense on the Incense-Altar, filling the Holy with fragrant smoke	5.8: *GOLD CENSERS FULL OF INCENSES* 8.3 & 9.13: *THE GOLD INCENSE-ALTAR BEFORE THE THRONE*, and also *FACING GOD* 15.8: *THE TEMPLE WAS FILLED WITH SMOKE FROM THE GLORY OF GOD AND HIS POWER*
He splits the ram's corpse and burns its parts on the Sacrificial-Altar	6.9–11: *I SAW BENEATH THE SACRIFICIAL-ALTAR THE SOULS OF THOSE SLAIN*
He recites: • The Ten Commandments, Deut. 5.6–22 • *Hear O Israel*, Deut. 6.4–9 • Deut. 11.13–21 • Num. 15.37–41	1.3: *THE PERSON WHO READS OUT* 5.1–8: *A SHORT SCROLL ON THE RIGHT HAND OF THE ENTHRONED-ONE* 10.1–2: *ANOTHER MIGHTY ANGEL… IN HIS HAND HOLDING AN OPEN TINY SCROLL*
He prays *May the Lord bless you and keep you*, Num. 6.22–26	1.3, 14.13, 16.15, 19.9, 20.6 & 22.7, 9 & 14: *BLESSED IS THE ONE/ARE THOSE WHO….*
He closes with: *Put My name on the people of Israel and I will bless them*, Num. 6.27	7.3–8: *WE STAMP THE SERVANTS OF OUR GOD ON THEIR FOREHEADS* 14.1: *WITH HIS NAME AND THE NAME OF HIS FATHER WRITTEN ON THEIR FOREHEADS* 22.4: *WITH HIS NAME ON THEIR FOREHEADS*

He and his Cohens prostrate themselves. The Levites sound trumpets, play harps, and sing a Psalm (on a Sunday Ps. 24, on a Monday Ps. 48, on a Tuesday Ps. 82, on a Wednesday Ps. 94, on a Thursday Ps. 81, on a Friday Ps. 93, and on a Sabbath Ps. 92)	4.10, 5.14 & 11.16: *THE 24 ELDERS FELL (FACE-)DOWN* 7.11 & 19.4: *THE 24 ELDERS AND FOUR LIVING-BEINGS FELL (FACE-)DOWN* 1.10, 4.1, ETC: *TRUMPETS* 5.8, 14.2 & 15.2: *HARPS* 5.9, 14.3 & 15.3: *A NEW SONG* 7.12, 19.1, 3–4 & 3.8: *PRAISE GOD* 8.13, ETC: *TRUMPET-BLASTS*
He pours out the wine at the base of the Sacrificial-Altar	16.1, ETC: *POUR THESE SEVEN PITCHERS*
BREAK BETWEEN THE DAWN AND SPECIAL SERVICES	**PERTINENT APOCALYPSE VERSES**
This break echoes the ten repentance *days of awe* that precede Yom Kippur	4.8, 6.11, 14.11 &14.13: *REST* 8.1: *SILENCE SETTLED IN THE SKY FOR ABOUT HALF-AN-HOUR*
YOM KIPPUR SPECIAL SERVICE	**PERTINENT APOCALYPSE VERSES**
The High Priest washes himself	1.5: *HIM...WHO WASHED...US*
He confesses for himself and his family over his own sacrificial ox (bullock)	4.7: *THE SECOND LIVING-BEING LIKE AN OX*
He utters God's otherwise unutterable name ***YHWH*** seven times	1.4, 1.8, 4.8: *THE-IS, THE-WAS, THE-IS-COMING* 11.17 & 16.5: *THE-IS, THE-WAS*
He draws lots over two sin-offering goats—one for the fire and the other, the scapegoat, for the fall. He tags the scapegoat with a skein of scarlet wool	1.1–22.21: Many double-meanings and word-plays 12.3, 13.11, 17.3: *DRAGON* and *BEASTS*
He confesses for the sins of Israel over each goat	1.5: *FREED US FROM OUR SINS*
He sacrifices the ox and collects its blood in a pitcher swirled by a Cohen to stop it clotting	4.7: *THE SECOND LIVING-BEING LIKE AN OX*

He takes a **double** handful of incense in a censer, plus a panful of embers from the Sacrificial-Altar	8.3: *MANY INCENSES WERE HANDED TO HIM* 8.5: *THE ANGEL…HAS TAKEN UP THE CENSER…FILLED IT FROM THE FIRE OF THE ALTAR*
He carries the incense and embers through the Veil (*Paroket*), into the Holy of Holies	1.1: *AN UNVEILING* 11.19 & 15.5: *THE TEMPLE OF GOD OPENED UP*
He burns the incense[A] on the floor before the Ark, filling the Holy of Holies with fragrant smoke	8.3–5: *MANY INCENSES…TO OFFER* 15.8: *THE TEMPLE WAS FILLED WITH SMOKE FROM THE GLORY OF GOD AND HIS POWER* 11.19: *WITHIN HIS TEMPLE APPEARED ITS ARK OF HIS COVENANT*
He collects the ox-blood, takes it into the Holy of Holies, and sprinkles it on the Ark-Lid, once up and seven times down	1.5, ETC.: Many mentions of *BLOOD*
He sacrifices the first goat on the Sacrificial-Altar, takes its blood in a pitcher back to the Holy of Holies, and sprinkles it on the Ark-Lid as above	1.5, ETC.: Many mentions of *BLOOD*
He returns to the Holy, sprinkles the bull and goat bloods on the Veil, mixes them, then sprinkles them onto the Incense-Altar, as above	1.5, ETC.: Many mentions of *BLOOD* 9.13: *THE FOUR HORNS OF THE GOLD INCENSE-ALTAR FACING GOD* 16.1, ETC.: *POUR THESE SEVEN PITCHERS*

[A] Temple incense was a mix of 11 spices as follows: 70 parts each of balsam sap, onycha (treated with Carshina lye and Cyprus wine), galbanum, and frankincense; 16 parts each of myrrh, cassia, spikenard, and saffron; 12 parts of costus; 3 parts of aromatic bark; 9 parts of cinnamon; plus catalytic amounts of Sodom salt, smoke-raising herb, and Jordan amber (*Talmud Kereitot* 6a)

He pours out what remains of the mixed blood at the base of the Sacrificial-Altar	1.5, ETC.: Many mentions of *BLOOD* 16.1, ETC: *POUR THESE SEVEN PITCHERS*
He dispatches the scapegoat 12 km eastwards to be thrown backwards alive off a specific cliff into the Dudael gorge, in order to return the sins of Israel to Azriel, the chief rebel angel	9.2, 11, 11.7, 17.8, 20.1: *THE ABYSS* 12.9: *THIS HUGE DRAGON…WAS CAST DOWN* 19.20: *THESE TWO WERE TOSSED INTO THE POOL OF FIRE* 20.1: *HE SEIZED THE DRAGON….HE TOSSED IT INTO THE ABYSS*
He burns parts of the ox and goat on the Sacrificial-Altar and sends their other parts to be burned outside the city	14.20: *THIS WINEPRESS WAS TRAMPLED OUTSIDE THE CITY*
He utters prayers and blessings, Lev. 16.1–34, 23.26–32, Num. 29.7–11	20.12: *SOME SHORT SCROLLS WERE OPENED*
Seven lambs are also sacrificed, timing uncertain[154-J]	1.4, ETC: Many mentions of sets of *SEVEN*
Yom Kippur ends with the sighting of three stars/planets	2.28 & 22.17: *THE DAWN-STAR* doubling as THE *DUSK-STAR*
THE BANQUET AFTER YOM KIPPUR	**PERTINENT APOCALYPSE** VERSES
The High Priest again dons his golden garments and begemmed breastplate	21.19–20: *THE FOUNDATIONS OF THE WALL OF THE CITY ARRAYED WITH ALL KINDS OF PRECIOUS GEMSTONE*
He throws a celebratory banquet	19.9: *THE WEDDING BANQUET OF THE RAM* 19.17: *GOD'S GREAT BANQUET*

Jewish Temples, Physical and Visionary

A single holy spot in Jerusalem has served as a site for several physical Jewish Temples. The first Temple of Solomon stood for three centuries until Nebuchadnezzar destroyed it in 586 BC. Jews back from Babylon built the Second Temple in 516 BC, Herod restored it around 16 BC—AD 30, and Titus razed for Rome in AD 70. The Third Jewish Temple exists only on the drawing boards of certain Jews and Christians awaiting their chance to rebuild it and restart its services, celebrations, rituals, and sacrifices.

Visionary Jewish Temples exist too, all vast. The Ezekiel Temple measures 250 yards (500 cubits). The Qumran Temple extends 800 yards (1600 cubits). The Apocalypse Temple encompasses 1500 miles (12,000 furlongs). These visionary Temples portray global **divine civilization**, with their size symbolizing its majestic grandeur.[155-JR]

John's visionary Temple displays and echoes a medley of detail. But he cannot describe it too clearly. An overly clear description could threaten Rome and alert its censors. So John plays safe and uses linguistic veils to hide his visionary Temple. He shows it in the bits and pieces of a *temple.doc* file, as it were fragmented across the hard disk of his Apocalypse as scattered sightings of an ethereal eerie for Angels.[156-J]

John spots Temple players in various vistas, snaps them amid sacred objects, and sculpts them onto sundry pedestals. He presents its High Priest dressed as a ghostly divine Human-Being. He watches its 24 classes of Cohens conduct services as 24 elders.[157-J] He hears its Levites chanting praises, sounding trumpets, strumming harps, waving victory palms, and singing a new song. He enthrones its Sanhedrin as judges. He abandons its outer courtyard to gentiles like Romans. He hears its Altar speak. He spatters its sacrificial-blood and wafts its fragrant incenses as pagans do. He routinely calls its all-important central Ark "the Throne" (only once calling it "the Ark"). He shines its breastplate-gemstones as foundations of New Jerusalem. And he escorts its bride of the Sabbath.

Then at the end, amazingly, John does not see the Temple any longer. It has simply vanished! Where on earth or in heaven has it gone? The answer is simply **EVERYWHERE! THE TEMPLE OF JERUSALEM CITY HAS GROWN INTO GRAND NEW JERUSALEM, AND IT IS SIMPLY TOO BIG TO BE SEEN**. From inside, neither we nor John can see it. The physical Temple has become the spiritual Temple of the visionary **divine civilization of New Jerusalem**. The humble Temple pupa has burst into flashing flight as the beautiful New Jerusalem butterfly, the wings of its divine civilization embracing the globe.

This divine civilization of New Jerusalem's grand *Tabernacle of the Cause of God will gather together the whole of mankind beneath its shelter.*[158-B] But when? On his dying day, Moses received an answer to this question in a vision that showed

> *God build the Temple of jewels and pearls, while between the separate gems and pearls shimmered the radiance of the Shekinah* [sic], *brighter than all jewels. Moses asks, 'When will this Temple built here in heaven come down to earth below?...Give me a sign'. God replies, 'I shall first scatter Israel as with a shovel over all the earth...among all nations ....Then shall I set My hand again the second time, and gather them in'.*[159-J]

In other words, the visionary Temple of heavenly New Jerusalem has been waiting for the People of Israel to return. Ever since 1844, this has been happening. The Temple of Baha'u'llah and his Baha'i Faith has indeed *come down to earth below* and begun to build global divine civilization. Baha'u'llah has taken the symbolic *form of the human temple* and has been *calling from this manifest Temple*, as other Messengers did before him. His *Tablet of the Temple* is written in the graphic form of a pentacle that represents his human shape, and addresses his own self as a *living Temple*, from body-part to body-part, stating:

> *Thus have We built the Temple with the hands of power and might....Which is preferable, this, or a temple which is built of clay? Set your faces towards it.*[160-BAS]

Thus, Baha'u'llah as the

> *man named the 'Shoot' shall branch out from his place and build the temple of the Lord* and *assume majesty and sit and rule on his throne.*[161-J]

In a similar vein, prior Messengers too did

> *build the Temple of the Lord...clothed in divers attire...soaring in the same heaven, seated upon the same throne, uttering the same speech, and proclaiming the same Faith....The Cause of Baha'u'llah is the same as the Cause of Christ...the same temple and the same foundation.*[162-BA]

Isaac Newton viewed the Temple as a *template of the cosmos.* Religious Jews likewise view the Temple as a microcosm of the universe whose sacred objects emanate

> *sublime and holy concepts that work at many symbolic levels of meaning...the garments of the High Priest and the vessels ...made in a way of imitation and representation of the universe*, with his breastplate as *an emblem of heaven.*[163-J]

Sacred Temple Objects

The Patmos storm projected its vision of the Temple onto the backdrop of the wall of John and Prochorus's cave, for them to walk us east to west into the Temple's *Hall*, *Holy*, and *Holy of Holies* as its three main chambers, and for us to examine its seven most sacred objects serially as its:

- **Sacrificial-Altar** set outside the main Door. Alas, *sacrifice*, involving some sort of exchange, the only word available in English, is an inaccurate mistranslation of the original core Hebrew word *korban*, which means *something that brings close*. Once, the symbolic Sacrificial-Altar helped Jews to face death to draw closer to God vicariously. Now it rallies all of us to face death and to draw closer to God. Further, the Sacrificial-Altar signifies God's only two Messengers to be martyred, namely Jesus and the Bab;
- **Door** opening into the Hall. Once, the symbolic Door and Hall drew Jews closer to God and to each other. Now they draw all of us closer to God and to each other. In addition, the Door signifies the only two of God's Messengers to take *Door* as a title, namely Jesus and the Bab;
- **Gold Incense-Altar** set centrally in the Holy. Once the symbolic Incense-Altar and its smoke wafted Jewish prayers for the unity of Israel, Now they emanate the spirit of Baha'u'llah's superb love bearing unity for all of us. The Incense-Altar marries the material meaning of the Showbread-Table with the spiritual meaning of the Menorah;
- **Gold Showbread-Table**, stacked with 12 loaves, standing in the Holy to the right of the Incense-Altar. Once, the symbolic Showbread-Table and loaves promised material bounty to Jews. Now it pledges worthy prosperity to all of us. Yet the Apocalypse does not mention the Showbread-Table, for John wants to avoid confusing the worthy prosperity that it signifies with the Malignant Materialism that its big bad brother of Babylon signifies. Only after the Chapter 18 fall of Babylon does the hidden Chapter 19 Showbread-Table function as a dining-table that is spread with the banquet of worthy prosperity on its tablecloth of spiritual economics;
- **Menorah** standing in the Holy to the left of the Incense-Altar. Once, the symbolic Menorah-Lamp shone Judaism as a *light to the nations*. Now it blazes the spiritual light of God's One Religion to all of us;

- **Veil**, the double red *Paroket* curtain veiling and unveiling the Holy of Holies. Once, the symbolic veil unveiled the Presence of God over the Ark to the High Priest only once a year. Now it reveals God's latest Presence enthroned on the Ark-Throne to all of us for a spiritual Cycle;
- **Ark of the Covenant** set on the foundation stone from which God's big bang created everything. Jews sight and cite this site as the "navel of the universe".164-R

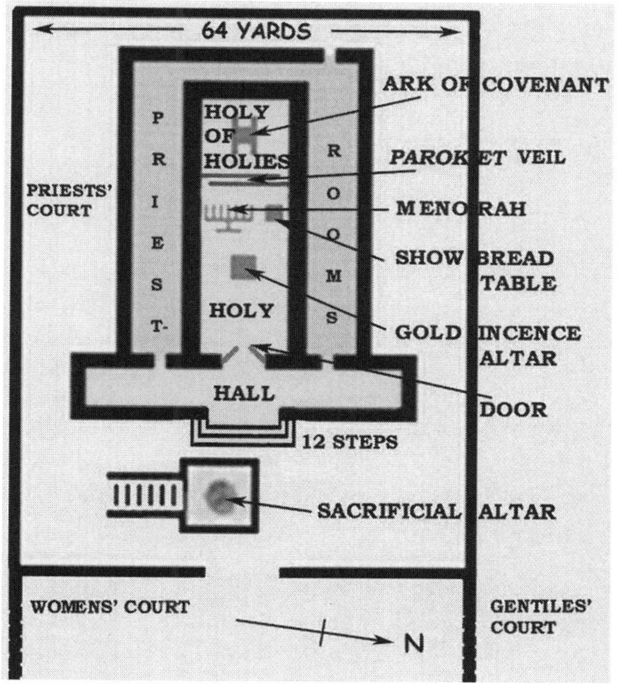

Plan showing the Temple's Sacred Objects

The Ark of the Covenant

The Ark is the most important sacred object in the Temple and the only item in its Holy of Holies, where it symbolizes the Presence of God. Even though it is known as "the lost Ark", the Ark is far from lost, just **hidden**. The Ark was last very long ago, in 608 BC to be precise, when, anticipating trouble,

> *King Josiah hid the Ark...in the intricate underground labyrinth of passageways and secret chambers built by King Solomon when he erected the Temple.*165-J

Therefore 22 years later, when Nebuchadnezzar destroyed the Temple in 586 BC, he found no Ark in it. The Second Temple had no Ark either. The Ark had simply gotten "lost".

Just the weight of the Ark—its gold cover alone weighed over a ton—favored King Josiah hiding it on the spot. So centuries later, when a Temple-Priest saw an odd-looking paving-stone near the wood chamber in the Women's Court, he

> *dropped dead, thereby it was known to a certainty that the Ark of the Covenant was hidden...under the wood chamber.*

Nonetheless, the exact location of the Ark would *remain unknown until God gathers his people together again and shows them mercy.* Now that Jews have returned, a few do claim to know the Ark's hiding place under the Temple—but just orally/aurally![166-J]

Yet, at the same time, a contrary apocryphal tale reports how the prophet

> *Jeremiah went to the mountain* [Nebo] *where Moses had gone up...found a cave, and brought there the tent, the ark, and the altar of incense.*[167-J]

Is this likely? Hardly! The notion that the priceless two-ton Ark could be carried safely and secretly from 2600–foot high Jerusalem down 3900 feet past enemy territory to the Dead Sea some 1300 feet below sea level then back up again onto 2680-foot high Mt. Nebo fails to hold water, let alone the Tablets of Moses! Instead, what Jeremiah was hiding in that Mt. Nebo cave was not a gold Ark but a red herring! His fishy tale was simply a tricky apocryphal Apocryphal cover story!

The Ark had a gold-plated 45″ × 27″ × 27" Ark-Cabinet *Aron* and a pure gold 45″ × 27″ × 3″ Ark-Cover *Kaporet*. The Cabinet was *God's Footstool*. The Cover was God's *Throne* (*Mercy-Seat*). Over the Throne hovered solid gold male and female cherubs, face to face, wings unfurled.[168-J] Throughout Revelation John calls the Ark "the Throne" (except for calling it "the Ark" just one time[169-R]). In addition, he sights and cites the site of the gold Incense-Altar as *before the Throne* and *facing God*.[170-R] Thus, he locates the Throne to the Holy of Holies, where only the Ark can be. Hereby John identifies the "Ark" and the "Throne" as one and the same object.

The Ark protects and proclaims God's Law. The symbolic Ark-Cabinet protects it. The symbolic Ark-Cover proclaims it. Once the Cabinet protected the Law of Moses and the Cover enthroned him proclaiming it to the Israelites. Now the Cabinet protects the Law of the Bab and Baha'u'llah and the Cover enthrones them proclaiming it to all of us. The Bab and Baha'u'llah are the latest *Divine Presence... seated upon the Throne of might and glory.*[171-BSJ]

The *Shechinah* Presence of God

The *Shechinah* of the *Presence of God* appeared to the People of Israel in the Sinai desert as a column of shining cloud that they saw rising

> *above the Ark-Cover between the two cherubim on top of the Ark* as the *aspect of God which He reveals to Man* as *an explanation of the Biblical anthropomorphisms and the appearance of God in the vision of the prophets.*[172-J]

The Shechinah projects the female aspect of God. Early on, He/She *created humankind* ***male and female in His/Her own image.***[173-J] Aptly, the Hebrew word *Shechinah* is feminine.

Every Friday night for thousands of years, Jews have welcomed the Shechinah as the **Sabbath Bride** of God the King,[174-J] with food and wine, candlelight and song. Likewise, Christians welcome the Shechinah as the ***bride* of New Jerusalem** painting a rainbow of promise and singing a new song. Now, similarly, Baha'is welcome the Shechinah as ***a maid of heaven****...veiled, beauteous, and unique,*[175-A] who is also a

> ***Maid of Eternity****...from the exalted paradise...with harp and with song...with amorous glances....With dance and with song she came....With musky tresses, with beauteous ruby lips from nigh unto God....to pierce our hearts...all souls in her path, all hearts in her embrace....With raven locks, like the dragon of Moses....This sweet Davidic voice... came with the Messianic Spirit....With the allurement of fidelity...with guiding light from the morn of the Divine Encounter, with Mount Sinai....With the joyful tidings of reunion this Divine Maiden came....From the city of Sheba... this Eternal Countenance...came with snow-white hand from the divine command....This pardoning visage...came with fetching allure....This Nightingale of mystic meaning came from the sacred rose bush with the hand of ecstasy. This luminous page came with light and splendour from the Midian of Spirit....This Witness of the Omnipotent, this heady Wine of the Beloved came with the goblet of sovereignty....That essence of the Beauty of the True One, that jewel of the Glory of the True One, she came....That Countenance of the desired One, that face of the adored One, she came with the most-supreme mercy....Souls to her reunion...hearts to her Bestowal, as the Most Exalted Lord she hath come! Hallelujah, Hallelujah, Hallelujah!*[176-B]

This *Most Exalted Lord* is Baha'u'llah who as
the Glory of God…identifies with the Shechinah.[177-J]

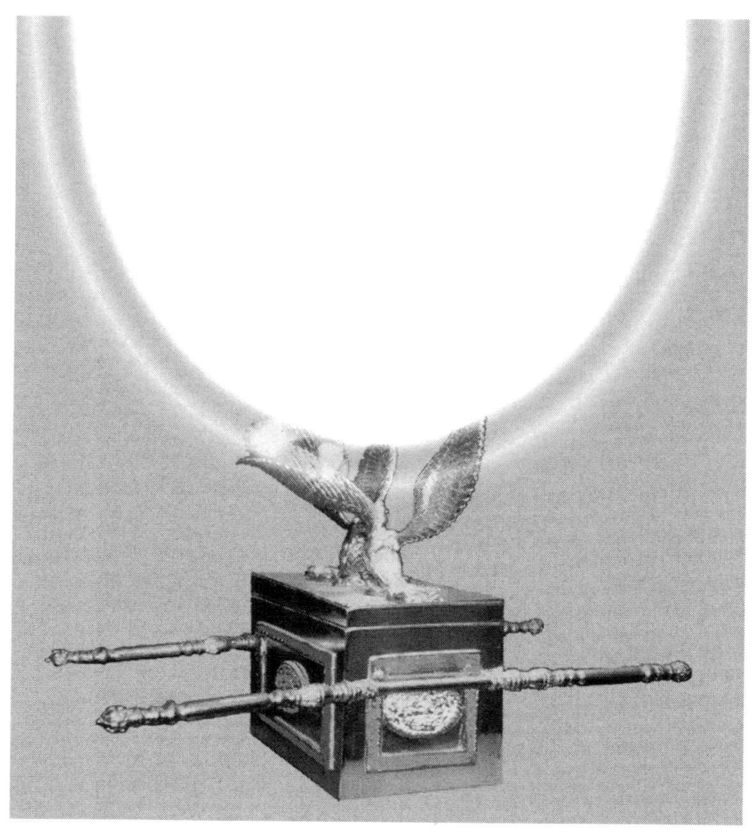

God's *Shechinah* Presence
hovering over the Ark-Throne

The Millennium is the Jewish Seventh Millennium

In addition, the Shechinah symbolizes the long-awaited Sabbatical Millennium of global justice, peace, and prosperity. In weekly terms, the Shechinah is welcomed as the regular Bride of the Sabbath-Day. In millennial terms, the Shechinah is welcomed as the Bride of the Sabbatical-Day of the Jewish Seventh Millennium.

In our trying end-times leading up to this grand Millennial Day,

> *the world shall be prepared to enter the Seventh Millennium as a person who prepares himself on the sixth day (Friday) as the sun sets to enter the Sabbath....Because at the end of times, when Moses will appear, the Shechinah will rise up. The students of the Torah on earth will be watered by her.*[178-J]

This *end of times when Moses will appear* and *the Shechinah will rise up* decipher as the four pre-Millennial centuries from AD 1844 to 2240. By the Jewish calendar and lore, the *world exists for 6,000 years* up to the Millennium.[179-J] The Jewish calendar began in *Anno Moshe* year AM 1, namely 3760 BC. Its 19-year cycle interdigitates 12 short 354-day years with 7 long 384-day years with. Its 12 short years alternate 29-day and 30-day months. And its 7 long years have an extra 30-day leap month to keep its years with the sun.

The multi-faith *a-day-for-a-thousand-years* formula[A] defines a prophetic *Day* as a millennium. Accordingly, the past millennial *Week* has had an

- AM 1–1000 (3760–2760 BC) millennial *Sun**Day***
- AM 1000–2000 (2760–1760 BC) millennial *Mon**Day***
- AM 2000–3000 (1760–760 BC) millennial *Tues**Day***
- AM 3000–4000 (760 BC to AD 240) millennial *Wednes**Day***
- AM 4000–5000 (AD 240–1240) millennial *Thurs**Day***
- AM 5000–6000 (AD 1240–2240) millennial *Fri**Day***
- AM 6000–7000 (AD 2240–3240) Millennial *Sabbath **Day*** (with which the Christian Third AD 2000–3000 Millennium overlaps just enough to pass arguably as *The Millennium* too).

The Millennial Sabbath Day crowns the six-Day millennial Week, just as a regular Sabbath Day crowns a normal six-day workweek.[180]

Each millennial Day was the Era of a Messenger producing a Revelation from his Ark-Cabinet and proclaiming it from his Ark-Throne, rather as a magician produces a bouquet from his hat and displays it from his stage. Then the Messenger of each millennial Day was *entrusted with a divinely-revealed Book* as his bouquet for the[181-B]

[A] For Judaism, *a thousand years are like a yesterday* (Psalm 90.4). For Christianity, *one day is as a thousand years and a thousand years as one day* (2Peter 3.8). For Islam, *a day is like a thousand years* (Quran 22.47 & 32.5)

- Jewish *SunDay*'s *Ghenza Rama* and *Torah* of Abraham and Moses
- Zoroastrian *MonDay*'s *Avesta* of Zoroaster
- Hindu *TuesDay*'s *Vedas* of Krishna
- Buddhist *WednesDay*'s *Tipitaka* of Buddha
- Christian *ThursDay*'s *Gospel* of Jesus
- Muslim *FriDay*'s *Quran* of Muhammad
- Baha'i ***Sabbath Day***'s *Bayan* of the Bab and *Aqdas* of Baha'u'llah. The double bumper Millennial Baha'i Bouquet shines the spiritual colors and emanates the spiritual fragrances of the bouquets of all prior Faiths.

The above Scriptures are

> *the Word of God revealed in every age and dispensation...in the days of Moses...the Pentateuch; in the days of Jesus, the Gospel; in the days of Muhammad...the Qur'án; in this day, the Bayan; and in the Dispensation of Him Whom God will make manifest* [Baha'u'llah], *His own* [Aqdas] *Book...to which all the Books of former Dispensations must needs be referred....Each believer of God will be able to explain and interpret all of the holy Books.*[182-BA]

The *Zohar* predicted our pre-Millennial end-times, stating that

> *in the year 600 of the sixth millennium...the world shall be prepared to enter the Seventh Millennium.*[183-J]

The short-form *year 600* interprets as Jewish year AM **5600**, namely AD 1840 (almost 1844). This prophecy fits AM 5600–6000 or AD 1840–2240 as four centuries of end-times/beginning-times. Now, 2012, we are near the central nadir of these four centuries, We are beginning to feel the two ending centuries tipping into two beginning centuries leading up to the AD 2240 (AM 6000) start of the Millennium.

The beginning-times will see six masculine, testosterone-driven, millennial Eras of war winding down. The new feminine, estrogen-boosted, Millennial Era of peace will dawn the divine global civilization of New Jerusalem and make

> *happy...all those who shall remain in the world at the end of the sixth millennium and enter the Shabbat which is the seventh millennium.*[184-J]

The AD 2240 start-date of the Sabbatical Millennium is the wedding date of Baha'u'llah as the Shechinah Bride. Maybe some wonderful major global event will mark it. Maybe the world's nations shall sign a truly binding enforceable global constitution. Maybe some key country like Israel shall find its Messiah and declare itself as the world's first Baha'i state (as, in AD 311, Armenia declared itself as the world's first Christian state).

NEW JERUSALEM IS DIVINE CIVILIZATION

Furthermore, the Jewish Seventh Sabbatical Millennium is to bring the divine civilization portrayed by the Shechinah Bride as

> *the Holy City, the Jerusalem of God...compared sometimes to a bride...a prophetic symbol, meaning the coming again of the Divine Teaching to enlighten the hearts of men....It is long since this Holy Guidance has governed the lives of humanity. Now, at last, the Holy City of the New Jerusalem has come...to lighten the whole world....**The heavenly Jerusalem is none other than divine civilization*** [my emphasis], *and it is now ready. It is to be and shall be organized, and the oneness of humankind will be a visible fact. Humanity will then be brought together....The Orient and Occident will be conjoined, and the banner of international peace will be unfurled. The world shall at last find peace, and the equalities and rights of men shall be established.*[185-A]

Thus,

> *the City of God hath appeared...in full adornment* as *the heavenly religion which secures the prosperity of the human world* and as *the guarantor of human happiness.... This Day Jerusalem hath attained unto a new Evangel,* namely **the *Law which the Prophet Isaiah...anticipated, and which the writer of the Apocalypse...described as the 'new heaven' and the 'new earth', as 'the Tabernacle of God', as the 'Holy City', as the 'Bride', and as the 'New Jerusalem coming down from God'*** [my emphasis].[186-BAS]

In this vein,

> *material civilization is one of the means for progress of the world of mankind, yet until it becomes combined with divine civilization the desired result, which is the...felicity of mankind, will not be attained....**Material civilization is like a globe of glass. Divine civilization is the light itself*** [my emphasis] *and the glass without the light is dark. Material civilization is like the body. No matter how infinitely graceful, elegant and beautiful it may be, it is dead. Divine civilization is like the spirit, and the body gets its life from the spirit, otherwise it becomes a corpse....As heretofore material civilization has been extended, the divine civilization must now be promulgated* to *accomplish the progress effected by religion.*[187-A]

Apropos, America has

> *attained a marvelous material civilization,* so *now let spiritual forces...animate this great body.*[188-A]

New Jerusalem is a Precious Diamond of Unity

For the shape of its visionary New Jerusalem, the Apocalypse supplies these specifications:

- *It is laid out as a square*
- *Its length equal to its breadth*
- *Its length, breadth, and height are equal.*

Three candidate shapes fit these specs: the diamond, the cube, and the square pyramid:[189-R]

- **The diamond**, the most favored, beautiful octahedral shape, is a "perfect solid" whose *number of edges = number of faces + number of corners - 2* (Euler's formula[190]). As a prism, the diamond refracts the white light of truth from the seven rainbow colors of the Faiths. As a frame, the diamond fits snugly between the poles and equator of the globe of the human world. As a gemstone, diamond is the hardest material suitable for the city wall's matrix and first foundation. The 12 gates of the city are also *diamonds of immortality*. The twelve *12,000–furlong* edges of the diamond total 144,000 furlongs that code for many believers progressively perfecting Faiths with hard work, each a *diamond blazing in the sun*, and all *chips hewn from the Diamond of Divine Knowledge* that *shine and sparkle with such brilliancy*, so that *'ere long the diamond age...will be established in the hearts.*[191-BAS]

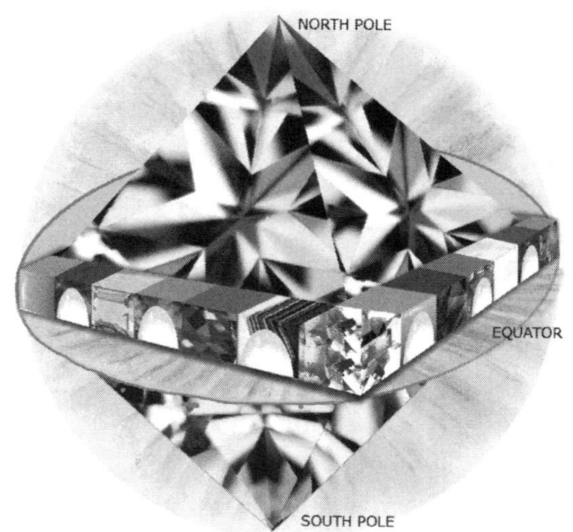

New Jerusalem is a precious diamond of unity

- **The cube** is another perfect solid But it rides lower than the diamond in the series of the five perfect solids. The cube is the shape for New Jerusalem favored by Christians. For Muslims too, the cube invokes the *City of God that hath descended from heaven, the celestial Kaaba*.[192-B] Mecca's Kaaba (*cube* in Arabic) is Islam's holiest site. It is an 11-meter-cubed black building set with Islam's most precious relic, the black stone of Abraham.
- **The square pyramid** is a half-diamond which—when reflected about its base—doubles as the favored full octahedral diamond.

The 24 Gemstones of New Jerusalem

The New Jerusalem **wall** of spiritual Law with its **12 foundations** and **12 gates** protects divine civilization. The wall's 12 foundations are Revelation's 12 gemstones. The wall's 12 gates are *jewels and pearls twenty cubits high and ten cubits wide*, also *12 pearls, each single gate from a single pearl*.[A] Altogether, the 12 foundation-gemstones and 12 gate-gemstones of the New Jerusalem wall of Law form a **unitary structure of 24 gemstones**. The 24 Revelation elders man the wall of spiritual New Jerusalem as once 24 watches of Cohens and Levites manned the wall of the physical Temple.[193-JC]

Identifying the New Jerusalem gemstones: Christian scholars believe that the 12 foundation-gemstones are

> *the same, beyond any reasonable doubt, as those...set into the breastplate of the Jewish High Priest*.[194-C]

In other words, the breastplate-gemstones of the High Priest are probably a template for the foundation-gemstones of New Jerusalem.

Alas, the Hebrew names for the breastplate-gemstones defy neat translation. For generations, Jewish sages have been debating about 30 candidates for the 12 breastplate-gemstones. After all, over millennia, gemstone names have changed frequently between languages, due to trends in sources, markets, cultures, and fashions.[B] The sages have been debating from the time when

> *two angels in heaven, Gabriel and Michael, dispute the meaning of 'kadkod'....One of them says that 'kadkod' means stones of shoham* [onyx] *and the other says it means stones of jasper. The Holy One...said to them: 'Let it be both as this and that'*.[195-J]

In other words, God is really telling Gabriel and Michael that what truly counts is each gemstone's *inner symbolical significance ...not the outward or literal meaning*![196]

[A] Pearl is a natural gemstone, like amber or coral

[B] Similarly, the names of items like musical instruments, vegetables, or birds have also varied tremendously over time due to shifts in their sources, markets, cultures, and fashions

Regardless, the gemstones of the breastplate and of New Jerusalem still need English names. Discovering these English names calls for first considering gemstone **hardness**, **names in Greek**, and **color**.

Gemstone hardness lets gemstones and their engravings last. Hardness is measured scientifically on the Mohs scale. Aptly, all the top candidates for the breastplate and New Jerusalem gemstones score high on this 1–10 scale. Out of 10 as its top possible score, diamond scores 10, ruby 9, sapphire 9, topaz 8, emerald 8–7.5, beryl 8–7.5, jacinth 7.5–6.5, amethyst 7, chalcedony 7–6.5, onyx 7–6.5, chrysolite 7–6.5, chrysoprase 7–6.5, carnelian 7–6.5, jasper 7–6.5, and sardonyx 6.5. Further, layered gemstones engrave well. They show their colored under-layer intaglio through their engraved upper-layer. For example, the *two very large and very excellent onyxes* on the shoulders of the High Priest[197-J] displayed their white lower layer tribal names intaglio through their engraved black upper layer.

The hardest gemstone diamond identifies as both the breastplate Hebrew *yashfeh* and as the New Jerusalem wall Greek *yaspis*. Jewish sources state that the **twelfth last** breastplate-gemstone yashfeh

- *Is lighted up*
- *Has the colors of the twelve colors* [of breastplate-gemstones]
- *Turns color, being now red, now green, now even black.*[198-J]

These characteristics let the yashfeh identify as diamond. Apropos, the mysterious *shamir* that engraved the breastplate-gemstones was probably itself a special diamond, with faces of different hardnesses that let it engrave even diamond.[199-J]

The template breastplate's last yashfeh matches the New Jerusalem first *yaspis*, with which it shares the same *Y/S/P-F* triconsonantal root. Revelation mentions the New Jerusalem foundation-yaspis in regard to its

- Enthroned-One *gleaming as an apparition of* ***yaspis***
- New Jerusalem *brilliance...resembling a most precious gemstone like a gemstone of crystallizing* ***yaspis***
- New Jerusalem wall with ***yaspis*** as its matrix
- New Jerusalem wall with ***yaspis*** as its first foundation.[200-R]

These characteristics let the Greek yaspis identify as diamond too.

Thus, the massive New Jerusalem diamond has diamond as also the matrix of its wall, its first foundation, and its first pearly gate. The usual translation, *jasper*, dismally fails to fit the bill of either *yashfeh* or *yaspis*. Jasper is lackluster, opaque, and quite soft, not at all lit up, multicolored, brilliant, hard, or crystallizing.

Gemstone names in Greek help to identify names in English for them too. The top place goes to the Revelation list of John. He evidently knew the Temple intimately, including the gemstones on the High-Priest's breastplate as the template for the New Jerusalem gemstones in his vision. So he knew their Hebrew names, their tribal names, and their colors, and importantly their Greek names (for Greek-speaking pilgrims) too. Here is John's list:[201-R]

(1) *Yaspis* (diamond)
(2) *Sappheiros* (sapphire)
(3) *Chalcedon* (chalcedony)
(4) *Smaragdos* (emerald)
(5) *Sardonux* (sardonyx)
(6) *Sardion* (ruby)
(7) *Chrusolithos* (chrysolite)
(8) *Beirulos* (beryl)
(9) *Topazion* (topaz)
(10) *Chrusoprasus* (chrysoprase)
(11) *Huakinthos* (jacinth)
(12) *Amethustos* (amethyst).

Most of the Greek and English names sound similar, excepting *yaspis* as *diamond* and *sardion* as *ruby.*

Three older Greek lists of breastplate-gemstones exist too. All differ from John's list by the same four names. All have the same three names in each of the same four rows. The Septuagint has a 1st row sardion, topazion, and smaragdos; a 2nd row anthrax, sappheiros, and yaspis; a 3rd row ligurion, achateis, and amethustos; and a 4th row chrusolithos, beirulos, and onux. One Josephus list has a 1st row sardion, topazion, and smaragdos; a 2nd row anthrax, yaspis, and sappheiros; a 3rd row achateis, amethustos, and ligurion; and a 4th row onux, beirulos, and chrusolithos. The other Josephus list has a 1st row sardonyx (intending presumably sardion), topazion, and smaragdos; a 2nd row anthrax, yaspis, and sappheiros; a 3rd row ligurion, amethustos, and achateis; and a 4th row chrusolithos, onux, and beirulos. The lists of Josephus seem less reliable. The varying sequences of their gemstones probably result from Josephus jumbling script-directions while he cross-translated his religious right-to-left Hebrew, his secular left-to-right Greek, and his native right-to-left Aramaic.[202-J]

Gemstone color is their most important hallmark (despite trace elements causing most gemstone color). The key *Midrash Rabah* source states that the vivid colors of the military standards of the Israelite tribes matched *the color of the precious gemstones on the breastplate.* The source paints its point pertinently by punning *tsev'a* (*color*) with *tsava* (*army*). Listing the tribal names in mixed seniority and birth order, it assigns each breastplate-gemstone a color as follows:

(1) Reuben's ***odem*** as ***red***
(2) Simeon's ***ptidah*** as ***green***
(3) Levi's ***bareket*** as ***a third white, a third black, a third red***
(4) Judah's ***nofech*** as ***like a type of sky***
(5) Issachar's ***safir*** as ***black like blue***
(6) Zebulon's ***yahalom*** as ***white***
(7) Dan's ***leshem*** as ***like safir***
(8) Gad's ***shvo*** as ***not black, not white, but mixed black-white***
(9) Naphtali's ***achlamah*** as ***like clear wine whose redness is not harsh***
(10) Asher's ***tarshish*** as ***a stone that women adorn themselves with***
(11) Joseph's ***shoham*** as ***deep black***
(12) Benjamin's ***yashfeh*** as having ***the colors of the twelve colors***.[203-J]

Other sources lend further support, adding that the

- All-important *yashfeh changes color, being now red, now green, now even black*
- *Odem*, *yahalom*, and *nofech* are respectively *red*, *white*, and *green*
- *Bareket beams like lightning*
- *Leshem* is *glittering*
- *Tarshish* has the *color of the great sea*
- *Yahalom* or *bareket* is *calf-eye*.[204-J]

The 12 Breastplate-Gemstones: Considering gemstone hardness, Greek names, and color helps us to identify the gemstones and tribal names as shown in page 97's illustration.

The Tribal and Apostolic names on the 24 Gemstones of New Jerusalem

Out of character, John uses the following wordy ways to describe the New Jerusalem gates, foundations, and their tribal names:

- *12 gates and over the gates 12 Angels, with names engraved that are the names of the 12 tribes of heirs of Israel*
- *12 foundations, upon them the 12 names of the 12 Apostles*.[205]

John's atypical wordiness infers more than meets the eye. It suggests that a **full list of 12 tribal names** is engraved on each of the 12 gates and a **full list of 12 apostolic names** on each of the 12 foundations. Thus, 288 repeating names are engraved on the 144-cubit-thick wall of Law, symbolically echoing the historical Temple's 288 singers and, as it were, tripling, the strength of New Jerusalem's wall of Law.[206-J]

The breastplate of the High Priest
showing its gemstones and tribal names in
top-right to bottom-left Hebrew direction

Still, each list of tribal and apostolic names needs a single leading name. The lead tribal names on the 12 gate-gemstones probably follow John's own listing of (1) Judah, (2) Reuben, (3) Gad, (4) Asher, (5) Naphtali, (6) Manasseh, (7) Simeon, (8) Levi, (9) Issachar, (10) Zebulon, (11) Joseph, and (12) Benjamin,[207-R] each tribal name bringing its breastplate-gemstone with it for double duty as a pearled New Jerusalem gate too.

Many lists of tribes of Israel exist. All are constant in naming 12 male names![A] Otherwise, the sequences of their names varies. Earlier lists tend to follow birth or seniority order.[B] Later lists tend to follow orders of breastplate-gemstones, blessings, censuses, exploration, territories, campsites, or Revelation seals. In addition, the names too can vary in that Manasseh and Ephraim often replace their father Joseph and the non-territorial priestly tribe of Levi.[208-J]

John's own one-of-a-kind Revelation list probably

- First followed the seniority listing of wife Leah's sons (1) Reuben, (2) Simeon, (3) Levi, (4) Judah, (5) Issachar, and (6) Zebulon; wife Rachel's sons (7) Joseph and (8) Benjamin; Leah's maid Zilpah's sons (9) Gad and (10) Asher; and Rachel's maid Bilhah's sons (11) Dan and (12) Naphtali[209-J]
- Next promoted Judah to top place as the tribe from whom the Messiah would come[210-J] and as the *king among* the tribes heading the tribal list engraved on the shoulder-onyxes of the High Priest (which otherwise follow birth order)
- Then advanced social equality by promoting maid-sons Gad, Asher, Naphtali, and Dan to 3rd, 4th, 5th, and 6th places[211-C]
- Finally substituted Joseph's elder son Manasseh (*making forget*) for Dan (*judgment*) whose tribe Jews scorn for worshiping idols and which Christians condemn as the tribe from which the Antichrist would come.[212]

On the 12 foundation-gemstones, the lead apostolic names probably follow Mark's earliest disciple listing of (1) Peter (Simon), (2) James (Jacob, son of Zebedee), (3) John (son of Zebedee), (4) Andrew (Andrai), (5) Philip, (6) Bartholomew (Nathaniel), (7) Matthew (Levi, son of Alphaeus), (8) Thomas (Judas), (9) James (Jacob, son of Alphaeus), (10) Thaddeus (Judas, Lebbaus), (11) Simon (Zealot, Canaanite), and (12) Matthias replacing Judas Iscariot.[213-C]

[A] Historically, the name *Judah* came to include the tribes of Benjamin, Simeon, and half of Levi absorbed by Judah, while *Israel* was the supra-tribal name of kept by the other 8½ of the 12 original tribes. Curiously, today's Jews embody the broad tribe of *Judah* while today's Palestinians probably embody the narrowed supra-tribe of *Israel* that the Jewish state took as its name

[B] Birth order includes wife Leah's sons (1) Reuben, (2) Simeon, (3) Levi, and (4) Judah; Rachel's maid Bilhah's sons (5) Dan and (6) Naphtali; Leah's maid Zilpah's sons (7) Gad and (8) Asher; wife Leah's sons (9) Issachar and (10) Zebulon; and wife Rachel's sons (11) Joseph and (12) Benjamin

The 12 New Jerusalem Gate-Gemstones, engraved with their lead tribal names, duplicating the breastplate-gemstones, now follow in John's own special tribal order:

(1) **Judah** heads the tribal list on the 4th **beryl** (nofech)
(2) **Reuben** heads the list on the 1st **ruby** (odem)
(3) **Gad** heads the list on the 8th **chrysoprase** (shvo)
(4) **Asher** heads the list on the 10th **amethyst** (tarshish)
(5) **Naphtali** heads the list on the 9th **jacinth** (achlamah)
(6) **Dan** heads the list on the 7th **chrysolite** (leshem)
(7) **Simeon** heads the list on the 2nd **emerald** (ptidah)
(8) **Levi** heads the list on the 3rd **sardonyx** (bareket)
(9) **Issachar** heads the list on the 5th **sapphire** (safir)
(10) **Zebulon** heads the list on the 6th **chalcedony** (yahalom)
(11) **Joseph** heads the list on the 11th **onyx** (shoham)
(12) **Benjamin** heads the list on the 12th **diamond** (yashfeh).

The 12 New Jerusalem Foundation-Gemstones, engraved with their lead apostolic names, now follow in John's own special gemstone order:

(1) **Diamond** (yaspis) with its apostolic list headed by **Peter**
(2) **Sapphire** (sappheiros) with its list headed by **Simeon**
(3) **Chalcedony** (chalcedon) with its list headed by **John**
(4) **Emerald** (smaragdos) with its list headed by **Andrew**
(5) **Sardonyx** (sardonux) with its list headed by **Philip**
(6) **Ruby** (sardion), with its list headed by **Bartholomew**
(7) **Chrysolite** (chrusolithos) with its list headed by **Matthew**
(8) **Beryl** (beirulos) with its list headed by **Thomas**
(9) **Topaz** (topazion) with its list headed by **James**
(10) **Chrysoprase** (chrusoprasus) with its list headed by **Thaddeus**
(11) **Jacinth** (huakinthos) with its list headed by **Simon**
(12) **Amethyst** (amethustos) with its list headed by **Matthias**.

The new foundation **topaz** replaces the old gate **onyx** that has been casting the shadow of those war-weary millennial *WeekDays*. Now it has been transformed into the new gold topaz that is shining the glory of universal education now so much needed to kick-start the new Millennial *Day*.

Furthermore, the gate and foundation gemstones link *the last* with *the first*. The **last** gate diamond links with the **first** foundation diamond. The **last** tribal name *Benjamin* on the **last** gate diamond becomes the **first** apostolic name *Peter* on the **first** foundation diamond. In both cases, *the last becomes the first*.

The 24 Gemstone Structure of New Jerusalem

John's vision shows the gates and foundations of New Jerusalem landing from the sky and lining up like Lego pieces to build the city-wall in standard Middle East style from its southeast foundation cornerstone. From this corner, the line of gates in the wall pincer the city, as it were, the first line hooking counter-clockwise to the East and North, then the other line hooking clockwise to the South and West.[214 R] The lead tribal name on each gate brings its own breastplate-gemstone with it, for double duty as a New Jerusalem gate too.

The first trio of the tribes Judah, Reuben, and Gad leads the lists on the three east gates. The second trio of the tribes Asher, Naphtali, and Manasseh leads the lists on the three north gates. The third trio of the tribes Simeon, Levi, and Issachar leads the lists on the three south gates. The last trio of the tribes Zebulon, Joseph, and Benjamin leads the lists on the three west gates.

Each tribal trio's first four names Judah, Asher, Simeon, and Zebulon lead the lists on the central gates of each sidewall. Each tribal trio's second four names Reuben, Naphtali, Levi, and Joseph lead the lists on the right-hand gates (leading **into** each sidewall—see *Comment 21:13* on page 272). Each tribal trio's last four names Gad, Manasseh, Issachar, and Benjamin lead the lists on the left-hand gates (again, leading **into** each sidewall).

Notably Judah, the tribe of the Jews, heads the list on the central gate of the special east wall. Notably too, the top four Christian Apostles, Peter, James, John, and Andrew lead the lists on the four foundation columns of this east wall. Thus, Jews and Christians face the East to greet the Baha'i Faith's two spiritual suns rising in Persia.

Each of the 12 New Jerusalem foundation gemstones has a layer projecting a column, in all 12 layers and 12 columns as follows:

- The 12 horizontal bedrock gemstone-layers stack up from the bottommost first strongest hardest diamond layer up to the topmost last majestic amethyst layer
- The 12 vertical gemstone-columns project up from the 12 gemstone-layers, again starting from the southeast cornerstone, each column rising between two of the 12 gemstone-gates, their array encircling the city counter-clockwise.[215-R]

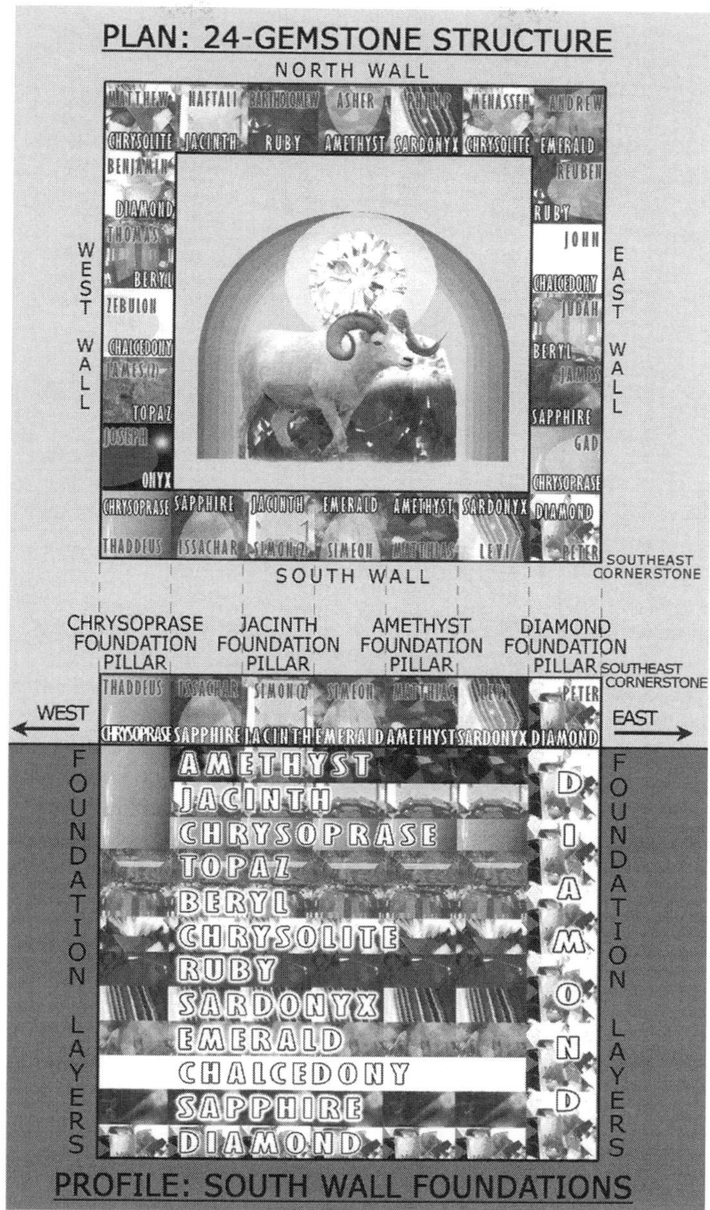

New Jerusalem's
24 gemstone gates and foundations

In addition, gemstones signify zodiac signs too. As for the breastplate-gemstones, *what else can they be emblems of, except...the months or the constellations, which the Greeks call the circle of the zodiac.*[216-J] As for the foundation-gemstones, the diamond signifies Pisces, the sapphire Aquarius, the chalcedony Capricorn, the emerald Sagittarius, the sardonyx Scorpio, the ruby Libra, the chrysolite Virgo, the beryl Leo, the topaz Cancer, the chrysoprase Gemini, the jacinth Taurus, and the amethyst signifies Aries.[217-J] Remarkably, John's list of the foundation-gemstones exactly **reverses** the normal sequence of the zodiac. Why? Did his vision simply want to reject esoteric horoscopic knowledge because it conflicts with faith?[218-C]

No, quite the opposite! The reverse zodiac sequence signifies the reverse-succession (precession) of Zodiac Ages.[219] The signs of the Zodiac mark both the 12 months of the seasonal year, but also the twelve Zodiac *Months* or 2,147–year Ages in a *Great Platonic Year* during whose 25,765-year (12 × 2,147) span the globe wobbles very slowly once in space like a giant spinning-top and generates two types of year:

- The normal seasonal year set by the sun
- The less-known cosmic year set by the stars.

These seasonal and cosmic years have almost the same length—but not quite. Each star-set cosmic year slips by just 20½ minutes slower than each sun-set seasonal year. The annual 20½–minute slippage means lets the cosmic and seasonal years drift steadily apart. Over 2,147 years, this steady 20½–minute/year separation adds up to the 43,830 minutes in a full month. This span of 2,147 years defines a Zodiac Month/Age. Every 2,147 years, a new Zodiac Age starts one calendar month earlier in the normal seasonal year. In other words, successive Zodiac Ages "precess" in reverse sequence to the months of the normal year. This phenomenon is called *the precession of the equinoxes*.

Each two-thousand-year Zodiac Age is a spiritual double Era, the latest being the:

- *Age of Gemini* (*Twins*), the Era of twin gods like Isis and Osiris
- *Age of Taurus* (*Bull*), the Era of Baal worship and its bull-sacrifice
- *Age of Aries* (*Ram*), the Era of the Jewish Faith and its ram-sacrifice
- *Age of Pisces* (*Fishes*), the Era of the Christian Faith and its spiritual fishing-for-men
- Present *Age of Aquarius* (*Water-Bearer*), the Era of the Baha'i Faith and its water of knowledge.

The Twelve Commandments of the Baha'i Faith

The 24 New Jerusalem gemstones shine solid old and brilliant new religious teachings. In John's time, they shone the solid old teachings of Judaism and the brilliant new teachings of Christianity. The 12 gate-gemstones shone the teachings of Judaism that Moses and his 12 tribal leaders had signed symbolically into law (their tribal names signify qualities of praise, vision, good-fortune, happiness, striving, forgiveness, understanding, unity, reward, exultation, productivity, and power[220-J]). The foundation-gemstones shone the teachings of Christianity that Jesus and his 12 Apostles had refined ("pearled") and signed symbolically into law.

Today the 24 gemstones of New Jerusalem shine solid old and brilliant new religious teachings. They shine the solid old teachings of the Cycle of Prophecy's seven Faiths that God's seven Messengers and their founding followers signed symbolically into law. The foundation-gemstones shine the Cycle of Fulfillment's Baha'i Faith's brilliant new 12 new commandments that Baha'u'llah and his 24 founding followers have refined ("pearled") and signed symbolically into law.

'Abdu'l-Baha made the commandments of Baha'u'llah a recurrent topic for his many lectures in his 1911–13 teaching tours delivered in Europe and America. He elaborated, combined, subdivided, and overlapped Baha'u'llah's commandments into lists of varying lengths for his different audiences.[221-A] Yet altogether, these commandments distil down neatly into the following comprehensive master-list of **Twelve Commandments**,[222-AS] each sequentially symbolized by a New Jerusalem gemstone:

(1) The Oneness of Humanity (diamond):
The gift of God to this enlightened age is the knowledge of the oneness of mankind, which all the divine Manifestations have proclaimed....People of the world...are the fruit of one tree and the leaves of one branch....Humanity is like unto a rose garden and the various races, tongues and people are like unto contrasting flowers. The diversity of colors in a rose-garden adds to the charm and beauty of the scene as variety enhances unity....Light is now dawning upon the world's darkened horizon. The first candle is unity in the political realm....the second candle is unity of thought in world undertakings....the third candle is unity in freedom....the fourth candle is unity in religion....the fifth candle is the unity of nations....the sixth candle is unity of races.... the seventh candle is unity of language.[223-ABS]

Unity and uniformity are poles apart. The brush of uniformity must not tar the concept of unity. **Unity** is what spins the earth, moon, and sun in smooth harmonious circuits, despite the discomforting disparity between the 24-hour rotation of the earth, the 27.3-day orbit and 29.5-day rotation of the moon, the 365.25-day revolution around the sun of the earth, and the 24.5-day rotation of the sun itself. To these arithmetic incongruences, calendars, tidal charts, and ephemerides all richly testify. In contrast, **uniformity** is what spins the second, minute, and hour hands of clocks in exact useful, but dreary, circuits of 60 seconds, 60 minutes, and 12 hours.

(2) THE INDEPENDENT INVESTIGATION OF TRUTH (sapphire): *Humanity must be saved from the darkness of imitation and attain to the truth....Tear off and cast away this ragged and outgrown garment of 1,000 years ago and....Put on the robe woven in the utmost purity and holiness in the loom of reality ....Science, education and civilization are most important necessities....If any religion rejected science and knowledge, that religion was false....By religion is meant that which is ascertained by investigation and not that which is based on mere imitation....Each person must be...fascinated and enraptured, and attracted to the divine bounty...like the butterfly who is the lover of the light from whatever lamp it may shine...like the nightingale who is the lover of the rose in whatever garden it may grow....Reality is one and not multiple...is not divisible...does not admit multiplicity.*[224-A]

(3) THE UNITY OF SPIRITUAL REALITY (chalcedony): *Spiritual perfections...are man's birthright....Man is, in reality, a spiritual being, and only when he lives in the spirit is he truly happy....Spiritual longing and perception belongs to all men alike....both material blessings and spiritual bestowals. ...Immortality of the spirit is...the fundamental basis of the divine religions....The spiritual world is an eternal reality, an indestructible reality, a reality belonging to the divine, supernatural kingdom; a reality whereby the world is illumined, a reality which grants unto man eternal life....Its power causes man to escape from nature's world. Escaping, he will find an illuminating reality, transcending the limited reality of man and causing him to attain to the infinitude of God....where there is neither separation nor disintegration. ...Spiritual existence is absolute immortality, completeness and unchangeable being....unlimited by the narrow restrictions of the mere human world of existence.*[225-A]

(4) THE ONE FOUNDATION FOR ALL RELIGIONS (emerald): *Light is good in whatsoever lamp it is burning....A star has the same radiance if it shines from east or west....A rose is beautiful in whatsoever garden it may bloom....In the East or the West, it is none the less a rose. For what mattereth...is not the outward shape and form of the rose, but rather the smell and fragrance which it doth impart....The sun of reality is one sun, but has different dawning places....Love the Sun of Truth from whatsoever point in the horizon it may arise!...If the Divine light of truth shone in Jesus Christ it also shone in Moses and in Buddha....It has now shone forth with the utmost brilliancy from the eastern horizon....If the nations of the world forsake imitations and investigate the reality underlying the revealed Word of God they will agree and become reconciled.... Religious reality is not multiple; it is one....The continuity of Divine Revelation widens the basis of all revealed religions, unravels the mysteries of their scriptures with unqualified recognition of the unity of their purpose, and pares away their priest-prompted superstitions ....The great religions...are divine...their basic principles in complete harmony...their teachings...facets of one truth...their functions... complementary.*[226-ASB]

(5) THE AGREEMENT OF RELIGION AND SCIENCE (sardonyx): *Science and Religion should go forward together...as the two wings with which humanity must fly. One wing is not enough....Should a man try to fly with the wing of religion alone he would quickly fall into the quagmire of superstition, whilst on the other hand, with the wing of science alone he would also make no progress, but fall into the despairing slough of materialism....The harmony of religious belief with reason is a new vista which Baha'u'llah has opened for the soul of man, for religion must be in harmony with science and reason. If it does not conform to science and reconcile with reason, it is superstition. Down to the present day it has been customary for man to accept a religious teaching, even though it was not in accord with human reason and judgment....Every religion which does not concern itself with Science is mere tradition....These two most potent forces in human life, will be reconciled, will co-operate, and will harmoniously develop....Sciences uplift the world of being, and are conducive to its exaltation....The knowledge of such sciences, however, should be acquired as can profit the peoples of the earth, and not those which begin with words and end with words....The best fruit of the tree of science and knowledge is that which benefits mankind and improves his condition....Science is the discoverer of the past* and draws *conclusions as to the future....Science without religion is lame, religion without science is blind...A legitimate conflict between science and religion cannot exist.*[227-AB]

(6) THE EQUALITY OF MEN AND WOMEN (ruby):
Of all the Faiths, the Baha'i Faith is the only one to teach the fundamental...principle of the equality of the sexes....The male and female...are equal before God, for so he created them. Why should woman be deprived of exercising the fullest opportunities offered by life? Whosoever serves humanity most is nearest God—for God is no respecter of gender. The male and female are like the two wings of a bird and when both wings are reinforced with the same impulse the bird of humanity will be enabled to soar heaven-ward to the summit of progress....Not until both wings are equally developed can the bird fly. Should one wing remain weak, flight is impossible. Not until the world of women becomes equal to the world of men in the acquisition of virtues and perfections, can success and prosperity be attained as they ought to be Man and woman are equally the recipients of powers and endowments from God....So why should we ever raise the question of superiority and inferiority?...Woman must be given the same opportunities as man....Both man and woman are servants of God before Whom there is no distinction....The sex distinction...is due to the lack of education for woman, who has been denied equal opportunity for development and advancement. Equality of the sexes will be established in proportion to the increased opportunities afforded woman in this age.[228-A]

(7) THE ABANDONMENT OF PREJUDICES (chrysolite):
Be free from prejudice...and adorned with equity and justice....Religious, racial, political and patriotic prejudice are the destroyers of human society. As long as these prejudices last the world of humanity will not attain to poise and perfection. As long as these threatening clouds are in the sky of humanity, the sun of reality cannot dawn....Until they are dispelled the advancement of the world of humanity is not possible, yet racial, religious and national bias are observed everywhere. For thousands of years the world of humanity has been agitated and disturbed by prejudices. As long as it prevails, warfare, animosity and hatred will continue. Moreover, *racial prejudice ...has bitten into the fiber, and attacked the whole social structure of American society and is the most vital and challenging issue confronting the Baha'i community at the present stage of its evolution.*[229-AS]

(8) Universal Peace (beryl):
All the divine Manifestations...taught that men should love and mutually help each other....The fundamental truth of the Manifestations is peace....The divine purpose is that men should live in unity, concord and agreement....All created things are expressions of the affinity and cohesion of elementary substances....But when these elements become discordant, repelling each other, decomposition and non-existence result. Everything partakes of this nature and is subject to this principle as an expression or outcome of love....War has been a factor of derangement and discomfort whereas peace and brotherhood have brought security and consideration of human interests....For thousands of years we have had bloodshed and strife....Now is the time to associate together in love and harmony....Let mankind for a time at least live in peace, free from savagery...religious warfare, political warfare or some other clash of human interests....Why should we kill our fellow-creatures? Warfare...violates the spirit and basis of all religion. Universal peace must be instilled into the minds of all...in order that they may become the armies of peace....Wars and disputes shall cease and over the world will spread the Most Great Peace...which is now at long last within the reach of the nations. For the first time in history it is possible for everyone to view the entire planet...in one perspective. World peace is...inevitable....Soon enough, the most Great Peace will hoist the Standard of God among all nations...in one common fatherland...the planet itself. Universal peace and concord will be realized between all the nations.[230-A]

(9) Universal Education (topaz):
Knowledge is as wings to man's life, and a ladder for his ascent.... ***The primary, the most urgent requirement is the promotion of education*** [my emphasis]. *It is inconceivable that any nation should achieve prosperity and success unless this paramount, this fundamental concern is carried forward. The principal reason for the decline and fall of peoples is ignorance....It is therefore urgent that beneficial articles and books be written, clearly and definitely establishing what the present-day requirements of the people are, and what will conduce to the happiness and advancement of society...published and spread throughout the nation....The publication of high thoughts is the dynamic power in the arteries of life; it is the very soul of the world. Thoughts are a boundless sea, and the effects and varying conditions of existence are as the separate forms and individual*

limits of the waves; not until the sea boils up will the waves rise and scatter their pearls of knowledge on the shore of life ....Children must be educated...taught a profession or trade, so that every member of the community will be enabled to earn his own living and...serve the community....All cannot be scientists and philosophers, but each should be educated according to his needs and deserts....All must receive training and instruction....Lack of mutual understanding will be remedied and the unity of mankind furthered and advanced...Every father to teach and instruct his children according to his possibilities:

First: whole-hearted service to the cause of education, the unfolding of the mysteries of nature, the extension of the boundaries of pure science, the elimination of the causes of ignorance and social evils, a standard universal system of instruction, and the diffusion of the lights of knowledge and reality.

Second: Service to the cause of morality, raising the moral tone of the students, inspiring them with the sublimest ideals of ethical refinement, teaching them altruism, inculcating in their lives the beauty of holiness and the excellency of virtue and animating them with the excellences and perfections of the religion of God.

Third: Service to the oneness of the world of humanity; so that each student may consciously realize that he is a brother to all mankind, irrespective of religion or race.

The mothers in their homes, the teachers in the schools, the professors in the college, the presidents in the universities, must teach these ideals to the young from the cradle up to the age of manhood.[231-BA]

(10) Spiritual Economics (chrysoprase):

For the immense economic problems that face humanity,

Baha'u'llah has set forth the solution and provided the remedy for the economic question. No religious Books of the past Prophets speak of this important human problem.[232-A]

To this end, the Baha'i Faith teaches **spiritual economics**, which provides multiple global remedies for fixing economic problems. These remedies appear separately later, in the section titled *Laws of Spiritual Economics* (pages 300–6).

(11) A UNIVERSAL AUXILIARY LANGUAGE (jacinth):
Leaders should choose one of the divers languages, and likewise one of the existing scripts, or...create a new language and a new script to be taught children in schools throughout the world...acquiring only two languages, one their own native tongue, the other the language in which all the peoples of the world...converse...relieved and freed from the necessity of acquiring and teaching different languages. This will be conducive to the concord and the unity of the peoples of the world...and a great means of dispelling the differences between nations....Then, to whatsoever city a man may journey, it shall be as if he were entering his own home.[233-BA]

Although Baha'i Writings recommend no specific universal auxiliary language, English has clearly already come to fill this role de facto, at least for now.

(12) A SUPREME GLOBAL TRIBUNAL (amethyst):
True civilization will raise its banner when some noble kings... step forth with firm resolution and keen mind and ***keeping fast hold of the means of enforcing their views they will establish a union of the states of the world, and conclude a definite treaty and strict alliance between them upon conditions not to be evaded. When the whole human race has been consulted through their representatives and invited to corroborate this treaty which verily will be accounted sacred by all the peoples of the earth*** [my emphasis]....*It will be the duty of the united powers of the world to see that this great treaty shall endure....Then, should any king take up arms against another,* ***all should unitedly arise and prevent him*** [my emphasis]. *If this be done, the nations of the world will no longer require any armaments, except for the purpose of preserving the security of their realms and of maintaining internal order within their territories. This will ensure the peace and composure of every people, government and nation* through a *global supreme tribunal...permanently established in order to arbitrate international questions. The members of this arbitral court of justice will be representatives of all the nations....In it all international difficulties will be settled.*[234-A]

The term ***all should unitedly arise and prevent him*** **requires the routine use of overwhelming force**. After all, en**force**ment **must** overwhelm, as a simple matter of definition! Overwhelms force will, paradoxically, **minimize** the price in death and destruction to be paid for peace.

War and Peace

A Lesser Peace shall lead to a Greater Peace

Now, ending warfare calls for a *Lesser Peace* to lead to a *Greater Peace*. A geopolitically-driven prior global Lesser Peace must lead to a spiritually-driven global Greater Peace.

But why a two-step Greater Peace? Why not **just a one-step** Greater Peace? Indeed, between 1867 and 1870, Baha'u'llah did initially write to the globe's most powerful leaders to urge them to establish directly a

> *Most Great Peace—the surest of all means for the protection of humanity...the supreme instrument that can ensure the security and welfare of all peoples and nations*, so that *these fruitless strifes, these ruinous wars shall pass away, and the 'Most Great Peace' shall come…and all men be as one kindred and one Family.* ***So let not a man glory in this, that he loves his country; let him rather glory...that he loves his kind*** [my emphasis].[235-S]

However, increasingly through the late-1800s,

> *the fire of war was blazing among the nations of the world... bloodshed was considered an honour to mankind...the carnage of thousands stained the earth...children were rendered fatherless ...mothers were spent with weeping...the darkness of inter-racial hatred and animosity seemed to envelope* [*sic*] *mankind and blot out the divine light...the wafting of the holy breath of God seemed to be cut off—in that time Bahá'u'lláh rose like a shining star from the horizon of Persia*, teaching that *the Most Great Peace should become a reality.*[236-A]

So the urgings of Baha'u'llah fell on deaf ears and his

> *appeals, the like of which neither the annals of Christianity nor...Islam have recorded, were disdainfully rejected. The dark warnings He uttered were haughtily scorned. The bold challenges He issued were ignored. The chastisements He predicted they derisively brushed aside.*[237-S]

Bu the close of the 1800s, world leaders had not missed their chance to miss their chance to establish a direct Greater Peace. They and the greedy tycoons backing them were playing and plying the awesome material progress of the new Era to profiteer from a massive arms race.

> *While peace is the pretext...night and day they are all straining every nerve to pile up more weapons of war....The smoke of corruption hath enveloped the whole world in such wise that naught can be seen in any direction save regiments of soldiers and nothing is heard from any land but the clashing of swords.*[238-B]

Already by 1890, alas, it had become all too clear that world leaders could not, or would not, establish a direct Greater Peace. So instead, in 1891, Baha'u'llah urged them:

Now that ye have refused the Most Great Peace, hold ye fast unto...the Lesser Peace....It is incumbent upon the Sovereigns of the world...unitedly to...achieve what will be conducive to the well-being of man...to convene an all-inclusive assembly ...to enforce whatever measures are required to establish unity and concord amongst men, to put away the weapons of war, to turn to the instruments of universal reconstruction and to *promote the Lesser Peace so that the people of the earth may be relieved from the burden of exorbitant expenditures. This matter is imperative and absolutely essential, inasmuch as hostilities and conflict lie at the root of affliction and calamity.*[239-B]

The Dual Peace of Jerusalem: The two Hebrew names for Jerusalem augured the initial concept of a direct Greater Peace being modified to the extended concept of a Lesser Peace leading to a Greater Peace:

(1) The earlier name *YOR'U-SHALEM* meant *they shall show the whole*, as if planning an initial concept of a one-step Greater Peace

(2) The later and present name *YIR'U-SHALAYIM* means *they shall see dual peace*, as if accepting and ensuing concept of a two-step Lesser Peace that will, one day, lead to a Greater Peace.

All Abrahamic Faiths teach the dual peace of Jerusalem in the various ways:

- **Judaism** cherishes *Lower Jerusalem* as a physical city and prays for the advent of *Upper Jerusalem* as a heavenly city[240-J] that inspires, explains, permeates, penetrates, and renews Lower Jerusalem. In the 1800s, Zionists settling in Palestine set out to regain Upper Jerusalem as a lost paradise by rebuilding Lower Jerusalem physically (plus the rest of Israel). Yet curiously and aptly, Zionist leader Theodore Herzl's utopian novel called *Old New Land* made Haifa its ideal city!
- **Christianity** prays in its Lord's Prayer for *peace on earth as in heaven*. However, early Christians demeaned earthly Jerusalem because *only pagans...sought God...in a particular place.*[241-C] In contrast, they adored heavenly New Jerusalem. They awaited its descent any day and read Revelation's New Jerusalem Chapter 21 more than any other Scripture. However, these early Christians were blithely ignoring that the main Revelation time-prophecy of 1,260 prophetic *days* of years demanded the passage of at least 1,260 years **before** any New Jerusalem could possibly appear!

- **Islam** paints heavenly Jerusalem as a huge tree with Judaism, Christianity, and Islam as three roots pouring its rivers of knowledge into earthly Jerusalem (*The Holy*). Jerusalem and Mecca have both served as holy cities for the Muslim direction of prayer (*qiblih*). Mecca to Jerusalem and back was the route flown by Muhammad on his night journey.[242-M] Mecca to Jerusalem is also set as the end-times flight route of the Kaaba. The duality of Jerusalem also echoes Islam's dual doctrine of *Abodes of Peace and War* (see page 125).

One day, the dual peace of Jerusalem will bless Holy Land Jews and Muslims for both peoples to prosper possibly as two states or preferably as a true Swiss-style cantonal confederation.

The Armageddon Century of Worldwide Warfare

The *Armageddon war of the Great Day of Almighty God* interprets as the worldwide warfare of the *Great Day* of a century begun by World War I in 1914 and continuing through World War II, the Cold War, the Korean War, the Viet Nam War, and many Middle East and other wars, until now.

Back in 1873, Baha'u'llah had already seen the blood and had smelled the smoke of two future World Wars for Germany specifically:

> *O banks of the Rhine! We have seen you covered with gore, inasmuch as the swords of retribution were drawn against you* [World War I], *and you shall have another turn* [World War II]. *And We hear the lamentations of Berlin, though she be today in conspicuous glory.*[243-B]

Also as early as 1860, Baha'u'llah had predicted *split the atom's heart, and lo! Within it thou wilt find a sun* (see page 176).[244-B]

Already in 1912, 'Abdu'l-Baha was predicting world war starting as the *Battle of Armageddon* in 1914:

> *We are on the eve of the Battle of Armageddon referred to in the sixteenth chapter of Revelation....Two years hence...all that which is recorded in the Revelation of John...*will *become fulfilled....Only a spark will set aflame the whole of Europe* as *a world-enkindling fire...in the Balkans....A great melee of the civilized nations is in sight...a tremendous conflict....a most tragic struggle...vast armies ...mobilized...for the fearful contest...a conflagration, the like of which is not recorded in the past history of mankind....By 1917 kingdoms will fall and cataclysms will rock the earth....Armed troops and artillery are to be found in every part of the field. The flash of the swords of enmity blind the eyes...the lightning effect*

of breastplate and lance and the sparkle of the bucklers of hatred light up the night and bewilder the sight....Strife, battle, slaughter and war are prepared in organized perfection....The flame of war is so ablaze that such terrible struggle finds no parallel in the war records....The most advanced and civilized countries have been turned into arsenals of explosives and the governments of the world are vying with each other as to who will first step into the field of carnage and bloodshed....In times gone by progress on the material plane was not so rapid, neither was there bloodshed in such profusion. In ancient warfare there were no cannons, no guns, no dynamite, no shells, no torpedo boats, no battleships, no submarines. Now, owing to material civilization, we have all these inventions, and war goes from bad to worse!...Warfare in former centuries had not attained the degree of savagery and destructiveness which now characterizes it. If two nations were at war...ten or twenty thousand would be sacrificed but in this century the destruction of one hundred thousand lives in a day is quite possible. So perfected has the science of killing become, and so efficient the means and instruments of its accomplishment that a whole nation can be obliterated in a short time.

In 1912, 'Abdu'l-Baha also warned of an evidently nuclear *stupendous force...able to destroy the whole earth* (see page 176).[245-A]

Then already in 1933, Shoghi Effendi was forecasting World War II starting in Europe as a

hotbed of strife and rancor. The political hatreds that exist there will if not subdued not only consume its inhabitants but will ravage the whole world and will bring devastation to the entire surface of the globe.[246-S]

In 1941, Shoghi Effendi further observed that World War II's

immediate cause can be traced to the forces engendered by the last war [World War I] *of which it may be truly regarded as the direct continuation....The internecine struggle, now engulfing the generality of mankind, is increasingly assuming, in its range and ferocity, the proportions of the titanic upheaval foreshadowed as far back as seventy years ago by Baha'u'llah....Its first sparks were kindled on the eastern shores of the Asiatic continent, enveloping two sister races of the world in a conflagration which no force seems able to either quench or circumscribe. This cataclysmic process was accelerated by the outbreak of a fierce conflict in the heart of Europe, fanning into flame age-long animosities and unchaining a series of calamities as swift as they were appalling. As the turmoil gathered momentum, it swept remorselessly into its vortex the most powerful nations of the European continent—the chief protagonists of that highly-vaunted yet lamentably defective civilization. The mounting tide of its havoc and devastation soon overspread the northernmost regions of that afflicted continent, subsequently ravaged the shores of the Mediterranean, and invaded the African continent as far as Ethiopia and the surrounding territories. The Balkan countries, as predicted by 'Abdu'l-Baha, were soon to sustain the impact of this tragic ordeal, communicating in their turn the commotions to which they had been subjected to both the Near and Middle East.*[247-S]

Its menace is overleaping the limits of the Old World and is plunging into consternation the Great Republic of the West [the USA], *as well as the peoples of Central and South America. The New World as well as the Old is experiencing the terrific impact of this disruptive force. Even the peoples of the Antipodes are trembling before the approaching tempest that threatens to burst on their heads. The races of the world, Nordic, Slavonic, Mongolian, Arab and African, are alike subjected to its consuming violence. The world's religious systems are no less affected by the* ***universal paralysis*** [my emphasis] *which is creeping over the minds and souls of men. The persecution of world Jewry, the rapid deterioration of Christian institutions, the intestine division and disorders of Islam, are but manifestations of the fear and trembling that has seized humanity in its hour of unprecedented turmoil and peril. On the high seas, in the air, on land, in the forefront of battle, in the palaces of kings and the cottages of peasants, in the most hallowed sanctuaries, whether secular or religious....Its heavy toll is steadily mounting—a holocaust sparing neither prince nor peasant, neither man nor woman, neither young nor old.*[248-S]

The Cold War brought the multiplication, the diversity and the increasing destructive power of armaments to which both sides [Communist and Capitalist] *caught in a whirlpool of fear, suspicion and hatred* were *rapidly contributing; the outbreak of two bloody conflicts* [Korean and Vietnam Wars] *entangling still further the American nation in the affairs of a distracted world, entailing a considerable loss in blood and treasure, swelling the national budget and progressively depreciating the currency.*[249-S]

Since 1914, the Armageddon century of worldwide warfare has seen *God...dethroned from the hearts of men,* as *an idolatrous world passionately and clamorously hails and worships the false gods which its own idle fancies have fatuously created, and its misguided hands so impiously exalted. The chief idols in the desecrated temple of mankind are...the triple gods of Nationalism, Racialism and Communism...at whose altars governments and peoples, whether democratic or totalitarian, at peace or at war, of the East or of the West, Christian or Islamic, are, in various forms and in different degrees, now worshiping. Their high priests are the politicians and the worldly-wise, the so-called sages of the age; their sacrifice, the flesh and blood of the slaughtered multitudes; their incantations outworn shibboleths and insidious and irreverent formulas; their incense, the smoke of anguish that ascends from the lacerated hearts of the bereaved, the maimed, and the homeless.*[250-S]

The theories and policies, so unsound, so pernicious, which deify the state and exalt the nation above mankind, which seek to subordinate the sister races of the world to one single race, which discriminate between the black and the white, and which tolerate the dominance of one privileged class over all others—these are the dark, the false, and crooked doctrines for which any man or people who believes in them, or acts upon them, must, sooner or later, incur the wrath and chastisement of God.[251-S]

Weakening of the pillars of religion...cannot but lead...to chaos and confusion....In the West, the nationalistic philosophy, which Christian rulers and governments have upheld, is an attack directed against the Church by those who were previously its professed adherents, a betrayal of its cause by its own kith and kin...assisted and encouraged by the prevailing spirit of modernism, with its emphasis on a purely materialistic philosophy, which...tends increasingly to divorce religion from man's daily life.[252-SB]

Soon, the Armageddon century of worldwide warfare is due to end. History alone will tell how this happens.

A New Supreme Global Tribunal

In 1919, the League of Nations emerged from World War I's clearing smoke. Alas, the League would prove weak, and by 1936 it failed to resolve the Abyssinia crisis, and collapsed. In 1945 arose the United Nations as a phoenix from the ashes of World War II and the League before it. Happily, the UN has come to embody

a unity of nations...securely established...in this [20th] *century,... causing all the peoples of the world to regard themselves as citizens of one common fatherland,* which would *lead through a series of victories and reverses, to the political unification of the Eastern and Western Hemispheres, to the emergence of a world government and the establishment of the Lesser Peace...foretold by Baha'u'llah and...the Prophet Isaiah.*[253-A]

The prime success of the UN has been to prevent nuclear war (thus far). Meanwhile, the streets of the global village still see nations brawl. Like the League, the UN is weak too. Soon some severe crisis will collapse it. From its ashes will a new Global Tribunal rise as a phoenix of already panting to emerge. Structured right, the new Global Tribunal will prove strong enough to forge a true global Lesser Peace.

In particular, America will play a major role in the

> *hoisting of the standard of the Lesser Peace, in the unification of mankind, and in the establishment of a world federal government on this planet, after it* [America] *stops clinging tenaciously to the obsolescent doctrine of absolute sovereignty and upholding a political system manifestly at variance with the needs of a world already contracted into a neighborhood and crying out for unity and is purged of its anachronistic conceptions, and prepared to play a preponderating role.*[254-S]

Soon enough, humanity shall conquer causes of war and achieve

> *the unfurling of the banner of the Most Great Peace, in the Golden Age of the Dispensation of Bahá'u'lláh…war shall cease between nations….All men will live as brothers.*

Nation shall no longer raise sword against nation. Instead, they will spare lives and resources by beating tanks into tractors.[255-AS]

Causes of Conflicts between Faiths

Meanwhile though, Faiths still fight. Across time, mother and daughter Faiths have fought from the day of the birth—Judaism and Christianity; Christianity and Islam; Hinduism and Buddhism. Across space, Faiths still fight over land—Jews and Muslims over Israel/Palestine; Hindus and Muslims over Kashmir; Catholics and Protestants over Northern Ireland; Christians and Muslims over the Balkans, the Philippines, Chechnya, Nigeria, and Sudan; and Muslims and Buddhists over part of Myanmar. And so on.

Yet if Abraham, Moses, Zoroaster, Krishna, Buddha, Jesus, and Muhammad would meet tomorrow, they would surely sit happily together over a meal, consorting as good friends in perfect amity, and shaking their heads sadly at the millennia of harm wreaked in their names, for even though

> *the foundations of the religious systems are one…the followers of these systems have disagreed* and *discord, strife and warfare have arisen among them, for they have forsaken the foundation and held to that which is but imitation and semblance* and have *made the Law of God a cause and pretext for perversity and hatred….The light of true religion has been extinguished.*[256-AB]

Faiths fight due to conflicts over major religious issues such as:

- Succession
- Literal interpretation of prophecies
- Dogmas if exclusive superiority
- A catch-22 definition of religious identity.

Succession

Believers in all Faiths conceive Messengers of God as rungs on spiritual ladders. Jews hear Adam, Noah, and Abraham as serial rungs on the spiritual ladder up to their Moses. Christians see Adam, Noah, Abraham, and Moses as serial rungs on the spiritual ladder up to their Jesus. Muslims accept Adam, Noah, Abraham, Moses, and Jesus as serial rungs on the spiritual ladder up to their Muhammad. Hindus savor Matsya, Kurma, Varaha, Nrisimha, Vamana, Bhrgupati, and Rama as serial rungs on the spiritual ladder up to their Krishna. Buddhists embrace Matsya, Kurma, Varaha, Nrisimha, Vamana, Bhrgupati, Rama, and Krishna as serial rungs on the spiritual ladder up to their Buddha. Zoroastrians accept prior Persian Prophets as serial rungs on the spiritual ladder up to their Zoroaster. And Baha'is welcome all these convening lines of serial Messengers as spiritual ladders leading up to their Bab and Baha'u'llah.

So far so good. With 20⁄20 hindsight, each believer spiritually sitting safe on the rung of his or her own Faith's Messenger look down fondly upon prior Messengers who functioned as spiritual rungs on their ladder and readily agree that *every ancient prophet gave the glad tidings of the future, and every future has accepted the past.*[257-A]

However, now looking up, 20⁄20 hindsight drops to 0/20 foresight! The same believers cannot accept the successor Messenger as the next rung on their spiritual ladder. A whole battery of theological blinkers, earplugs, nose clips, muffs, and handcuffs blocks them from seeing, hearing, scenting, tasting, or grasping the reality of the successor Messenger of their Faith. As a result,

> *those who were the seekers of Reality...attached to Abraham were deprived of its influences when* they *illuminated the reality of Moses....Those who held fast to Moses when the Sun of Reality shone from Christ...were also veiled.* So *the Jews await the Messiah, the Christians the return of Christ, the Muslims the Mahdi, the Buddhists the fifth Buddha, the Zoroastrians Shah Bahram, the Hindus the reincarnation of Krishna, and the Atheists—a better social organization!*[258-A]

Why all these theological blinkers, earplugs, nose clips, muffs, and handcuffs? One good reason is fear of false-messiahs. Statistically, the false-messiahs in any Faith outnumber its one true Messiah. As a result, all clergy reject potential Messiahs in a blink. In the process, they inevitably spin the baby of their Faith's true Messiah down the spiritual plughole with the bathwater of its false-messiahs.

So even though clergy in all Faiths have searched

> *with such earnestness and longing....their attack hath been more fierce than tongue or pen can describe. Not one single Manifestation of Holiness hath appeared but He was afflicted by the denials, the repudiation, and the vehement opposition of the people around Him....Each nation hath plotted darkly against their Messenger to lay violent hold on Him, and disputed with vain words to invalidate the truth....Leaders of religion have hindered their people....By their sanction and authority, every Prophet of God hath drunk from the chalice of sacrifice....What unspeakable cruelties they that have occupied the seats of authority and learning have inflicted....How many have...yearningly awaited the advent of the Manifestations of God....How often have they expected His coming....How frequently have they prayed that the breeze of divine mercy might blow, and the promised Beauty step forth from behind the veil of concealment, and be made manifest to all the world. And whensoever the portals of grace did open, and the clouds of divine bounty did rain upon mankind, and the light of the Unseen did shine above the horizon of celestial might, they all denied Him, and turned away from His face—the face of God Himself—*as *hath been recorded in every sacred Book.*[259-BSM]

As a result, believers cease to hope that their Faith's Promised One will come, close their minds and hearts, take the prophecies that predict him with a pinch of salt, and pay him just lip service as some ethereal dream. They simply continue firmly to hold onto their own safe and solid Messenger of God as His final Messenger. Thus, they ***limit the number of his* [God's] *appearances through his prophets*, which *is equal to limiting God himself*!**[260-A]

Literal Interpretations of Prophecies

In any case, clergy teach congregations to interpret prophecies about the Promised-One literally, not symbolically. So believers expect Messiahs to appear in impossible superhuman forms and settings. Jews expect their Messiah to deliver up a golden Millennium—instantly! Christians expect their Messiah to ride on clouds—bodily! Muslims expect their Messiah to land amid stars falling and angels descending—physically! **So the Messiah who comes is never the one expected!**

Accordingly, the Jewish

> *Pharisees...denied with the greatest obstinacy the explanations of Christ...saying 'These prophecies are...of the Promised One Who shall come later according to the conditions mentioned in the Bible'. Some of these conditions were that he must have a kingdom, be seated on the throne of David, enforce the Law of the Bible, and manifest such justice that the wolf and the lamb shall gather at the same spring.... Thus they prevented the people from knowing Christ....The words of the prophets were fulfilled, but because the Jews held tenaciously to hereditary interpretations, they did not understand the inner meanings of the Holy Bible; therefore, they denied Jesus Christ, the Messiah....Submerged in the sea of ancestral imitations, they could not comprehend the meaning of these prophecies...intoxicated with the wine of haughtiness...not...conscious even for a moment.*[261-AB]

Likewise, the

> *Christian divines have failed to apprehend the meaning of...'the Son of man shall appear in heaven'...and did not recognize their object and purpose, and have clung to the literal interpretation of the words of Jesus....They therefore became deprived of the streaming grace of the Muhammadan Revelation and its showering bounties...prevented from beholding the beauty of the King of glory, inasmuch as those signs which were to accompany the dawn of the sun of the Muhammadan Dispensation did not actually come to pass....The adherents of Jesus have never understood the hidden meaning of these words, and as the signs which they and the leaders of their Faith have expected have failed to appear, they therefore refused to acknowledge, even until now, the truth of those Manifestations of Holiness that have since the days of Jesus been made manifest.*[262-B]

Similarly,

> *the people of the Qur'án have perverted the text...concerning the signs of the expected Manifestation....Corruption of the text...in which all Muslim divines are engaged...is the interpretation of God's holy Book in accordance with their idle imaginings and vain desires....When Muslims say: 'These words...have no interpretation other than their outward meaning', then what objection can they raise against...people of the Book* [Jews and Christians] who *heard the literal interpretations of their divines* but *refused to recognize God in those who are the Manifestations of His unity...and failed to believe in them and submit to their authority* because *they did not see the sun darken, or the stars of heaven fall to the ground, or the angels visibly descend upon the earth.*[263-B]

Dogmas of Exclusive Superiority

Early in the history of each Faith, its clergy chose to exaggerate some of its teachings into dogmas of exclusive superiority. *Each sect* [Faith] *hath picked out a way for itself and is clinging to a certain cord.* For example, rabbis insist that **Jews are specially chosen by God—forever**. Priests assert that **Jesus is the only way to God—indeed is God**. Imams argue that **Muhammad is the supreme Word of God—His final Word**. Such superiority dogmas block recognition of Promised-Ones. By preaching them

> *leaders of religion...have hindered their people...some for the lust of leadership, others through want of knowledge and understanding....The beginnings of all great religions were pure; but priests, taking possession of the minds of the people, filled them with dogmas and superstitions, so that religion became gradually corrupt.*[264-BA]

Each Faith's dogmas of exclusive superiority act as a select operating system for its computer alone. No upgrades needed! Onto the bolts of its superiority dogmas, each Faith locks down nuts of material laws that control food, clothes, hair, marriage, sexual conduct, property, etc.. Preserved thus, these idolized idealized dogmas have forever festered, fueled, and flamed fights between Faiths, so that

> *religionists have anathematized religionists, each considering the other as deprived of the mercy of God, abiding in gross darkness and the children of Satan. For example, the Christians and Muslims considered the Jews satanic and the enemies of God. Therefore, they cursed and persecuted them. Great numbers of Jews were killed, their houses burned and pillaged, their children carried into captivity. The Jews in turn regarded the Christians as infidels and the Muslims as enemies and destroyers of the law of Moses. Therefore, they call down vengeance upon them and curse them even to this day.*[265-A]

A Catch-22 Definition of Religious Identity

Religious identity plays a very important driving role too. Believers who accept their Faith's true Messiah are staying true to the Faith, just as an adult is staying true to his or her own "child within". Nonetheless, they take on the mantle of the new daughter Faith in the form or new rituals and a fresh calendar. At the same time, the old-style believers in the mother Faith who reject its Messiah are also staying true to the Faith. So they brand their erstwhile coreligionists as heretics and regardless of their common belief in the same mother-Faith, the two groups split, and usually enmity arises between them.

An Apocalypse History of Muslim Militarism

The Apocalypse parades a menagerie of scary monsters that project different forms of Muslim Militarism. Its *ancient serpent* oozes primeval sinfulness that drives militarism, now of Middle East Muslim Empires. Its *dragon* (*serpent*) hisses as Muslim Militarism itself. Its *beast from the sea* bellows as Muslim Militarism's Umayyad Caliphate, with *ten horns* as dynastic Caliph-Names and *seven heads* as domains. Its *beast from the land* roars as Muslim Militarism's dynastic Ottoman Sultanate, with *two horns* as its titles *Sultan* and *Caliph*. Its *scarlet beast* reeks of Muslim brutality generally, with *seven heads* as the original seven territories of its Umayyad Caliphate and *ten horns* performing in two sets—one depicting 10 Shahs of Qajar Persia, the second depicting 10 rogue regimes and terrorist organizations of modern Muslim Militarism.[266-R]

Rashidun Caliphate (AD 632–659)

Ali was the true successor of Muhammad, as his cousin, stepson, son-in-law, and second follower. In his last oasis of Ghadir Khum sermon, Muhammad named Ali publicly as Islam's future *Leader* (*Imam*) and his successor. Muhammad was *desirous to see Ali's coronation celebrations being commemorated in the Islamic Society*. So he crowned him with a turban called the *Cloud* (*Sahab*) to signify his successorship.[267-M]

But Umar stopped Ali succeeding Muhammad. In AD 632,

> *as Muhammad lay dying...he said 'fetch me hither ink and paper, that I may record for you a writing which shall hinder you from going astray forever.' But Umar said, 'Pain is deluding Him. We have God's Book, which is enough.' So the companions wrangled at the deathbed, whether to bring the materials and write the words, and Muhammad sent them away.*[268-M]

Immediately after Muhammad's death, Umar endorsed the aged Abu-Bakr as his successor. So after two years, when Abu-Bakr died, Umar succeeded him, and after him Uthman, an Umayyad. These three took *Rashidun Caliphs*, meaning Muhammad's *Righteous Successors*, as their arrogant blasphemous title (Rev. 13.1), despite them being neither righteous nor true. Free of Muhammad's restraining hand, Umar unleashed the *Locust and Scorpion* cavalries and archers of Islam, who swarmed out of Arabia and drove back the Byzantine Christian and Zoroastrian Sassanid Empires (Rev. 9.5 & 10) Empires in short order. Thus began Muslim Militarism.[269]

Finally, in AD 656, Ali did succeed Muhammad as the fourth and only truly righteous Rashidun Caliph. But Ali is far better known as the First Imam of Shi'a Islam—ever since Ghadir Khum. Alas, the assassination of Ali squelched all hope of halting Muslim Militarism.

Umayyad Caliphate (AD 666–74)

The evil Umayyad Mu'awiya founded the Umayyad Caliphate in the notorious year of AD **666**. Mu'awiya was scion of a warrior line, great-grandson to tribal chief Umayya, grandson to Harb (*War*), son to Abu-Sufyan (*Father of a Sword*), and a kinsman of the third Rashidun Caliph Uthman. Abu-Sufyan, Mu'awiya, and their Umayyad tribe became Muhammad's arch-enemies, because his iconoclastic teachings had wrecked their lucrative idol-trade in Mecca on the watch of Abu-Sufyan as its mayor. In AD 640, Umar made Mu'awiya governor of Syria in Damascus.[A] After Ali was assassinated in AD 661, Mu'awiya seized control of the expanding Muslim world, proclaimed himself as the First Caliph of the Umayyad Caliphate in AD **666**, made militant Damascus the capital instead of holy Mecca, and desecrated the sites of Muhammad's birthplace in Mecca and tomb in Medina. Mu'awiya's destructive edicts crippled true Islam. His Umayyad Caliphate went on to carve out the world's then biggest Empire, from Pakistan to Portugal, and from Sudan to Samarkand. (Rev. 9.11, 13.1–2, 13.5–6 & 13.18.)

The Shi'a Imamate of Ali, Hasan, and Husayn (AD 656–873)

Ali began Shi'a Islam as its First Imam (*Leader*). His line of Imams ran through his Second Imam son Hasan (AD 661–668), his Third Imam son Husayn (AD 668–680), and eight more Imams descending from them (Rev. 12.1). In AD 873, the death of the Eleventh Imam interrupted the Imamate. Shi'a Muslims claim that the Eleventh Imam had a small Twelfth Imam son who vanished into "occultation" and whose return they still expect. In contrast, Baha'is believe that he was childless and that the Bab succeeded him as Twelfth Imam after a long gap.[270-M] The Shi'a Imamate made Kufa in Iraq its capital city.

Shi'a Islam and Sunni Islam

Mu'awiya fought the Imams just as his father AbuSufyan had fought Muhammad. He stole the cloak of successorship from the Imams just as Abu-Bakr, Umar, and Uthman had stolen the successorship turban from Ali.[271] Then the Umayyads killed four Imams as *one third of the stars in the sky* (Rev. 12.4). They beheaded the Third Imam Husayn and poisoned the Second Imam Hassan, and the Fourth and Fifth Imams (later Imams would be poisoned too). The martyrdom of

[A] Back then, *Syria* covered the territory of modern Syria, Lebanon, Jordan, and Israel

Husayn marked a point-of-no-return that split Islam into its Shi'a (*Follower*) branch following the Imams and its Sunni (*Way*) branch following the Caliphs. Each year Shi'a Muslims flagellate themselves openly on the street to memorialize the martyrdom of Husayn.

Spiritually, Shi'a Islam prevailed over Sunni Islam. For most of its history, it followed the true teachings of Muhammad and Ali quietly. It kept mosque and state separate. It waged just defensive war. It practiced true jihad as *spiritual striving in the way of God.* In contrast, Sunni Islam prevailed materially, the name *Sunni* deriving from another blasphemous title, *Sunna* or *Way* (Rev. 13.1). Mu'awiya expanded what the first three Rashidun Caliphs had begun. His puppet clergies twisted Islam's history, skewed its teachings, and bent its doctrines. Sunni Islam joined mosque with state, promoted militarism, justified war with Faith and Faith with war, and made jihad its military doctrine, its modus operandi, and its modus vivendi. Today, some 80–85% of Muslims are Sunni. The Shi'a minority live mostly in Iran, Iraq, Bahrain, Syria, and Lebanon.[A]

The Caliphates of the Sunni Abbasids (AD 750–1258) and the Spanish Umayyads (AD 756–1031)

The parallel Abbasid and Spanish Umayyad Caliphates displaced and replaced the Umayyad Caliphate in AD 749. Both new Caliphates were enlightened. But violence begat them. Abbasid rebels lured their Umayyad overlords to a death-dealing dynastic dinner near Damascus, killed all but one, and seized the Umayyad Empire. But the survivor Al-Rahman escaped to Spain and kept it Umayyad as *one of the beast's heads...fatally wounded...but its mortal wound healed up* (Rev. 13.3, 12 & 14).

The days of Damascus were done. The new Abbasid Empire built Baghdad as its capital city. The new Spanish Umayyad Caliphate of Al-Rahman made Cordoba its capital city. Both the Abbasid and Spanish Umayyad Caliphates flourished famously.

> *What a great civilization was established in Spain...What a powerful caliphate...in Baghdad!*

Umayyad Spain became an *Ornament of the World* where Jews, Christians, and Muslims prospered in mutual respect for several centuries. Regardless, later on, Spain's Catholic rulers changed all this. By 1492, they had succeeded to cleanse Spain ethnically of both Jews and Muslims, making 1492 the year of Spain's greatest shame as well as its greatest fame (Columbus).[272-A]

[A] Historically, other Shi'a-derived groups include the Alawi Muslims of Syria, the Alevi Muslims of Turkey, and the Druze of Syria, Lebanon, Jordan, and Israel

The Sunni Ottoman Sultanate and Empire (1299–1918)

In the 1100–1200s, tribes from Turkistan converted to Islam and migrated to Turkey. In AD 1299, their leader Othman founded his Empire and Sultanate (Rev. 13.11). The Ottoman Empire became as brutal as the earlier Umayyad Empire. It cloned its cruel system, revived its corrupt doctrines, waged its aggressive jihad, and enforced its cruel taxation and discrimination with jizya and kharaj tattoos (Rev. 13.12–18).

Further, the Ottomans militarized the Muslim *Doctrine of Abodes* that told citizens in Muslim *Abodes-of-Submission* peacefully to convert residents of non-Muslim *Abodes-of-War*. Instead, they made the doctrine an order to conquer and forcibly convert. The Balkans still bear painful witness to them militarizing the Abodes doctrine.

In 1453, the Ottoman Empire conquered Christian Constantinople and made it their capital city Istanbul (Rev. 9.14–15).[A] In the 1800s, the Empire fell into decline, with its Tanzimat reforms coming too late to save it, and it became history in 1918 (Rev. 17.11).

Shi'a Qajar Persia (1796–1924)

Dynastic Qajar Persia was ally to the Ottoman Empire. Its system, ruled by Shahs and their Shi'a clergy, made Qajar Persia as brutal as the Umayyad and Ottoman Empires. As a result, Persia's

> *Shi'i sect, which* [once] *regarded itself as the most learned, the most righteous, and the most pious of all the peoples of the world...hath shown a cruelty such as hath never been experienced.*[273-B]

The scarlet beast's first set of *ten horns* (Rev. 17.12) fits the ten Shahs of Qajar Persia. For Baha'is, Nasir-i-Din (1848–96) was the worst Shah. In the mid-1800s, he ordered the execution of the Bab and oversaw the massacre of 20,000 Babis and Baha'is (Rev. 6.9–11 & 7.13–17). After its brutal century, in 1924, Qajar Persia became history too (Rev. 17.12–14).

Modern Muslim Militarism

Over the past few decades, modern Muslim Militarism has waxed with a vengeance, driven by a mix of Sunni orthodoxy, Shi'a extremism, and a general Muslim revival.[274] Its rogue regimes and terrorist organizations have been relighting the fire of military jihad and fanning its flames just as furiously as the Umayyad Locusts and

[A] At the end of World War II, five centuries after the Ottomans took Constantinople, Winston Churchill was still pining that the name *'Constantinople' should never be abandoned*! (Churchill, *Prime Minister's Personal Minutes* Serial No. M387/5A)

Scorpions, the Ottoman cavalries, and the Qajar Shahs and clergy acted before them. Its jihad is plumbing horrendous new depths of brutal violence. Now it wears the cloak of Shi'a Iran too, whose Ayatollahs sprout Shihab rockets, nurture protégés like Hezbollah, Hamas, and Syria, centrifuge uranium, and dream nuclear dreams.

The scarlet beast's second set of *ten horns* (Rev. 17.16) fits the brutal rogue regimes and terrorist organizations of modern Muslim Militarism. From inside events, one can only guess who the ten horns are. But the Iran of the Ayatollahs, the Al Qaida of Bin Laden, and the Iraq of Saddam Hussein must surely top the list. Other potential candidates include Afghanistan, Algeria, Egypt, Hamas, Hezbollah, Libya, a Kurdish entity, Pakistan, a Palestinian entity, Tunisia, Turkey, Saudi Arabia, Sudan, Syria, and Yemen. Soon enough, history will show who these *ten horns* were.

As for Israel, Muslim Militarism views it as both a Jewish wing of the Christian West and a Jewish Abode-of-War island in a Muslim Abode-of-Submission sea. (Hypothetically, Islam would view a notionally Christian Lebanon in exactly the same way)

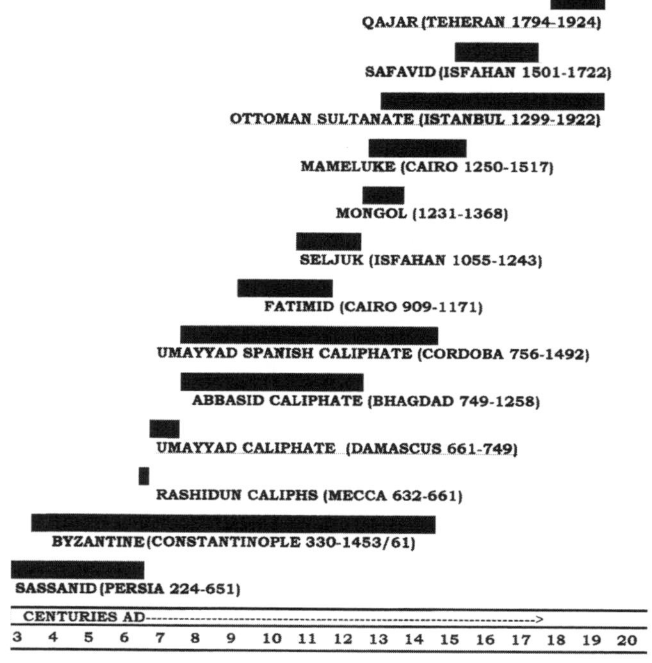

Timeline of Middle East Empires

Parallel Interpretation of the Apocalypse

This Parallel Interpretation of the Apocalypse is the real McCoy of *Apocalypse Secrets*. It harnesses every traceable Baha'i interpretation. It teases out John's hidden Greek and Hebrew codes. It topically focuses on the modern *beast* of Muslim Militarism and the modern *Babylon* of Malignant Materialism. It lists New Jerusalem's spiritual and material laws for the coming Millennium's divine civilization. And it keeps my own interpretive glosses separate.

A new sky and earth of spiritual and material Law seen from John's Patmos cave

The Parallel Interpretation sets out the two following parallel texts in this matching left- and right-column format:

THE ORIGINAL APOCALYPSE TEXT SET IN SMALL-CAPITAL OLD CLAUDE FONT.	**The interpretive Baha'i-based text set in this book's main Georgia font.**

The left-column's small-capital OLD CLAUDE FONT emulates the UNCIAL BLOCK-LETTER SCRIPT OF THE ORIGINAL GREEK. The original and interpretive texts match tightly, paragraph by paragraph, verse by verse, phrase by phrase, and word by word—down to the comma. The restrictive parallel format compels its primary thrust of a single Baha'i-based interpretation.

Alas, the close match between the texts in the two columns cannot be perfect, for the right-column interpretive text

- Runs 14% longer than THE LEFT-COLUMN TRANSLATION TEXT
- Assigns long names and titles to Messengers[A]
- Doubly interprets a few select items like *DEATH AND THE UNSEEN*; *THE GRASS, ANY PLANT, OR ANY TREE*; *FOUR ANGELS*; *FIRE, SMOKE, AND SULFUR*; *RULERS FROM THE RISING-PLACE OF THE SUN*; and last, but not least, *ARMAGEDDON*[B]
- Follows English, not Greek, usage and word order
- Tells its story in a real-time present-tense centered on the 40 years of Baha'u'llah's teaching in the second half of the 1800s
- Employs, for effect, stylish exaggerative jargon for interpreting terms like *INTO THE ERAS OF THE ERAS* as *from spiritual Cycle to spiritual Cycle*; *DAY AND NIGHT* as *as God's light lights the night*; and *A QUART OF WHEAT FOR A DAY'S PAY* as *a day's pay barely buys bread*[C]
- Imports some of John's internal interpretations, such as v. 17.15's *PEOPLES, POPULATIONS, NATIONS, AND LANGUAGE-GROUPS*, to interpret v. 17.1's *waters*
- Imports some telling Baha'i interpretive phrases, such as *kindles light* and *calamities and hardships*[D]
- Ignores terms that interpretation has rendered redundant, for example *LIKE*, and *IT WAS GIVEN TO IT TO*
- Interprets, for effect, certain singular nouns as plural and certain indefinite articles as definite, for example ***AN*** *ANGEL* interpreting as ***the*** *Messenger*.

Comments, listed by verse, follow each Apocalypse Chapter. These Comments address specific issues, cite Baha'i sources, incorporate extra topics, explain unusual translations, and expand interpretations. As for citing Old Testament prophecies, the Comments limit themselves to citing only especially pertinent ones (other Apocalypse works cite them abundantly).

To prepare the ground for the Parallel Interpretation, the following subjects deserve discussion first:

- Prophecies possess multiple meanings
- John's linguistic devices, and
- Baha'i-based summaries of the Parallel Interpretation's Apocalypse chapters.

[A] Rev. 4.5, 5.6
[B] Rev. 1.18, 9.4, 9.14–5, 9.17–8, 16.12, 16
[C] Rev. 1.18, 4.8, 6.6
[D] Rev. 7.17, 16.21

Prophecies possess Multiple Meanings

Biblically, prophecies possessing multiple meanings extend from the Bible's first Book of Genesis *story of Adam and Eve...as a symbol* with *numerous meanings*,[275-A] to the many centuries of interpretations of its last Book of Revelation.

For the Old Testament prophecies, Jews use the mnemonic Hebrew acronym ***PARDES*** (*orchard*) to spell out four levels of scriptural meaning. The four Hebrew consonants of ***PARDES***, its letters ***P***, ***R***, ***D***, and ***S***, stand for

- '***PESHAT***' *(the literal meaning of the Torah)*
- '***REMEZ***' *(hints and allusions)*
- '***DRASH***' *(the homiletical interpretation)*
- '***SOD***' *(secret)*.[276-J]

More widely, Baha'is teach that prophecies

> *speak a twofold language. One language, the outward language, is devoid of allusions, is unconcealed and unveiled; that it may be a guiding lamp and a beaconing light....The other language is veiled and concealed....Literal meaning, as generally understood by the people, is not what hath been intended. Thus it is recorded: 'Every knowledge hath seventy meanings, of which one only is known'* and *'We speak one word, and by it we intend one and seventy meanings; each one of these meanings we can explain'*.[277-B]

The multiple meanings of symbols in the Apocalypse group two ways. On one hand, several if its symbols depict a single topic, just as different rooms in the Apocalypse Palace serve as, say, a guest room. Thus,

- Many symbols portray its main Messenger in different roles
- Various sets of seven—*Spirits of God, Menorah-Lamps, stars, Angels, horns and eyes,* and *seals*—depict the seven Cycle of Prophecy Messengers and Faiths
- *A huge whore who sits over many waters, a woman mounted on a scarlet beast, a woman drunk, the Mother of the Whores, Confused Great Babylon,* and *the great city* all glint great greed.

On the other hand, a single Apocalypse symbol may also depict multiple entities across different eras, areas, and arenas, just as the library of the Apocalypse Palace can serve multiply for reading, writing, meeting, or flirting! Examples include certain compelling double interpretations in the Parallel Interpretation (Rev. 9.4, 17–8, 16.12, 16, and 20.9) as exceptions to the prime interpretive thrust. Less-compelling multiple interpretations appear in the Comments on other Apocalypse verses.

John's Linguistic Devices

John's five main linguistic devices were introduced in pages 20 and 21. They are his number-codes, floating-terms, verbal-thematic links, hidden-titles, and cover-names. Further examples of these five main devices follow here:

Number-Codes tag Messengers, their Faiths, and their foes:[278-R]

- ***1*** (*one*) tags the main Revelation Angel as its foremost Messenger
- ***7*** tags Messengers as *Spirits, churches, Menorah-Lamps, stars, seals, horns, eyes, thunders, Angels bearing trumpets,* and *Angels pouring pitchers*
- ***10*** tags foes of Messengers as *days, horns,* and *sovereign-crowns*
- ***12*** tags Faiths in the ways described on page 20
- ***24*** (as twice the usual *12* for Faiths) tags *elders* for teachers and *gemstones* for their New Jerusalem teachings
- ***1000*** codes for *many people*
- ***144,000*** contains embedded codes for *many believers progressively perfecting Faiths. Thousand* codes for *many believers*. The biblical square *144* codes for *perfecting*. Its square-root *12* codes for *Faiths*. As the 12th number in the Fibonacci series guiding growth and structure in nature and underpinning art, *144* codes also for *progressively*.[A] Curiously, the telephone directory enquiry number of modern Israel is "144" too.
- The units ***cubit*** and ***furlong*** code for *human standards* and for *hard work*.

More number-codes appear on pages 311–2 in the Translation Section.

Floating-Terms, such as *dressed in sackcloth*, inclusively and concurrently qualify both the prior and ensuing terms, in referring both backwards and forwards. A floating-term can be a word, phrase, or clause. The further examples of floating-terms that follow appear in bold:

- 2.22–23: *I am casting...those who commit adultery with her into great hardship,* ***unless they give up her practices****, I shall also deal death to her children*
- 7.15: *They are at God's Throne,* ***within His Temple****, conducting its worship*

[A] Each number in the Fibonacci series (1, 1, 2, 3, 5, 8, 13, 21, 34, 55, 89, **144**, 233, 377...) is the sum of the prior two numbers. The Fibonacci series governs the scientific structure of items like pinecone whorls, flower petals, seashell spirals, electron orbits, or reproductive trees, and it also underpins artistic truths like the Golden Mean (1·62...), the shape of the pentacle, or the number of notes in musical scales.

- 22.1–2: *He showed me a river of water of life...**between the main-square of the city and the river, here and there**, a Tree of Life*
- 22.2: *A Tree of Life producing 12 fruits **monthly** each yielding its fruit* (with *producing* and *yielding* as separate stages of fruiting).

More floating-terms appear on pages 311–2 in the Translation Section.

Verbal-Thematic links were first discovered tagging certain Old Testament verses. They include trigger-words like *drunken*, *roof*, and *shear* and key-phrases like *good-for-nothing*, *dried-up*, *weak eyes*, *spend the night*, *thirty pieces of silver*, *drew water from the well*, and *washed his feet*. The verses that these links tag can be then joined together to form a *Hidden Book in the Bible*, to uncloak a riveting tale of royal incest and adultery, and dynastic betrayal and assassination. No wonder it was hidden![A]

The Apocalypse has similar verbal-thematic links. Most track the roles played by its main Messenger as he slips in and out of its verses. Thus, the trigger-word *one* tags him as *an elder*, *a Living-Being*, *a Pitcher-Angel*, *a mighty Angel*, and *an Angel standing in the sun*. Likewise, the trigger-words *mighty*, *cloud*, and *rainbow* tag him too. Similarly, the key-phrase *in his hand* tags him holding various types of authority symbol as *stars*, *a short scroll*, *a tiny scroll*, *a sharp scimitar*, and *a big chain*.[279-R]

Other links tag the main Messenger weaving in and out of the Apocalypse verses. For example, he sets out as a divine Human-Being with his *face shining like the sun* (Rev. 1.11), reappears roaring *as a lion* (v. 10.1) who is the prior *Lion from the tribe of Judah, the root of a beloved David* (v. 5.5), who then grows into *the root and the shoot of a beloved David* (v. 22.16) as *the Spirit* (v. 22.17) who has been the *Spirit telling the churches* all along (vv. 2.7, etc.)!

Hidden-Titles result from the ORIGINAL TEXT IN BLOCK-LETTER GREEK having no separate capital letters. This has let simple words act as hidden Messenger titles. One, *WORD* itself, means *Divine Speaker*, already discussed on page 20. Other hidden-titles include:

- *Spirit* as a *Manifestation of God* for each Messenger
- *Witness* as *Delegates of God* for recent Messengers
- ***Trumpet-Blasts*** (*Woe, Ouai*) for the latest three Messenger heralds after Jesus wreaking their Eras of change
- *Glory of God* specifically for the main Messenger of Revelation
- *Dwell* and *dwelling* for all Messengers as the *Presence of God*

[A] Friedman, Richard E. *The Hidden Book in the Bible*

- *Anointed* is now a less-than-hidden-title for the Promised Jewish Messiah, since it has become formalized as the Hebrew title *Messiah* (*Mashiach*) and as the Greek title *Christ* (*Christos*).[280-BR]

Cover-Names are the flip-side of hidden-titles. Traditionally, cover-names appear as capitalized "**P**roper-**N**ames". But they are really literary Trojan-Horses bearing cargoes of hidden meanings. But in Chapter 1, John first presents his readers with a cluster of true Proper-Names—namely *God, Jesus, Christ, John, Asia, Patmos, Ephesus, Smyrna, Pergamos, Thyatira, Sardis, Philadelphia*, and *Laodicea*. This opening cluster of Proper-Names has decoyed translators and readers to expect simply more of the same. So when *HAIDOU* appears towards the end of Chapter 1, for example, it got all too readily read as the Proper-Name *Hades* instead of as its true literal cover-name of *unseen*.

In its context, each Apocalypse cover-name packs far more punch and makes far more sense as its literal meaning that it does as a "Proper-Name". Thus, *HAIDOU* stresses how unseen death is. *NICOLAITOS* conquers people. *SATAN* hates and opposes. *DIABOLOS* lies evilly. *ANTIPAS* stands against all. *BA'LAAM* swallows people. *BALAK* laps blood. *MANNA* aptly asks *What is it? JEZEBEL* (*IZABEL*) trashes God. *DAVID* is a beloved one. *ABSINTHE* is undrinkable. *ABBADON* and *APOLLYON* wreak destruction. *MICHAEL* is like God. *MOUNT ZION* beckons. *BABYLON* sows confusion. *GLORY OF GOD* means Baha'u'llah. *ARMAGEDDON* is a *Mountain of Preaching*. *HALLELUJAH* praises God. *GOG AND MAGOG* represent a future dictator and his forces. Comprehensively too, the *NAMES* of the tribes of Israel project qualities; *ISRAEL* was a man who saw God; *JERUSALEM* augurs folk seeing dual peace; and *EUPHRATES* surges new knowledge.[281-R]

Then too, some cover-names—*BA'LAAM, IZABEL, DAVID, ABBADON*, and *APOLLYON*—lack the honorific *the* normally due before Greek Proper-Names. This omission of *the* hints that these words are not Proper-Names at all. Indeed, many translators do already routinely render *ABBADON, APOLLYON*, and *ABSINTHE* as their literal meanings of *destruction, destroyer*, and *undrinkable*.

After AD 600, Greek developed cursive letters. Its new letters freed up Greek UNCIAL BLOCK-LETTERS—its only letters until then—to serve now as capital letters. This worsened matters for cover-names. The newly released capital letters acted as literary nuts screwed down upon the bolts on the rest of the new cover-names' cursive-letters. So, right into modern times, Greek's new cursive and capital letters helped to retain, maintain, and sustain John's cover-names as **P**roper-**N**ames rather than as their truer literal meanings.

Baha'i-Based Summaries of the Parallel Interpretation's Apocalypse Chapters

These Baha'i-based summaries now follow as an hor d'œvre for us to savor before relishing the main meal of the Parallel Interpretation.

Apocalypse Chapter 1:

The main master-of-ceremonies Angel of the Apocalypse is Baha'u'llah, God's Messenger of the new Cycle. The *seven Spirits* are His prior Messengers of the prior Cycle of Prophecy—Abraham, Moses, Zoroaster, Krishna, Buddha, Jesus, and Muhammad.

Apocalypse Chapters 2–3:

The main Messenger Baha'u'llah addresses the *Seven-Churches* as the extant monotheistic Faiths of Sabaeanism, Judaism, Zoroastrianism, Hinduism, Buddhism, Christianity, and Islam.

Apocalypse Chapter 4:

A Throne is the new Baha'i Revelation of Baha'u'llah as its Founder. A Door is its Bab. Four Living-Beings are its Primary-Figures. And 24 elders are its founders.

Apocalypse Chapter 5:

The sealed scroll is the Apocalypse itself. The Ram is the Bab as Co-Founder of the Baha'i Faith who will interpret the scroll.

Apocalypse Chapter 6:

The Bab breaks the seals of the scroll to reveal messages from and to the prior Cycle of Prophecy Faiths of Sabaean, Jewish, Zoroastrian, Hindu, Buddhist, Christian, and Muslim Faiths.

Apocalypse Chapter 7:

The four Angels are Abraham, Moses, Jesus, and Muhammad—four Messengers in the Abrahamic line who welcome a new Angel from the East as the Bab.

Apocalypse Chapter 8:

Seven Trumpet-Angels sound as Abraham, Moses, Zoroaster, Jesus, Muhammad, the Bab, and Baha'u'llah as seven Messengers of the Middle East. First, Abraham, Moses, Zoroaster, and Jesus lament the history of Christianity.

Apocalypse Chapter 9:

The fifth Trumpet-Angel, first Trumpet-Blast Messenger Muhammad, appears as the first Warner after Jesus, to proclaim Islam and lament its militaristic history. The sixth Trumpet-Angel, the Trumpet-Blast Messenger Bab, appears as the second Warner after Jesus, to proclaim Islam and lament its militaristic history further.

Apocalypse Chapter 10:

The mighty seventh Trumpet-Angel, third Trumpet-Blast Messenger Baha'u'llah, appears to proclaim and expound the hidden intent of God.

Apocalypse Chapter 11:

Two Witnesses identify first as Muhammad and Ali, then as their 1844 return as the Bab and Quddus. The 1,260–day, 42–month, and 3½–day time-prophecies all predict the same 1260–year Muslim Era. The seventh Trumpet-Angel, third Trumpet-Blast Messenger Baha'u'llah. appears as the third Warner after Jesus to proclaim his new Baha'i Era. The Temple is his Baha'i Faith.

Apocalypse Chapters 12–15:

Beasts are the Umayyad Caliphate and Ottoman Sultanate as Islam's worst Empires, whose Muslim Militarism crippled Muhammad and Ali's original true loving Islam.

Apocalypse Chapter 16:

Seven Pitcher-Angels are Abraham, Moses, Zoroaster, Jesus, Muhammad, the Bab, and Baha'u'llah as seven Middle East Messengers exerting spiritual influence from the mid-1800s into the 1900s in Persia, upon the Middle East, and across the globe.

Apocalypse Chapter 17:

The scarlet beast's horns are today's modern rogue regimes and terrorist organizations of Muslim Militarism fighting modern Babylon's whore of confused Malignant Materialism.

Apocalypse Chapter 18:

Babylon falling is modern confused Malignant Materialism collapsing of into a Greatest Depression.

Apocalypse Chapter 19:

The wedding banquet celebrates spiritual and economic wealth. Spiritually its wealth is the promised "bride" Baha'u'llah "marrying" or perfecting the Bab as his partner "groom". Economically, its wealth is the worthy prosperity that spiritual economics brings to the globe.

Apocalypse Chapter 20:

The Millennium is the Jewish Seventh Millennium. Gog and Magog are a global dictatorship that ends the Millennium.

Apocalypse Chapter 21:

The bride is the city of New Jerusalem as the divine global civilization of the Millennium.

Apocalypse Chapter 22:

The Tree of Life displays the wisdom of the *changeless Religion of God, eternal in the past and eternal in the future.*[282-B]

Apocalypse Chapter 1
A Messenger of a New Faith

An Unveiling by John

1.1An unveiling of Jesus Christ
that God gave him
to show to his servants
what had to happen fast,
which he made known by
transmitting through His
Angel to His servant John,
2who witnessed this Word of
God and this testimony of Jesus
Christ as all that he saw.

3Blessed is the one reading out
and those hearing the Words
of this prophecy and taking
to heart the visions recorded
in it, for the time is near.

4From John to the Seven-
Churches of Asia:

Blessings to you and Peace from

- ***The-Is,***
- ***The-Was,***
- ***The-Is-Coming,***

*from the seven Spirits who
are before His Throne, 5as
well and from Jesus
Christ, the trustworthy
Witness, the firstborn son
of the dead, and the ruling
power of the rulers of the
world.*

*To him who loves us, who
washed and freed us from
our sins with his blood. 6He
has made us a kingdom,
Priests of his God and
Father. To him be the glory
and the power into the Eras.
Amen!*

A Revelation by John

A revelation of Jesus Returned that God has given him to reveal to his servants events that shall flash fast, which he is transmitting by publishing through His Messenger to me His servant John, who has witnessed this Speaker of God and his testimony as Jesus Returned as all that I have seen.

Blessed am I writing and you reading about the Divine Speakers in my interpretation and taking seriously the events described in it, for its time has come.

From John to the seven Faiths from Asia:

Blessings to you and Shalom from

- ***The-God-of-Later-Eras,***
- ***The-God-of-Earlier-Eras,***
- ***The-God-of-a-New-Era,***

from the seven Manifestations who have proclaimed His Revelation, and from Jesus Returned, His true Delegate, the chosen one of a spiritually dead nation, and the power of the leaders of the planet.

To him who loves us, who has cleaned and freed us from our sins through his death. He is turning us into a spiritual order, teachers for his God and spiritual Father. To him be the glory and the power for a whole spiritual Cycle. Indeed so!

7*Look! He comes on the
clouds. Every eye shall see
him, even those who pierced
him. All the tribes of the
world shall mourn him. Yes!
Amen!*

Look! He has returned in his glory amid human limitations. Everybody can identify him, even the Persians who pierced him with bullets. All families on the planet shall come to mourn him. Yes! Indeed so!

The Lord God says,

- 8 ***'I Myself am the A and the Z,***
- ***The-Is,***
- ***The-Was,***
- ***The-Is-Coming,***
- ***The Almighty One'.***

The Lord God says,

- ***'I Myself am the Founder and the Fulfiller of Faiths,***
- ***The-God-of- Later-Eras,***
- ***The-God-of-Earlier-Eras,***
- ***The-God-of-a-New-Era,***
- ***The Almighty God'.***

9I myself John, your brother
and partner in the distress yet
reign and endurance in Jesus,
came to be on the island called
Patmos, due to this Word of
God and this testimony of Jesus
Christ, 10I was soaring in spirit
on the Lord's Day.

I your author John, your fellow and partner in the distress yet rule and tenacity of Jesus, have returned to the island of Patmos, due to this Speaker for God and his testimony of Jesus Returned, I am soaring in spirit in God's new Era (as I was in Jesus's Era).

Then behind me I heard a
loud voice like a trumpet
11sounding:
*What you are seeing write
down in a short scroll and
send to the Seven-Churches:*

- *To Ephesus,*
- *To Smyrna,*
- *To Pergamos,*
- *To Thyatira,*
- *To Sardis,*
- *To Philadelphia,*
- *To Laodicea.*

Then echoing from my cave wall I hear a Proclaimer herald commanding:
What you are hearing record in a short Revelation tale and publish for the seven Faiths:

- *For Sabaeanism,*
- *For Judaism,*
- *For Zoroastrianism,*
- *For Hinduism,*
- *For Buddhism,*
- *For Christianity,*
- *For Islam.*

12At this, I turned to look for
the voice that was speaking
with me. Having turned, I saw
seven gold Menorah-Lamps;
13amid these Menorah-Lamps an
apparition of a Human-Being
clad in a long robe; looped
about the breasts with a gold

At this, I turn to see the herald who is speaking with me. Having turned, I see an assembly of seven glorious Revelators; amid this assembly of Revelators a divine Human-Being emanating complete virtue; a glorious loving guide; his head, meaning his hair,

GIRDLE; 14 HIS HEAD, MEANING HIS HAIR, LIKE WOOL AS WHITE AS SNOW; HIS EYES LIKE A FLAME OF FIRE; 15 HIS FEET LIKE WHITE-HOT MOLTEN BRONZE REFINED IN A FURNACE; HIS VOICE RUSHING LIKE MANY WATERS; 16 HOLDING IN HIS RIGHT-HAND SEVEN STARS; PROJECTING FROM HIS MOUTH A SHARP TWO-EDGED SWORD; AND HIS FACE SHINING LIKE THE SUN IN ITS FULL STRENGTH.

white from suffering, shining like snow; his spirit blazing divine love; his justice glowing reward and gleaming punishment; his words broadcasting bountiful teachings; his power uniting seven spiritual Teachers; uttering with his speech true wise perceptive words; and his presence emanating the radiance of God in its full power.

17 WHEN I SAW HIM, I FELL AT HIS FEET AS IF DEAD. BUT HE PUT HIS RIGHT-HAND UPON ME, SAYING:

DO NOT FEEL AFRAID. I MYSELF AM THE FIRST AND THE LAST, 18 THE LIVING-BEING LIVING ON, I HAVE ALSO GONE THROUGH DEATH. SEE, I AM A LIVING-BEING LIVING ON INTO THE ERAS OF THE ERAS. MOREOVER, I POSSESS THE KEYS OF DEATH AND THE UNSEEN.

As I see him, I submit to him stunned. But he restores me with his power, reassuring:

Do not be afraid. I as the Messenger am the First-to-Last Manifestation of God, a Primary-Figure living on, I have also experienced death. See, I am His Primary-Figure living on from spiritual Cycle to spiritual Cycle. Moreover, I bear remedies for atheism and agnosticism.

19 *ACCORDINGLY, RECORD:*

- *THE VISIONS THAT YOU HAVE BEEN SEEING,*
- *THE VISIONS THAT ARE OCCURRING, AND*
- *THE VISIONS THAT ARE DUE TO OCCUR AFTER THESE VISIONS.*

Accordingly, publish:

- *The events that you have been watching,*
- *The events that are happening, and*
- *The events that are due to happen after these events.*

20 *AS FOR THE MYSTERY OF THE SEVEN STARS THAT YOU HAVE SEEN IN MY RIGHT-HAND, AND THE SEVEN GOLD MENORAH-LAMPS:*

THE SEVEN STARS ARE ANGELS OF THE SEVEN-CHURCHES
THE SEVEN MENORAH-LAMPS ARE SEVEN CHURCHES.

As for the hidden intent of the seven spiritual Teachers that you see my power unite, and the assembly of seven glorious Revelators:

The seven spiritual Teachers represent Messengers of the seven Faiths
The assembly of seven Revelators represents their four earlier and three later Faiths.

Comments, listed by verse number, follow each Apocalypse chapter.

1.1, Title: *'An Unveiling' by John* is a title-author Inscription (and Subscription) that typically opens and closes Greek scrolls. In addition, the verbless clause *'An Unveiling of Jesus Christ that God gave him to show his servants what had to happen fast' was intended by the author to function as a title.*[A]

1.1: *Kai* renders legitimately as *which* in *which he made known*, so as to qualify *what had to happen fast* as its subject-clause.

1.1 etc.: ***Christos*** means literally *Anointed* but renders as its Greek equivalent *Christ* (vv. 1.1, 5 & 9) or Hebrew equivalent *Messiah* (vv. 11.15, 12.10, 20.4 & 20.6).

1.1, also 10.1, 5, 8–10, 11.15, 17.7, 18.1, 18.21, 19.17, 20.1, 22.6, 22.8 & 22.16: ***His/the Angel***, the main Messenger of the Apocalypse, takes the definite article *the* at v. 1.1's very first mention of him as ***the*** *Angel of His*. His instant familiarity makes him immediately known or special.

1.2, see also 22.20: ***Witnessed*** finds favor here over its other valid translation of ***witnessed to***.

1.2: ***Word*** acts as a hidden-title for the main Messenger as the *Word of God…the first bestowal of the Almighty…the first instructor in the University of existence…the Primal Emanation of God…illumining the realm of thought and morals*.[B]

1.3 & 22.10: Always *the time is near* for faithful believers who await the advent of the Messenger of God promised by their Faith.

1.3: *Prophecy* interprets as specifically Baha'i-based interpretation of the Book of Revelation.

1.4: *Asia* in AD 95 was the Roman province of Asia Minor (now Turkey), the home of the seven original AD 95 churches. *Asia* today Asia Major, the home of the seven Faiths that the AD 95 churches portray.

1.4, 3.1, 4.5, 5.6 & 22.6: ***Spirit*** is a hidden-title for a *Manifestation of God*.

1.4, 1.8, 4.8, 11.17 & 16.5: ***THE-IS, THE-WAS, THE-IS-COMING*** reads for v. 1.1's *God*, rather than for its *Jesus Christ* or *Angel*), with *THE-IS/I AM* (Hebrew *YHWH/EHIYEH*) as God's ineffable name.[C] The full formula is no simple past-present-future formula: its tenses run out of order chronologically; *THE-IS-COMING* replaces its expected *THE-SHALL-BE*; and later (vv. 11.17 & 16.5) *THE-IS-COMING* gets dropped from the formula.

1.4, etc.: ***The Seven-Churches*** take the definite article *the* at v. 1.4's very first mention of them. Their instant familiarity makes them immediately known or special. Indeed, out of the scores of Christian churches already established in Turkey by AD 95, these seven churches were indeed special. On the map, from their Ephesus-tip to

[A] Aune *52A*.4
[B] Baha'u'llah *Scriptures* 50.130; 'Abdu'l-Baha *PUP* 94
[C] Exod. 3.14, also John 8.58

their Laodicea-tail, they trace a geographic 7-shape that points toward the Holy Land, as if to address its Jews. Consequently, *the seven churches* render in compound form as *the Seven-Churches*.

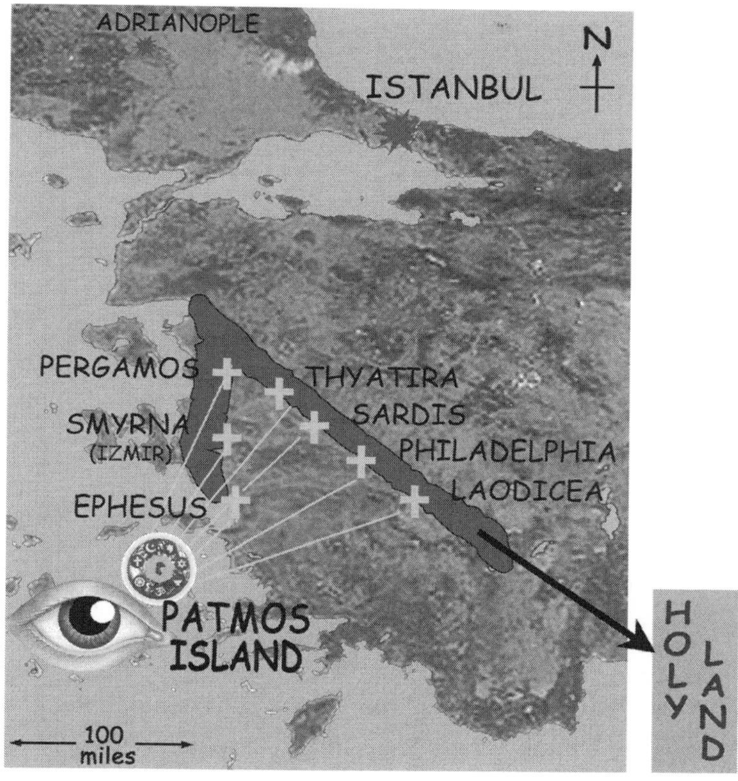

Map showing the Seven-Churches of Asia and Patmos

1.5: ***Witness*** is a hidden-title for *divine Delegate.*[A]
1.5: This *firstborn son of the dead...a Jew from among the Jews,* who *revivified the people till they were transferred from one state of existence into a higher state of existence* was Jesus in AD 95 and his return as the Bab in 1844.[B]
1.6, 5.10 & 20.6: ***Priests***, in this Temple context, means the *Cohen* Temple-Priests descended from the first High Priest Aaron, brother of Moses. Cohens were not regular rabbis but special clergy preordained to serve specifically in the Temple.

[A] As Muhammad in vv. 11.3, 17.6, the Bab in vv. 1.5, 2.13, 17.6, and Baha'u'llah in 3.14, 17.6
[B] 'Abdu'l-Baha *DP* 44

1.7, 10.1, 11.12 & 14.14–16: ***Clouds***

signify, in one sense, the annulment of laws, the abrogation of former Dispensations, the repeal of rituals and customs current amongst men, the exalting of the illiterate faithful above the learned opposers of the Faith. In another sense, they mean the appearance of that immortal Beauty in the image of mortal man, with such human limitations as eating and drinking, poverty and riches, glory and abasement, sleeping and waking, and such other things as cast doubt in the minds of men, and cause them to turn away. All such veils are symbolically referred to as 'clouds' that *cause the heavens of the knowledge and understanding of all that dwell on earth to be cloven asunder....This is what is meant by coming in the clouds....Tear asunder the veils and curtains of these dogmas, remove these accumulated, suffocating increments, dispel these dark impenetrable clouds, that the sun of reality may shine from the horizon of eternity....The promised One...riding upon the clouds...will be made manifest from the heaven of the will of God....They shall see the Son of Man* [divine Human-Being] *coming in the clouds of heaven with power and great glory.*[A]

The archetypical cloud both hid and signified the glory of God as it hovered over the Ark in the Sinai desert.[B]

1.7: A Persian firing squad *riddled the breast of the Bab with bullets*[C] as Roman nails had pierced his hands at his first coming as Jesus.

1.8, 17, 2.8, 21.6 & 22.13: ***The A and the Z* (*the Alpha and the Omega*), *the Beginning and the Ending*, *the First and the Last*** are titles that honor Messengers of God, each as

the 'Beginning' and the 'End,' the 'First' and the 'Last' just as *Christ has said: 'I am Alpha and Omega, the first and the last'—that is to say, there has never been and never shall be any change and alteration in Me....*Thus, if *one of these Manifestations of Holiness proclaim saying: 'I am the return of all the Prophets,'* or if *He Who is the...End...say: 'Verily, I am the Point of the Beginning', He would indeed be speaking the truth.* Likewise, to Baha'u'llah, *the Author of the Apocalypse...alluded as...'Alpha and Omega', 'the Beginning and the End,' 'the First and the Last'...the Manifest and the Hidden.*[D]

[A] ***Signify, in one sense***, Baha'u'llah *KI* 71–2. ***Cause the heavens***, Baha'u'llah *KI* 72. ***This is what is meant***, Baha'u'llah *KI* 25, 66–7; 'Abdu'l-Baha *TAB* 1.145, *SAQ* 26.110; Shoghi Effendi *PDC* 52. ***Tear asunder the veils***, 'Abdu'l-Baha *DP* 4.162; Shoghi Effendi *GPB* 95–6. ***The promised One***, Baha'u'llah *KI* 25, 66–7; 'Abdu'l-Baha *TAB* 1.145, *SAQ* 26.110; Shoghi Effendi *PDC* 52. ***See the Son of man***, Baha'u'llah *KI* 61; 'Abdu'l-Baha *TAB* 1.145.

[B] Exod. 33.9

[C] Shoghi Effendi *PDC* 90

[D] ***The 'Beginning' and the 'End'***, Baha'u'llah *Gems* 45.34, *KI* 179, 161, 163. ***Christ has said***, 'Abdu'l-Baha *SAQ* 58.219. ***One of these Manifestations***, Baha'u'llah *KI*

Hinduism too awaits the advent of a *Divine Being…who is the beginning and the end.* Likewise, Buddhism teaches that everything that has a beginning has also an end.[A]

1.10: ***Day*** interprets as a full spiritual *Era*, per the *a-day-for-a-thousand-years* formula of Judaism, Christianity, and Islam.[B]

1.10, also 12.10 & 16.15: ***A loud voice*** signifies Baha'u'llah as *the Proclaimer of all this—the 'Great Voice' as He is called.*[C]

1.12–13: Baha'u'llah is now *the lamp burning before the Throne* amid the seven Menorah-Lamps symbolizing the seven Messenger Revelators who established Faiths in the Cycle of Prophecy.[D]

The Menorah stands for seven Faiths

153–4, *Gems* 40.30–1. ***The Author of the Apocalypse***, Shoghi Effendi *GPB* 95–6; 'Abdu'l-Baha *SWA* 3.13; Baha'u'llah *Gems* 46.34, *Scriptures Tablet to the Jews* 47.117 to Eliahu Cohen in (1) *Aqdas* 16.25 (2) *Taaje Wahhaj* 28 compiled by Zabihullah Azizi (3) *Amr va'l-Haqq* 2.242–3 (4) *Bishaarat* compiled by Hosaam Noqabaa'ee

[A] ***That Divine Being***, *Vishnu Purana* 4.24. http://www.unification.net/ws/theme161.htm#14. **Everything that has a beginning**, Kelen, Betty, *Guatama Buddha* 102

[B] Ps. 90.4, 2Peter 3.8; *Quran* 22.47, 32.5

[C] 'Abdu'l-Baha cited by Brittingham, *Commentary 16.15*

[D] Baha'u'llah *GWB* 136.295

1.13 & 14.14, ***Human-Being*** renders the original literal term *Son of Man* in Greek and Hebrew idiomatically. This particular *Human-Being/Son of Man* lacks any *the*, which lets him interpret as a **new** divine Human-Being, namely Baha'u'llah, to whom

> *Jesus Christ had referred as...the 'Son of Man' Who 'shall come in the glory of His Father'...upon the clouds of heaven with power and great glory* and *the sound of the great trumpet.... Fatherhood and sonship are allegorical and symbolical....Jesus was truthful when he said, 'The Father is in me'.* Baha'u'llah *unequivocally admitted and repeatedly announced...the identification of His advent with the coming of the Father Himself,* saying *the Father is come....*the *everlasting Father... foretold by Isaiah...*the *establisher of the Kingdom of the Father foretold by the Son,* to whom *all previous Dispensations led up.* Yet *do the sons recognize the Father...or do they deny Him, even as the people aforetime denied Him (Jesus)?*[A]

1.14: Recalling his incarceration in Teheran's *Black Pit* dungeon, Baha'u'llah reported that its *cruelties...bowed Me down, and turned My hair white.*[B] Later, after being pressed by family and followers (and not from vanity), he dyed his hair to a black shine to dye.

1.14, 2.18 & 19.12: ***Eyes like a flame of fire***

> *alludeth but to the keenness of sight and acuteness of vision of the Promised One, Who with His eyes burneth away every veil and covering, maketh known the eternal mysteries in the contingent world, and distinguisheth the faces that are obscured with the dust of hell from those that shine with the light of paradise. Were His eyes not made of the blazing fire of God...how could He see all things?*[C]

The eyes of Baha'u'llah shone famously bright. Eyewitnesses reported them burning with divine intensity and reading into their very souls. Some found it too hard to return his gaze.

1.15, 2.18 & 10.1: ***Feet like bronze*** signify

> *justice and equity* as *twin guardians that watch over men.... Justice hath a mighty force at its command. It is none other than reward and punishment for the deeds of men. By the power of this force...the wicked...restrain their natures for fear*

[A] ***Jesus Christ had***, Shoghi Effendi *GPB* 95. ***Upon the clouds***, Baha'u'llah *WOB* 360, *KI* 61–2. ***Fatherhood and***, 'Abdu'l-Baha *DP* 5.152. ***Unequivocally admitted***, Baha'u'llah *Tablets* 2.11, *ESW* 57, *PB* 27, 84; Shoghi Effendi *Summons of the Lord of Hosts*, *PDC* 109.52. ***Everlasting Father***, Shoghi Effendi *PDC* 37.20. ***Foretold by Isaiah***, Baha'u'llah *Summons of the Lord of Hosts* 1.122.63. ***Establisher of***, Shoghi Effendi *PDC* 302.123. ***All previous Dispensations***, Shoghi Effendi *Letter* 1952/08/06, *PDC* 52. ***Do the sons recognize***, Baha'u'llah *PB* 97, *Tablets* 2.14–5; Shoghi Effendi *PDC* 256.103

[B] Baha'u'llah *Ministry of Custodians* 148; Shoghi Effendi *PDC* 9, 90

[C] Baha'u'llah *Gems* 75.54, *KI* 79

of punishment....The structure of world stability and order hath been reared upon, and will continue to be sustained by, the twin pillars of reward and punishment....As to the words 'brass-like were His feet'...is meant His [Baha'u'llah's] *constancy....He shall so persevere in the Cause of God, and evince such firmness in the path of His might...not waver in the proclamation of His Cause, nor flee from His command in the promulgation of His Laws....He will stand as firm as the highest mountains and the loftiest peaks....No obstacle will hinder Him.*[A]

1.15, 14.2 & 19.6: ***Voice rushing like many waters*** echoes Baha'u'llah's *faculty of speech like a rushing torrent* that left religious scholars *astounded...filled with amazement and astonishment at the seething and the roaring of the Ocean of his utterance.*[B]

1.16, 2.12, 16, 19.15 & 21: This ***two-edged sword*** is

the sword of spiritual truth and of the Word and *of wisdom and of utterance....Unsheathe the sword of your tongue from the scabbard of utterance* and *conquer the citadel of men's hearts.... The sword of metal has been working over six thousand years and has become dull. We must look...for another sword to take its place. The greatest sword is the tongue....The sword of steel sheds blood; the sword of speech bestows life. One takes away life; the other grants it. This one is temporal in action and effect; the other is eternal. This one is of metal; that one is the Love of God...The real sword is the tongue...We must take it out and use it more and more* just as *Christ conquered the East and the West by the sword of His utterance.* Hinduism too expects its Lord Kalki to come with *sword in hand...blazing like fire, bringing harmony back to the planet.*[C]

1.16 & 10.1: ***Face shining like the sun*** portrays Baha'u'llah as **THE GLORY OF GOD** who emanates the radiance of God and

*resembleth the physical sun, His verses are like its rays....An atmosphere of majesty haloed Him as the sun at midday....*and he *shone forth from the horizon of Persia* as a *Sun of Wisdom, declaring 'I am the sun of perception and the ocean of science...I am that light which illumines the path of insight'...shining into the eyes of those who sleep, awaking them to behold the glory of*

[A] ***Justice and equity***, Shoghi Effendi *GPB* 95; Baha'u'llah *ESW* 13. ***Justice hath a mighty force***, Baha'u'llah *Tablets* 11.164. ***As to the words "brass-like...***, Baha'u'llah *Gems* 76.54

[B] 'Abdu'l-Baha *Traveler's Narrative* 36

[C] ***The sword of spiritual truth***, 'Abdu'l-Baha *Traveler's Narrative* 64; Baha'u'llah *GWB* 136.296, 139.303. ***Unsheathe the sword***, Baha'u'llah *ESW* 25, 55; Shoghi Effendi *Light* 1936.570, *Messages to the Baha'i World* 49. ***The sword of metal***, 'Abdu'l-Baha SW (1919/12/31) 3.16.9. ***Christ conquered the***, 'Abdu'l-Baha *PUP* 199. ***Sword in hand***, *Srimad-Bhagavatam* 12.2.19–20. ***Blazing like fire***, *Todala Tantra* 2.10

a new dawn....In the spiritual realm of intelligence and idealism there must be a center of illumination, and that center is the everlasting, ever-shining Sun, the Word of God...illumining the realm of thought and morals....This Sun of Reality...is the prophet or Manifestation of God who *confers illumination upon the human world.*[A]

1.17–18: As John falls *as if dead*, the Angel empathizes that he has *gone through death* too.

1.18, 6.8, 20.13 & 14: ***HAIDOU*** (*HADES*) is a Greek cover-name that means literally *un-seen* (*A-IDĒS*), to echo our ignorance about death. Similarly, its Hebrew versions *SHEOL* and *SHE'OL* mean *asking*[B] and *a hollow underground cavity suitable for burial.*

1.18, 3.7, 9.1 & 20.1: ***Keys*** symbolize Baha'u'llah's teachings as *keys to all the doors...the keys of the heaven and the earth*, which let humankind *unlock the cities with the keys of* [*His*] *name* and *the gates of the hearts of men with the keys of remembrance of Him Who is the Remembrance of God.*[C]

1.20: In addition, the seven Menorah-Lamps burn symbolically for the letters that spell the given name of Baha'u'llah *Husayn Ali*, for those that spell the given name of the Bab *Ali Muhammad*; for the seven original names shared by the 12 Apostles of Christ; and for those shared by the traditional 12 Imams of Islam.[283]

1.20, also 1.4, 11 & 20: Suddenly, v. 1.20's **second** mention of *Seven-Churches* lacks *the*, which lets them interpret as **new** religious communities, namely Faiths.

[A] ***Resembleth the physical sun***, *Selections from the Writings of the Bab* 92. ***An atmosphere of majesty***, Abdu'l-Baha *BWF* 222. ***Sun of Wisdom***, Baha'u'llah *Scriptures* 50.131–2, *KI* 208–9. ***Shining into***, 'Abdu'l-Baha *Paris Talks* 32. ***In the spiritual realm***, 'Abdu'l-Baha *BWF* 254–5, *PUP* 94, *Foundations of World Unity* 11.

[B] *Midrash Avot* 5.9 about Job 17.13–6

[C] ***Keys to all the doors***, 'Abdu'l-Baha *TAB* 3.692. ***The keys to the heaven and the earth***, Quran 39.63, 42.12. ***Unlock the cities with***, Baha'u'llah *GWB* 105.212. ***The gates of the hearts of men***, Baha'u'llah *GWB* 136.296

Apocalypse Chapter 2
His Messages for Four Earlier Faiths

His Message to Sabaeanism

2.1 *Write to the Angel of the Church in Ephesus:*

Publish for Abraham to his Sabaean Faith from Iraq:

'These things says he who firmly holds the seven stars in his right-hand, who walks amid the seven gold Menorah-Lamps.

'This message comes from your Almighty's Friend who unites the seven spiritual Teachers with his power, who advances its assembly of seven glorious Revelators.

2 *I have seen your very deeds and your tireless labor and endurance, and that you cannot bear bad people. You have tested people who call themselves spiritual emissaries but are not, and you have exposed them as liars.*

I know of your own good deeds and of your tireless labor and tenacity, and that you could not stand bad people. You tested people who said they were spiritual envoys but were not, and you proved them to be liars.

3 *You had endurance. You bore up because of my name and did not tire.*

You had tenacity. You stood up for me in Abraham and did not tire.

4 *On the other hand, I hold
against you that you lost
your first love.* 5 *Accordingly,
recall from where you fell,
repent, and perform those
original deeds.*

On the other hand, I hold against you that you lost your original love. Accordingly, you should have recalled what you had let lapse, reformed, and revived your original good deeds.

But if not, I am coming to you and shall shake your Menorah-Lamp from its place, if you do not repent.

But since you have not, I have returned to you as Moses, Jesus, and Muhammad and have been demoting your Sabaeanism from its status as a Faith, since you have not reformed.

6 *On the other hand, you do have this, that you detest the acts of those who win people over, which I too also detest.*

On the other hand, you do have this, that you detest the ways of heretics who deceive true Sabaeans, whose ways I too also detest.

7 *Let you who have ears hear what this Spirit is telling the Churches.*

Let alert Sabaeans hear what your Almighty's Manifestation is telling His Faiths.

As for the one who prevails, I shall feed him or her from the Tree of Life that grows in the orchard of God.'	*As for you Sabaeans who prevailed, I have been feeding you with the wisdom of Judaism, Christianity, and Islam that have fruited in the Eden tradition of God.'*

Comments:

2.1–3.22: Designating Faiths as *earlier* or *later* comports with their *Scriptures of both the former and latter generations.*[A]

2.1–3.22: The Angel praises and criticizes all churches and Faiths through each specific one, just as the dying Moses praised and criticized all of Israel's tribes through each specific one.[B] After all, no church or Faith or tribe can monopolize vice or virtue!

2.1–7: ***Sabaeanism*** began as the Faith of the Sabaean Empire straddling the Red Sea from Arabia to Ethiopia. The name derives from its capital *Sheba* (possibly its later ritual of baptism).[C] Both Old Testament and Quran mention Sabaeans.[D] But it was in Chaldea that *Sabeanism* [*sic*] *became widespread and flourished* as a Faith.[E] Its prime proponent was Abraham as a *divinely-sent Messenger*[F] and *follower of that Faith.*[G] The People of Israel who practiced the Faith of Abraham before the Judaism of Moses were—in effect—Sabaeans. The Sabaean Faith was *originally monotheistic* but *became gradually corrupted.*[H] Under early Islam, many vague monotheists converted to Sabaeanism in order to gain protected status as People of the Book.[I] But today, a confusing mix of Sabaean groups exists, including vague groups of primal monotheists scattered across Africa.[J] But today the main group is of Iraq and Iran (also called *Nasoreans, Harranians*, or *'Baptists'*), whose *distinct Abrahamic Faith*[K] is *an ancient religion* that came to include *John the Baptist* yet *failed to*

[A] Baha'u'llah *Aqdas* 138.69
[B] Deut. 33
[C] Chris Buck, personal communication 99/11/16
[D] Job 1.15; Isaiah 45.14; Quran 2.62, 5.69, 22.17
[E] Shoghi Effendi *Light* 1694.502–3, *Compilation of Compilations* 56.20
[F] Baha'u'llah cited by the Universal House of Justice (1996/08/06) in *Sabeans, UFOs, Alien Abduction and Genetic Engineering.* http://bahai-library.com/uhj_sabeans_mary_ufos#s1.1; Shoghi Effendi *Light* 1694.502
[G] Shoghi Effendi, *Compilation of Compilations* 4.15
[H] Shoghi Effendi, *Compilation of Compilations* 4.15
[I] Chris Buck, personal communication 99/11/16
[J] Chris Buck, personal communication 99/11/16
[K] Sinasi Gunduz, *The Knowledge of Life: The Origins and Early History of the Mandaeans and Their Relations to the Sabians of the Qu'ran and to the Harranians* in Journal of Semitic Studies, Supplement 129–31 (1993), Oxford University Press

recognize Jesus as the Manifestation of God.[A] Their central Scripture is the *Great Treasure* (*Ghenza Rama*). Having recently suffered persecution by Muslims and destruction of their *Shat-el-Arab* marshland homeland by Saddam Hussein, Mandeans have migrated worldwide. They have to be born into and marry within the Faith, so unsurprisingly, their number has fallen to some 100,000, in keeping with v. 2.5's prophecy.

2.1: ***The Almighty*** (*El Shaddai*) was the title by which God introduced Himself to Abraham. Abraham's own title was *Friend of God*, echoed by his city of Hebron whose Hebrew name *Chevron* means *Place of the Friend* and Arabic name *Chalil* means *Friend.*[B]

2.1–7: Baha'u'llah was doubly descended from Abraham separately through his two wives Sarah and Keturah.

2.6 & 15: ***NICOLAITOS*** is a Greek cover-name that means literally *conquer-people* (*NICO-LAITOS*) and interprets for Sabaean heretics here and Zoroastrian heretics later (v. 2.15).

2.7, 11, 17, 29, 3.6, 13, 22, 14.13, 19.10 & 22.17: Baha'u'llah is *designated as the Spirit of Truth...in the Gospel.*[C]

2.7: *As soon as Moses appears at the end of times, he will plant the children of Israel in the holy Garden of Eden.*[D]

His Message to Judaism

2.8 *NOW WRITE TO THE ANGEL OF THE CHURCH IN SMYRNA:*	*Now publish for Moses to his Jewish Faith from Israel:*
'THESE THINGS SAYS THE FIRST AND THE LAST, WHO HAS GONE THROUGH DEATH, YET LIVES ON.	*'This message comes from your Adonai's First-to-Last Manifestation, who went through death as Moses, yet lives on as His Messiah Ben David.*
9 *I HAVE SEEN YOUR DISTRESS AND POVERTY (YET YOU ARE WEALTHY), ALSO THE BLASPHEMY OF THOSE WHO CALL THEMSELVES JEWS YET ARE NOT. INSTEAD, THEY ARE AN ASSEMBLY OF OPPOSITION.*	*I know of your distress and poverty (yet you are rich in spirit) also of the blasphemy of Jews who say they are Jews yet are not. Instead, they are an atheist "minyan" who oppose Judaism.*
10 *DO NOT FEAR WHAT YOU ARE TO SUFFER. LOOK, THE LYING EVIL ONE WILL CAST SOME OF YOU INTO PRISON, SO THAT YOU*	*You have endured the persecutions that you have had to suffer. Look, lying evil Hitler will gas you in concentration*

[A] Baha'u'llah in above footnote E

[B] ***The Almighty (El Shaddai)***, Gen 17.1. ***Friend of God***, Isaiah 41.8; 2Chron. 20.7; James 2.23; Quran 4.125

[C] Shoghi Effendi *WOB* 104

[D] *Zohar* 1.21.243

MAY BE TESTED, YOU SHALL ALSO BE TROUBLED FOR TEN DAYS. BE FAITHFUL INTO DEATH AND I SHALL GIVE TO YOU THE PRIZE OF LIFE.	*camps, so that you shall be sorely tested, you shall also suffer from 1935 to 1945. Remain faithful through this genocide and in 1948 I shall give you Israel as your prize of life.*
11 *LET YOU WHO HAVE EARS HEAR WHAT THIS SPIRIT IS TELLING THE CHURCHES.*	*Let alert Jews hear what your Adonai's Manifestation is telling His Faiths.*
THE ONE WHO PREVAILS SHALL NEVER BE HURT BY THE SECOND-DEATH.'	*You Jews who prevail shall never be hurt by spiritual death.'*

Comments:

2.8: *YHWH (JEHOVAH)*, God's unutterable name, is how He introduced Himself to Moses, saying: *I appeared to Abraham, Isaac, and Jacob as 'The Almighty' but I did not tell them My name 'YHWH' (Jehovah)*. In prayer, *YHWH* (*Yahweh/Jehovah*) may not be voiced, but only enunciated as *The Name* or as *Lord*.[A]
2.8: Baha'u'llah is the *return of Moses at the End of Days*.[B]
2.8–11: Baha'u'llah's *Tablet to the Jews* draws on Jewish concepts in urging:

> *The promised God says: 'O Concourse of Jews! Ye were of Me, appeared from Me and returned to Me. How is it that ye do not recognize Me now when I have appeared with all the signs? Ye have taken foes for friends and abandoned the real Friend!...Gaze with pure eyes....Turn with attentive ears.... Hear the voice of God....All things call unto you and invite you unto the Lord, while ye...have not become conscious even for a moment. The ear is to hearken unto My voice, and the eye is to behold My beauty....Only a new eye can perceive and a new mind can end this station* so that *the wanderers may attain to the real native land and the blind ones may receive discerning sight.*[C]

2.9, 2.13 × 2, 24, 3.9, 12.9, 20.2 & 7: ***Satan*** is a Hebrew cover-name that means *hate* (*SATAN*; its close sister-word *SATAM*, means *oppose /block*). *Satan is utter hate....Whenever you meet hatred and enmity know that these are the evidences and attributes of Satan.* As an *evil spirit Satan...refers to the lower nature in man....Human*

[A] Exod. 6.3
[B] *Zohar* 1.21.234
[C] Baha'u'llah *Scriptures Tablet to the Jews* 47.116–7

personality appears in two aspects: the image or likeness of God, and the aspect of Satan.[A]

2.9, also 3.9: *The blasphemy of those who call themselves Jews, yet are not* alludes to atheist Jews who despise Judaism. A *minyan* is the quorum of ten men required for worship.

2.10, 12.9, 12.12, 20.2 & 20.10: ***Devil*** is a Greek cover-name meaning literally *thrower-through* (of words; *DIA-BOLOS*). Renderings include *lying evil* (favored), *liar, slanderer,* or *accuser*. Although

> *there is no independent force of evil in creation...terms such as 'devil' or 'Satan' are used in sacred books as symbols of the promptings of the lower nature of man* and *of evil and dark forces yielding to temptation.*[B]

2.10: These particular *ten days* of years of Jewish suffering ran from the 1935 Nürnburg race-laws up to the 1945 Holocaust end.

2.10: *In this cycle Israel will be gathered in the Holy Land....The Jewish people who are scattered to the East and West, South and North, will be assembled together.*[C]

His Message to Zoroastrianism

2.12 *NEXT, WRITE TO THE ANGEL OF THE CHURCH IN PERGAMOS: 'THESE THINGS SAYS HE WHO BEARS THE SHARP TWO-EDGED SWORD.*	*Next, publish for Zoroaster to his Zoroastrian Faith from Persia: 'This message comes from your Ahura Mazda's Bearer of Benefit who utters true wise perceptive words.*
13 *I HAVE SEEN WHERE YOU LIVE, WHERE THE THRONE OF HATRED IS. YET YOU HOLD FIRMLY TO MY NAME AND HAVE NOT DENIED MY FAITH EVEN IN THOSE AGAINST-ALL DAYS OF MY OWN TRUSTWORTHY WITNESS WHO WAS EXECUTED AMONG YOU WHERE HATRED DWELLS.*	*I know Persia where you and I dwell, where the Qajar regime of hatred rules. Yet you have been loyal to me in Zoroaster and have not rejected my Faith even in those oppositional 1844–1850 years of my own true Delegate Hushidar who has been executed among us in Persia where Qajar hate has its home.*
14 *ON THE OTHER HAND, I HOLD SOME THINGS AGAINST YOU, THAT*	*On the other hand, I hold some matters against you, that in*

[A] ***Satan is utter hatred***, 'Abdu'l-Baha *PUP* 40. ***Evil spirit Satan***, 'Abdu'l-Baha *Foundations of World Unity* 77. ***Human personality appears***, 'Abdu'l-Baha *PUP* 464, *Foundations of World Unity* 108

[B] ***There is no independent force***, Universal House of Justice (1985/12/2) *Child Abuse, Psychology and Knowledge of Self.* ***Of evil and dark forces***, Shoghi Effendi *Light* 1738.513

[C] 'Abdu'l-Baha *SAQ* 12.65; *Quran* 5.20–1, 17.100–4

THERE YOU HAVE FOLK HOLDING FIRMLY TO THE TEACHING OF A PEOPLE-SWALLOWER WHO TAUGHT THE BLOOD-LAPPER TO SET A TRAP BEFORE THE HEIRS OF ISRAEL TO EAT SACRIFICIAL-MEAT AND TO FORNICATE.	*Persia you have Zoroastrians snared by the heresy of an arch-heretic who has led a bloodthirsty leader to entrap us successors of the People of Israel who first saw God into profiteering and into exploitation.*
15 *SO YOU TOO HAVE FOLK HOLDING FIRMLY TO THE TEACHING OF THOSE WINNING PEOPLE OVER LIKEWISE.*	*So you too include Zoroastrians snared by the heresy of heretics deceiving believers as Sabaean heretics did likewise.*
16 *THEREFORE, MEND YOUR WAYS. BUT IF NOT, I AM COMING TO YOU SOON AND SHALL FIGHT THEM WITH THE SWORD OF MY MOUTH.*	*Therefore, you had to reform. But since you have not, I have come to you in 1863 just after Hushidar and am fighting your heretics with the words of my speech.*
17 *LET YOU WHO HAVE EARS HEAR WHAT THIS SPIRIT IS TELLING THE CHURCHES.*	*Let alert Zoroastrians hear what your Ahura Mazda's Manifestation is telling His Faiths.*
AS FOR THE ONE WHO PREVAILS, TO HIM OR HER I SHALL GIVE SOME OF THE HIDDEN "WHAT-IS-IT". I SHALL ALSO GIVE HIM OR HER A WHITE TABLET, AND WRITTEN ON THIS TABLET ***A NEW NAME*** *THAT NO ONE BUT THE RECIPIENT KNOWS.'*	*As for you Zoroastrians who prevail, with you I am sharing some hidden secrets. I am also showing you Hushidar's true tablet, and penned on this tablet* **THE MOST GLORIOUS** *as Ahura Mazda's new name that all can now learn.'*

Comments:

2.12–17: ***Zoroastrianism*** (also *Zarathustrianism, Magianism,* or *Mazdeism*) has influenced religious history probably more than any other Faith. Zoroaster (*Zarathustra*) was

> *a divinely-appointed and fully independent Manifestation of God* whose *flame…is still burning….Had the Zoroastrians comprehended the reality of Zoroaster, they would have understood Moses and Jesus.*[A]

Zoroastrianism was the state religion of Persia and its rulers Cyrus, Darius, Xerxes, and Artaxerxes. For Judaism, it respected the Israelites taken captive by Nebuchadnezzar. For Christianity, its

[A] **Zoroastrianism…has probably influenced**, Boyce Mary Foreword *Textual Sources for the Study of Zoroastrianism*, University of Chicago Press, 1990. ***A divinely-appointed***, Shoghi Effendi *Light* 1694.502. ***Flame…is still burning***, 'Abdu'l-Baha *PUP* 346. ***Had the Zoroastrians***, 'Abdu'l-Baha *DP* 32

three wise men were the Magi *Melchior, Caspar,* and *Balthazar* who came late for the first Christmas. For Islam, its followers were known favorably as *Magians.*[A]

2.12–17: Baha'u'llah's *Tablet to the Persian Zoroastrian Baha'is* draws on Zoroastrian concepts in urging and presenting him as the

> *First Emanation...from the Sun of Wisdom,* the *skillful physician* who *diagnoses the illness and wisely prescribes the remedy....The Primal Word appeared in these latter days* as *the Sun of Knowledge....The heaven of righteousness has no star...brighter than this....Turn from the darkness of foreignness to the shining of the sun of unity....The tree of the Word has no better blossom, and the ocean of wisdom never shall have a brighter pearl than this....I am that light which illumines the path of insight. I am the falcon on the hand of the Almighty. I bear healing in My wings, and teach the knowledge of soaring to the heaven of truth. The past is the mirror of the future, look and perceive....After the acquirement of knowledge, ye may know the Friend.*[B]

2.12–13: Zoroastrianism calls God *Lord of Wisdom* (*Ahura Mazda*). Zoroastrianism's lesser and greater Promised-Ones are its *Door of Wisdom* (*Hushidar*) and its *Bearer of Benefit* (*Saoshyant*).

2.13: ***ANTIPAS*** is a Greek cover-name that means literally *against-all* (*ANTI-PAS*). It interprets for the speaking-out of the Bab against Qajar Persia's cruel unjust system from 1844 until his 1850 execution. Earlier, also another Antipas had been martyred. He was the first Bishop of Pergamos who had spoken out against idolatry.

2.13: *A world in which naught can be perceived save strife, quarrels and corruption is bound to become the seat of the throne, the very metropolis, of Satan.*[C]

2.14: ***BA'LAAM***, the name of a prophet, acts as a Hebrew cover-name that means literally *he-swallowed-a-people* (*BA'LA-AM*).

2.14: ***BALAK***, the name of a king, acts as a Hebrew cover-name that means literally *he comes-to-lap-up* (*BA-L'LAKEK*, contracted down to *BA-LAK*) presumed Israelite blood, and interprets as *blood-lapper.*

2.14, 7.4 & 21.12: ***ISRAEL*** is a Hebrew cover-name that means literally *a man who saw God* (*ISH-SHE-RAAH-EL*) as the new name of *Jacob who had his name changed to Israel.* But comprehensively, *Israel* interprets for *the Israelites who first saw God* as *a royal priesthood...seeing God* and the first folk in the old Cycle of Prophecy to honor God enduringly. Baha'is are their spiritual heirs, as *a kingdom of Priests* and the first folk in the new Cycle of

[A] Quran 22.17
[B] Baha'u'llah *Scriptures, Tablet of Unity,* 50.130–2
[C] *Tablets of Baha'u'llah* 11.177

Fulfillment to honor God enduringly.[A] (But, in addition, *ISRA-EL* may also punnily render as *he strove with God*).

2.16, 3.11, 11.14, 22.7, 12 & 20: ***Soon*** interprets for the rapid advent of the proclamation of Baha'u'llah in 1863, just a short nineteen years after the 1844 proclamation of the Bab.

2.17: ***MANNA*** is a Hebrew cover-name that means literally *What-Is-It* (*MAN-HU*)? that the surprised hungry People of Israel shouted one morning when they saw bread from heaven covering the Sinai sand.[B]

2.17: The ***white tablet*** depicts the *long epistle* that the Bab wrote just before execution. It was *penned in the most graceful manner...in the shape of a man*, comprising *three hundred and sixty derivatives from the word Bahá* [Glory]. The Bab left instructions for it to *be delivered to the hands of Jinab-i-Baha* [Baha'u'llah] *in Tihran* [*sic*].[C]

2.17 & 3.12: **God's *new name*** is ***THE MOST GLORIOUS*** (***EL-ABHA***).[D]

His Message to Hinduism

2.18 *THEN WRITE TO THE ANGEL OF THE CHURCH IN THYATIRA:* *'THESE THINGS SAYS THE SON OF GOD WITH HIS EYES LIKE A FLAME OF FIRE AND HIS FEET RESEMBLING WHITE-HOT MOLTEN BRONZE.*	*Then publish for Krishna to his Hindu Faith from India:* *'This message comes from your Son of Brahman, His Kalki Avatar with his soul blazing divine love and his justice glowing reward and gleaming punishment.*
19 *I HAVE SEEN YOUR VERY DEEDS, ALSO YOUR LOVE, FAITH, SERVICE, AND ENDURANCE, WITH YOUR LATEST DEEDS BIGGER AND BETTER THAN THE FIRST.*	*I know of your own good deeds, also your love, loyalty, service, and tenacity, with your recent deeds bigger and better than the first Hindus' deeds.*
20 *ON THE OTHER HAND, I HOLD AGAINST YOU THAT YOU TOLERATE THAT GOD-TRASHING WOMAN WHO CALLS HERSELF A PROPHETESS, YET TEACHES AND SEDUCES MY SERVANTS TO FORNICATE AND TO EAT SACRIFICIAL-MEAT.*	*On the other hand, I hold against you that you have been tolerating that God-trashing greed that poses as visionary, yet misleads and lures my servants into exploiting and into profiteering.*

[A] ***A man who saw God***, Philo *Change of Names* 20.12.81, *Abraham* 22.12.56, *Unchangeableness of God* 30.144, *Dreams* 2.26.17 2, *Confusion of Tongues* 8.56. *Midrash Tanna Debe Eliyahu* 138–9. ***A royal priesthood***, Philo *Abraham* 22.12.56. ***A kingdom of priests***, Rev. 16

[B] Exod. 16.15

[C] ***Long epistle***, 'Abdu'l-Baha *Traveler's Narrative* 25–6. ***Be delivered***, Nabil *Dawnbreakers* 505; 'Abdu'l-Baha *BWF* 221, *PUP* 26; Shoghi Effendi *GPB* 69

[D] Isaiah 62.2, 65.15; Baha'u'llah *Summons of the Lord of Hosts* 1.103.54, *Scriptures* 41.98

21 *I have given her time to repent, but she does not want to give up her fornicating.*	*I have given it time to reform, but it does not want to stop its exploiting.*
22 *See, I am casting her into a sickbed and those who commit adultery with her into great hardship, unless they give up her practices,* 23 *I shall also deal death to her children.*	*See, I am condemning it to suffer and you who have profiteered from it to great distress, since you have not stopped its misbehavior, I am also visiting fatal events upon your youth.*
All the Churches shall know that I myself am the sifter of hearts and minds. I shall reward each of you according to your deeds.	*All the Faiths have had to learn that I your Kalki Avatar assess hearts and minds. I reward each of you as your deeds deserve.*
24 *But I am telling the rest of you in Thyatira, as many as do not hold this same teaching, the ones who have not learned "the depths of hatred" as folk say, I lay no other burden on you.* 25 *Just firmly hold to what you have, until wherever I shall come.*	*But I am telling the rest of you in Hinduism, as many as did not get bound up by this same heresy, those of you who have not learned "deep hatred" as folk call it, I ask no more of you. You just had to remain loyal to the Hinduism that you have, until to Persia I came.*
26 *As for the one who prevails and takes to heart my actions right to the end, I shall give him or her authority over nations,* 27 *so that he or she shall guide them with an iron rod as clay pots to be broken up, as I too have also attained from my Father,* 28 *so I shall assign the Dawn-Star to him or her.*	*As for you Hindus who prevail and take seriously my actions into these end-times, I shall give you authority over nations, so that you shall direct them with my strong Law as countries dividing up into cantons, as I too have also attained from my Father, so I shall appoint the role of Teacher of the next spiritual Era to a Hindu.*
29 *Let you who have ears hear what this Spirit is telling the Churches.'*	*Let alert Hindus hear what your Brahman's Manifestation is telling Its Faiths.'*

Comments:

2.18–29: Hinduism is as monotheistic as Christianity, despite their Trinities (Brahma[A]/Vishnu/ Shiva, and Father/Son/Holy Spirit).[B]

2.18: *The Message of Krishna is the message of love. The reincarnation of Krishna* is Baha'u'llah to whom *the Bhagavad-Gita...referred as the 'Most Great Spirit,' the 'Tenth Avatar,' the 'Immaculate Manifestation of Krishna'*[C]

2.20: ***IEZABEL*** (*JEZEBEL*), the name of a vile queen, is a Ugaritic-Hebrew cover-name that means literally *God-Trash* (*AY-ZEVEL*).

2.20–29: Directly interpreting *fornicating* sexually fits a Hindu prophecy predicts how, at the end of its Kali Yuga Cycle, the

> *masters of the High Tantras stray like dogs...spirits of wantonness possess maidens...spirits of depravity possess nuns; passion... the sole bond of union between the sexes...women...objects merely of sensual gratification.*[D]

2.22: In this context, rendering *klinē* as *coffin* takes the meaning of *arsa*, the equivalent Aramaic word in the *Crawford Aramaic Text*.[284-C]

2.23: Also directly interpreting *deal death to her children* sexually fits the early fatal forms of venereal disease such as biblical syphilis[E] and early AIDS.

2.23: Baha'u'llah *was styled...'Sifter of Men'*.[F]

2.25: The translation *until wherever I shall be present* relates to place rather than time (for which *whenever* would be appropriate).

2.27: *Clay pots to be broken up* interprets constructively for countries dividing down smoothly into cooperative united cantons worldwide. Apropos, US President Jimmy Carter noted that *human beings are still divided into nation states, but these states are rapidly becoming a single global civilization.*[G]

2.28 ***Dawn-Star***: Just as the dawn-star Venus heralds the rising of the sun of a new day, so each *Dawn-Star* heralds the *Day of Revelation of each Prophet of God* as *the advent of that most great light* in *the heaven of justice.*[H] This particular *Dawn-Star* augurs the Messenger dawning the post-Baha'i spiritual Era having a Hindu origin.

[A] *Brahman* is the Hindu Godhead and *Brahma* is one of the Hindu Trinity (http://en.wikipedia.org/wiki/Brahman, http://en.wikipedia.org/wiki/Brahma)

[B] But *the Hindu doctrine of metempsychosis...is fallacious* since the material *reality of things cannot be made to return* (Shoghi Effendi *Dawn of a New Day* 201)

[C] ***The Message of Krishna***, 'Abdu'l-Baha *Paris Talks* 35. ***The reincarnation of Krishna***, 'Abdu'l-Baha *TAB* 1.7; Shoghi Effendi *Aqdas* 160.234, *GPB* 94. ***The Bhagavad-Gita...referred***, Shoghi Effendi *GPB* 95

[D] *Vishnu Purana* 4.24, *Legend of the Great Stupa Jarungkhasor 1*

[E] Num. 25.9

[F] Shoghi Effendi *GPB* 94

[G] **Countries dividing down**, Alesina *Number and Size of Nations* 1027–56
Human beings are still, Jimmy Carter cited by Sagan in *Murmurs of the Earth* 28

[H] Baha'u'llah *KI* 62

Apocalypse Chapter 3
His Messages for Three Later Faiths

His Message to Buddhism

3.1 *Now write to the Angel of the Church in Sardis:*
'These things says he who holds the seven Spirits of God, namely the seven stars.

Now publish for Buddha to his Buddhist Faith from Nepal:
'This message comes from your Eternal Essence's Maitreiya Fifth Buddha who unites Its seven Manifestations, namely Its seven spiritual Teachers.

I have seen your very deeds, that you have a name, that you are alive, but you are dead!

I know of your own good deeds, that you Buddhists became renowned, that your spirit was alive, but you have died!

2 *Wake up and strengthen the rest who are about to die, for I have found your very deeds incomplete in the sight of my God.*

You should have become enlightened and have revived your Buddhist remnant whose spirit had almost died, for I had found your own deeds lacking as viewed by our Eternal Essence.

3 *Therefore, recall how you heard and have received, then repent and obey.*

Therefore, you had to recall how you had learned and gained from Buddha, then repent and obey.

However, if you do not wake up, I shall be present like a thief, so that you will not at all at know at what specific hour I shall come upon you.

However, since you have failed to be enlightened, I have appeared unexpectedly in Persia, so that you have not at all recognized this century of the 1800s as when I am present for you.

4 *On the other hand, you do have some people in Sardis who have not soiled their garments, because they are worthy, they shall walk with me in white.*

On the other hand, you have believers in Buddhism who did not blemish their nobility, because they are worthy, they are advancing with me in purity.

5 *As for the one who prevails, this same person shall thus wear white garments. I shall never delete his or her name from the Full Book of Life and shall acclaim his or her*

As for you Buddhist believers who prevail, you same Buddhists thus display pure nobility. I shall always include you with all morally decent folk and am acclaiming you in the

NAME BEFORE MY FATHER AND HIS ANGELS.	*service of my Father and His Messengers.*
6 *LET YOU WHO HAVE EARS HEAR WHAT THIS SPIRIT IS TELLING THE CHURCHES.'*	*Let alert Buddhists hear what your Eternal Essence's Manifestation is telling Its Faiths.'*

Comments:

3.1–6, ***Buddhism***: *The real teaching of Buddha is the same as the teaching of Jesus Christ....Buddha...was a divinely-appointed and fully independent Manifestation of God...a wonderful soul* who *established the Oneness of God....In the time of the Buddha ...civilization in Asia and in the East was very much higher than in the West and ideas and thoughts of the Eastern peoples were much in advance of, and nearer to the thoughts of God than those of the West....Later the original principles of his doctrines gradually disappeared, and ignorant customs and ceremonials arose and increased.*[A]

3.1: For God, Buddhism applies titles like *Eternal Essence, Infinite, Boundless Essence, Causeless Cause*, or *Ultimate Reality*. Similarly, Judaism writes *God* as only *G-d* or *Gcd* or utters Its/His/Her unutterable name *YHWH* as just *Adonai* or *The Name*. Likewise, the Baha'i Faith calls God the *innermost Spirit of Spirits* or *eternal Essence of Essences*.[B] All such titles show how impossible it is to define the It/Him/Her we call "God".

3.2: ***Buddha*** means literally *awakened/enlightened one*. Buddhism's five enlightened-ones are its First Buddha Gautama, its Second Buddha Jesus, its Third Buddha Muhammad, and now its Fourth Buddha the Bab and Fifth Buddha Baha'u'llah. Its Fifth or *Maitreiya/Kindness Buddha* or *Amitabha Buddha of Limitless Light* is *expected to appear to the West of India and to the East of Israel...Blessed is the slumberer who is awakened by* [his] *Breeze.*[C]

3.3–7: By the 11–15th AD centuries, Buddhism had spread through India. But the rulers of India found that Buddhist teachings were too peaceful for waging war, so they displaced and supplanted

[A] ***The real teaching of Buddha***, *'Abdu'l-Baha in London* 63. ***Buddha...was a divinely***, Shoghi Effendi *Light* 1694.502. ***A wonderful soul***, *'Abdu'l-Baha in London* 64. ***In the time of the***, *'Abdu'l-Baha in London* 69. ***Later the original principles of***, 'Abdu'l-Baha *SAQ* 43.165, *'Abdu'l-Baha in London* 64

[B] Baha'u'llah *KI* 179

[C] ***Buddha* means literally *awakened***, http://en.wikipedia.org/wiki/Buddha. ***Expected to appear***, *William Sears, Thief in the Night* 108. ***Blessed is the slumberer***, Baha'u'llah *TB* 16, *Scriptures* 49.124; Shoghi Effendi *GPB* 210

Buddhism by promoting Hinduism and Islam.[A] Buddhism went offshore and thrived in Sri Lanka, Southeast Asia, Tibet, China, and Japan.

3.3 & 16.15: Baha'u'llah, the Maitreiya Fifth Buddha, appeared *as comes a thief...secretly...born below...leaving behind the highly exalted throne to bring salvation* and *coming* as *a thief into a house, the owner of which is utterly unaware*.[B]

3.4–5, etc.: ***Garments*** *signify...good qualities...such as love, sincerity, etc....White garments signify holy dignity and a station sanctified from color...free from the universal conditions and material qualities. Adorn yourselves with the raiment of goodly deeds...with works of righteousness.*[C] The rich wardrobe of the Apocalypse contains many dressing-words, each imparting a specific meaning:

- *A long robe* as *complete virtue* (v. 1.13)
- *Garments* as *nobility* (vv. 3.4–5, 18, 4.4, 16.15, 19.13 & 16)
- *Robe* as *virtue* (6.11, 7.9, 13, 14 & 22.14)
- *Linen* as *goodness* (15.6)
- *Fine-linen* as *righteousness* (19.8 & 14) or *self-righteousness* (18.12 & 16)
- *Clad in* as *emanating* (1.13, 15.6 & 19.14)
- *Wearing* as *displaying* (3.5, 3.18, 4.4, 7.9, 13, 10.1, 17.4, 18.16, 19.8 & 13), or *promoting* (11.3) or *shining* (12.1)
- *Arrayed* as *presenting* (21.2 & 19)
- *White* as *pure* (2.17, 3.4, 5, 18, 4.4, 6.11, 7.9, 7.13, 14.14, 19.11, 19.14 × 2, & 20.11) or impure (6.2)
- *Clean* as *true* (15.6, 19.8 & 14)
- *Shining* as *radiant* (15.6 & 19.8).

3.5, 13.8, 17.8, 20.12, 20.15 & 21.27: ***The Book of Life*** is laid open in Jewish lore over the month before Yom Kippur for recording the names of morally decent Jews as *letters inscribed upon His* [God's] *sacred scroll*, as *verses of perfection on the page of the universe*, and as *words of oneness in the Book of Life*.[D]

[A] Gard, *Great Religions of Modern Man: Buddhism* 25–6

[B] ***As comes a thief...secretly***, Japanese Buddhist Scripture: *Sekai Kyusei Kyo. Inori-no-Shu* in www.unification.net/ws/theme161.htm#16. ***Coming as a thief into a house***, 'Abdu'l-Baha *SWA* 168.198–9; cited by Brittingham 3

[C] ***Garments signify***, 'Abdu'l-Baha cited by Brittingham 3. ***White garments***, Baha'u'llah *Aqdas* 73.45, *Tablets* 11.178, *KI* 73.45

[D] ***The Book of Life***, Ps. 69.28–9; Exod. 32.32–3; Dan. 12.1; Mal. 3.16. ***Letters inscribed upon***, Baha'u'llah *GWB* 96.196; Shoghi Effendi *Advent of Divine Justice* 75. ***Verses of perfection***, 'Abdu'l-Baha *SWA* 193.232, *Compilation of Compilations* 1.782.371

His Message to Christianity

3·7 *Next write to the Angel of the Church in Philadelphia:*	*Next publish for Jesus to his Christian Faith from Israel:*
'These things says the Holy One, the True One who holds the key of a beloved David, who opens so that no one shall close, and closes so that no one opens.	*'This message comes from your God's unique Messenger, His true Messenger who brings the remedy of the beloved Bab, who has begun a new Era that no one can close, and has ended an old Era that no one can reopen.*
8 *I have seen your very deeds.*	*I know of your own good deeds.*
Look, I have placed open in front of you your own door that none of you can close, for you have little strength.	*Look, I am revealing to you your own Door of Jesus as the Bab whom none of you can close off, for disunity makes you weak.*
Yet you have taken my Word to heart and have not denied my name.	*Yet you have taken me seriously as a divine Speaker and have not rejected me in Jesus.*
9 *Look, I am handing over some from that assembly of opposition who call themselves Jews yet are not, but are lying. Listen, I shall have them come and worship at your feet, so that they shall learn that I myself have loved you.*	*Look, I have assigned some Jews from that atheist "minyan" opposing Judaism who call themselves Jews yet are not, but are posturing. Listen, I am having them come and worship humbly with you, so that they can know that I, their Messiah, love you Christians.*
10 *Because you have preserved this Word of my endurance, I too shall also preserve you from the hour of test that shall come upon the whole inhabited earth to test those living on the earth.*	*Because you have kept Jesus as the divine Speaker of my eternal truth, I too shall also keep you safe from the end-time trials that have come upon the whole Middle East society to try those living across the Middle East.*
11 *I am coming soon. Hold onto what you have, so that no one may remove your prize.*	*I have come in 1863, just after the Bab. You have stayed loyal to the Christian Faith that you have, so that no one can remove me as your prize.*
12 *As for the one who prevails, I shall make him or her a pillar in the Temple of my God, so that he or she shall*	*As for you Christians who prevail, I am turning you into champions for the new Faith of my God, so that you shall never*

NEVER LEAVE. UPON HIM, HER, AND IT, I SHALL WRITE:	*leave. Through you and it, I broadcast:*
• ***THE NAME*** *OF THIS GOD OF MINE,*	• ***THE MOST GLORIOUS*** *as the name of this God of ours,*
• ***THE NAME*** *OF THE CITY OF THIS GOD OF MINE, THE NEW JERUSALEM LANDING FROM THE SKY FROM MY GOD, AND*	• ***DIVINE CIVILIZATION*** *as the name of the system of this God of ours, the New Jerusalem arriving from the One Religion of our God, and*
• ***THIS NEW NAME*** *OF MINE.*	• ***GLORY OF GOD*** *as my own new name of.*
13 *LET YOU WHO HAVE EARS HEAR WHAT THIS SPIRIT IS TELLING THE CHURCHES.'*	*Let alert Christians hear what your God's Manifestation is telling His Faiths.'*

Comments:

3.7–13: Baha'u'llah's *Tablet to the Christians* draws on Christian concepts in urging:[A]

> *Christians! Are ye hidden from Myself because of My Name? Ye have called for your Lord…night and day, and when He hath come…have not approached….Consider those who turned away from the Spirit (Christ) when He came to them with manifest power. How many of the Pharisees were abiding in the Temples in His Name….But when the gate…opened…no one…approached….Likewise look at this time. How many monks were abiding in churches and were calling for the Spirit, and when He came in truth, they approached Him not….He hath come from Heaven as He came from it the first time….The Son…beareth witness to Me and I bear witness to Him….Priests, leave the bells…come out from the churches…. Proclaim in this Greatest Name among the nations.*[B]

Further, Baha'u'llah's *Tablet to the Pope* (Pius IX) urges him:

> *O Pope! Rend asunder the veils!…He hath come from heaven another time, as He came from it the first time; beware lest thou oppose Him as the Pharisees opposed Him…without evidence or proof….The Promised One hath appeared….Beware lest theology prevent thee from the King…lest celebration preventeth you from the Celebrated, and worship from the Worshipped….Ye read the Gospel and still do not acknowledge the Glorious Lord…The Word, which the Son (Christ) concealed hath appeared…in the form of man in this time….Sell that which*

[A] Baha'u'llah *Tablet to the Christians, Scriptures* 49.124
[B] Baha'u'llah *Scriptures* 49.124; Shoghi Effendi *GPB* 210

thou hast of decked ornaments....come out from the Vatican.... He [Jesus] *said, 'Come, that I may make you fishers of men,' and today We* [Baha'u'llah] *say, 'Come, that We may make you vivifiers of the world....People of the Gospel...We have revealed Ourselves unto you on a previous occasion and ye did not know Me. This is another time* [Muhammad], *this is the Day of God, come unto Him.*[A]

3.7–8, 3.20 & 4.1: The *Holy One,* the *True One* interprets for one party as Baha'u'llah. His *key* and *beloved David* interpret for a second party as the Bab.[B]

3.7, 5.5 & 22.16: ***BELOVED DAVID*** is a comprehensive rendering of the Hebrew cover-name *DAVID* that means literally *a beloved one.*

3.8, 3.20 × 2, & 4.1: ***Door*** appears in Revelation these four early times. Then the *Door* disappears and gets replaced from v. 5.6 to the end by the *Ram.* Both this *Door* and that *Ram* portray the Bab as the return of Jesus.

3.8: In Christianity, *dissentions among various sects have opened the way to weakness.*[C]

3.10 & 12.2: Christianity's testing *end-times* correspond with Judaism's *birth pangs of the Messiah* and Hinduism's *dark events* ending its Kali Age.

3.12: *Revelations* [*sic*] *3.12 refers to the Revelation of Baha'u'llah.*[D]

3.12, etc.: ***The Temple*** symbolizes the new Baha'i Revelation whose *pillar of God is being erected and hath become manifest* as *all things are made new.*[E]

3.12, also vv. 15.8, 21.11 & 21.23: ***The NEW NAME*** of God is ***THE MOST GLORIOUS.*** The new name of Baha'u'llah as the return of Jesus is **GLORY OF GOD** (which is what *Baha'u'llah* means).

3.12, 21.2 & 21.11: ***JERUSALEM*** is a Hebrew cover-name that means literally *they shall see-dual-peace* (*YIR'U-SHALAYIM*). But it still translates traditionally as *Jerusalem.*

[A] Baha'u'llah *Summons of the Lord of Hosts* 1.101.54–5, *PB* 83, *Scriptures* 41.98–104
[B] Isaiah 22.22
[C] *Tablets of Baha'u'llah* 6.60
[D] Shoghi Effendi *Letters to Aust. and N.Z.* 41
[E] Baha'u'llah *Scriptures Tablet to the Jews* 47.116–7

His Message to Islam

3.14 *THEN WRITE TO THE ANGEL OF THE CHURCH IN LAODICEA: 'THESE THINGS SAYS THE AMEN, THE TRUSTWORTHY AND TRUE WITNESS, AND THE BEGINNING OF THE CREATION OF GOD.*	*Then publish for Muhammad to his Muslim Faith from Arabia: 'This message comes from your Allah's Last Qayyum Raiser, His Trustworthy and True Delegate, and His Opener of the new world order of your Allah.*
15 *I HAVE SEEN YOUR VERY DEEDS, THAT YOU ARE NEITHER COLD NOR HOT. IF ONLY YOU WERE COLD OR HOT!* 16 *ACCORDINGLY, BECAUSE YOU ARE TEPID AND NEITHER HOT NOR COLD, I SHALL VOMIT YOU FROM MY MOUTH,* 17 *FOR YOU GUSH:* • *"I AM RICH.* • *"I HAVE GROWN RICH.* • *"I NEED NOTHING!"*	*I know of your very deeds, that you are neither serene nor striving. If only you were serene or striving! Accordingly, because you are complacent and neither striving nor serene, I denounce you, for you have been boasting:* • *"We have wealth.* • *"We became prosperous.* • *"We need no more!"*
YET YOU HAVE NOT SEEN THAT YOU YOURSELF ARE THE WRETCHED AND PITIFUL ONE: • *POOR!* • *BLIND!* • *NAKED!*	*Yet you have not learned that you yourselves are spiritually wretched and pitiful folk:* • *Empty!* • *Unaware* • *Ignorant!*
18 *I ADVISE YOU TO BUY FROM ME* • *GOLD REFINED BY FIRE, FOR YOU TO BE RICH,* • *WHITE GARMENTS, FOR YOU TO WEAR AND YOUR SHAMEFUL NAKEDNESS NOT SHOW,* • *OINTMENT TO ANOINT YOUR EYES, FOR YOU TO SEE.*	*I urge you to gain from me* • *Glory refined by love, for you to fill your emptiness,* • *Pure nobility for you to display and your stark ignorance not show,* • *Perception to hone your insight, for you to become aware.*
19 *I MYSELF TRAIN AND REBUKE WHOMEVER I LOVE. SO GET SERIOUS AND MEND YOUR WAYS.*	*I, your Last Qayyum Raiser, train and rebuke whomever I love. So sober up and reform.*
20 *LOOK! I WAS, AND I HAVE BEEN, STANDING AT THE DOOR. NOW I AM KNOCKING. IF ANYBODY HEAR MY VOICE AND OPEN THIS DOOR, FOR THEM I SHALL ENTER. WITH THEM I SHALL BANQUET, AND THEY WITH ME.*	*Look! From 1844 I was, and up to 1850 I have been, championed by the Bab as Jesus's Door. In 1863 I proclaimed. Since some of you Muslims greeted me and accepted the Bab as Jesus's Door, for you I have come. With you I am celebrating, and you with me.*

21 *As for the one who prevails, I shall appoint him or her to join me on my Throne, as I too have also prevailed and have joined my Father on His Throne.*	*As for you Muslims who prevail, I have appointed you to join me in establishing my new Revelation, as I too have also prevailed and have joined our Father Allah in establishing His new Revelation.*
22 *Let you who have ears hear what this Spirit is telling the Churches.'*	*Let alert Muslims hear what your Allah's Manifestation is telling His Faiths.'*

Comments:

3.14–22: The Apocalypse predicting Islam surprises Christians. But like it or not, as a prophet, John was duty-bound to report important spiritual news, good and bad, and Islam was important spiritual news. as the Faith after Christianity. As good news, John's visionary eye reported Muhammad's true Islam conceived as large as life in his Apocalypse bride. As bad news, he reported military Islam parading its Umayyad Locust cavalries, zinging its Umayyad Scorpion arrows, and billowing its Ottoman cannon smoke.

3.14: The first six churches depict the six Faiths already in existence in the AD 95 of John. To them the Angel has introduced himself using titles from his debut in Chapter 1. To Ephesus, for example, he was *he who firmly holds the seven stars in his right-hand*. But the seventh church of Laodicea depicts Islam that did not yet then exist. So to introduce himself to Laodicea the Messenger takes three new titles. As the *Amen*, he is *the Seal of the Prophets* like Muhammad. As the *Beginning of the Creation of God*, he *reproduce*[s] *creation as...the first time* like Muhammad. And as the *True Witness*, he is a *Messenger...your witness* like Muhammad.[A]

3.14: The *Qayyum Raiser* is the greater Promised-One of Shi'a Islam, equivalent to the *Muhdi Guider* of Sunni Islam.

3.18: *Wherever in the Holy Books...the blind received sight...he obtained the true perception*, and wherever *a deaf man received hearing...he acquired spiritual and heavenly hearing*.[B]

3.20, also 19.9: *We...have opened unto you the gates of the Kingdom....Every favoured soul is seated at the banquet table of the Lord, receiving his portion of that heavenly feast*.[C]

3.21: *A Messenger has come from among yourselves* as *the Lord of the mighty throne*.[D]

[A] **The first six churches**, Aune, *52A*.263. ***Seal of the Prophets***, Quran 33.40. ***Reproduc*[*ing*] *creation***, Quran 21.104. ***Messenger...to be***, Quran 73.15

[B] 'Abdu'l-Baha *SAQ* 22.101–2

[C] 'Abdu'l-Baha *SWA* 28.57

[D] Quran 9.128–9

Apocalypse Chapter 4
His Message of a New Faith

4.1 After these visions, I look, and behold, a door open in the sky. Then that first voice that I had heard like a trumpet was speaking with me, saying:

Come up here, and I shall show you the visions that must flash after these visions.

After these events, I watch and behold, the Bab as Jesus's Door of 1844 revealed by God's One Religion. Then that first Proclaimer whom I had heard as a herald is speaking with me, inviting:

Rise up with me, John, and I shall reveal to you the events that must pass after these events.

2 Immediately, I soared in spirit and behold:

At once, I soar in spirit, and behold:

- A Throne set in the sky, with a person seated on the Throne,

- A Revelation from God's One Religion, with him Baha'u'llah establishing his Baha'i Revelation,

- 3 The enthroned person gleaming as an apparition of diamond and ruby gemstone,

- He its Founder emanating strong justice as brilliant as diamond and ardent love as fiery as ruby,

- Around the Throne a rainbow like an apparition of emerald,

- Supporting the Revelation his promise of harmonious unity for the seven Faiths,

- 4 Also around the Throne, 24 thrones,

- Also supporting his Revelation, 24 revelatory roles,

- On these thrones, 24 elders seated, wearing white garments, with gold crowns on their heads,

- In these revelatory roles, 24 founders established, displaying pure nobility, as leaders with superb authority,

- 5 Out of the Throne poured lightnings, voices, and thunders,

- Resulting from his Baha'i Revelation flashes God's anger at the voices rising against it, and at the violations shaking it,

- Blazing in front of the Throne, seven fiery torches that are God's seven Spirits,

- Passionately serving his Baha'i Revelation, seven loving Revelators who have been God's seven Manifestations Abraham, Moses, Zoroaster, Krishna, Buddha, Jesus, and Muhammad,

6 • Also in front of the Throne a seeming sea of glass like crystal,

- Also serving his Baha'i Revelation transparent truth in all its excellence,

• At the center of the Throne and around the Throne, four Living-Beings studded with eyes front and back:

• Central to his Revelation and guarding his Revelation, four Primary-Figures [two Founders, two guardians] predicting the future and explaining the past:

7The first Living-Being like a lion,
The second Living-Being like an ox,
The third Living-Being with the face like a human-being's,
The fourth Living-Being like a flying eagle.

The first Primary-Figure its regal Founder Baha'u'llah,
The second Primary-Figure its Co-Founder sacrificial Bab,
The third Primary-Figure its kind servant of his Glory, 'Abdu'l-Baha,
The fourth Primary-Figure its scholarly guardian of his Glory, Shoghi Effendi.

8The four Living-Beings, each and every one bearing aboard six wings, studded with eyes outside and in, get no rest day or night, calling out:

The four Primary-Figures, one and all soaring tandem amid the 24 founders, uttering prophecies spiritual and material, are getting no respite as God's light is lighting the night, proclaiming:

Holy! Holy! Holy!
Almighty Lord God,
• *The-Was,*
• *The-Is,*
• *The-Is-Coming!*

Unique! Unique! Unique!
Almighty Lord God,
• ***The-God-of-Earlier-Eras,***
• ***The-God-of-Later-Eras,***
• ***The-God-of-a-New-Era!***

9As the Living-Beings glorify, honor, and thank the Enthroned Living-Being living on into the Eras of the Eras, 10the 24 elders are to fall down before this Enthroned-One, to worship this Living-Being living on into the Eras of the Eras, and to toss their crowns down before the Throne, saying:

As the Primary-Figures glorify, honor, and thank the Founder Primary-Figure Baha'u'llah living on from the old Cycle of Prophecy into the new Cycle of Fulfillment, the 24 founders are devoting themselves to the service of this Founder, are adoring this Primary-Figure living on from Cycle to Cycle, and are yielding their leadership to the service of his Baha'i Revelation, saying:

11*Worthy are You, our Lord and God, to receive the glory and the honor, now the power, for You Yourself have created all things. Through Your will they existed, then they were created.*

Worthy are You, our Lord and God, to assume the glory and the honor, now the power, for You Yourself create all things. Through Your will their essence exists, then it takes physical form!

Comments:

4.1–2 & 21.10: Baha'u'llah, *the falcon on the hand of the Almighty*, taught *knowledge of soaring to the heaven of truth.*[A]

4.2–3, also 4.9, 10, 5.1, 7, 13, 6.16, 7.10, 15, 19.4, 20.11, 21.5 & 22.5, ***The Enthroned-One***: The prophet Ezekiel also saw

> *what looked like a throne...an apparition of a human-being...the brilliance all around him like a rainbow in cloud on a rainy day...the appearance of the glory of God.*[B]

To his Day Jesus Christ Himself...referred as 'the regeneration when the Son of Man shall sit in the throne of His glory'. Open your eyes, O concourse of bishops, that ye may behold your Lord seated upon the Throne.[C]

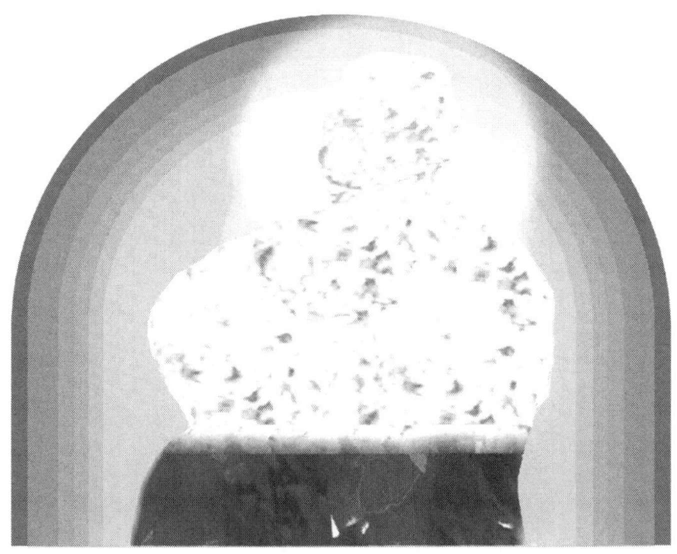

An Enthroned-One
as an apparition of diamond and ruby

4.2–3: This rainbow seals God's promise of unity to the seven Faiths, as an Old Testament rainbow once sealed God's promise never to flood the earth again. The green of the rainbow unites the rainbow colors of the seven monotheistic Faiths, just as the green of leaves unites all flower-colors.[D]

[A] Baha'u'llah *Scriptures Tablet to the Persian Zoroastrian Baha'is* 50.132

[B] ***What looked like a throne***, Ezekiel 1.28.

[C] ***To his Day Jesus Christ Himself***, Baha'u'llah *Summons of the Lord of Hosts* 1.122; Shoghi Effendi *GPB* 96

[D] Gen. 9.12–7. An arc of green gardens also spans Mount Carmel's Baha'i World Center

4.5, 8.5, 11.19 & 16.18–20: ***Lightnings, voices, thunders*** roar the turmoil that typically opens spiritual Eras, when

> *the lightnings of the anger and the wrath of God will flash, the noise of the thunder of the violation of the Covenant will resound, the earthquake of doubts will take place, the hail of torments will beat upon the violators of the Covenant, and even those who profess belief will fall into trials and temptations....* Thus *when (for example) Christ...appeared, a storm of trials arose, afflictions appeared, the winds of tests blew, the thunder of temptation descended and hosts...surrounded the houses of the friends; then the weak ones were shaken and were misled after once being* guided. Similarly, once *the Covenant of Baha'u'llah had...been manifestly violated...the storm foreshadowed by the writer of the Apocalypse had broken....the 'lightnings', the 'thunders', the 'earthquake' which must needs accompany the revelation...had all come to pass.*[A]

4.4, 7.4, 14.1 & 14.3: ***The 24 elders*** interpret as the 24 (small-*f*) **f**ounders of the Baha'i Faith as the first *worshipers of the appearance of the universal Manifestation.*[B]

4.5, also 8.10: These *torches* interpret positively as Revelators. Later (v. 8.10), *a torch* interprets negatively for Constantine as a would-be revelator.

4.6: *How manifold the emanations of knowledge from that ocean of divine wisdom,*[C] which contains *all the knowledge of the past and all the knowledge of the future.*[D]

4.7: ***The four Living-Beings*** portray spiritual, not secular, kings.[E]

4.7: The lion Living-Being bears *the flag of the Messiah son of David ...of Judah, with a lion marked on it.* In its turn, the ox Living-Being bears *the flag of the Messiah son of Joseph, on which is the sign of an ox* (the ox was a central Yom Kippur sacrifice in the Temple).[F]

4.7, also 4.1–2, 4, 6–10, 5.6–7, 8, 11, 14, 6.1, 6, 7.11, 11.16, 14.3, 15.7 & 19.4: Inclusively, the 24 elders, four Living-Beings, and two Enthroned-Ones **total 24 parties** (not 24 + 4 + 2 = 30 parties).

[A] ***The lightnings of the anger***, 'Abdu'l-Baha *SAQ* 11.60–1. ***When (for example) Christ,*** 'Abdu'l-Baha *TAB* 1.13. ***The Covenant of Baha'u'llah***, Effendi *GPB* 249.

[B] ***The 24 elders,*** Shoghi Effendi *GPB* 8. ***Worshipers of the appearance***, 'Abdu'l-Baha *SAQ* 11.57–8

[C] Baha'u'llah *KI* 234, *Aqdas* 180.85, *ESW* 3, 19, 93, *TB* 4.34, 6.67, *Gems* 19.16

[D] Baha'u'llah *Prayers and Meditations* 84

[E] The Baha'i World Center Research Department could find no Pilgrim Note claimed by Moffett's *New Keys to the Book of Revelation* p. 20 to interpret the four Living-Beings as secular kings spreading the Baha'i Faith (letter to the author, 1999/11/15)

[F] ***The flag of the Messiah***, *Zohar* 10.18.483, 479, 481. **The ox was a central**, Levit. 16.3

Stars shining inclusively for Revelation's 24 elders.
The two biggest stars shine for Enthroned-Ones.
The four big stars shine for Living-Beings
All 24 stars (big and small) shine for elders

4.8: Grammatically and arguably, the eyes stud the Living-Beings as well as just their wings.
4.8: The triple praise *Holy! Holy! Holy!* (*Kadosh! Kadosh! Kadosh!* in Hebrew, *Agios! Agios! Agios!* in Greek) heralds God's three successor Messengers after Jesus, namely Muhammad, the Bab, and Baha'u'llah.

Apocalypse Chapter 5
The Apocalypse Ram

5.1 Next, I saw a short scroll on the right-hand of the Enthroned-One, written inside yet outside sealed with seven seals.

Next, I hear my short Revelation tale authorized by Baha'u'llah as Founder of the Baha'i Revelation, revealed yet veiled for the seven Faiths.

2 Now I saw a mighty Angel proclaiming in a loud voice:

Who is worthy to open this short scroll and break its seals?

Now I hear the Bab as a powerful Messenger Proclaimer demanding:

Who is worthy to interpret John's short Revelation tale and reveal it for the Faiths?

3 But nobody in the sky, on the earth, or under the earth was able to open the short scroll or look into it.

But no spiritual, materialistic, or simple person has been able to interpret my short Revelation tale or explain it.

4 I wept a lot, because nobody worthy was found to open the short scroll or to look into it.

Since AD 95, I have felt very sad, because nobody worthy has been found to interpret my short tale or explain it.

5 Then one of the elders tells me:

Stop crying! Look, the Lion from the tribe of Judah, the root of a beloved David, has won through to open this short scroll, along with its seven seals.

Then foremost Founder Baha'u'llah tells me:

Cheer up John! Look, I, the first Primary-Figure descended from the Jews, the source of the beloved Bab, have succeeded to interpret your short Revelation tale, along with its seven Faiths.

6 Now I saw at the center of the Throne and the four Living-Beings, and at the center of the elders, a young Ram standing as if slain, with seven horns and seven eyes that are God's seven Spirits sent out into the whole world.

Now I see at the center of the Baha'i Revelation and its four Primary-Figures, and at the center of its founders, the young Bab championing justice until his 1850 execution, speaking the names and shining the faces of Abraham, Moses, Zoroaster, Krishna, Buddha, Jesus, and Muhammad who have been God's seven Manifestations sent out to the whole of humanity.

7 He came and he has taken the short scroll from the right-hand of the Enthroned-One.

The Bab comes and takes up my short tale empowered by Baha'u'llah as the Baha'i Revelation Founder.

8As he took the short scroll,
the four Living-Beings and the
24 elders fell down before the
Ram, each bearing a harp and
gold censers full of incenses
that are the prayers of the
faithful, 9they are also singing
a new song, saying:

You are worthy to take this short scroll and break its seals, for you have been slain and have with your blood bought folk for God from every tribe, language-group, people, and nation.
*10 You have made them
a kingdom and Priests for our God. They shall reign over the earth.*

As he takes up my short tale, the four Primary-Figures and the 24 founders devote themselves to serving the Bab, each heralding harmony and uttering splendid prayers that express the hopes of faithful Baha'is, they are also celebrating his new Gospel, rejoicing:

You are worthy to take up John's short Revelation tale and interpret it for the Faiths, for you have been executed and have through your death gained folk for God from every Persian family, language-group, people, and nation. You have turned them into a spiritual order and teachers for our God. They shall lead the planet.

11Now I saw and heard a sound of
many angels around the Throne,
the Living-Beings, and the
elders, their number millions,
now hundreds of millions,
12calling out in a loud voice:

The slain Ram is worthy to assume the power, along with wealth, wisdom, might, honor, glory, and praise

Now I see and hear many divine envoys supporting the Baha'i Revelation, its Primary-Figures, and its founders, in their millions, now hundreds of millions, loudly proclaiming:

The executed Bab is worthy to assume spiritual power, along with spiritual wealth, wisdom, might, honor, glory, and praise.

13Next, I heard all creatures
in the sky, and on the earth,
under the earth, now on the
ocean, along with everything
in them, responding:

All praise, all honor, all glory, now all dominion, to the Enthroned-One and to the Ram, into the Eras of the Eras.

Next, I hear all spiritual, material, and simple people, now wise people, along with all that they represent, responding:

All praise, all honor, all glory, now all dominion, to the Founder Baha'u'llah and to the Bab, from the old Cycle into the new Cycle.

14The four Living-Beings said:

Amen!

And the elders fell down and worshiped.

The four Primary-Figures concur:

Indeed so!

And the founders submit themselves in adoration.

Comments:

5.1–14, etc.: ***Short scroll*** (*BIBLION*), a diminutive of the standard book-word *BIBLOS*, is what the Apocalypse calls itself. The Apocalypse's almost exclusive use of *BIBLION* reflects own the very brevity.
5.2: The usefully ambiguous term *for the Faiths* implies both *from the Faiths* and also *to the Faiths*.
5.2 & 10.1: This particular *mighty Angel* interprets as the Bab. The later (v. 10.1) *mighty Angel* interprets as Baha'u'llah.
5.5 & 6: Now the Ram sets out to interpret the Apocalypse from here up to Chapter 10. From Chapter 10, John will interpret it to the end.
5.6, ***Young Ram* or *ARNION*** is the diminutive of *ARĒN/ARNOS* that means *male sheep*. The word ARNION is specific to Revelation. Previous New Testament Books use *AMNOS* (*Lamb*) or *PASCHA* (*Paschal Lamb*),[A] both clearly for Jesus. But suddenly this ARNION Ram runs onto the Revelation stage, displaying horns and later anger and leadership (vv. 5.6, 6.16 & 7.17), all characterizing rams, not lambs. So to ram the point home and buck centuries of tradition, *Ram* is the most accurate translation of *ARNION*! Apropos, it is now the Ram and no longer the Door that portrays the Bab as the second coming of Jesus.

This Revelation *Ram*
is not the Gospel *Lamb*

[A] **Previous New Testament**, John 1.29, 1.36; Mark 14.12; Luke 22.7; Acts 8.32; 1Peter 1.19. **Displaying horns and later anger**, Rev. 5.8, 6.16, 7.17. ***Ram*** **is the most accurate translation of** ***ARNION***, Aune 52A.323.6d

5.6: Arguably, the Ram still retains his two natural horns and his two natural eyes in addition to his visionary *seven horns and seven eyes*! If so, then his total of **nine** horns/eyes portray the **nine** Manifestations of God. His visionary *seven horns/eyes* portray God's seven prior Manifestations. His two natural horns/eyes portray the Bab and Baha'u'llah as God's two new Manifestations.
5.6, see also 7.17: *At the center of the Throne*, the Co-Founder of the new Baha'i Revelation, is the Ram as a second Enthroned-One.
5.8 & 15.7: *Censers* are *chalices of utterance*.[A]
5.8: This Temple context calls for rendering the generic Greek *kithara* (literally *large lyre*) as *harp*. The Temple's 22-stringed harp outplays its 8- and 10-stringed lyres. In addition, the harp also strums out the 22 letters of the Hebrew alphabet and the 22 chapters of Revelation.[B]
5.8, 14.2–3 & 15.2: *Each bearing a harp* is a verbal-thematic link coding for the Living-Beings and elders.
5.8: The recurring Revelation term *the faithful* (*hoi hagioi*) defines devotion to God, rather than holiness. Thus, *the faithful* interprets for *faithful believers* generally, and it interprets as *faithful Jews, Christians, Muslims* or *Baha'is*, etc. specifically.[C]
5.10: By the term *kingdom as recorded in Revelation...is intended ...a religion*.[D]
5.11, also 3.3 (× 2), 3.19 & 6.2 (see also 19.1 & 6): The translated term *millions, now hundreds of millions* has reluctantly reversed the last-first order of the literal original phrase *hundreds of millions, now millions*. (see page 326).

[A] Baha'u'llah *Scriptures Tablet to the Jews* 47.116
[B] Ps. 92.4
[C] Aune *52A* 359
[D] 'Abu'l-Fadl SW (1916/04/28) 7.3.23

Apocalypse Chapter 6
The Four Horses of the Apocalypse are Forces

6.1Now I looked as the Ram opened the first of the seven seals. At this, I heard one of the four Living-Beings calling out as a voice of thunder: *Come out!*	Now I watch as the Bab interprets my short Revelation tale for Sabaeanism as first of the seven Faiths. At this, I hear foremost Primary-Figure Baha'u'llah thunder: *Exposed!*
2I looked, and behold, a white horse, and the rider on it holding a bow. A crown was given to him. He rode out in order to conquer, then to conquer.	I watch, and behold, the impure force of Power Politics, and the false faith driving it meting out empty justice. Leadership is assigned to it. It sets out in order to win, then to win.
3Next, as he opened the second seal, I heard the second Living-Being calling: *Come out!*	Next, as the Bab interprets my short tale for the second Faith of my own Judaism, I hear this second Primary-Figure as himself shouting: *Exposed!*
4At this, out came another horse, a fiery-red one. The rider on it was allowed to take peace from the planet, so that people might slay each other. Additionally, a huge sword was given to him.	At this, out races another force, bloody Widespread Warfare. The national greed driving it has taken peace from the planet, so that people have been slaughtering each other. Additionally, the atomic bomb has been consigned to it.
5Then as he opened the third seal, I heard the third Living- Being calling: *Come out!*	Then as the Bab interprets my short tale for the third Faith of Zoroastrianism, I hear the third Primary-Figure 'Abdu'l-Baha shouting: *Exposed!*
I looked, and behold, a black horse. And the rider on it holding a yoke in his hand. 6I heard a sound of a voice amid the four Living-Beings calling out: *A quart of wheat for a day's pay! Three quarts of barley for a day's wages! Even: 'Don't abuse the olive oil or wine'!*	I watch, and behold, the black-hearted force of Economic Injustice, and the corporate greed driving it yoking folk with its power. I hear joint input from the four Primary-Figures denouncing: *A day's pay barely buys bread! A month's wages scarcely pays for the train! Even: 'Don't waste money on clothes or shoes'!*

7 Then as he opened the fourth
seal, I heard the voice of the
fourth Living-Being calling:
Come out!

Then as the Bab interprets my short tale for the fourth Faith of Hinduism, I hear input from the fourth Primary-Figure Shoghi Effendi shouting:

Exposed!

8 I looked, and behold, a pale-
green horse, and the rider
astride it whose name was
Death, and *The Unseen* followed
it. They were given power over
one quarter of the earth, to
kill by sword, famine, and
deadly disease, also through
the world's wild animals.

I watch, and behold, the sickening force of Callous Selfishness, and the lazy neglect dominating it dealing death, and skepticism accompanies it. They hold power over the Poor South, to kill by war, starvation, and fatal epidemics, also through human bestiality.

9 Then as he opened the fifth
seal, I saw beneath the
Sacrificial-Altar the souls of
those slain for this Word of
God and for this testimony
that they were bearing 10 They
also cried out in a loud voice,
demanding:
*Master, holy and true, until
when are You not judging
and avenging our blood shed
by those living on the
earth?*

Then as the Bab interprets my short tale for the fifth Faith of Buddhism, I see sustaining his sacrificial love the souls of Persian believers martyred for this Speaker for God and for his testimony that they bear they loudly proclaim, demanding:

Master, unique and true, until when are You not to judge and avenge our deaths caused by enemies living on across the Middle East?

11 At this, each of them was
given a white robe. But they
were told to rest a bit longer
until their fellow servants
and their brothers and sisters
due to be killed (as they had
been) would be fully counted.

At this, each of them is honored for his or her pure virtue. But they are told to wait a while until their fellow-Baha'is and their brothers and sisters in other Faiths due to be martyred (as they have been) will reach a final tally.

12 Then I watched as he
opened the sixth seal. A
violent earthquake erupted.
The sun turned as black as
mourning-haircloth. The
whole full moon turned as
red as blood. 13 The stars of
the sky fell to earth as a
fig-tree, shaken by a gale,

Then I hear the Bab interpret my short tale for the sixth Faith of my own Christianity. Severe turmoil shakes Islam in the 1800s. The Shi'a Islam of Persia is eclipsed by deadly ignorance. The Sunni Islam of the whole Ottoman Empire runs red with blood. The Cadis and Imams of Islam are deposed as

CASTS OFF ITS STERILE-FIGS. [14]THE SKY SNAPPED ASIDE LIKE A SCROLL SCROLLING UP.

their Islam, shaken by stormy change, casts aside these impotent leaders. The true Faith collapses as fast as a Quran scroll scrolls up.

EVERY MOUNTAIN AND ISLAND WAS SHAKEN FROM ITS PLACE. [15]THE EARTH'S RULERS, THE TOP PEOPLE (THE MILITARY LEADERS, THE WEALTHY, AND THE MIGHTY), AND EVERY SLAVE AND FREE PERSON HAVE HIDDEN THEMSELVES IN THE CAVES AND IN THE CRAGS OF THE MOUNTAINS. [16]THEY ARE URGING THE CRAGS AND THE MOUNTAINS:

FALL OVER US! HIDE US FROM THE PRESENCE OF THE ENTHRONED-ONE AND FROM THE ANGER OF THE RAM, [17]*BECAUSE THE GREAT DAY OF HIS ANGER HAS COME. WHO CAN STAND FIRM* [7.1]*AFTER THIS VISION?*

Small countries are annihilated and influential leaders vanish. The Middle East's Caliphs, Sultans, and Shahs, its top people (the military, the rich, and the powerful), and its every worker and owner, seek safety in their homes and from the governments of their nations. They beg their governments and their nations:

Protect us! Save us from the advent of the Founder Baha'u'llah and from the punishment of the Bab, for the Grand Era of their punishment has begun. Who can champion Islam after this event?

Comments:

6.2–8, also vv. 14.20 & 19.11, 14, 18, 19 & 21: ***The Four Horses of the Apocalypse*** depict the dark forces of *Power Politics, Widespread Warfare, Economic Injustice*, and *Callous Selfishness* whose

breeding-ground...is prejudice: prejudice of race and nation, of religion, of political opinion; and the root cause of prejudice is blind imitation of the past—imitation in religion, in racial attitudes, in national bias, in politics. These corrupt systems ensure that *civilization will prove as prolific a source of evil as it had been of goodness when kept within the restraints of moderation*, not least *the civilization of the West* that *hath agitated and alarmed the peoples of the world.*[A]

6.2–8: Exactly the same verse numbers 6.2–8 in the Hebrew Book of Zechariah describe black and white horses blowing as winds towards the (industrialized) North, gray-green horses as winds to the (impoverished) South, and red horses as winds across the whole earth.

6.2–8: Aptly, the four horses of the Apocalypse depict also AD 96's planetary conjunction of Venus's white horse in Sagittarius's bow;

[A] ***Breeding-ground is***, 'Abdu'l-Baha *SWA* 202.247, *Letter to Root*. ***Civilization will prove***, Baha'u'llah *BWF* 138, *GWB* 164.343; Shoghi Effendi *Advent of Divine Justice* 31. ***The civilization of the West***, *Tablets of Baha'u'llah* 6.69

Mars's red horse in Orion's sword; Saturn's black horse in Libra's scales; and Jupiter's green horse in Scorpio's Hades.[A]

6.2: An arrowless bow depicts judgment lacking justice. A non-gold crown depicts leadership lacking divine direction.

6.4: **Atomic Bomb**: In 1860, Baha'u'llah said

> *Split the atom's heart, and lo! Within it thou wilt find a sun.*

In 1912, 'Abdu'l-Baha warned the Ambassador of Japan (of all countries) to Spain about a

> *a stupendous force, as yet, happily undiscovered by man.... Supplicate God...that this force be not discovered by science until spiritual civilization shall dominate the human mind. In the hands of men of lower nature, this power would be able to destroy the whole earth.*[B]

6.5–6: ***Yoke*** and ***scales*** are both valid meanings of *zugos* (whose Hebrew sister-word *zug* means *pair* or *couple*). Hung **down**, *zugos* means *yoke*. Hung **up**, *zugos* means *scales*. Both versions represent economic injustice. Here the *yoke* here binds workers, while *scales* would weigh volumes (here *quarts*) falsely.

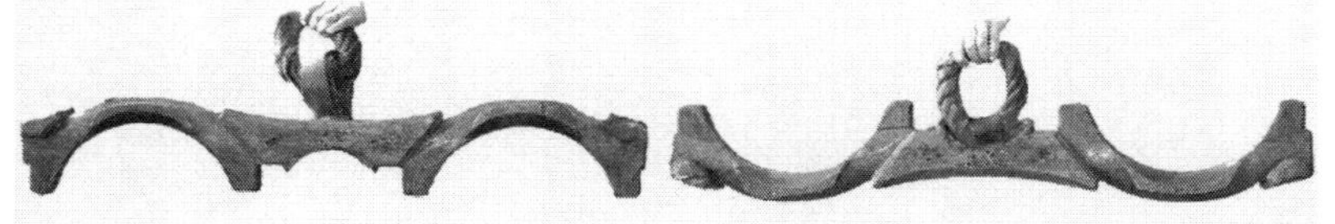

Zugos can mean either *yoke* or *scales*

6.5–6: Wheat for baking bread used to cost about thrice the price of barley for feeding animals.

6.5–6: ***A denarius*** was a day's pay for laborer in AD 95, some $50 in minimum USA wage terms (2009). So *denarius*[C] renders idiomatically as a *day's pay*.

Silver Domitian denarius

[A] Bilderback 33–4

[B] ***Split the atom's heart***, Baha'u'llah *The Seven Valleys and the Four Valleys, the Valley of Knowledge* 12. ***A stupendous force***, 'Abdu'l-Baha (1912) to Viscount Arakawa in *Japan Will Turn Ablaze* 1.9.51

[C] Casey, *Roman Coinage* 7

6.5–6: *Don't abuse the olive oil or wine* also evokes Roman Emperor Domitian's hated AD 91–92 economic edict to destroy vines.
6.9, 8.3a, 8.5, 11.1, 14.18 & 16.7; &; 8.3b, 9.13 & 11.1: ***Temple Altars*** were the Sacrificial and gold Incense Altars. The former burns with the sacrificial love incarnated by Jesus and the Bab. The latter shines the superb love incarnated by Baha'u'llah.
6.10–11, also 10.7 & 19.5–6: *Until when?* gets its answer as v. 10.7's *mystery of God* being fulfilled from vv. 19.5–6 to the end.
6.8: The following grammatical ambiguities echo the uncertainty surrounding death. *Death* rides ***astride***, rather than just ***upon***, its horse. The *Unseen* follows on the **same** or a **different** horse. And *it* may mean ***horse*** or ***death***.

Salvador Dali's *Cosmic Athletes* depicting *Callous Selfishness* and *lazy neglect*,

6.12–14, also 12.1: *The sun...and the moon...are...the Persian and Ottoman kingdoms; for the emblem of Persia is the sun, and that of the Ottoman Empire is the crescent moon....The collapse and fall of the Muslim Caliphate and the virtual collapse of the Shi'ih hierarchy in Persia, were the visible and immediate consequences of the treatment meted out to the Cause of God by the clergy of the two largest communions of the Muslim world....The sun of the heavenly teachings hath been eclipsed, the stars of the divinely-established laws have fallen, and the moon of true knowledge—the educator of mankind—hath been obscured....The standards of guidance and felicity have been reversed, and the morn of truth and righteousness hath sunk in night.*[A]

Alternatively, the *violent earthquake* may interpret as the 1755 Lisbon earthquake that killed 60,000 people; *the sun turned black* as the 1780 *Dark Day*; and *the stars of the sky fell* as the 1833 *Starfall*.

6.13: ***Sterile-figs*** (*olunthoi*) contain clear interpretive meaning. Each fig-tree bears not just its normal tasty summer figs but also small hard sterile-figs that stay on the tree into winter. Mediterranean languages give the two types of fig different names: in Greek *sukona* and *olunthoi*; in Hebrew *te'enim* and *pagim* (*pagim* means preterm babies too); and in Arabic *t'in* and *faj*.

Sterile winter figs

6.14: *The heaven of divine Revelation...is elevated with every Manifestation, and rent asunder with every subsequent one. By 'cloven asunder' is meant that the former Dispensation is superceded and annulled....My decree be such as to cause the heaven of every religion to be cleft* asunder as the *sky is torn apart....The day is approaching when we will have rolled up the world and spread out a new order in its stead.*[B]

[A] ***The sun...and the moon***, Baha'u'llah *KI* 221. ***The collapse and fall***, Shoghi Effendi *PDC* 238.95, 226.90. ***The sun of the heavenly teachings***, Baha'u'llah *KI* 61; 'Abdu'l-Baha *TAB* 1.145

[B] ***The heaven of***, Baha'u'llah *KI* 44. ***My decree be***, Baha'u'llah *PB* 121, *GWB* 18.45, 155.333, 17.42. ***The sky is torn apart***, Quran 82.1, 78.19, 21.104. ***The day is approaching when***, Baha'u'llah *GWB* 143.313, 4.6, *PB* 121, 98–9

6.14 & 16.20: *Islands and the mountains...mean people of influence, and also small kingdoms, which will be destroyed and annihilated at that time...*to *vanish like a mirage, scattered in dust, passed away.*[A]

6.17: *The Day is God's.*[B]

6.17: *Who can stand firm?* finds its answer in Baha'is and their new Baha'i Faith spiritually withstanding the decline of Islam.

6.17/7.1: Here *after this vision* repeats ahead of itself to close Chapter 6 before it goes on to open Chapter 7.

A ***Islands and the mountains***, 'Abdu'l-Baha cited by Brittingham 3. ***Vanish like a mirage***, Quran 78.19–20; Baha'u'llah *ESW* 132, *PB* 98–9, *GWB* 18.45

B Baha'u'llah *Tablets* 8.117, *ESW* 118

Apocalypse Chapter 7
A 144,000 Diamond of Unity

7.1After this vision, I saw four Angels standing at the four corners of the earth, holding back the earth's four winds, so that no wind would blow over the land, across the sea, or upon any tree.	After this event, I see Abraham, Moses, Zoroaster, and Jesus championing their Faiths across the whole Middle East, averting the Middle East's four forces of change, so that no Power Politics, Widespread Warfare, Economic Injustice, or Callous Selfishness could harm their material prosperity, spiritual knowledge, or any of their clergy.
2Then I saw another Angel arising from the rising-place of the sun, bearing a seal from the living God, he cried out in a loud voice to the four Angels who were entrusted with power to harm the land and the sea, saying:	In 1844 I hear the Bab as another Messenger arising from Persia in the East, endorsed by the living God, he calls out as a Proclaimer to the four Messengers who had been entrusted with power to harm material prosperity and spiritual knowledge, urging:
3*Let no harm hurt the land, the sea, or the trees until we stamp the servants of our God on their foreheads.*	*Let no harm hurt our material prosperity, our spiritual knowledge, or our clergy until we have endorsed the servants of our God openly.*
4At this, I heard the number of those stamped, 144,000 persons, stamped from every tribe of heirs of Israel:	At this, I see the emblem of those endorsed, a diamond of unity of many believers progressively perfecting Faiths, endorsed with every quality as successors of the People of Israel who first saw God:
5From a tribe of Judah 12,000 persons stamped	With praise, its first edge of many believers endorsed,
From a tribe of Reuben 12,000 persons,	With vision, its second edge of many believers,
From a tribe of Gad 12,000 persons,	With good-fortune, its third edge of many believers,
6From a tribe of Asher 12,000 persons,	With happiness, its fourth edge of many believers,
From a tribe of Naphtali 12,000 persons,	With striving, its fifth edge of many believers,
From a tribe of Manasseh 12,000 persons,	With forgiveness, its sixth edge of many believers,

7FROM A TRIBE OF SIMEON 12,000 PERSONS,
FROM A TRIBE OF LEVI 12,000 PERSONS,
FROM A TRIBE OF ISSACHAR 12,000 PERSONS,
8FROM A TRIBE OF ZEBULON 12,000 PERSONS,
FROM A TRIBE OF JOSEPH 12,000 PERSONS,
FROM A TRIBE OF BENJAMIN 12,000 PERSONS STAMPED.

With understanding, its seventh edge of many believers,
With unity, its eighth edge of many believers,
With reward, its ninth edge of many believers,
With exultation, its tenth edge of many believers,
With productivity, its eleventh edge of many believers,
With power, its twelfth edge of many believers endorsed.

9AFTER THESE VISIONS I WATCHED, AND BEHOLD, A HUGE CROWD, WHOSE NUMBER NO ONE COULD COUNT, FROM A WHOLE NATION—TRIBES, PEOPLES, AND LANGUAGE-GROUPS—STANDING IN FRONT OF THE THRONE AND THE RAM, WEARING WHITE ROBES, WITH PALMS IN THEIR HANDS,
10CRYING OUT IN A LOUD VOICE, CALLING:

VICTORY TO OUR GOD, TO THE ENTHRONED-ONE, AND TO THE RAM!

After these events I watch, and behold, the Bab's many followers, too many to count, from the whole of Persia—families, peoples, and language-groups—championing the new Baha'i Revelation and its Bab, displaying pure virtue, with victory in their power, loudly proclaiming, calling out:

Victory to our God, to Baha'u'llah His Revelation Founder, and to its Bab!

11ALL THE ANGELS HAD BEEN STANDING AROUND THE THRONE, THE ELDERS, AND THE FOUR LIVING-BEINGS. THEY FELL FACE-DOWN BEFORE THE THRONE AND WORSHIPPED GOD,
12SAYING:

AMEN! TO OUR GOD BE THE PRAISE, THE GLORY, THE WISDOM, THE THANKS, THE HONOR, THE STRENGTH, AND THE MIGHT, INTO THE ERAS OF THE ERAS. AMEN!

All God's Messengers have championed the Baha'i Revelation, its founders, and its Primary-Figures. They have submitted fully to serving the Baha'i Revelation and adoring God, saying:

Indeed so! To our God be all praise, glory, wisdom, thanks, honor, strength, and might, from His old Cycle of Prophecy into His new Cycle of Fulfillment. Indeed so!

13NOW ONE OF THE ELDERS CUTS IN, ASKING ME:

THESE PEOPLE WHO ARE WEARING THE WHITE ROBES, WHO ARE THEY? WHERE HAVE THEY COME FROM?

Now foremost Founder Baha'u'llah cuts in, asking me:

These souls who displaying pure virtue, who are they? Where have they come from?

14 I rejoined, *My Lord, you yourself know!*	I rejoin, *My Lord Baha'u'llah, you yourself know!*
At this, he told me: *These are the ones who are emerging from the great tribulation. They have washed their robes and have bleached them in the blood of the Ram.*	At this, he tells me: *These are the souls of the 20,000 Babi martyrs who passed through Persia's massive mid-1800s massacre. They have refined their virtue and have purified themselves as martyrs like the Bab.*
15 *Due to this they are at God's Throne, within His Temple, conducting its worship day and night. The Enthroned-One shall manifest God's Presence over them.* 16 *They shall neither hunger any longer nor thirst any longer. Neither shall the sun strike them, nor any type of heat.* 17 *For the Ram up at the center aboard the Throne shall guide them. He shall lead them to life on living sources of waters of life. God shall wipe every tear from their eyes.*	*Due to this they have become partners in God's new Revelation, within His new Baha'i Faith, leading its worship as His light has been lighting the night. I the Founder of the Baha'i Revelation manifest God's Presence over them. They lack neither material assets any more nor spiritual sources any more. Neither can Persia hurt them, nor any of its fire-tortures. For the Bab in tandem at the center as Co-Founder of our Baha'i Revelation has guided them. He has led them to spiritual life through living sources of knowledge of life. God has soothed away their sorrows and has kindled light in their eyes.*

Comments:

7.1, also 6.17: This time, *vision* is atypically singular. It interprets as the most recent sixth seal that predicts Islam's spiritual decline.
7.1, also 9.14–5: Here *four angels* interprets validly as four Messengers. But later (vv. 9.14–5) it as validly interprets as four Baha'i Primary-Figures.
7.1, also 6.2–8: ***The four winds*** are the four horses shape-shifted now as the malevolent winds seen by Zechariah (whose Hebrew *ruchot* can mean either *winds* or *spirits*). Apropos, so *long as...the foundations of the social order be blown to the four winds, just so long will humanity be continually exposed to direst peril.*[A]

[A] ***The four winds***, Zech. 6.2–8. ***So long as***, 'Abdu'l-Baha *SWA* 202.247, *Letter to Root*

7.2 & 16.12: The literal translation *rising-place of the sun* works interpretively better for the Bab as a spiritual sun rising in Persia east of Israel than the usual idiomatic translation of *in the East*.

7.3–8: *Every forehead which is illuminated with these lights will be a lamp of guidance and a star whereby all horizons will be lighted* and *glisten with manifest light*.[A]

Apropos, male Jews wear phylactery prayer-boxes (*tefillin*) on their foreheads for worship.

7.5–8, **Tribal Names**, oddly, all lack *the*, which lets them interpret for Baha'is as **new** believers with various human qualities (praise, vision, etc.). The twelve tribal names derive from the tale of how Jacob conceived each son in a wife or maid. In addition, tribal names represent zodiac signs: Judah represents Aries, Issachar Taurus, Zebulon Gemini, Reuben Cancer, Simeon Leo, Gad Virgo, Ephraim Libra, Manasseh Scorpio, Benjamin Sagittarius, Dan Capricorn, Asher Aquarius, and Naphtali has Pisces.[B] Hereby the tribes of Israel signify Zodiac Eras too (see page 102).

7.9: This time, *whole nation* is unexpectedly singular. It interprets specifically as the Persia of the mid-1800s.

7.9–17: From the mid-1800s into modern times Persia's Qajar regime and clergy killed the Bab, his eighteen founder disciples, 20,000 Babis, and many Baha'is. Thus, *the old pattern of herald, prophet, martyrs and establishment of the Faith has been repeated in our times*.[C]

7.15, 12.12, 13.6, 15.5 & 21.3: ***DWELL*** and ***DWELLING*** (***SKĒNOŌ/SKĒNĒ***) act as hidden Greek titles for the *Shechinah Presence* of God. Likewise, lending support, the Onkelos Aramaic Torah also renders the Hebrew word *SHACHNATI* comprehensively as *I will cause My Presence to dwell*.[D] Apropos, the Greek ***skēnoō/skēnē***, the Hebrew ***shechinah/shachnati*** (as the Presence of God), the Arabic ***saken*** (*dwell*), the English ***skein*** (*tent-skin*) and even ***skin*** itself are all sister-words sharing the same *SH-S/CH-K/N* triconsonantal root.

7.17, 21.6, 22.1 & 22.17, **Water** *is knowledge and life....When Christ speaks of water He is symbolizing that which is the cause of Everlasting Life*.[E]

7.17 & 21.4: *Kindled light* is an imported Baha'i interpretive phrase.[F]

[A] 'Abdu'l-Baha *TAB* 1.106, 3.672

[B] **The twelve tribal names**, Gen. 29.32–30.24, 35.17–8, 49.3–27. **In addition, tribal names represent zodiac signs**, Philo *Life of Moses* 2.24.124–6, *Special Laws* 1.16.87; Josephus *Antiquities* 3.7.7

[C] Marzieh Gail, *Introduction ESW* 5.xviii

[D] **The Onkelos Aramaic Torah**, *Targum Onkelos* Aramaic Torah. ***I will cause My Presence to dwell***, Exod. 25.8

[E] Abdu'l-Baha *Paris Talks* 82, *SAQ* 19.92

[F] 'Abdu'l-Baha *SWA* 3.12

7.17, also 5.6: ***Two Enthroned-Ones*** were augured by Judaism as *a man called the Shoot* who *shall sit on his Throne and rule, and ...a Priest...seated on his Throne....Harmonious understanding shall prevail between them.*[A]

The Ram is a second Enthroned-One

[A] Zech. 6.12–3

Apocalypse Chapter 8
A History of Christianity

8.1Next, as he opened the seventh seal, silence settled in the sky for about half-an-hour.

Next, as the Bab interprets my short Revelation tale for the seventh Faith of Islam, peace settles over the young Baha'i Faith for a decade from 1853 to 1863.

2Then I saw the seven Angels standing before God. Seven trumpets were handed to them.

Then I see the seven Middle East Messengers as champions in the service of God. Seven warnings of change had been issued by them.

3Now another Angel, bearing a gold censer, came and stood upon the Altar. Many incenses were handed to him to offer with the prayers of all the faithful at this gold Incense-Altar before the Throne.

In 1863, Baha'u'llah, another Messenger uttering splendid verses, appears and champions his superb love. Abundant prayers are assigned to him to fulfill the hopes of believers in all Faiths through his superb love serving the Baha'i Revelation.

4From the hand of the Angel before God, the smoke of the incenses arose with the prayers of the faithful.

Empowered by Baha'u'llah serving God, the loving spirit of his sprayers inspires the hopes of all faithful believers.

5The Angel has taken up the censer, filled it from the fire of the Altar, and swung at the earth.

Baha'u'llah utters his verses, fills them with the ardor of his superb love, and broadcasts across the Middle East.

At this, thunders, voices, lightning, and an earthquake broke out.

At this, violations shake his Baha'i Revelation, voices rise against it, God's anger flashes, and doubts quake it, as once violations shook my own Christian Revelation, as voices rose against it, as God's anger flashed, and as doubts quaked it.

6Then the seven Angels bearing the seven trumpets prepared to trumpet them.

Back then the seven Middle East Messengers bearing seven warnings of change had been issuing them.

7The first Angel trumpeted. Hail and fire broke out, mixed with blood that was dashed into the earth. One third of

Abraham had warned of change. From AD 110 to 238, persecution and violence by Rome began, mixed with bloodshed that engulfed my

THE EARTH WAS BURNED UP. THIS
THIRD OF THE TREES WAS BURNED
UP. ALL GREEN GRASS WAS BURNED
UP.

Christian world. The western third of my Christian world was crushed. This third of Christian clergy was engulfed. All new converts were lost.

8 THEN THE SECOND ANGEL
TRUMPETED. A KIND OF HUGE
BLAZING MOUNTAIN WAS CAST
INTO THE SEA. ONE THIRD OF THE
SEA TURNED TO BLOOD. 9 THIS
THIRD OF THE CREATURES LIVING
LIVES IN THE SEA DIED. THIS THIRD
OF THE SHIPS WAS DESTROYED.

Then Moses had warned of change. From AD 249 to 311, the vigorously growing Church was crushed by Rome's full fury. The western third of the Church had suffered violence. This third of folk running their lives by the Church had died in spirit. This third of its churches had been wiped out.

10 THEN THE THIRD ANGEL
TRUMPETED. A LARGE STAR,
BLAZING LIKE A TORCH, FELL
FROM THE SKY. IT FELL UPON ONE
THIRD OF THE RIVERS AND UPON
THE SOURCES OF THE WATERS.
11 THE NAME OF THIS STAR WAS
CALLED THE *UNDRINKABLE*. THIS
THIRD OF THE WATERS BECAME
UNDRINKABLE. MANY HUMAN-
BEINGS DIED FROM THESE WATERS
BECAUSE THEY HAD TURNED
BITTER.

Then Zoroaster had warned of change. As a Teacher Emperor Constantine, as passionate as a revelator, made Christianity the Rome's state religion. His AD 325 Council of Nicea corrupted the Byzantine third of Christian knowledge and the sources of its teachings. The infamy of this Emperor had been the *Incredible Creed* of Nicea. This third of Christian teachings had become incredible. Many Christians had died in spirit from these teachings because they had turned harsh.

12 THEN THE FOURTH ANGEL
TRUMPETED. ONE THIRD OF THE
SUN WAS STRUCK, ALONG WITH
ONE THIRD OF THE MOON AND
ONE THIRD OF THE STARS, SO THAT
THIS THIRD OF THEM GREW DARK.
FOR THIS THIRD OF IT, THE DAY
WOULD LACK LIGHT AND THE
NIGHT LIKEWISE.

Then Jesus had warned of change. In AD 410, the western third of Christendom was seized by barbarian tribes, along with this third of its clergy and this third of its teachers, so that this third of them fell into ignorant times. For its last AD 410–622 third, our Christian AD 1–622 Day lacked spiritual light and our dark AD 622–1844 night of Islam lacked light likewise.

[13]NOW I SAW AND HEARD ONE EAGLE FLYING IN MID-HEAVEN, CRYING WITH A PIERCING CRY:	In AD 622 I see and hear foremost spiritually soaring soul Muhammad crying out as a Proclaimer:
TRUMP-TA-RA,	***I, A WARNER, AM HERALDING MY ERA OF CHANGE***
TRUMP-TA-RA,	***THE WARNER BAB SHALL HERALD HIS ERA OF CHANGE***
TRUMP-TA-RA,	***THE WARNER BAHA'U'LLAH SHALL HERALD HIS ERA OF CHANGE,***
TO YOU WHO LIVE ON THE EARTH, FROM THE REMAINING TRUMPET-BLASTS OF THE THREE ANGELS WHO ARE ABOUT TO TRUMPET!	*for you who dwell in the Middle East, from the coming warnings of us three Messengers who are about to proclaim!*

Comments:

8.1: ***Silence...for about half-an-hour*** interprets as the young Baha'i Faith's 1852–1863 peaceful *Baghdad period* as a

> *'delay' of no less than a decade, divinely interposed between the birth of Baha'u'llah's Revelation in the Black Pit and its announcement.*[A]

Tightly, the half-hour of silence interprets for Baha'u'llah's eight years in Baghdad (another two years he was out of the city) as 1/48th part of a 360-year prophetic *day*. The half-hour of silence also echoes two silences of Yom Kippur: the ten *days of woe* before it, and the silent break between its two morning Services.

8.2, etc.: ***Seven Trumpet-Angels***, with Temple-style trumpets and later with pitchers as Pitcher-Angels, fit them into the Abrahamic line of the Middle East Messengers Abraham, Moses, Zoroaster, Jesus, Muhammad, the Bab, and Baha'u'llah (the Bab and Baha'u'llah replace Krishna and Buddha rather as Manasseh and Ephraim replace Joseph and Levi in some tribal lists). The three last loudest 5th, 6th, and 7th Trumpet-Angels are also the three Trumpet-Blast Messengers Muhammad, the Bab, and Baha'u'llah.[B] Jewish folklore says that Angels always stand because they lack knees!

8.2: For a prior spiritual Era, the seven standing angels portrayed the *holy angels Uriel, Raphael, Raguel, Michael, Sariel, Gabriel, Remiel.*[C]

8.3: The term *many incenses* invokes the extra special double-handful of incense burned by the High Priest in the Holy of Holies on Yom Kippur.[D]

[A] Shoghi Effendi *GPB* 151
[B] 'Abdu'l-Baha *SAQ* 56
[C] 1Enoch 20.1–8
[D] Ariel, Richman, *Holy Temple of Jerusalem* 150

8.5: Now the interpretation jumps back to the Christian Era.
8.7: *Kai* renders legitimately as *which* in *which was dashed*, so as to qualify *blood* as its subject.
8.8: In AD 79, the *huge blazing mountain* of Vesuvius had also erupted.
8.10: ***The Council of Nicea***: In AD 325, Constantine wanted to Christianize his new Byzantine Empire. He summoned 300 Christian bishops to Nicea, and held, lodged, dined, and wined them for months until they agreed to agree what Christianity was. The Council was convened under duress and important bishops stayed away. Out of fifty or more Christian scriptures, the Council canonized just the four most neutralist Gospels.[A] For many Christians, the Nicene Creed was, and still is, blasphemous. Flawed, the Council of Nicea split, rather than united, Christianity.
8.10, also 9.1: ***Fallen star*** interprets here negatively for Constantine, and later (v. 9.1) positively for Muhammad.
8.11: ***ABSINTHE/APSINTHE*** is a Greek cover-name that means literally *un-drinkable* (*A-PSINTHOS*). As a herb, absinthe embitters spirits like *Vermouth* and *Absinthe*. As *wormwood,* absinthe cures worm-infestations. As a draught, absinthe was drunk by repentant adulteresses in their cleansing ritual in the Temple.[B]
8.12: In space, *this third of it* fits the territorial Roman third of Christendom seized by barbarian tribes. In time, *this third of it* fits the last AD 410–622 third of the AD 1–622 Christian *Day* from the AD 410 conquest of Rome by Alaric the Goth to the AD 622 rise of the Muslim moon that opened the AH 1–1260 Muslim *Day* as the AD 622–1844 Christian *Night*.
8.13: This spiritually soaring eagle Muhammad was one of the

> *birds of the celestial Throne...sent down from the heaven of the Will of God...to proclaim His irresistible Faith.*

Apropos, the eagle of mythology appears on the US dollar bill and passport landing in the field of time bearing laurels of peace in its right talon and gripping arrows of war in its left talon.[C]
8.13, 9.12, 11.14, 12.12, 18.10, 16 & 19: The three ***Trumpet-Blasts*** or ***Woes*** herald the Days of Eras of Jesus's three successor Messengers, as Temple trumpets once heralded the three High Holy Days of *Passover, Weeks*, and *Tabernacles*.

[A] The many Scriptures discarded by the Council of Nicea included, for example, the Gospels of *Thomas, Mary, Bartholomew, James, the Hebrews, Mark's Secret Gospel, Pseudo-Matthew, The Ebionites,* and the *Latin Infancy Gospel* (*Other Bible*, http://www.earlychristianwritings.com, http://www.gnosis.org/welcome.html)
[B] Ariel, Richman, *Holy Temple of Jerusalem* 103.
[C] ***Birds of the celestial Throne***, Baha'u'llah *KI* 152, 211. **Apropos, the eagle of mythology**, Campbell *Power of Myth* 27, 37

Apocalypse Chapter 9
A History of Islam

9.1 Then this fifth Angel trumpeted.

In AD 622, this Messenger Muhammad warns of his Era of change.

At this, I saw a star fallen from the sky into the earth. He was given the key to the shaft of the Abyss 2 and opened up the shaft of the Abyss. But smoke like the fumes of a huge furnace billowed out of the shaft.

At this, I see Muhammad arriving urgently as a spiritual Teacher from God's One Religion amid the barbarous tribes of Arabia. He bears the remedy for their escape from spiritual error and reveals their escape from spiritual error. But the evil influence of smothering Umayyad propaganda blocks their escape.

From the fumes from the shaft, the sun and the air have turned dark. 3 Out of these fumes swarmed locusts onto the earth. To them has been given power as yellow-scorpions possess power over the earth.

From the evil Umayyad influence blocking their escape, the radiance and the Spirit of Allah are eclipsed. Resulting from this evil influence swarm the Umayyad *Locust* cavalries across the Middle East. To them is given power as their *Scorpion* archers wielding arrow-power over the Middle East.

4 But they have been told not to hurt the grass of the land, or any plant, or any tree, but only the human-beings who do not have God's stamp on their foreheads. 5 Them they have not been allowed to kill but to torment for five months, their torment like torment from a yellow-scorpion when it stings a human-being. 6 In those there days, human-beings will seek death but shall never find it. They will long to die but death shall flee from them.

But they are told not to hurt the People of the Book, or their houses of worship, or their clergy (nor to fire their fields, or flame their fodder, or fell their forests), but only infidels who do not proclaim any Faith openly. Them they are not allowed to kill but to torment for the 150 Muslim years from AH 11 to 161 (AD 632 to 778), their suffering as painful as Scorpion arrows when they pierce infidels. In these yonder years, infidels seek death but cannot find it. They long to die but death eludes them.

7 The appearance of the locusts was like horses ready for battle, with some sort of crowns on their heads, shining like gold.

Their swarming Locust cavalries were forces on the attack, with brass helmets on their heads, shining like gold. Their faces

THEIR FACES LIKE MEN'S FACES, 8YET THEY HAD HAIR LIKE WOMEN'S TRESSES. THEIR TEETH WERE LIKE FANGS OF LIONS. 9THEY HAD CHESTS LIKE IRON BREASTPLATES, WITH THE SOUND OF THEIR WINGS LIKE THE RUSH OF MANY HORSE-CHARIOTS RACING INTO BATTLE.

bearded, yet they wear their hair long like women. Their teeth are dressed like fangs of lions. They have chests with iron breastplates, with the roar of their cavalries like the rush of many future fighter jets swooping into battle.

10THEY POSSESS TAILS WITH STINGERS LIKE YELLOW-SCORPIONS, AND IN THESE TAILS OF THEIRS THEIR POWER TO HURT HUMAN-BEINGS FOR FIVE MONTHS.

They have rear-riders raining arrows as their Scorpion archers, and with these archers of theirs lies their power to hurt infidels for 150 Muslim years from AD 632 to 778.

11AS RULER OVER THEM, THEY HAVE THE EVIL-ANGEL OF THE ABYSS, HIS NAME IN HEBREW *DESTRUCTION*, WHILE IN GREEK HE HAS *DESTROYER* AS A NAME.

As ruler over them, they have the evil Umayyad envoy of error Mu'awiya, his infamy spelling destruction for Jews, while for Christians he is a destroyer notorious.

12THIS NUMBER ONE TRUMPET-BLAST HAS FADED.

THIS FIRST WARNER MUHAMMAD HAS ISSUED HIS WARNING.

LISTEN, A DUO OF TRUMPET-BLASTS IS STILL COMING AFTER THESE VISIONS.

LISTEN, A PAIR OF WARNERS SHALL STILL HERALD THEIR ERAS OF CHANGE AFTER THESE EVENTS.

13THEN THE SIXTH ANGEL TRUMPETED.

IN AD 1844, THE MESSENGER BAB HERALDS HIS ERA OF CHANGE.

AT THIS, I HEARD A SINGLE VOICE FROM THE FOUR HORNS OF THE GOLD INCENSE-ALTAR FACING GOD, 14TELLING THIS SIXTH ANGEL WITH THE TRUMPET:

RELEASE THE FOUR ANGELS BOUND DOWN AT THE RIVER EUPHRATES!

At this, I hear joint input from the four Primary-Figures for the superb love of Baha'u'llah serving God, telling their Messenger Bab as the herald:

You have released us four Messengers whose surging knowledge has been suppressed across the Persian and Turkish Empires!

15SO THE FOUR ANGELS WHO HAD PREPARED FOR THIS HOUR (A DAY PLUS A MONTH PLUS A YEAR) WERE RELEASED TO KILL ONE THIRD OF HUMAN-BEINGS.

So the four Baha'i Primary-Figures who have been waiting for 1844 (ending 391 years) have been released to convert the Shi'a third of Muslims.

16The number of the horse-
troops was 200 million. I
heard this number of them.
17Thus I saw the horses in
the vision and the riders
on them: wearing fiery-red,
hyacinth-blue, and sulfur-
yellow breastplates, with
the heads of the horses like
heads of lions. 18From their
mouths pour fire, smoke, and
sulfur. From the same three
afflictions—from the fire,
smoke, and sulfur pouring
from their mouths—one third
of human-beings was killed.

The number of the cavalries from the Umayyads to the Ottomans has mounted to 200 million. I hear this number of them galloping from AD 632 to 1453. Thus I see the cavalries in my Revelation tale and the riders on them: sporting brilliant red, bright blue, and shining yellow armor, with the thrust of their forces as the power of their cannons and Sultans. From their cannon-muzzles spit flames, fumes, and flashes. From their Sultan-edicts spit terror, evil influence, and despair. From the same three severe lessons—from the flames, fumes, and flashes spat by their muzzles, and from the terror, evil influence, and despair spat by their edicts—the Byzantine third of Christians converts to Islam.

19For the power of the horses
within their mouth is also
within their tails, for their
tails are like serpents with
heads. With them, they wreak
ruin.

For the power of the forces within their muzzle is also within their shafts, for their shafts recoil like serpents with cannon-balls as heads. For the power of the Sultans within their edict is also within their spy-systems, for their spy systems slip as snakes with spies as eyes. With them both, they wreak ruin.

20However, the remaining
human-beings—the ones not
killed by these same afflictions
—have not given up the
products of their hands, so as
not to worship these demonic
spirits and idols, those of
gold, silver, brass, stone, and
wood that cannot see, hear,
or walk!

However, other believers—the Jews and Christians not converting to Islam from these same severe lessons—do not forsake the possessions in their power, so as to stop adoring such fiends and idols—their ornaments of gold, trappings of silver, fittings of brass, statues of marble, and furnishings of mahogany that cannot appreciate, understand, or advance!

21Moreover, they do not
repent of their murders, or
their sorceries, or their
fornication, or their thefts!

Moreover, they do not repent of their murdering, or their drug-dealing, or their exploiting, or their thieving!

Comments:

9.1–2, also 9.11, 11.7, 20.1 & 20.3: The ***Abyss*** is a bottomless *pit of error* whose *gates of Hell have opened wide* and *whose existence thou didst day and night deny,*[A] which invokes the Dudael gorge into which a scapegoat was thrown every Yom Kippur.

9.2–3, also 8.4, 9.18, 14.11, 15.8, 18.9, 18 & 19.3: ***Smoke/fumes*** *denotes grave dissensions, the abrogation and demolition of recognized standards.*[B] Here, *fumes* waft evil the Umayyad influence crippling early Islam. Elsewhere (vv. 8.4 & 15.8), *smoke* wafts a loving spirit.

9.3: ***Locusts and Scorpions*** were the apt nicknames of the first terrifying Muslim cavalries and archers.[C]

9.3: The deadly desert yellow-scorpion fits Arabia better than the less lethal black-scorpion of greener climes.

9.4–6, 12.17, 13.7 & 13.17: ***People of the Book*** is the title that Muhammad gave to his fellow monotheist Jews, Christians, and Sabaeans (extended later to Zoroastrians). In conquered territories, Umayyad generals initially protected People of the Book, forbade harming them, treated them justly, bothered them little, and did not force them to convert to Islam. But later Muslim rulers treated them more harshly, in order for them to *turn to God, maintain the prayer, and pay the prescribed alms.*[D]

9.5 & 10: ***5 months*** decodes as 150 (5 × 30) *days* of Muslim years for the military reign of the Umayyad Locust and Scorpion forces from Muhammad's AH 11 (AD 632) death up to their AH 161 (AD 778) Pyrenees rout of Frankish forces that gained peace for Muslim Spain.[E] Apropos, five months also happens to be the life-span of a locust.[F]

9.6: Under dire circumstances, *death is better than life, and nonexistence better than existence.*[G]

9.11: ***ABBADON*** and ***APOLLYON*** are Hebrew and Greek cover-names whose literal meanings are *destruction* and *destroyer*. Umayyad Caliph Mu'awiya is the best candidate for *the evil-angel of the Abyss*, and as a runner-up his father Abu-Sufyan. Against both Abu-Sufyan and Mu'awiya, Shi'a Muslims pray:

[A] ***Pit of error***, 'Abdu'l-Baha *SAQ* 11.51. ***Gates of Hell***, Baha'u'llah *Summons of the Lord of Hosts* 4.11–2

[B] Baha'u'llah *KI* 76–7

[C] Runciman *Fall of Constantinople 1453* 228 cited by Riggs *Apocalypse Unsealed* 136, 141, 310

[D] **Initially in conquered territories**, **Umayyad generals**, Holt *Cambridge History of Islam* IA 87–92; Lapidus *History of Islamic Societies* 37–45; Riggs *Apocalypse Unsealed* 135. ***Turn to God***, Quran 9.5

[E] Bullough 57–9. Menocal *Ornament of the World* 56–8

[F] Hoyt *Insect Lives* 94–5

[G] 'Abdu'l-Baha *PUP* 53

Allah, curse Abu-Sufyan, Mu'awiya, son of Abu-Sufyan...and make it a never-ending curse.[A]

Even Sunni Muslims are ashamed of Mu'awiya. He died aged 78 from a festering battle-wound and is buried in a town called *Mu'awiya* after him (but Damascus claims another tomb for him).

The tomb of Mu'awiya in a town called *Mu'awiya*

9.12: Coming together, the simultaneous second and third Trumpet-Blasts heralded a single *Day of two Manifestations* for whom *the blast reverberates and the second blast follows* as *a single blast.*[B]

9.14–15, also 7.1: Here *four angels* interpret as Baha'i Primary-Figures. But in v. 7.1 they interpret also as Abraham, Moses, Zoroaster, and Jesus, whose Faiths Islam suppressed over the same 391–year (1453–1844) period across a Middle East ruled by the Ottoman Empire's four Sultans of Asia, Syria, Mosul, and Miyapharekin.[C]

9.14–15 & 16.12: ***THE RIVER EUPHRATES*** *signifies the Turkish and Persian kingdoms* through which the river ran.[D] *Euphrates* is a Greek-Hebrew cover-name meaning literally *good-surging-water* (*EU-FRATĒ*).[E] It traditionally translates as *Euphrates*, but comprehensively interprets as *surging knowledge.*

9.14–15, 18, 11.5, 13 & 19.21: Conversion to a new Faith demands being *killed* spiritually to a prior Faith.

[A] Jalali *Karbala & Ashura: Ziyarah of Ashura* 142

[B] ***Day of two Manifestations***, 'Abdu'l-Baha *SAQ* 39; Shoghi Effendi *GPB* 92. ***The blast reverberates***, Quran 79.6–7, 79.13

[C] Isaac *Newton's Secrets* 29, Yahuda MS1.8f.17v, *Map of the Middle East*

[D] 'Abdu'l-Baha cited by Brittingham 2

[E] Gesenius *Hebrew-Chaldean Lexicon. Fratē/frear* appears also in v. 9.2 for *shaft*

9.14–15: For a prior spiritual Era, *four angels* portrayed Islam's four Primary-Figures Muhammad, Ali, Hasan, and Husayn.
9.15: The interpretation presumes that, in the mid-1800s, some third of Muslims were Shi'a, based on higher Sunni birth-rates.
9.16: The figure *200 million* is a number that is credible historically as the total number of the huge Muslim cavalry hordes that ranged widely between AD 632 and 1453, lured by salvation, land, booty, and women. Just the single horde of thirteenth-century Shah Muhammad of Kharesm numbered 400,000 men.[A]
9.17: Historically, bright red, blue, and yellow were the fashionable colors of Ottoman cavalries.

Ottoman cavalries in their fashionable red, blue, and yellow colors

9.17–19: *Fire, smoke, and sulfur* interpret for cannons militarily and for Sultans politically. The first cannons, invented by Hungarian engineer Orban, were charged and loaded by the muzzle, and hurled 1200-lb missiles. In 1453, these cannons let Ottoman Sultan Mehmet II and his 80,000 troops conquer Constantinople.[B]

[A] Lamb *Gengis Khan* 115
[B] Riggs *Apocalypse Unsealed* 140

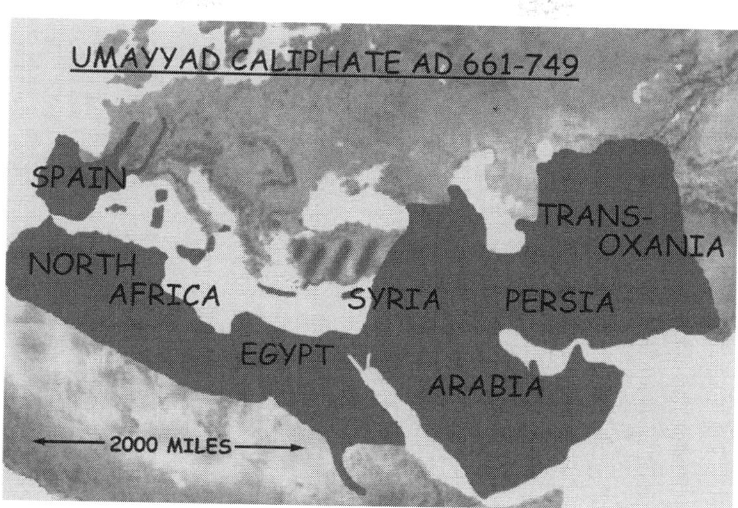

Map of the Umayyad Caliphate
at its greatest territorial extent

Map of the Ottoman Sultanate
at its greatest territorial extent

Apocalypse Chapter 10
The Glory of God

10.1 Next, I saw another mighty
Angel landing from the sky,
wearing a cloud, over his head
that rainbow, his face shining
like the sun, his legs like
pillars of fire, 2 and holding
in his hand an open tiny
scroll.

In 1863, I see Baha'u'llah as another mighty Messenger arriving from God's One Religion, displaying glory amid his human limitations, a leader promising unity to the seven Faiths, his presence emanating the glory of God, his justice glowing reward and gleaming punishment, and his power authorizing a revealed summary of my Revelation tale.

He put his right foot on the
ocean but his left one on the
land. 3 He cried out in a loud
voice just as a lion roars. As he
cried out, the seven thunders
boomed their own voices. 4 As
the seven thunders boomed, I
was about to record. But I
heard a voice from the sky
commanding:

Seal up whatever things the seven thunders have boomed. Do not record them.

He champions spiritual truth but also material prosperity. He calls out as a Proclaimer just as the Lion Primary-Figure asserting his system of justice. As he proclaims, the prior seven Messengers assert their systems of justice. As the seven Messengers assert their systems, I begin to record. But I hear the God of the One Religion commanding:

Set aside the systems of justice that the prior seven Messengers have been asserting. Do not bother to publish them.

5 Then this Angel, whom I had
seen standing on the ocean
and the land, raised his right-
hand to the sky 6 and swore to
the One Who lives into the
Eras of the Eras, Who created
this sky and the things in it,
this land and the things in it,
and this ocean and the things
in it:

No moment shall exist
7 other than these days of the sound of the seventh Angel when he is due to trumpet and the mystery of God will have been fulfilled after He has joyfully proclaimed His own servants the Prophets.

Then Baha'u'llah, whom I see championing spiritual truth and material prosperity, draws power from God's One Religion and promises to the God Who lives from Cycle to Cycle, Who has created His One Religion and what it represents, material prosperity and what it represents, and spiritual truth and what it represents:

No moment matters other than these 40 years (1852–92) of I as the Messenger Baha'u'llah teaching as I announce myself and the hidden intent of God is achieved after He has joyfully proclaimed the Bab and me as His own servant Prophets.

8Now that voice, which I had heard from the sky, was speaking with me again and saying: *Go on! Take this short scroll open in the hand of the Angel standing on the ocean and the land.*	Now God, Whom I had heard for His One Religion, speaks with me again and says: *Go ahead John! Take up your short Revelation tale revealed though the power of Baha'u'llah championing spiritual truth and material prosperity.*
9So I went up to the Angel, asking him to give me the tiny scroll. He tells me: *Take it! Eat it up! It will burn that stomach of yours. Yet in your mouth, it shall taste as sweet as honey.*	So I approach Baha'u'llah, asking him to share with me his brief of my Revelation tale. He tells me: *Take it up! Take it in! Its pain will hurt the core of your being. Yet from the start, it shall reveal its loving spirit.*
10So from the hand of the Angel I took the tiny scroll and ate it up. Indeed, in my mouth, it did taste as sweet as honey. But when I swallowed it, my stomach turned bitter.	So authorized by Baha'u'llah I take up the brief of my Revelation tale and take it in. Indeed, from the start, it does reveal its loving spirit. But as I take it in, the core of my being hurts.
11Now they tell me: *You yourself must again prophesy about and against many peoples, nations, language-groups, and rulers.*	Now God and Baha'u'llah tell me: *You must now interpret about and against many peoples, nations, language-groups, and leaders.*

Comments:
10.1, also 1.16: ***Face shining like the sun*** portrays Baha'u'llah as the ***Glory of God*** emanating the glory of God.[A]
10.2: In this context, rendering *podes* as *legs* takes the meaning of *reglayim*, the equivalent Aramaic word in the *Crawford Aramaic Text*.[285-C]
10.2–4: ***Tiny scroll*** interprets also as the *Most Holy Book* (*Kitab-i-Aqdas*) of Baha'u'llah, which is the *principal repository of that Law...the writer of the Apocalypse...described.* The *Most Holy Book* details the new system of justice of Baha'u'llah.[B]
10.10–11: Up to this point, the Ram as the Bab has been interpreting Revelation. Since the Bab is soon to die in v. 11.12, in his stead the mighty Angel Baha'u'llah appoints John to interpret Revelation to the end.

[A] The Bab *Selections from the Writings of* 92
[B] Shoghi Effendi *Aqdas* 12–6. *GPB* 213

Apocalypse Chapter 11
The Central Apocalypse Prophecy

11.1 NOW THERE WAS GIVEN TO ME A REED LIKE A ROD SAYING: *COME AND MEASURE THE TEMPLE OF GOD, THE ALTAR, AND THE WORSHIPERS WITHIN IT.*

Now there is introduced to me Baha'u'llah as a guide and source of divine inspiration saying: *Come and present the Faiths of God, their sacrificial and superb love, and the believers in them.*

2 *BUT SET ASIDE THE COURTYARD OUTSIDE THE TEMPLE. DO NOT MEASURE IT, FOR IT HAS BEEN GIVEN OVER TO GENTILE NATIONS. THEY WILL TRAMPLE THE HOLY CITY FOR 42 MONTHS.*

But ignore the external material part of His Faiths. Do not bother to present it, for it has been assigned to gentile nations. They will crush unique Jerusalem for the 1,260-year Muslim Era (AD 622–1844).

3 *REGARDLESS, I SHALL APPOINT*
MY TWO WITNESSES. THEY WILL
PROPHESY FOR 1,260 DAYS,
WEARING SACKCLOTH,
4 *THESE*
MEN ARE THE TWO OLIVE TREES
AND THE TWO LAMPS STANDING
BEFORE THE MASTER OF THE
UNIVERSE.

Regardless, I have appointed my two Delegates Muhammad and Ali. They are revealing Islam for the 1,260-year Muslim Era (AD 622–1844), promoting the Torah and Gospel, these men are Arabia's anointed Revelators and Islam's Founder and Promoter championing the service of the Master of the Universe.

5 *IF ANYBODY WANTS TO HURT THEM, FIRE FLAMES FROM THEIR MOUTHS AND CONSUMES THESE ENEMIES OF THEIRS. IF ANYBODY SHOULD WANT TO HURT THEM, THIS IS HOW HE IS DOOMED TO DIE.*

If Umayyads hurt them, teachings shoot from their mouths and demolish these enemies of theirs. Whenever any Umayyad tries to hurt them, this is how he gets converted to Islam.

6 *THESE MEN HAVE THE POWER TO SHUT OFF THE SKY, SO THAT RAIN MAY NOT FALL DURING THE DAYS OF THEIR PROPHESYING. THEY ALSO HAVE POWER OVER THE WATERS TO TURN THEM TO BLOOD AND TO STRIKE THE LAND WITH EVERY TYPE OF AFFLICTION WHENEVER THEY WANT.*

These men have Elijah's power to curb the knowledge provided by God's One Religion, so that its spiritual bounty is limited during the years of them revealing it. They also have Moses and Aaron's power over knowledge to turn it violent and to punish Arabia's barbarous tribes with every type of severe lesson as often as they like.

*7 But when they end their
testimony, the beast rising
from the Abyss will wage war
against them. It shall defeat
them. It shall kill them,
8 with their dead body strewn
across the main-square of the
great city that is spiritually
called 'Sodom and Egypt',
where also their Lord was
crucified.*

But as Muhammad and Ali finish testifying for God, the brutal Umayyad Caliphate arising in its spiritual error wages jihad against their true Islam. It corrupts their true Islam. It destroys their true Islam, with its spiritless shell exposed to public view across the central Umayyad region that spiritually tested Abraham at Sodom and Moses in Egypt, where also Jesus, their Lord too, was crucified in Jerusalem.

*9 For 3½ days, folk from the
peoples, tribes, language-
groups, and nations watch
over their dead body and will
not let their corpses be
buried in a tomb.*

For the 1,260-year Muslim Era (AD 622–1844), Muslims from the peoples, families, language-groups, and nations make a spectacle of their Islam's spiritless shell and do not let its prayer or fasting rituals fade.

*10 At this, the people living
across the earth rejoice over
them. They shall be glad
and exchange gifts, because
these same two Prophets have
tormented the people living
across the earth.*

At this, Europeans and Asians around the Middle East gloat over them. They make merry and join against them, because these same two Prophets, Muhammad and Ali, have afflicted the citizens around the Middle East.

*11 But after the 3½ days, a
spirit of life from God
entered them. They stood
back on their feet, so that
deep dread fell on those who
were watching them.*

But after the 1,260-year Muslim Era, a spirit of life from God revives them as the Bab and Quddus in 1844. They champion justice again, so that deep dread strikes their enemies who have begun to recognize them.

*12 Next, they heard a loud voice
from the sky, telling them:
'Rise up here!'*

Next, they hear God proclaim for His One Religion, commanding them:

'Ascend to heaven!'

*At this, they rose into heaven
on that cloud as their
enemies were watching them.*

In 1849 and 1850, they return martyred to the divine realm in clouds of smoky glory as their enemies begin to recognize them.

13 *On that there day, a large earthquake erupted. One tenth of the city fell. In this earthquake, 7,000 individual human-beings were killed. The rest were terrified. Yet they glorified the God of heaven.*

In this yonder time, large earthquakes erupt in Istanbul and Shiraz. One tenth of Shiraz falls. Due to this earthquake, many faithful Muslims are converted. The rest are terrified. Yet they celebrate the Glory of the God of His One Religion.

14 This second Trumpet-Blast has faded.

The second Warner Bab has issued his warning.

Listen! The third Trumpet-Blast is soon coming.

Listen! The third Warner is now heralding his Era of change.

15 Then this seventh Angel trumpeted.

In 1863 this Messenger Baha'u'llah heralds his Era of change.

At this, loud voices arose in the sky, saying:

The kingdom of the world-order of our Lord and of His Messiah has come to exist. He shall reign into the Eras of the Eras.

At this, all Proclaimers of God's One Religion announce:

The spiritual order of the global civilization of our Lord God and of His Messiah Baha'u'llah is launched. He has led the Cycle of Prophecy into the Cycle of Fulfillment.

16 The 24 elders seated on their thrones before God fell face-down and worshipped God, 17 saying:

We thank You, Almighty Lord God,

- ***You The-Is***
- ***You The-Was,***

that You have assumed Your great power and have begun to reign.

The 24 Baha'i founders established in the service of God submit fully and adore God, saying:

We thank You, Almighty Lord God,

- ***You-God-of-Later-Eras***
- ***You-God-of-Earlier-Eras,***

that You have engaged the great power of Your teaching and have assumed control.

18 *Meanwhile, nations have been raging. But Your anger has come, along with the time for the dead to be judged; to award the reward to Your servants the Prophets, to the faithful, and to those who honor Your name, the*

Meanwhile, nations have been acting punishingly. But Your punishment has come, along with the time for the spiritually dead to be judged; to award Baha'u'llah to Your servant Prophets, to faithful believers, and to folk who honor You by many names, the

HUMBLE AND THE IMPORTANT; AND TO RUIN THOSE WHO RUIN THE PLANET.	*humble and the important; and to strip abusers who are stripping the planet.*
19 NOW THE TEMPLE OF GOD OPENED UP IN THE SKY.	In 1863 the Baha'i Faith of God is revealed by His One Religion.
WITHIN HIS TEMPLE APPEARED ITS ARK OF HIS COVENANT.	Within God's Baha'i Faith appears 'Abdu'l-Baha as its Center of His Covenant.
LIGHTNINGS, VOICES, THUNDERS, AN EARTHQUAKE, AND HEAVY HAIL BROKE OUT.	The anger of God flashes as voices rise against His Revelation, as violations shake it, as doubts quake it, and as severe torments beat down on its Covenant-Breaker heretics.

Model of the Jewish Temple viewed from the Northeast

Comments:

11.1–19: **'Abdu'l-Baha's 1918 *Commentary on the Eleventh Chapter of the Revelation of St. John***[A] addresses all of Chapter 11 and supplies most of the following citations for it.

11.1: *This reed is a Perfect Man who is likened to a reed...emptied from all save God....Whatever He utters is not from Himself, but...is a divine inspiration....That reed is like a rod....the helper of every impotent one, and the support of human beings....the rod of the Divine Shepherd.*[B]

11.1: Although this Altar is **within** the Temple, it is not gold, so interprets generically for both the Sacrificial-Altar and the Incense-Altar.

11.1–2: ***The Temple*** symbolizes *the One Religion or Law of God....Measuring is the discovery of proportion....Compare the Temple and the altar and them that are praying therein ....Investigate...their true condition and discover in what degree and state they are, and what conditions, perfections, behavior and attributes they possess....In the...seventh century...when Jerusalem was conquered...the outer court was taken and given to the Gentiles* [Muslims] *to govern and control Jerusalem forty and two months, signifying twelve hundred and sixty days; and as each day signifies a year...twelve hundred and sixty years...prophesies the duration of the Dispensation of Islam when Jerusalem was trodden under foot....As the period of twelve hundred and sixty years has expired, Jerusalem, the Holy City, is now beginning to become prosperous, populous and flourishing. Anyone who saw Jerusalem sixty years ago* [1844], *and who sees it now* [1912], *will recognize how populous and flourishing it has become, and how it is again honored....the 'cleansing of the Sanctuary', prophesied by Daniel... accomplished....The 'forty and two months,' during which the 'Holy City,' as predicted by St. John the Divine, would be trodden under foot, had elapsed. The 'time of the end' had been ushered in.*[C]

The *times of the gentiles* describes primarily the 1,260-year Muslim Era that ran from AD 622 to 1844, but also other gentile nations like polytheistic Romans, Christian Byzantines, and Zoroastrian Persians who had occupied Jerusalem before the Muslims.

[A] 'Abdu'l-Baha *SAQ* 11.45–61

[B] 'Abdu'l-Baha *SAQ* 11.45

[C] ***The Temple symbolizes the One Religion or Law of God***, 'Abdu'l-Baha *SAQ* 11.46–8. ***Measuring is the discovery of***, 'Abdu'l-Baha *SAQ* 11.46–8. ***The 'cleansing of the Sanctuary'***, Shoghi Effendi *GPB* 58

11.3: ***Two Witnesses*** *refers to Muhammad and Ali...Muhammad ...the root, and Ali the branch, like Moses and Joshua...clothed in old raiment....Nor would their Cause appear new; for Muhammad's spiritual Law corresponds to that of Christ in the Gospel, and most of His laws relating to material things correspond to those of the Pentateuch,* which made the Quran *the truth confirming...the Torah and the Gospel.*[A]

11.4: **Muhammad and Ali**: Muhammad, *a prophet like Moses,* along with Ali, were *two souls...likened to olive trees...Lamps were lighted by olive oil....The candlestick is the abode of the light and from it the light shines forth...from these illumined souls...standing in the service of God, and educating...the barbarous nomad Arab tribes of the Arabian peninsula....They reached the highest degree of civilization, and their fame and renown became worldwide.*[B]

11.5: *No one would be able to withstand them....If a person wished to belittle their teachings and their law, he would be surrounded and exterminated by this same law which proceedeth out of their mouth; and everyone who attempted to injure, to antagonize and to hate them would be destroyed by a command which would come out of their mouth.*[C]

11.6: *The law and teachings of Muhammad, and the explanations and commentaries of Ali, are a heavenly bounty; if they wish to give this bounty, they have power to do so. If they do not wish it, the rain will not fall....Rain stands for bounty....The prophethood of Muhammad was the same as that of Moses....The power of Ali was the same as that of Joshua: if they wished, they could turn the water of the Nile into blood, so far as the Egyptians and those who denied them were concerned....The cause of their life, through their ignorance and pride, became the cause of their death,* just as *the kingdom, wealth and power of Pharaoh and his people... became, through their opposition, denial and pride, the cause of death, destruction, dispersion, degradation and poverty. Hence these two witnesses have power to destroy the nations....'Smite the earth with all plagues, as often as they will'* means *that they also would have the power and the material force necessary to educate the wicked and those who are oppressors and tyrants...educate and correct the ferocious, bloodthirsty, tyrannical nomad Arabs, who were like beasts of prey.*[D]

[A] ***Two Witnesses refers to***, 'Abdu'l-Baha *SAQ* 11.49. ***Muhammad...the root***, 'Abdu'l-Baha *SAQ* 11.48–9. ***The truth confirming***, Quran 3.2

[B] ***A prophet like Moses***, Deut. 18.18; Quran 73.15, 61.5–6. ***Two souls***, 'Abdu'l-Baha *SAQ* 11.49 (for ***likened to olive trees***, *Zech.* 4.2–3, 11.14).

[C] 'Abdu'l-Baha *SAQ* 11.49–50

[D] ***The law and teachings of Muhammad***, 1Kings 17.1; 'Abdu'l-Baha *SAQ* 11.50.

11.7–8: *'When they shall have finished their testimony' means when they...have delivered the divine message, promoting the Law of God and propagating the heavenly teachings, to the intent that the signs of spiritual life might be manifest in souls, and the light of the virtues of the world of humanity might shine forth, until complete development should be brought about among the nomad tribes.*[A]

11.7–8: ***'The beast'****...means the Umayyads who attacked them from the pit of error, and who rose against the religion of Muhammad and against the reality of Ali—in other words, the love of God. The beast made...spiritual war, meaning that the beast would act in entire opposition to the teachings, customs and institutions of these two witnesses, to such an extent that the virtues and perfections which were diffused by the power of those two witnesses among the peoples and tribes would be entirely dispelled, and the animal nature and carnal desires would conquer. Therefore, this beast making war against them would gain the victory—meaning that the darkness of error coming from this beast was to...kill those two witnesses... destroy the spiritual life which they spread abroad in the midst of the nation, and entirely remove the divine laws and teachings, treading under foot the Religion of God.*[B]

11.8: ***Great city***: Here *polis* in Greek may mean not just city, but also *country*,[C] rather as *medineh* in Arabic means *city* while its Hebrew sister-word *medinah* means *country*. This lets *great city* interpret big as the central Umayyad Caliphate domains of Syria and Egypt.

11.8–9: ***'Their bodies'*** *means the Religion of God, and 'the street' means in public view. The meaning of 'Sodom and Egypt', the place 'where also our Lord was crucified', is....this region of Syria, and especially Jerusalem, where the Umayyads then had their dominions....Here the Religion of God and the divine teachings first disappeared....like a dead body without spirit....The nations, tribes and peoples would...make a spectacle of the Religion of God: though they would not act in accordance with it, still, they would not suffer their bodies—meaning the Religion of God—to be put in the grave....In appearance they would cling to the Religion of God and not allow it to completely disappear from their midst, nor the body of it to be entirely destroyed and annihilated. Nay, in reality they would leave it, while outwardly preserving its*

The prophethood of Muhammad, 'Abdu'l-Baha *SAQ* 11.50
[A] 'Abdu'l-Baha *SAQ* 11.51
[B] 'Abdu'l-Baha *SAQ* 11.51
[C] Liddell-Scott *Greek-English Lexicon* 570–1

name and remembrance. Those 'kindreds, people and nations' signify those who are gathered under the shadow of the Qur'án, not permitting the Cause and Law of God to be... entirely destroyed and annihilated—for there are prayer and fasting among them—but the fundamental principles of the Religion of God, which are morals and conduct, with the knowledge of divine mysteries, have disappeared; the light of the virtues of the world of humanity, which is the result of the love and knowledge of God, is extinguished; and the darkness of tyranny, oppression, satanic passions and desires has become victorious. The body of the Law of God, like a corpse, has been exposed to public view for...the cycle of Muhammad. The people forfeited all that these two persons had established, which was the foundation of the Law of God, and destroyed the virtues of the world of humanity, which are the divine gifts and the spirit of this religion, to such a degree that truthfulness, justice, love, union, purity, sanctity, detachment and all the divine qualities departed from among them. In the religion only prayers and fasting persisted...as if these two persons were dead.[A]

11.10: *Other nations and races, such as the peoples of Europe and distant Asia...saw that the character of Islam was entirely changed, the Law of God forsaken* and they *became happy, and rejoiced that corruption of morals had infected the people of Islam, and that they would...be overcome by other nations.... This people which had attained the summit of power, how degraded and downtrodden it is now* [1908]. *The other nations ...'send gifts to one another,' meaning that they should help each other, for 'these two prophets'...overcame the other nations and peoples of the world and conquered them.*[B]

11.11: **The Bab and Quddus** were the returns of Muhammad and Ali. *After...twelve hundred and sixty years...the teachings and the law that Muhammad established and Ali promoted...were again established....The spirituality of the Religion of God had been changed into materiality, and virtues into vices, love...into hatred, enlightenment into darkness, divine qualities into satanic ones, justice into tyranny, mercy into enmity, sincerity into hypocrisy, guidance into error, and purity into sensuality....These divine teachings, heavenly virtues, perfections and spiritual bounties were again renewed by the appearance of the Bab and the devotion of Quddus....Holy breezes were diffused, the light of truth shone forth, the season of the life-giving spring came, and*

[A] 'Abdu'l-Baha *SAQ* 11.52–3
[B] 'Abdu'l-Baha *SAQ* 11.53–4

the morn of guidance dawned. These two lifeless bodies again became living, and these two great ones—one the Founder and the other the Promoter—arose and were like two candlesticks, for they illumined the world with the light of truth.[A]

11.12: In 1849, a crazed mob tore Quddus apart alive and burned him in *a death which even Jesus Christ...had not faced in...His greatest agony.* In 1850, a firing squad executed the Bab, and *the very moment the shots were fired a gale of exceptional violence arose and swept over the city. From noon till night a whirlwind of dust obscured the light of the sun, and blinded the eyes of the people.* During their martyrdoms, they heard *the voice of God, saying: You have performed all that was proper and fitting in delivering the teachings and glad tidings; you have given My message to the people and raised the call of God, and have accomplished your duty. Now, like Christ, you must sacrifice your life...and be martyrs. And that Sun of Reality* [the Bab], *and that Moon of Guidance* [Quddus], *both, like Christ, set on the horizon of the greatest martyrdom and ascended to the Kingdom of God....Many of their enemies, after witnessing their martyrdom, realized the sublimity of their station and the exaltation of their virtue, and testified to their greatness and perfection.*[B]

The clouds of smoke that engulfed the Bab and Quddus at death shone their glory too.

11.13: ***A large earthquake*** struck Istanbul in 1850, the day after the execution of the Bab. But it was in 1852 that the prophesied large

Shiraz...'earthquake', foreshadowed in no less weighty a Book than the Revelation of St. John...threw the whole city into turmoil and wrought havoc amongst its people...greatly aggravated by the outbreak of cholera, by famine and other afflictions. As this *earthquake occurred in Shiraz....Many people were destroyed....All the remnant lamented and cried day and night, and were occupied in glorifying and praying to God.*

The *7,000 killed* codes for *many faithful Muslims are converted* (see page 312). In addition, the figure of *7,000 killed* fits a likely immediate traumatic death-toll of the Shiraz earthquake given that its full death-toll was some 13,000 persons.[C]

[A] 'Abdu'l-Baha *SAQ* 11.54–5, also Shoghi Effendi *GPB* 58

[B] ***A death which even Jesus Christ***, Shoghi Effendi *GPB* 49–50. ***The very moment***, Shoghi Effendi *GPB* 53. ***The voice of God, saying***, 'Abdu'l-Baha *SAQ* 11.55.

[C] **A *large earthquake* struck Istanbul in 1850**, Alexis Perrey, *Note sur les tremeblements de terre*, Academie Royal des Sciences des letters et de Beaux Artes Bulletin 18.4.291–308, 1st series, 1855 cited by Riggs *Apocalypse Unsealed* 310. ***The Shiraz...'earthquake'***, Shoghi Effendi *GPB* 53–4. ***Earthquake occurred***

1.14–5, also 8.13, 9.12, 12.12, 18.10, 16 & 19: The three ***Woes*** or ***Trumpet-Blasts*** herald the spiritual Era of the last three loudest 5th, 6th, and 7th Angels after Jesus, each appearing *with the sound of the great trumpet,*[A] as:

- The Muslim AH 1–1260 (AD 622–1844) Era of Jesus's ***Comforter*** Muhammad. This ***first woe*** *is the appearance of the Prophet, Muhammad, sent as a warning*. By *'trumpet' is meant the trumpet call of Muhammad's Revelation.*[B]
- The Babi AH 1260–80 (AD 1844–63) Era of Jesus's ***Door*** the Bab. This ***second woe*** *is the appearance of the Bab* as *the Blast...blown on the Trumpet of the Bayan.*[C]
- The Baha'i AH 1280 (AD 1863) Era of Jesus's spiritual ***Father*** Baha'u'llah. This ***third woe*** *is the day of the manifestation of Baha'u'llah, the day of God...near to the day of the appearance of the Bab...none other than* Baha'u'llah's *Pen of Glory* emitting the *stunning trumpet-blast* to which *St. Paul...alluded as the hour of the 'last trump'...of God'.*[D]

11.15: **Baha'u'llah** as *the seventh angel is a man qualified with heavenly attributes, who will arise with heavenly qualities and character....In that day of God, the Spiritual and Divine Kingdom will be established, and the world will be renewed; a new spirit will be breathed into the body of creation; the season of the divine spring will come; the clouds of mercy will rain; the sun of reality will shine; the life-giving breeze will blow; the world of humanity will wear a new garment; the surface of the earth will be a sublime paradise; mankind will be educated; wars, disputes, quarrels and malignity will disappear; and truthfulness, righteousness, peace and the worship of God will appear; union, love and brotherhood will surround the world; and God will rule for evermore—meaning that the Spiritual and Everlasting Kingdom will be established. Such is the day of God....The Kingdom is God's...invested with radiant sovereignty....By 'kingdom' as recorded in Revelation...is intended... a religion....The Kingdom here means the manifestation of Himself;*

in Shiraz, 'Abdu'l-Baha *SAQ* 11.55. **Its full death-toll**, Nasser Engheta, Editor *Sobhe Emruz*, personal communication Los Angeles 1999

[A] 'Abdu'l-Baha *TAB* 1.145

[B] ***Comforter***, *Comforter* (*Menachem* in Hebrew) is one name for the Jewish Messiah. New Testament *references* [John 14.16, 26, 15.26, 16.7, 13–4] *to...'Paraclete'* [*Comforter*] *refer to Muhammad's Revelation*, Shoghi Effendi *Letters from the Guardian to Aust. and N.Z.* 41, *Light* 494. ***This first woe is***, 'Abdu'l-Baha *SAQ* 11.56. ***Sent as a warning***, Quran 33.45. ***'Trumpet' is meant***, Baha'u'llah *KI* 116

[C] ***Second woe is***, Shoghi Effendi *GPB* 95–6; 'Abdu'l-Baha *SWA* 3.13. ***The Blast...blown***, *Tablets of Baha'u'llah* 17.244, 8.118, 8.131

[D] ***Third woe is***, 'Abdu'l-Baha *SAQ* 11.56, *GPB* 92. ***None other than***, *Tablets of Baha'u'llah* 6.61. ***Stunning trumpet-blast***, *Tablets of Baha'u'llah* 8.117. ***St. Paul...alluded***, Shoghi Effendi *GPB* 96

and He will issue all the laws and teachings which are the spirit of the world and everlasting life and will *subdue the world by spiritual power...by true love...promote these divine teachings by kindness and righteousness...educate the nations and people that, notwithstanding their various conditions, their different customs and characters....will...like the wolf and the lamb, the leopard, the kid, the sucking child and the serpent, become comrades, friends and companions....Barriers between nations will be completely removed, and all will attain perfect union and reconciliation.*[A]

11.18: God's *teachings opposed the passions of the other peoples ....They do not follow* [His] *precepts, counsels and teachings ....They will be deprived...veiled from the light....Those who are deprived of the spirit of the love of God...will be judged with justice....They will arise to receive that which they deserve....He will distinguish the righteous by endless bounty....He will entirely deprive the neglectful....The ignorance and want of knowledge of the people of error will be recognized.... Consequently, the destroyers will be destroyed.*[B]

11.18 & 16.5, also 1.4, 1.8 & 4.8: The term *THE-IS-COMING* no longer follows *THE-IS and THE-WAS*, for the Baha'u'llah's of as the 7th Trumpet-Angel and 3rd Trumpet-Blast Messenger makes *THE-IS-COMING* passé.

11.19: ***The Temple*** or *sanctuary of Jerusalem is likened to the reality of the Law of God....The laws, conventions, rites and material regulations are the city of Jerusalem....'There was seen in His temple the ark of His Testament'* means that *the Book of His Testament will appear in His* [New] *Jerusalem, the Epistle of the Covenant will be established, and the meaning of the Testament and of the Covenant will become evident....The Cause of God will fill the world. The violators of the Covenant will be degraded and dispersed, and the faithful cherished and glorified ..firm and steadfast in the Covenant.*[C]

11.19: 'Abdu'l-Baha was *extolled by the writer of the Apocalypse as 'the Ark'* to denote his *rank and station...designed by the Lord of the Covenant Himself to shield and support, after His ascension* as *the appointed Center of His Faith*. The *Book of the Covenant*, the will of Baha'u'llah, named 'Abdu'l-Baha as his successor and the *Centre of the Covenant.*[D]

[A] ***The seventh angel is*** 'Abdu'l-Baha *SAQ* 11.56–7; Shoghi Effendi *GPB* 92. ***The Kingdom is God's***, Baha'u'llah *GWB* 17.42. ***By 'kingdom'***, 'Abu'l-Fadl SW (1916/04/28) 7.3.23. ***The Kingdom here means***, 'Abdu'l-Baha *SAQ* 11. 58

[B] 'Abdu'l-Baha *SAQ* 58–9

[C] ***The Temple or Sanctuary of Jerusalem***, 'Abdu'l-Baha *SAQ* 11.60. ***'There was seen in His Temple'***, 'Abdu'l-Baha *SAQ* 11.59–60

[D] ***Extolled by the writer***, Shoghi Effendi *GPB* 239. ***Baha'u'llah's will***, Baha'u'llah *Tablets, Book of the Covenant* 15.221–2

Apocalypse Chapter 12
Muslim Militarism cripples True Islam

11.19 Then the Temple of God opened up in the sky.	In AD 622 the Muslim Faith of Allah is revealed by His One Religion.
Within His Temple appeared its Ark of His Covenant.	Within Allah's Muslim Faith appears Ali as its Center of His Covenant.
Lightnings, voices, thunders, an earthquake, and heavy hail broke out.	The anger of Allah flashes as voices rise against His Revelation, as violations shake it, as doubts quake it, and as severe torments beat down on its Umayyad heretics.
12.1 Now a magnificent sign has appeared in the sky: a woman wearing the sun, beneath her feet the moon, over her head a crown of 12 stars, 2 and pregnant. She shrieks in labor and in the throes of childbirth.	Now a magnificent scene is being played out by God's One Religion: noble Islam shining the spiritual sun of Muhammad and the emblem sun of Persia, based on the spiritual moon of Ali and the emblem moon of Turkey, led by 12 divine Imams, and bearing a mission. It labors painfully and suffers severely to deliver its Twelfth Imam as the Bab.
3 But an additional sign has appeared in the sky. Behold, a huge fire-red dragon with seven heads, ten horns, and seven sovereign-crowns on its heads.	But an extra scene is playing out within God's One Religion. Behold, Muslim Militarism's monstrous bloodthirsty Umayyad Caliphate with seven domains, ten dynastic Caliph names, and seven caliphs sovereign over its domains.
4 Its tail is sweeping down one third of the stars of the sky and has cast them into the earth.	It finally kills four of 12 of the Shi'a Imams of God's One Religion and publicly shames them.
The dragon was, and has been, standing in front of the woman due to give birth, so that whenever she would deliver her child, her child it would devour. 5 Regardless, she bore an heir, a male who is destined to guide all nations	Muslim Militarism from AD 632 has been, and up to 1844 is, opposing the true Islam due to produce its successor, so that when it does deliver him, him it kills. Regardless, it delivers its successor, the 1844 Bab who is to direct all nations with his strong

with an iron rod. This child of hers was snatched up to God and to His Throne.

Law. This young Bab of true Islam is plucked up by firing squad to God and into His Baha'i Revelation in 1850.

6 The woman had fled to the desert where there she had a spot prepared by God, so that there they would nourish her for 1,260 days.

True Islam had retreated to the Arabian desert in AD 666 where here it had Mecca and Medina prepared by Allah, so that here true Muslims sustained it for the 1,260-year Muslim Era.

7 Next, war broke out in the sky—Michael-like-God and his angels having to fight the dragon. The dragon and its evil-angels fought back. 8 But they lacked the might. Nor was any place left for them in the sky any longer. 9 So the huge dragon, the ancient serpent, known as the lying evil and the hatred that deceives the whole inhabited world, was cast down to the earth and its evil-angels were cast down with it.

Next, war breaks out for God's One Religion—Baha'u'llah-manifesting-God and his envoys fighting Muslim Militarism. Muslim Militarism and its evil envoys fight back. But they prove impotent. Nor is any role left for them in God's One Religion any more. So monstrous Muslim Militarism, the primeval sinfulness, known for its lying evil and hatred that has tricked the whole Middle East society, is publicly shamed and its evil envoys are shamed with it.

10 Then I heard a loud voice in the sky proclaiming:

Launched right now is the victory, the power, and the rule of our God with the authority of His Messiah, for the accuser of our brothers and sisters, denouncing them before our God day and night, has been cast down. 11 They themselves have defeated it through the blood of the Ram. Through this Word of their testimony, they have not clung to life, right into death.

Then I hear Baha'u'llah as the Proclaimer of God's One Religion announcing:

Launched right now is the victory, the power, and the rule of our God with my authority as His Messiah, for Qajar Persia falsely accusing our fellow-Baha'is, denouncing them before our God as His light has been lighting the night, has been shamed. They themselves have defeated it through the death of the Bab. Through this divine Speaker in their testimony, they have not clung to life, right into martyrdom.

12 *Thanks to this, rejoice you heavens, meaning you manifesting God's Presence in them!* ***Trump-Ta-Ra*** *to you earth and sea, for lying evil has razed down into you with intense fury, knowing that it has little time.*

Thanks to this, rejoice you Faiths, meaning you Messengers manifesting God's Presence in them! **My Baha'i Era is warning** *you material and spiritual realms of Persia, for lying evil is slashing down into you with great fury, knowing that its time is done.*

13 When the dragon saw that it had been cast into the earth, it hunted for the woman who bore the boy.

When Muslim Militarism realizes that it is publicly shamed, it hounds the true Islam that is to deliver the Bab.

14 However, the great eagle's two wings were given to the woman for her to fly to her spot in the desert where she might be nourished there for 3½ seasons, far from the face of the serpent.

However, great Muhammad's Hasan and Husayn were given to true Islam for it to retreat to its place in the Arabian desert where it has been sustained in Mecca and Medina for the 1,260-year Muslim Era, far from the Caliphates, Sultanates, and Imamates fronting for primeval sinfulness.

15 From its mouth the serpent spewed a river of water after the woman, so as to wash her
away. 16 But the land helped
the woman. The land opened up its mouth and swallowed up the river that the dragon had spewed from its mouth.

From its capitals primeval sinfulness gushes out floods of lies against true Islam, so as to overwhelm it. But decent desert folk help true Islam. Salt-of-the-earth Bedouin joke at and laugh off the lies that Muslim Militarism has been gushing from Damascus, Baghdad, Cairo, Istanbul, and Teheran.

17 Consequently, the dragon got angry over the woman. Furthermore, it set out to fight the rest of her children who were keeping the commands of God and bearing this testimony of Jesus. So it was standing firm on the sand of the sea.

Consequently, Muslim Militarism punishes true Islam. Furthermore, it fights its Sabaean, Jewish, and Zoroastrian People of the Book who obey the teachings of God, and its Christians who bear this testimony of Jesus. So it is championing over the many descendants of Abraham.

Comments:
11.19: This verse has closed Chapter 11, and now goes on to repeat in opening Chapter 12. This time, the Temple and its Ark of the Covenant depict the earlier Muslim Revelation and its custodian Ali. Like 'Abdu'l-Baha, Ali was the true successor of the Founder of his Faith as the adopted son, cousin, and son-in-law of Muhammad. For his part, 'Abdu'l-Baha was the son of Baha'u'llah. Both Faiths also had their heretics: Islam had its Umayyads, the Baha'i Faith had its *Covenant Breakers*.
12.1–17: **'Abdu'l-Baha's *Commentary on the Twelfth Chapter of the Revelation of St. John***[A] addresses much of Chapter 12 and supplies many of the following citations for it.
12.1: ***A woman wearing the sun*** *is that bride, the Law of God that descended upon Muhammad*, a spiritual *Sun of Prophethood* and Ali, a *Moon of divine guidance...the sun of the heavenly teachings...and the moon of true knowledge....These twelve stars are the twelve Imams...the promoters of the Law of Muhammad and the educators of the people, shining like stars in the heaven of guidance....The sun with which she was clothed, and the moon which was under her feet, are the two nations which are under the shadow of that Law....The emblem of Persia is the sun, and that of the Ottoman Empire is the crescent moon. Thus the sun and moon are the emblems of two kingdoms which are under the power of the Law of God....The brightest 'star' shining in the 'crown' mentioned in the Revelation of St. John* is *Imam Husayn, the most illustrious of the successors of the Apostle of God....Genesis 17.20 refers to the twelve Imams* as the *twelve princes* that Ishmael begat.[B]
12.2: For prior spiritual Eras, the *woman wearing the sun* portrayed Zion promoting Judaism or Hagar and Fatima promoting Islam; and her *crown of 12 stars* fitted the 12 tribes of Ishmael, the 12 tribes of Jacob, or the 12 Apostles of Jesus.
12.2: Far from repetitive hype, *shrieking in labor and in the throes of childbirth* is accurate in resounding the double pain of the first stage, and then of the second stage, of childbirth.
12.2: The Law of God *fell into the greatest difficulties and endured great troubles and afflictions until a perfect offspring was produced —that is, the coming Manifestation.*[C]

[A] 'Abdu'l-Baha *SAQ* 11.68–72
[B] ***A woman dressed in the sun is that bride***, 'Abdu'l-Baha *SAQ* 13.68. ***Sun of Prophethood***, Baha'u'llah *KI* 221. ***The sun of the heavenly teachings***, Baha'u'llah *KI* 61–2. ***These twelve stars are***, 'Abdu'l-Baha *SAQ* 13.68. ***The brightest 'star' shining***, Shoghi Effendi *GPB* 94. ***Genesis 17.20 refers to***, Shoghi Effendi *Light* 1662.494
[C] 'Abdu'l-Baha *SAQ* 13.68–9, *SWA* 145.172

Morning Star portraying Shi'a Islam as
a woman wearing the sun, beneath her feet
the moon, over her head a crown of 12 stars

12.3: **The Umayyad Caliphate** is depicted by the dragon. *These signs are an allusion to the dynasty of the Umayyads who dominated the Muhammadan religion. Seven heads and seven crowns mean seven countries and dominions over which the Umayyads had power: they were the Roman dominion around Damascus; and the Persian, Arabian and Egyptian dominions, together with the dominion of Africa—that is to say, Tunis, Morocco and Algeria; the dominion of Andalusia, which is now Spain; and the dominion of the Turks of Transoxania. The Umayyads had power over these countries. The ten horns mean the names of the Umayyad rulers—that is, without repetition...ten names....Several of them bear the same name...two Muaviya, three Yazid, two Valid, and two Marvan....The first was Abu Sufyan, Amir of Mecca and chief of the dynasty of the Umayyads, and the last was Marvan.*

The dragon of mythology was a serpent that had an eagle's wings. The dragon of the Umayyad Caliphate was a serpent of primeval sinfulness possessing that had the wings of the corrupted eagle of crippled Islam.[A]

12.4: *The Umayyads...destroyed the third part of the holy and saintly people of the lineage of Muhammad who were like the stars of heaven.*[B] Respectively in AD 670, 713, 733, and 680, they poisoned the Second Imam Hasan, the Fourth Imam Ali, and the Fifth Imam Muhammad, and beheaded the Third Imam Husayn.

12.5: **The Bab** was *this child...the promised Manifestation, the offspring of the Law of Muhammad. The Umayyads were always waiting to get possession of the Promised One...from the line of Muhammad, to destroy and annihilate Him; for they much feared the appearance of the promised Manifestation, and they sought to kill any of Muhammad's descendants who might be highly esteemed....This great son is the promised Manifestation...born of the Law of God and reared in the bosom of the divine teachings. The iron rod is a symbol of divine power and might* with which *He will shepherd all the nations of the earth....'Her child was caught up unto God and to his throne'...is a prophecy of the Bab, Who ascended to the heavenly realm, to the Throne of God, and to the center of His Kingdom....Because of the despotism of the dragon the child was carried up to God. After twelve hundred and sixty days the dragon was destroyed, and the child...the Promised One, became manifest...*this *'Man Child'...in the Book of Revelation, destined to 'rule all nations with a rod of iron', had released, through his coming, the creative energies, which, reinforced by the effusions of a swiftly succeeding and infinitely mightier Revelation,*

[A] ***These signs are an allusion***, 'Abdu'l-Baha *SAQ* 13.69–70 (Persian *v*'s replace Arabic *w*'s). **The dragon of mythology**, Campbell *Power of Myth* 37

[B] 'Abdu'l-Baha *SAQ* 13.69–70

were to instill into the entire human race the capacity to achieve its organic unification, attain maturity and thereby reach the final stage in its age-long evolution.[A]

For prior spiritual Eras, the male heir portrayed Jesus or Muhammad.

12.6: *The Law of God fled to the wilderness, meaning the vast desert of Hijaz....The Arabian Peninsula...became the abode and dwelling place, and the center of the Law of God....Twelve hundred and sixty days mean the...years that the Law of God was set up in the wilderness of Arabia.*[B]

For prior spiritual Eras, the *woman* who *fled into the desert* portrayed Hagar saving Ishmael in the Paran desert, or Mary saving Jesus in the Egyptian desert.

12.7: ***MICHAEL-LIKE-GOD*** is a comprehensive rendering of a Hebrew cover-name that means literally *One-who-is-like-God* (*MI-CHA-EL*).

12.9–15 & 20.2: **Serpent [dragon]** means *attachment...of the spirit to the human world* that *led the soul and spirit of Adam from the world of freedom to the world of bondage....From the height of purity and absolute goodness he entered into the world of good and evil....Attachment of the spirit to the human world, which is sin, was inherited by the descendants of Adam ....That enmity continues and endures....This bondage is identical with sin....Because of this attachment...men have been deprived of essential spirituality and exalted position....Jealousy, greed, the struggle for survival, deception, hypocrisy, tyranny, oppression, disputes, strife, bloodshed, looting and pillaging all emanate from the world of nature.*[C]

12.14: The two wings of the great eagle of Muhammad could also portray Ali and Fatima as Islam's earlier (small-*f*) founders.

12.14: Eagles fighting serpents is a classic mythological theme.[D]

12.17, also 22.16: The seed of Abraham now populates the Middle East. No wonder! Four thousand years ago, Abraham sired three sets of fraternal tribal leaders: 12 through his maid Hagar and their son Ishmael; 12 through his first wife Sarah and their son Isaac and grandson Jacob; and 10 through his second wife Keturah and their six sons. Thus, God kept His promise to make the seed of Abraham *as many as grains of sand on the seashore.*[E] The Bab descended from Abraham and Hagar. Baha'u'llah descended doubly, from both Abraham and Sarah, and separately from Abraham and Keturah.

[A] ***The Bab was this child***, 'Abdu'l-Baha *SAQ* 13.68–9, *SWA* 145.172. ***'Man Child'...in the Book of Revelation***, Shoghi Effendi *GPB* 58

[B] 'Abdu'l-Baha *SAQ* 13.70–1, *SWA* 145.172

[C] ***Serpent means attachment...of the spirit***, 'Abdu'l-Baha *SAQ* 30.123–5. ***Jealousy, greed, the struggle for***, 'Abdu'l-Baha *SWA* 180.206

[D] Campbell *Power of Myth* 37

[E] Gen. 22.17–8, 12.2–3, 18.18, 26.4

Apocalypse Chapter 13
The Number of the Beast is AD 666

13.1The dragon was standing firm on the sand of the sea. From this sea I saw a beast arising, with ten horns and seven heads: on its horns ten sovereign-crowns and on its heads blasphemous titles.

Muslim Militarism is championing over the coast of the sea. From this Red Sea I see the brutal Umayyad dynasty arise in AD 666, sporting ten names and seven domains: its ten dynastic ruler names of supreme Caliphs and the rulers of its domains blasphemously titled caliphs.

2The beast that I saw was like a leopard, its feet like a bear's, and its mouth like a lion's maw. To it, the dragon gave its power and its throne, plus great authority.

The brutal Umayyad Caliphate that I see expands as fast as the Greek *Empire of the Leopard*, has the strength of the Persian *Empire of the Bear*, and makes Damascus its capital like the Assyrian *Empire of the Lion*. To it, Muslim Militarism supplies its power and its capital Damascus, plus great authority.

3Also I saw one of its heads as if fatally wounded. But its mortal wound healed up.

Also I see its foremost lone domain of Umayyad Spain all but destroyed by the Abbasids in AD 749. But its decisive destruction is thwarted.

The whole earth became fervent after the beast. 4People worshiped the dragon that had given power to the beast. They also worshiped the beast, boasting:

Who is like the beast?
Who can fight it?

The whole Middle East has gone mad after the brutal Umayyad Caliphate. Muslims adore the Militarism that supplies power to the brutal Caliphate. They also adore its brutal dynasty, boasting:

No dynasty is as brutal!
No one can fight it!

5It was given a mouth speaking boasts and blasphemies. It was assigned authority to act for 42 months. 6It opened its mouth with blasphemies against God, insulting His name and His Presence (those who manifest God's Presence in heaven).

It has been given Damascus gushing pomp and profanity. It has been assigned authority to operate for the 1,260-year Muslim Era. It exploits Damascus in uttering profanities against God, cursing his name *Allah* and His *Presence* (Messengers who manifest Allah's Presence in Revelations).

7It was even allowed to wage war against the faithful and

It even wages jihad against faithful believers and defeats them. It gains

DEFEAT THEM. IT WAS GRANTED POWER OVER EVERY TRIBE, PEOPLE, LANGUAGE-GROUP, AND NATION.

power over all Middle East families, peoples, language-groups, and nations.

8ALL THOSE PEOPLE LIVING ON THE EARTH WHOSE NAME WAS NOT TO HAVE BEEN LISTED IN THE *BOOK OF LIFE* OF THE RAM-TO-BE-SLAIN, DUE TO A FOUNDING OF A WORLD-ORDER, WILL WORSHIP IT.

All those Middle Easterners who go unacclaimed as morally decent per the executed Bab, due to the founding of a militaristic Muslim world-order, adore it.

9LET WHOEVER HAS EARS HEAR.

Let alert readers understand.

10WHOEVER IS DESTINED FOR CAPTIVITY, INTO CAPTIVITY HE GOES. WHOEVER IS TO BE KILLED WITH A SWORD, WITH A SWORD HE SHALL BE KILLED. THIS INDEED SHOWS THE ENDURANCE AND BELIEF OF THE FAITHFUL.

True Muslims whom God captivates, Umayyad captives must become. True Muslims who succumb to the sword of the words of Muhammad, to swords of Umayyad steel must succumb. This indeed displays the tenacity and truth of faithful Muslims.

11NEXT, I SAW ANOTHER BEAST ARISING FROM THE LAND. IT HAD TWO HORNS LIKE A RAM'S, BUT IT HISSED LIKE A DRAGON.

Next, I see another brutal dynasty of the Ottoman Sultanate rise from the Asian steppes in 1299. It sports the titles *Sovereign* (*Sultan*) and *Successor* (*Caliph*) as its sheep's clothing, but it menaces as Muslim Militarism.

12IT EXERCISES THE FULL AUTHORITY
OF THE FIRST BEAST ON ITS BEHALF.
IT MAKES THE EARTH AND THE
PEOPLE LIVING ON IT WORSHIP
THAT FIRST BEAST WHOSE MORTAL
WOUND HAD HEALED.
13IT WORKS
MAGNIFICENT WONDERS, SO AS
EVEN TO MAKE FIRE FALL FROM
THE SKY TO THE LAND IN FRONT OF
HUMAN-BEINGS.

It exercises the full authority of the first brutal Umayyad Caliphate on its behalf. It forces the Middle East and the citizens in it to adore that first brutal Caliphate whose decisive destruction of Spain has been thwarted. It runs magnificent schemes, so as even to make fire flash from heaven to earth in front of its Sunni Muslims.

14WITH THE WONDERS THAT HAVE BEEN GIVEN TO IT TO WORK ON BEHALF OF THAT BEAST, IT DECEIVES THOSE LIVING ON THE EARTH, TELLING THOSE LIVING ON THE EARTH TO MAKE A COPY OF THAT BEAST THAT HAD THE WAR-WOUND, YET LIVED ON.

With the schemes that it runs on behalf of that brutal Caliphate, it tricks those living in the Middle East, telling Middle Easterners to create an Ottoman clone of that brutal Caliphate that has faced destruction, yet lives on as Umayyad Spain.

15 INTO THIS COPY OF THAT BEAST IT HAS BEEN ALLOWED TO BREATHE AN EVIL SPIRIT, SO THAT THIS COPY OF THE BEAST MIGHT BE DICTATORIAL AND CAUSE TO BE KILLED WHOEVER HAS NOT WORSHIPED THIS COPY OF THE BEAST.	Into its Ottoman clone of that brutal Caliphate it instills its own evil spirit, so that its clone of the brutal Caliphate is dictatorial and is sentencing to death whoever refuses to adore this Ottoman clone of the brutal Caliphate.
16 IT MAKES EVERYBODY—THE HUMBLE AND THE IMPORTANT, THE WEALTHY AND THE POOR, THE FREE AND THE SLAVE—TO BE GIVEN A TATTOO ON THEIR RIGHT-HAND OR ON THEIR FOREHEAD, 17 SO THAT NO ONE CAN BUY OR SELL EXCEPT THE BEARER OF THE TATTOOED NAME OF THE BEAST OR THE NUMBER OF HIS NAME.	It forces everybody—the humble and the important, the rich and the poor, the owners and the workers—to take Mu'awiya's right-wrist *kharaj* tax-tattoo on landowners or his forehead *jizya* pole-tax tattoo on non-Muslims, so that no trader can function except somebody wearing the tattooed name of brutal Mu'awiya or the code of his authority.
18 HERE INDEED IS WISDOM. LET THE PERSON WITH A MIND FIGURE-OUT THE NUMBER OF THE BEAST, FOR IT IS A NUMBER OF A HUMAN-BEING. HIS NUMBER IS *666.*	Here indeed is insight. Let the reader with a mind discern the code of brutal Mu'awiya, for it is a code of this evil Muslim. His code is the AD 666 year that he proclaimed as Caliph.

Comments:

12.17/13.1: *It was standing firm on the sand of the sea* closed Chapter 12 and now goes on to repeat in opening Chapter 13. This time the sea surges a different meaning.
13.1: For a prior Era, the *beast* depicted also Rome's regime and rulers.
13.1–18: *This prophecy was related to the Holy Land.*[A]
13.1: *In Revelation...by a 'beast' is intended an earthly government.* The term *beast* sometimes *signifies a body politic and sometimes a single person which heads that body.*[B]'
13.1: ***Ten horns and seven heads*** continue to depict the names and domains of Umayyad Caliphs.
13.1, The ***blasphemous title*** *Caliph* (*Successor*) was a title first assumed by the Rashidun Caliphate, then by the Umayyad Caliphate to help it usurp Muhammad's successorship from Ali and his line of Imams.

[A] 'Abdu'l-Baha *Má'idih-i-Ásmání* 2.82 translated by Badi Daemi
[B] ***In Revelation...by***, 'Abu'l-Fadl SW (1916/04/28) 7.3.23. ***Beast* sometimes *signifies a body politic***, Isaac *Newton's Secrets* 19, *Rules for Interpreting the Words and Language of Scripture*, Yahuda MS1.1f.12r

13.2 & 11: These sea and land beasts call up the Old Testament sea monster *Leviathan* and land monster *Behemoth*.[A] Apropos, Abyss (Greek *A-BUSSOS* or *NO-BASE*) originally applied to the bottomless sea.
13.2: The prophet Daniel saw *a lion, a bear, a leopard,* and a fourth *dreadful, horrible, extremely strong, beast* with *ten horns*. The first three beasts interpret as the serial Assyrian, Persian, and Greek Empires. The fourth beast interprets as the Umayyad Caliphate.[B]
13.3: The terse clause *one of its heads as if fatally wounded...but its mortal wound healed up* augurs how the sole Umayyad domain of Spain, under Abd Al-Rahman, escaped the Abbasid conquest of the other six Umayyad domains in AD 749.
13.8 & 17.8: Both *founding* (*katabolēs*) and *a world-order* (*kosmou*) lack *the*, which lets them interpret for the Umayyad Caliphate founding Muslim Militarism as its **new** world-order.
13.13: Making *fire fall from the sky onto the land* fits *Greek fire*, as early napalm and/or concave mirrors focusing the sun.
13.14: For prior spiritual Eras, *a copy of the beast* depicted brutal Domitian (AD 81–96) succeeding Nero (AD 54–68); Umayyads (AD 666–749) displacing Romans (AD 95–476); or Yazid (AD 645–83) poisoning his poisoner father Mu'awiya (AD 602–680).
3.15: Ottoman Sultans often strangled high-ranking people **at** the dead of night, **as** the dead of night![C]
13.16–17, etc.: Cruel ***tax-tattoos***, begun by the evil Umayyad Mu'awiya, were revised by the Ottomans to enforce the jizya poll tax on non-Muslims and the kharaj tax on landowners. Even today, some Ethiopian Falasha women and Egyptian Copts still take the jizya (the Copts as a mark of honor, and now on the wrist).
13.18: ***The number of the beast 666*** *refers to the year....That beast is the Umayyad King who appeared in the year 666 AD*, the first Umayyad Caliph Mu'awiya who proclaimed himself in AD 666.[D] Further, his two Revelation titles numerologically total 666 too:

- ***The Caliph*** as *O KALIPH* spelt with the Greek letters ***O*** (*omicron*) = 70, ***K*** (*kappa*) = 20, ***A*** (*alpha*) = 1, ***Λ*** (*lambda*) = 30, ***Λ*** (*lambda*) = 30, ***E*** (*epsilon*) = 5, ***I*** (*iota*) = 10 and ***Φ*** (*phi*) = 500
- ***Beast*** as *THĒRION* spelt with the Hebrew letters **ת** (*tav*) = 400, **ר** (*resh*) = 200, **י** (*yud*) = 10, **ו** (*vav*)= 6, and **נ** (*nun*) = 50.

[A] ***Leviathan*** Isaiah 27.1, Job 3.8, 41.1 & 12, Ps 74.14, 104.26; ***Behemoth*** Job 40.15
[B] Dan. 7.4–7, 23–4; Riggs *I, Daniel* in http://bci.org/prophecy-fulfilled/id1.htm under *Chapter 13*
[C] Wheatcroft 75–6
[D] ***The number of the beast 666***, 'Abdu'l-Baha *Má'idih-i-Ásmání* 2.82 translated by Badi Daemi. **The first Umayyad Caliph Mu'awiya who proclaimed**, http://encyclopedia.stateuniversity.com/pages/15490/Muawiyah-I.html,http://en.wikipedia.org/wiki/Muawiya_I

Other cross-cultural interpretations of 666 include

- The sum total of the 6×6 Muslim magic sun square (each of whose rows, columns, and diagonals totals 111)[A]
- Its Arabic (*sete-sete-sete*) other meaning *woman-woman-woman*
- The sum of the first six digitalized Latin numbers *I* (1), *V* (5), *X* (10), *L* (50), *C* (100), and *D* (500)
- The gematric Hebrew *w-w-w* (now pronounced *v-v-v*) standing for ***world-wide-web***
- The barcode skeleton, whose three long pairs of thin lines at its two sides and center each codes for *6*. Take a look!

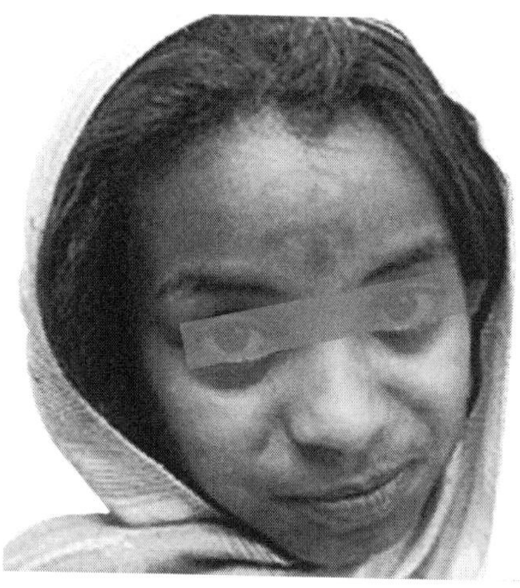

Jizya cross tattooed on the forehead of a Falasha Ethiopian girl

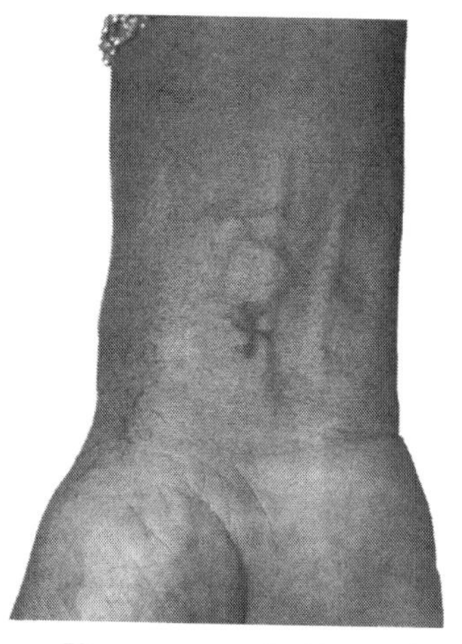

Jizya cross tattooed on the right wrist of an Egyptian Copt

[A] http://www.calendersign.com/images/soquadr.JPG

Apocalypse Chapter 14
A New Gospel

14.1 Now I looked, and behold,
the Ram standing on the
beacon Mount Zion, and with
him some 144,000 persons with
his name and the name of his
father written on their
foreheads.

Now I watch, and behold, the Bab championing and beckoning to Mount Carmel, and with him his diamond of unity of many followers progressively perfecting the Faiths endorsing him and his spiritual Father Baha'u'llah openly.

2 Next, I heard a sound from
the sky like a rushing of many
waters and like a pealing of
powerful thunder. This sound
that I heard was like harpists
playing their harps.

Next, I hear broadcast by God's One Religion bountiful knowledge and powerful justice. This music to my ears echoes the Primary-Figures and founders heralding harmony.

3 They are singing some sort of
new song before the Throne
and before the four Living-
Beings and the elders.

They are celebrating the Bab's new Gospel in serving the Baha'i Revelation and in serving their own selves as its four Primary-Figures and its founders.

Nobody, except these 144,000
people bought from the earth,
has been able to learn this
song. 4 These are the ones
unspoiled by women, for they
are celibates. These are the
ones who follow the Ram
wherever he may go, whenever
he may come. These are the
ones who have been bought
from among human-beings as a
prime-pick of God and for the
Ram. 5 No falsehood is heard
from their mouths, for they
are faultless.

Nobody, except this diamond of unity of believers progressively perfecting Faiths, recruited from the Middle East, can yet grasp his new Gospel. These are faithful Muslims unspoiled by materialism, for they are pure spiritually. These are unspoiled Muslims who are true followers of the Bab in the Persia of 1844. These are true followers who have been recruited from among Muslims as the first choice by God and for the Bab. No lies cross their lips, for they are beyond reproach.

6 Next, I saw another Angel
flying in mid-heaven, bearing
eternal good news to proclaim
joyfully to those seated over
the earth and over every
nation, tribe, language-group,
and people, 7 calling out in a
loud voice:

Next, I see another Messenger, Jesus, soaring spiritually, bearing a new eternal Gospel to proclaim joyfully to the rulers of the Middle East and to all of its nations, families, language-groups, and peoples, calling out as a Proclaimer:

FEAR GOD AND GLORIFY HIM, FOR THE HOUR OF HIS VERDICT HAS COME. WORSHIP THE CREATOR OF THE SKY AND THE LAND AND OF AN OCEAN AND SOURCES OF WATERS.	*Revere God and celebrate the glory of God, for the century of His verdict has come. Adore the Creator of the spiritual and material realms and of new spiritual truth and new sources of knowledge.*
8 ANOTHER ANGEL, A SECOND, FOLLOWED, CALLING:	Another Messenger, Muhammad as a second, joins in, calling:
IT HAS FALLEN! GREAT CONFUSED BABYLON HAS FALLEN. IT HAS MADE ALL NATIONS COLLAPSE INTOXICATED FROM THE WINE OF THE FURY OF ITS FORNICATING!	*It must be destroyed! Monstrous Malignant Materialism must be destroyed. It has been driving all nations mad from the grip of its furious exploitation!*
9 ANOTHER ANGEL, A THIRD, FOLLOWED THEM, CALLING OUT IN A LOUD VOICE:	Another Messenger, Baha'u'llah as a third, joins them, calling out as a Proclaimer:
AS FOR WHOEVER WORSHIPS THE BEAST (MEANING THIS COPY OF IT) AND TAKES A TATTOO ON HIS FOREHEAD OR HIS HAND, 10 THEY TOO SHALL DRINK FROM THE WINE OF THE FURY OF GOD POURED FULL-STRENGTH INTO THE CUP OF HIS ANGER	*As for you Persians who adore the brutal Muslim system (meaning this Qajar Persian clone of it) and run its religious discrimination or its cruel taxation, you too shall be gripped by the fury of Allah focused in the full fate of His punishment.*
FACING THE HOLY ANGELS AND FACING THE RAM, THEY SHALL BE TORMENTED IN FIRE AND SULFUR.	*Facing God's unique Messengers and facing the Bab, you shall be afflicted with unbelief and despair.*
11 THE SMOKE FROM THEIR TORMENT RISES INTO ERAS OF ERAS. THESE WORSHIPERS OF THE BEAST (MEANING THIS COPY OF IT), AND WHOEVER TAKES THE TATTOO OF ITS AUTHORITY, GET NO REST DAY OR NIGHT.	*The effects of your torment send a signal from an old Cycle to a new Cycle. You Persians adoring the brutal Muslim system (meaning this Qajar clone of it), and you running cruel taxation on its authority, shall get no respite as God's light is lighting the night.*
12 HERE INDEED IS THE ENDURANCE OF THE FAITHFUL WHO TAKE TO HEART THE COMMANDMENTS OF GOD, INCLUDING THE FAITH OF JESUS.	Here indeed is the tenacity of faithful believers who take seriously the teachings of God, including the Faith of Jesus.
13 NEXT I HEARD A VOICE FROM THE SKY SAYING:	Next I hear the God of the One Religion recalling:

Record how blessed are those who die in a Lord, from now on— *Certainly so,* says the Spirit, *so that they may rest from their tireless labors, for their deeds follow after them.*	*You published in AD 95 how blessed would be the folk who die believing in a Messenger, from that time on—* *Certainly so,* adds His Manifestation Baha'u'llah, *so that they get respite from their tireless labors, for their good deeds have blazed their trail.*
14 Now I looked, and behold, a white cloud, and seated on the cloud an apparition of a Human-Being wearing on his head a gold crown and bearing in his hand a sharp scimitar.	Now I watch, and behold, pure glory, and established in his glory amid human limitations, that divine Human-Being Baha'u'llah leading with superb authority and exacting keen judgment with his power.
15 Then another Angel came from the Temple, crying out in a loud voice to the one seated on the cloud: *Swing this scimitar of yours to reap, because the hour to reap has come, for the grain-harvest of the earth has dried out.*	Then another Messenger, Muhammad, appears for the Muslim Faith, crying out as a Proclaimer to Baha'u'llah established in glory amid his human limitations: *Execute this judgment of yours to reward, because your century to reward has begun, for goodness in the Middle East has faded.*
16 So the one seated on the cloud cast his scimitar out across the earth and the earth was reaped.	So Baha'u'llah established in glory amid his human limitations judges the Middle East and the Middle East is rewarded.
17 Next came another Angel from the Temple in the sky, he himself also bearing a sharp scimitar.	Next the Bab appears as another Messenger for the Bahai Faith of God's One Religion, he himself also exacting keen judgment.
18 Then another Angel from the Sacrificial-Altar, in charge of the fire, called out in a loud voice to the person bearing the sharp scimitar, saying: *Swing out this sharp scimitar of yours to gather the grape-clusters from the vintage of the earth, for the grape of the earth has peaked.*	Then Jesus as another Messenger of sacrificial love, emanating this love, calls out as a Proclaimer to the Bab exacting keen judgment, saying: *Execute this keen judgment of yours to punish the amassed evil from the wickedness in the Middle East, for the evil in the Middle East is peaking.*

[19]SO THE ANGEL CAST HIS SCIMITAR INTO THE EARTH. HE GATHERED THE VINTAGE OF THE EARTH AND TOSSED IT INTO THE HUGE WINEPRESS OF THE FULL FURY OF MAGNIFICENT GOD. [20]THE WINEPRESS WAS TRAMPLED OUTSIDE THE CITY. OUT OF THIS WINEPRESS FLOWED BLOOD UP TO THE BRIDLES OF THE HORSES—FOR 1,600 FURLONGS.

So the Bab judges the Middle East. He confronts the wickedness in the Middle East and dooms it to the great crushing lesson of the full grapes-of-wrath of magnificent God. The crushing lesson proceeds separately from the system of Malignant Materialism. Resulting from this crushing lesson emerges violence suffocating Power Politics, Widespread Warfare, Economic Injustice, and Callous Selfishness—calling for hard work leading to perfection over a long period.

Comments:

14.1, *THE BEACON MOUNT ZION*: is a comprehensive rendering of a Hebrew cover-name that means literally *mountain beacon* (*MOUNT TSIŌN*). This Mount Zion spiritual beacon beckons us to the divine civilization of New Jerusalem, just as Mount Zion's physical beacon beckoned the People of Israel to the Temple of Jerusalem.

> *Isaiah hath announced...get thee up into the high mountain....The Great City hath descended from heaven and Zion is re-vivified and rejoiced, by the appearance of the Manifestation of God....Out of Zion hath gone forth the Law of God...filled with the glory of His Revelation....Zion trembleth and exulteth with joy.*[A]

14.2–3 & 15.2, also 5.8: The verbal-thematic link *harpists playing their harps* codes for the Living-Beings and elders.

14.4: Temple-Priests (*Cohens*) had to be physically celibate to enter the Temple. Likewise, the Bab's first 18 disciples (the Letters of the Living) had to be spiritually pure to follow him.

14.4: These Letters of the Living were

> *the first who followed the commandments of God...the first fruits of all good and its consummation.*[B]

Each Letter of the Living was inspired by God to seek out the Bab.

14.6: *Eternal good news* lacks *the* (this only time in the New Testament), which lets it interpret for the Baha'i Gospel as **new** glad tidings, just as it portrayed the Gospel of Jesus as glad tidings in a prior Era.[C]

[A] ***Isaiah hath announced***, Baha'u'llah *Scriptures Tablet To An Oriental Jew* 48.120. ***Out of Zion***, Baha'u'llah *PB* 111, ***Zion trembleth***, Baha'u'llah *ESW* 145

[B] 'Abdu'l-Baha *Traveler's Narrative* 76

[C] Baha'u'llah *Scriptures Tablet to the Jews* 47.117

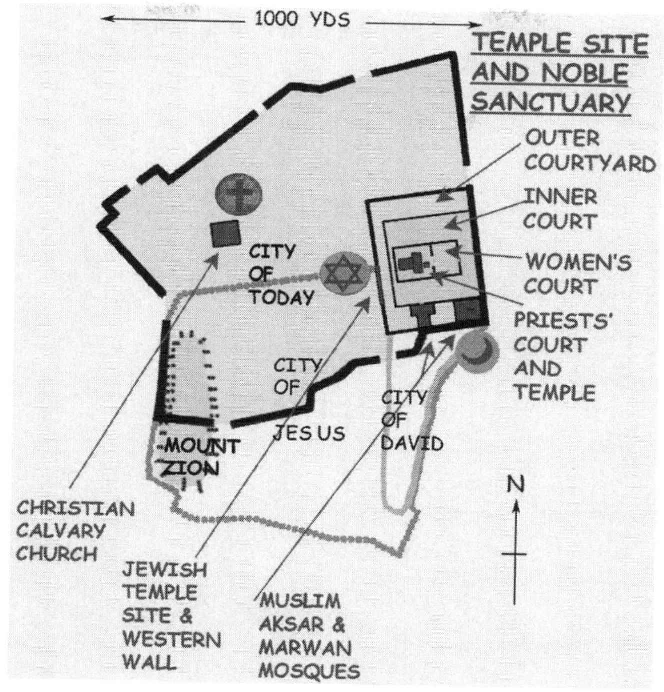

Map showing Mount Zion,
a beacon for Jerusalem and its Temple

14.7, 16.9, 19.7, also 11.13: *Glorify God* implicitly calls up ***Glory of God***, which is what the title *Baha'u'llah* means.
14.6–9: These three *Angels* can interpret in other sequences too, for example the first as Muhammad *flying in mid-heaven*, as he already did in v. 8.13.
14.8, 16.19, 17.5, 18.2, 10 & 21: ***Confused Babylon*** comprehensively renders a Hebrew cover-name that means literally *confusion* (*babel*). For a prior spiritual Era, the ignoble whore of Babylon glinting greed depicted Rome.
14.7: Both *ocean* and *sources of waters* lack *the*, which lets them interpret for the **new** truth and **new** knowledge of the Baha'i Faith.
14.11: *Eras of eras* lacks *the* (this single time in the New Testament). This lets it interpret for the **new** Baha'i Cycle.
14.13: *Lord* lacks *the*. This lets it interpret for not just specifically and traditionally for Jesus but also for all of God's Messengers generically.

14.14: *They shall see the Son of man* [divine Human-Being] *coming in the clouds of heaven with power and great glory.*[A]
14.18: ***Fire*** *is the love of God.*[B]
14.20: *Furlong* (*furrow-long*), a unit of farm work, codes for *hard work.*

[A] Baha'u'llah *KI* 61; 'Abdu'l-Baha *TAB* 1.145
[B] Abdu'l-Baha *SAQ* 19.92

Apocalypse Chapter 15
God's Presence opens our End-Times

15.1Now I saw another extensive
and amazing sign in the sky:
seven Angels bearing seven
afflictions—the last, for
with them God's fury has
ended.

Now I see another extensive and amazing scene played out by God's One Religion: the seven Middle East Messengers dispensing seven severe lessons—the end-time lessons, for through them God's fury is finally felt.

2Then I saw a seeming sea of
glass mixed with fire, and
standing on this sea of glass
those who had prevailed over
the beast (meaning over this
copy of it) and over the
number of its name, bearing
the harps of God, 3they are
also singing the song of God's
servant Moses and the song of
the Ram, saying:

Then I see clear truth shining love, and championing this clear truth the Primary-Figures and founders prevailing over the brutal Muslim system (meaning over this Qajar clone of it) and over the 666 code of its Mu'awiya, heralding the harmony of God, they are also celebrating the Torah of God's servant Moses and the Gospel of the Bab, chanting:

Extensive and amazing are Your
deeds, Almighty Lord God.
Just and true are Your ways,
Ruler of Nations.
4 *Who, Lord, does not fear*
You and glorify ***Your name****?*
For You alone are sacred,
For all nations shall come
and worship before You,
For Your righteous
requirements are clear.

Extensive and amazing are Your
acts, Almighty Lord God.
Fair and true are Your ways,
Leader of Nations.
Who, Lord, does not revere
You ***The Most Glorious****?*
For You alone are holy,
For all nations shall come
and adore serving You,
For Your loving
Law is clear.

5After these visions, I looked,
and the Temple of the Presence
of God in the Covenant opened
up in the sky. 6The seven Angels
bearing the seven afflictions
emerged from the Temple,
clad in clean shining linen,
with gold girdles looped
around their chests.

After these events, I watch, and the Baha'i Faith of the Presence of God in His Law is revealed by His One Religion. The seven Middle East Messengers dispensing the seven severe lessons appear for His One Religion, emanating true radiant goodness, as glorious loving guides.

7One of the four Living-
Beings handed the seven Angels

The foremost Primary-Figure, Baha'u'llah allots the seven

SEVEN GOLD PITCHERS FILLED WITH THE FURY OF THE GOD LIVING INTO THE ERAS OF THE ERAS.	Messengers seven splendid doses of the fury of the God living from Cycle to Cycle.
8 AT THIS, THE TEMPLE WAS FILLED WITH SMOKE FROM THE GLORY OF GOD AND HIS POWER. YET NOBODY COULD ENTER THE TEMPLE UNTIL THE SEVEN AFFLICTIONS OF THE SEVEN ANGELS ENDED.	At this, the Baha'i Faith is filled with the loving spirit of Baha'u'llah and his power. Yet nobody can live his Baha'i Faith until after the seven severe lessons of the seven Middle East Messengers are finally felt.

Comments:

15.1, also 8.2: **The *seven Pitcher-Angels*** and the seven prior Trumpet-Angels are, per Isaac Newton, *synchronous*, meaning the same.[A] Their pitchers and trumpets fit them as Middle East Messengers in the Abrahamic line. Now as Pitcher-Angels, they expand the concepts that they heralded as Trumpet-Angels into further lessons.

15.2, also 5.8 & 14.2–3: The verbal-thematic link *bearing the harps of God* codes for the Living-Beings and elders.

15.4: *You alone are sacred* echoes the beautiful Arabic word-play *La ilaha illa Allah* meaning *There are no gods but God.*

15.5: *Covenant* interprets specifically for the Revelation of the Baha'i Faith as the most recent Law evolved by the One Religion of God.

15.7, also 5.8: *Pitchers* are *pitchers of knowledge*,[B] filled now with God's fury.

15.8: In the Temple, the smoke of burning incense filled the *Holy* in its daily Dusk and Dawn Services, and filled the *Holy of Holies* in its annual Yom Kippur Special Temple Service.

15.8, 21.11 & 23: ***GLORY OF GOD*** is both a cover-name and hidden-title for Baha'u'llah to whom *the author of the Apocalypse...alluded as the 'Glory of God'.*[C] *Bahá-'Ulláh* is Arabic for *Glory of God.*[D] In applying this title to himself, Baha'u'llah recommends that Jews too read about it in Revelation, even though it is a Christian Book.[E] Likewise, the prophet Ezekiel saw in a vision a person like the

> *glory of the God of Israel from the east, his voice like the rush of many waters. The earth was lit up* as *the Glory of God came into...and filled the Temple.*[F]

[A] Isaac *Newton's Secrets* 31, *Synchronism of the Seven Trumpets and Seven Vials*, Yahuda MS.3f.1r

[B] Baha'u'llah *Scriptures Tablet to the Jews* 47.116

[C] Shoghi Effendi *GPB* 95

[D] For *glory of God*, the Scottish Bible Society's Arabic New Testament switched from *bahá-'Ulláh* in its 1833 edition to another term, *magd-'Ulláh*, in its 1858 edition!

[E] Baha'u'llah *Scriptures Tablet to the Jews* 47.117

[F] Ezek. 43.1–4

Apocalypse Chapter 16
Armageddon is Mount Carmel

16.1 Then I heard a loud voice from the Temple telling the seven Angels:

Off you go! Pour these seven pitchers of God's fury into the earth!

In 1863 I hear Baha'u'llah as Proclaimer of the Baha'i Faith telling the seven Middle East Messengers:

Off we go! Let us dispense these seven doses of God's fury into the Middle East!

2 So the first one set out and poured his pitcher into the earth. A foul and evil ulcer festered upon the human-beings who had the tattoo of the beast and those who worshiped this copy of it.

So Abraham sets out and dispenses his dose of God's fury into Qajar Persia. Malignant and evil wickedness eats up its Muslims who run discrimination and cruel taxation for its brutal Shah and adore this Qajar clone of his.

3 Next, the second one poured his pitcher into the sea. It congealed like blood in a corpse. Every living soul in the sea died.

Next, Moses dispenses his dose of God's fury into Persia's Ulema. They are confounded by spiritual death. Every once-vital Muslim under their influence dies in spirit.

4 Then the third one poured his pitcher into the rivers and the sources of the waters. They turned to blood.

Then Zoroaster dispenses his dose of God's fury into Persia's lesser clergy and the sources of their knowledge. They turn violent.

5 At this, I heard the Angel of the waters declaring:

- *You The-Is,*
- *You The-Was,*
- *You Divine One*

Are just, because You have
judged these things, 6 for
they have shed the blood of the faithful and the Prophets. So You have given them blood to drink. They deserve it!

At this, I hear Baha'u'llah the Messenger of knowledge stating:

- ***You-God-of-Later-Eras,***
- ***You-God-of-Earlier-Eras,***
- ***You Divine God***

are just, because You are punishing these things, for Persia's leaders are shedding the blood of faithful followers and us Prophets. So you are serving them violence to suffer. They (and we) deserve it!

7 I heard speaking from the Sacrificial-Altar:

Yes, Almighty Lord God, these verdicts of Yours are true and just.

I hear speaking with the sacrificial love of the Bab:

Yes, Almighty Lord God, these verdicts of Yours are true and just.

8 Now the fourth one poured
his pitcher over the sun. It
was allowed to burn human-
beings with fire. 9 Human-
beings were burned beyond
belief. They cursed the name
of the God with power over
these same afflictions. But
they did not repent so as to
glorify Him.

Now Jesus dispenses his dose of God's fury over the Ottoman Sultanate. Its Sultan kills its Sunni Muslims ferociously. Its Muslims are being butchered beyond belief. They curse Allah as the God with power over these same severe lessons. But they show no regret so as to celebrate the glory of God.

10 Next, the fifth one poured
his pitcher over the throne of
the beast. His kingdom grew
dark. People bit their tongues
from the pain. 11 They cursed
the God of heaven due to
their pains and their ulcers.
Regardless, they did not
repent of their bad deeds.

Next, Muhammad dispenses his dose of God's fury over the Teheran of the brutal Shah of Qajar Persia. His Persia falls into ignorant times. Its Muslims eat out their hearts from the suffering. They curse the Allah of the One Religion due to their sufferings and their wickedness. Regardless, they show no regret for their bad deeds.

12 Then the sixth one poured
his pitcher over the River
Euphrates. Its waters dried up
in order to prepare the way
for the rulers from the
rising-place of the sun.

Then the Bab dispenses his dose of God's fury over the knowledge surging though the Persian and Turkish Empires. Their knowledge fades in order to prepare the way for the Shah of Persia and the Sultan of Turkey to dispatch Baha'u'llah and the Bab to the Holy Land.

13 At this, I see coming from the
mouth of the dragon, from
the mouth of the beast, and
from the mouth of the false-
prophet three foul spirits like
frogs, 14 for they are demonic
spirits working wonders pouring
out over the rulers of the
whole inhabited earth to
gather them for the war of this
Great Day of Almighty God.

At this, I hear Persia's slyly-spoken hateful Prime Minister, its sharply-shouting brutal Shah, and its slickly-subtle antichrist Alem[A] as three shifty lying souls, for they are evil fiends running schemes rousing all the rulers of the whole Middle East society to gather them for the worldwide warfare starting this Grand Era of Almighty God.

[A] *Alem* is the singular form of the plural *Ulema*

15 *Listen, I am coming like a thief. Blessed is the one who stays awake and protects his or her garments, lest they walk naked and people see their shameful state.*

Listen, I Baha'u'llah have come unexpectedly to Persia. Blessed are you Persians who have stayed alert and maintained your nobility, so that you advance in knowledge and folk recognize your noble state.

16 Now he and they have gathered them to the spot called *Mountain of Preaching* or *Armageddon* in Hebrew.

Now Baha'u'llah and the evil fiends gather these rulers, he to his Carmel Mountain of Preaching for peace, they to their Armageddon Mountains of the Balkans for war.

17 Then this seventh one poured his pitcher over the air. A loud voice came from the Temple, declaring from the Throne:

It has happened!

Then Baha'u'llah dispenses his dose of God's fury over the spirit of the globe. 'Abdu'l-Baha proclaims for their Baha'i Faith, warning for its Revelation:

Armageddon has begun!

18 Hereupon lightnings, voices, and thunders have broken out. A massive earthquake has erupted, such as has never erupted since any human-being evolved on the earth, so terrible an earthquake, so massive. 19 The great city has split into three parts. The cities of the nations have fallen. Great Confused Babylon has been kept in mind before God to inflict it with the cup of the wine of the fury of His anger. 20 Every island has fled and mountains have vanished.

From 1914 flames flash, people shout, and bombs burst. Worldwide warfare erupts, such as has never erupted since human-beings arose on the planet, such devastating warfare, so extensive. The monstrous economic system is splitting the globe into the capitalist West, the communist East, and the poor South. Cities in many nations are destroyed. Monstrous Malignant Materialism is put on God's agenda for Him to inflict it with the fateful grip of the fury of His punishment. Influential rulers are exiled and small kingdoms are annihilated.

21 Heavy hail falls from the sky by the hundred-weight onto human-beings. Human-beings have been blaspheming God for this affliction of the hail, for its affliction has been so extensive.

Barrages of bombs beat down from the sky by the ton onto believers. Believers curse God for this battering by the bombs, for its calamities and hardships are so overwhelming.

Comments:

16.1–4, 8, 10, 12 & 17: The Angels pour their *seven pitchers of God's fury* in two grammatical ways: the first three Angels pour ***into*** (*eis*)—as if locally into Persia; and the last four Angels pour ***over*** (*epi*)—as if broadly over the Middle East and globe.

16.1–21: ***Abdu'l-Baha to Mrs. Brittingham—Apr. 1909 Book of Revelation Chapter 16***[A] is a trusted Pilgrim Note that addresses all of Chapter 16 and supplies most of the following citations for it.

16.1: *The events mentioned in the first part of chapter 16... happened before the coming of the Manifestation. The seven angels signify seven Powers, which will have authority...over the world of existence* as *the world will be disturbed, i.e., sins and wickedness will abound, and the darkness of error will surround the world.*[B]

16.2: *The first angel is a power who will give forth wonderful signs. The first vial (or cup) really means influence. Through that influence some who were apparently good, but inwardly bad, were destroyed...deprived of the light.*[C]

16.3: *The sea here symbolizes the Ulema—the great and learned people....They, as well as those under their authority and guidance, were deprived.*[D] Persia's Muslim Ulema had a status corresponding to that of Christian bishops.

16.4: *Rivers and fountains of water signify less influential men than the Ulema, who were likewise affected, because the knowledge of the people which should be, like water, the cause of life, became like blood; that is, it becomes the cause of misleading the people and so the cause of death, for they changed the teachings of God.*[E] Persia's lesser Muslim leaders had a status corresponding to that of Christian priests.

16.5–6: *The angel of the waters: i.e. the power of knowledge, is addressing God. Another angel or power speaking, confirms this, that God is just and righteous to have thus judged the people.*[F]

16.6: In this context, *they* is usefully ambiguous as both shedders of blood or their victims.

16.8–9: *The sun here means an Eastern potentate or king....The heat of the sun signifies his rule and authority, and the people*

[A] 'Abdu'l-Baha cited by Brittingham in her 3-page distribution copy in the Barstow-Lovejoy Archives, by kind permission of Thellie Lovejoy: *'Abdu'l-Baha to Mrs. Brittingham—Apr. 1909 Book of Revelation Chapter* 16, titled also *I. D. Brittingham—Translated in Akka—Received April, 1909*, and *Translated in Acco by Monever Khanum*

[B] 'Abdu'l-Baha cited by Brittingham 1

[C] 'Abdu'l-Baha cited by Brittingham 1

[D] 'Abdu'l-Baha cited by Brittingham 1

[E] 'Abdu'l-Baha cited by Brittingham 1

[F] 'Abdu'l-Baha cited by Brittingham 1–2

will be scorched or burnt through the fierceness of his rule. This Eastern King was Sultan Mahmoud, who ruled the Turkish people. All his time he was slaying....Once he slew many thousands of soldiers in one day. But, in spite of these events and trials, the people did not repent, and did not come to themselves.[A] Mahmoud's *Reign of Terror* lasted from 1808 to 1839.

16.10: *The 'seat of the beast' means the King of Persia, seated on his throne, upon whom the cup of the 5th angel was poured. But the people were not admonished by all the calamities which occurred.*[B]

16.10–11, also 2: *The* and *their* before *pain/pains* makes these pains familiar, probably arising from the prior *foul and evil ulcer* (16.2).

16.12, ***The River Euphrates****...signifies the Turkish and Persian kingdoms. The drying up of the water means that all learning and science was abolished, and that ignorance prevailed. This made the way easy for the kings of the East to become powerful and arbitrary.*[C]

16.12: *The way...prepared for the rulers from the rising-place of the sun* was the way that the Shah and Sultan as secular *rulers* of chose to dispatch Baha'u'llah and the Bab as spiritual *rulers* from Persia to the Holy Land. This was the *way* from Teheran to Acco that they exiled Baha'u'llah between 1853 and 1868, and the *way* from Persia to Haifa that their execution of the Bab indirectly dispatched him as bodily remains between 1899 and 1900.

16.13, ***Beast, dragon, false-prophet***: The *beast* who *sought with his utmost power to destroy the Cause of God...was the King of Persia*, brutal Nasir-i-Din Shah (1848–96). The *dragon is Hadji Mírzá Aghassi...Grand Vizier* [Prime Minister] *of Persia....The false prophet was Karim Káhn, one of the greatest of the Ulama* [*sic*] *of that country* who *used to say 'My words are revealed from above'. These three persons tried their utmost to turn all the people against the Cause of God, so that they might all oppose it, and so make war against God. The spirits like frogs signify their words which were spread throughout Persia.*[D]

The term *false-prophet* overlaps with the term *antichrist*. Apropos, *anyone who violently and determinedly sought to oppose the Manifestation could be called an 'anti-Christ'*. Thus, Karim Kahn was the antichrist of the Babi Revelation and *Siyyid Muhammad, the Antichrist of the Baha'i Revelation.*[E]

[A] 'Abdu'l-Baha cited by Brittingham 2
[B] 'Abdu'l-Baha cited by Brittingham 2
[C] 'Abdu'l-Baha cited by Brittingham 2
[D] **The *Beast* who *sought***, Nabil, *Dawnbreakers* 2.39–40. **The *dragon is Hadji Mírzá Aghassi***, 'Abdu'l-Baha cited by Brittingham 2–3
[E] ***Anyone who violently***, Shoghi Effendi *High Endeavours, Messages to Alaska* 85.69. ***Siyyid Muhammad***, Shoghi Effendi *GPB* 164–5, 112, *Aqdas* 192.249;

16.12: Frogs croaking lies slip slickly between water and land (in contrast, birds warbling truth fly freely through the air!).

16.14: Qajar Persia and Ottoman Turkey's late-1800s *jihad* against the early Baha'i Faith helped to begin the Armageddon century of worldwide warfare.

16.15, also 1.10 & 12.10: *The words 'Behold I come as a thief, etc.' are spoken by the Proclaimer of all this* [Baha'u'llah]*—the 'Great Voice' as He is called at the beginning of the chapter* coming *suddenly, like a thief—as Christ said He would come—so that no one will know it....Blessed is the one who is awake and watches...when a Manifestation comes.*[A]

16.15, also 3.4–5: *Garments signify the good qualities...such as love, sincerity, etc. He 'that watcheth' must keep that good character...like a robe adorning him.*[B]

16.16: ***ARMAGEDDON***[C] *signifies Roumelia and Macedonia* [the Balkans] *....Often the kings have been gathered together on subjects concerning these places.*[D] Armageddon serves as not just a symbol of war but also as a Hebrew cover-name meaning literally *Mountain of Preaching* (*HAR-MAGIDON*). So Armageddon comprehensively renders both traditionally as *Armageddon* and anew as *Mountain of Preaching*. In concert, the subject of the singular verb *has gathered* (*sunēgagen*) can be both

- A neuter plural *they*[E] for v. 16.14's *rulers* as the world leaders who ran a massive arms race in the second half of the 1800s that sparked a century of worldwide warfare in 1914 at their Balkan mountains Armageddon
- A singular *he* for v. 16.15's Baha'u'llah *coming like a thief* from 1860 to 1870 to write letters urging world leaders to disarm and build global peace at his *Mount Carmel of Preaching* Armageddon.

16.16–7: In 1912, 'Abdu'l-Baha predicted.

We are on the eve of the Battle of Armageddon referred to in the sixteenth chapter of Revelation. The time is two years hence....All that which is recorded in the Revelation of John and the Book of Daniel will *become fulfilled....The seventh angel poured out his influence upon all the world...on the air, because the air fills every place, and the continuing verses mean the Great War that is to come.*[F]

'Abdu'l-Baha *Child of the Covenant* 61, 82, 105, 82; Baha'u'llah *KI* 247

A 'Abdu'l-Baha cited by Brittingham 3

B 'Abdu'l-Baha cited by Brittingham 3

C The English *ARMAGEDDON* lacks the opening *H* of the Greek/Hebrew *HARMAGEDDON*. Alternative versions arguably construe *HARMAGEDDON* as (1) *'IR MAGEDDON* (spelt with ' /*ayin* not *h*/*he*) as *Mageddo city*, (2) *HAR MO'ED* (spelt with ' /*ayin* not *g*/*gimmel*, Isaiah 14.13) as *mountain of assembly*, and (3) *HAR MEGUDAD* (Zech. 12.11) as *mountain cutting through* the Megiddo pass (Aune *52b*, 899)

D 'Abdu'l-Baha cited by Brittingham 3

E Aune *52B* 858.16a–a

F ***We are on the eve***, 'Abdu'l-Baha cited by Corinne True in *Chicago North Shore*

In 1918, the Turks sentenced 'Abdu'l-Baha to death. But he and *his whole family narrowly escaped crucifixion*, for the British War Office in London had alerted General Allenby about the execution order and Allenby's

> *unexpectedly swift advance* drove *the Turkish authorities out of Haifa before they even had time to carry out their terrible threat.*[A]

In recognition of his charitable works, 'Abdu'l-Baha later received a knighthood and became *Sir 'Abdu'l-Baha.*

16.18–21 (also 4.5, 8.5 & 11.19): ***Lightnings, voices, thunders, earthquake, and hail*** resound to open the Baha'i Era with the turmoil of military *conflagration, the like of which is not recorded in the past history of mankind.*[B]

16.19: *The city which was cut in three pieces means that kingdom of Babylonia, which is under three kings: England, Persia and Turkey.*[C] Indeed, also today's Iraq seems set to split into Shi'a, Sunni, and Kurdish states. But, writ bigger here, *great city split into three parts* here fits the world of the 1900s divided into the capitalist West, communist East, and poor South.

16.19: World War II in particular saw *flourishing lands...ruined, cities completely wrecked and thriving towns annihilated,*[D] especially Russia's Stalingrad, Germany's Dresden, and Japan's Hiroshima and Nagasaki.

16.21: *The 'great hail' means both the bombs, shells, instruments of destruction, and the calamities and hardships which...cause people to blaspheme.*[E] The right-column interpretation has imported the Baha'i interpretive phrase *calamities and hardships.*[F]

Review September 26 1914, cited by Dr J.E. Esslemont in *Baha'u'llah and the New Era* 243. ***All that which is recorded***, 'Abdu'l-Baha (1912) *Tablets of the Divine Plan* 22–3. ***The seventh Angel poured***, 'Abdu'l-Baha cited by Brittingham 3

[A] Major W. Tudor-Pole SW (1922/12/31) 12.16.252–3. Maudes 90–3, 122–3

[B] 'Abdu'l-Baha cited by *Esslemont, J.E., Baha'u'llah and the New Era* 243

[C] 'Abdu'l-Baha cited by Brittingham 3

[D] 'Abdu'l-Baha *Letter to Martha Root*

[E] 'Abdu'l-Baha cited by Brittingham 3

[F] 'Abdu'l-Baha *SWA* 3.12

Apocalypse Chapter 17
Interpreting Prophetic Symbols

17.1Then one of the seven
Angels bearing the seven
pitchers came and spoke with
me, saying:

Then Baha'u'llah as foremost of the seven Middle East Messengers dispensing the seven doses of God's fury, comes and speaks with me, inviting:

*Come! I shall show you the
condemnation of the huge
whore who sits over many
waters, 2with whom the
rulers of the world have
been fornicating and the
people living on the earth
have gotten drunk from the
wine of her fornicating.*

Come! I shall reveal to you the justice meted out to the monstrous seductive greed that drives many peoples, populations, nations, and language-groups, with which the leaders of humanity have been exploiting and the citizens of the planet have gone crazy from the grip of its exploitation.

3At this, he soared me in
spirit into a desert. I saw a
woman mounted on a scarlet
beast, blanketed by blasphemous
titles, possessing seven heads
and ten horns. 4This woman was
wearing purple and scarlet,
gilded with gold, precious
gemstone, and pearls, holding
in her hand a gold cup full of
vile things and with the
foulness of her fornicating,
5with a title written on her
forehead as a mystery:

Great Confused Babylon,
Mother of the Whores and
the Vile Things in the World:

At this, he soars my soul over a spiritually barren world. I see greed borne by Muslim brutality, sporting blasphemous titles, boasting seven territories and ten ruler-names. This greed displays pomp and power, flashes riches, brute strength, and cunning, authorizing an inglorious destiny filled by vile deeds and with the corruption of its exploitation, with a slogan endorsing it as flagrantly as a brothel light gleaming its hidden intent:

Monstrous Malignant Materialism, Breeder of Greed and the Vile Deeds of Humanity

6Next, I saw this woman drunk
from the blood of the faithful
and from the blood of the
Witnesses of Jesus. Seeing her, I
grew bewildered beyond belief.

Next, I hear this greed crazed with violence against faithful believers and with violence against the three Delegates of Jesus. Hearing it, I get bewildered beyond belief.

7At this the Angel told me:

*Why be bewildered? I myself
will explain to you the
mystery of this woman and the
beast bearing her, possessing*

At this Baha'u'llah tells me:

John, why be bewildered? I the Messenger will teach you the hidden intent of this greed and the Muslim brutality bearing it,

*The seven heads and the ten
horns.*

boasting the seven territories and the ten ruler-names.

8 *The beast that you saw did
exist. Then it does not exist.
Then it is due to rise from
the Abyss. Now it heads to
destruction. The people living
on the earth whose name was
not to have been listed in
the Book of Life, due to a
founding of a world-order,
will become fervent at seeing
this beast, for it did exist, next
it does not exist, then it will
be present*

The Muslim brutality that you see was began by the Umayyad Caliphate. Then it ceased. Then it returned as the Ottoman Sultanate in its spiritual error. Now it is doomed to destruction. The Middle Easterners who went unacclaimed as morally decent, due to the founding of a militaristic Muslim world-order, have gone mad from learning this Muslim brutality, for it came, then it ceased, then it came back

—9 Here indeed a wise mind!—

—Here indeed deep insight!—

*The seven heads are seven
mountains where the woman
sits over them. Over them
are seven rulers.* 10 *Five have
fallen. One exists. The other
has not yet come. But when it
does come, it must stay small.*

The seven territories were seven Empires where greed ruled over them. Over them ruled seven regimes. Egypt, Assyria, Media, Persia, and Greece had fallen by AD *95. In* AD *95, Rome ruled. Byzantium had not yet come. But when it came in* AD *330, it began to shrink steadily.*

11 *As for the beast that did
exist, then does not exist, this
same one is also an eighth, as
well as of the seven. Now it
too heads for destruction.*

As for the Muslim brutality that began, then ceased, this same brutality has been driving also our eighth Ottoman Empire as well as the prior seven Empires. Now it too is doomed to destruction.

12 *As for the ten horns that you
saw, they are ten rulers, those
who have not received royal
power, but will receive
authority as rulers with the
beast for a single hour.*

As for the ten names that you have heard, they are Persia's ten Qajar Shahs who did not have sovereignty, but now have power as rulers with Muslim brutality during these 1800s.

13 *These rulers possess a single
purpose. They have submitted
their power and authority to
the beast.* 14 *These rulers shall
fight the Ram. Yet the Ram
shall defeat them, for he is a*

These Qajar Shahs are pursuing a single goal. They are devoting their power and authority to Muslim brutality. These Shahs have fought the Bab. Yet the Bab has defeated them, for he is a

LORD OF LORDS AND KING OF KINGS. MOREOVER, THE ONES WITH HIM ARE CALLED, CHOSEN, AND TRUSTWORTHY.

LORD OF LORDS *and* **LEADER OF LEADERS**. *Moreover, the disciples with him are motivated, select, and true.*

15 CONTINUING, HE TELLS ME:
THE WATERS THAT YOU SAW, WHERE THE WHORE SITS, ARE PEOPLES, POPULATIONS, NATIONS, AND LANGUAGE-GROUPS.

Continuing, he tells me:
The peoples, populations, nations, and language-groups that you have seen, whom seductive greed rules, are the seven billion people who will populate the planet in the early 2000s.

16 *AS FOR THE TEN HORNS THAT YOU SAW, ALONG WITH THE BEAST, THESE SHALL DETEST THE WHORE. THEY SHALL RAVAGE AND STRIP HER NAKED, CONSUME HER FLESH, AND BURN HER UP IN A BLAZE.* 17 *FOR GOD HAS PUT INTO THEIR HEARTS TO CARRY OUT THIS WILL OF HIS, TO CARRY OUT A SINGLE INTENT, AND TO SUBMIT THEIR ROYAL POWER TO THE BEAST UNTIL THESE WORDS OF GOD SHALL BE FULFILLED.*

As for the ten rogue regimes and terrorist organizations that you hear, along with their Muslim brutality, these detest seductive greed. They are attacking and stripping it bare, consuming its wealth, and destroying it ferociously. For Allah has fueled their fanaticism to carry out this plan of His, to shoot for a single goal, and to devote their rule to brutality until we Speakers for God, the Bab and I, are manifest.

18 *AND THE WOMAN THAT YOU SAW IS THE GREAT CITY THAT RETAINS RULE OVER THE RULERS OF THE EARTH.*

And the greed that you are seeing, John, is the monstrous economic system that lords it over the leaders of the lands of the world.

Comments:

17.1, ***The whore of Babylon*** symbolizes greed blinding the soul as *the thin eyelid prevents the eye from seeing the world and what is contained therein....The curtain of greed covers the sight of the heart....The darkness of greed and envy obscures the light of the soul, as the cloud prevents the penetration of the sun's rays.*[A]

17.1 & 15: The right-column imports John's v. 17.15 internal interpretation of *waters* as *peoples, populations, nations, and language-groups.*

17.5: Greedy Babylon's *title written on the forehead* displays open adoration for Malignant Materialism instead of for a Faith.

17.6: The *Witnesses of Jesus* may portray also the 18 Letters of the Living as the first disciples of Jesus returned as the Bab.

[A] Baha'u'llah *Scriptures* 50.132

17.9: Bishop Andreas (AD 563–614) was the first to interpret *seven heads* and *seven mountains* as seven ancient Empires notorious for militarism and materialism, here identified as Egypt, Assyria, Media, Persia, Greece, Rome, and Byzantium.[A]

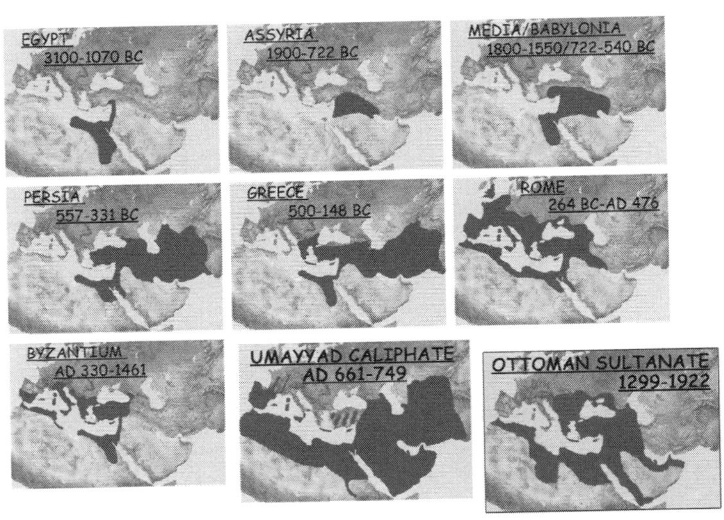

Map showing militaristic Middle East Empires, seven ancient ones and two recent Muslim ones

17.8 & 10: For a prior spiritual Era, the beast that *did exist* depicted Mu'awiya snatching power, the beast that *does not exist* as him ostensibly returning power to Hasan, and the beast that *is due to rise* as him seizing power back from Hasan.[286] Likewise, *five have fallen* depicted Abu Sufyan, Abu-Bakr, Umar, Uthman, and Ali, *one exists* as Mu'awiya, *the other...must stay small* as Hasan holding power briefly, and *the eighth as well as of the seven* as Mu'awiya seizing power back from Hasan.[287]

17.10: In AD 330, the territorial extent at which the Byzantine Empire began was its greatest. After that, the Empire shrank steadily from the military advances of the Persian, Hunnic, and Muslim Empires. In 1453, the Empire lost Constantinople to the Ottomans and came to its end in 1461.

[A] Aune *52A*.lxiii

17.8: *The beast...did exist...then it does not exist...then it is due to rise* and *five are fallen, one exists, and the other has not yet come... this one is both an eighth and also of the seven*, interpret per this

Revelation timeline of Middle East Empires

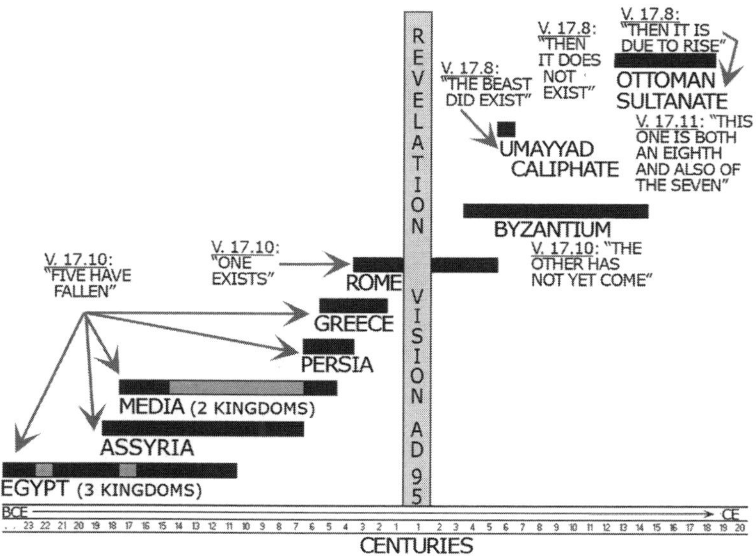

17.12: For prior spiritual Eras, *ten rulers, the ones who…will receive …authority…for a single hour* depicted ten Spanish Umayyad Caliphs, ten Abbasid Caliphs, or ten Seljuk Caliphs.[288] Likewise, *a single hour* depicted the AD 666–749 century of power of the Umayyad Caliphate.

17.12: The first set of *ten horns* fits the ten brutal dynastic Shahs of Qajar Persia, namely (1) Fath-Ali Kahn, (2) Aqa-Muhammad, (3) Sadiq, (4) Fath-Ali, (5) Adil, (6) Muhammad, (7) Nisir-i-Din, (8) Muzaffaru-Din, (9) Muhammad-Ali, and (10) Ahmad.[A]

17.14, also 19.16: ***Lord of lords** and **King of kings*** in this verse serve as titles for the Bab and in v. 19.16 for Baha'u'llah.

17.16: The second set of *ten horns* fits the top ten rogue regimes and terrorist organizations of modern Muslim Militarism. Soon enough, history will show who they were.

[A] Nabil *Dawnbreakers, The Qajar Dynasty* lx

Apocalypse Chapter 18

The Fall of Babylon is a Greatest Depression

18.1 After these visions I saw
another Angel landing from
the sky with great authority.
The globe was lit by his glory.
2 He cried out in a mighty
voice saying:

It has fallen,
Great Confused
Babylon has fallen!

She has grown into a den of
demons, a haunt for every foul
spirit, and a haven for every
foul and hateful bird, 3 for
all nations have collapsed
intoxicated from the wine from
the fury of her fornicating;
the rulers of the globe have
been fornicating with her; and
the businessmen of the planet
have gotten rich from the
power of her extravagance.

4 Next I heard another voice
from the sky urging:

Leave her, my people, lest you
take part in her sins or lest
you take on her afflictions,
5 for her very sins have scaled
the sky. But God has recalled
her crimes. 6 Pay back to her as
she herself has paid out.
Double and double again,
according to her dealings,
fix a double draught for her
in the cup that she has fixed.

7 In as much as she has
glorified herself and lived
lavishly, inflict on her as
much torment and grief, for
in her heart she gushes:

- *'I sit as Queen!*
- *'I am no widow.*
- *'I shall never see sorrow!'*

After these events I see another Messenger as Baha'u'llah arriving from God's One Religion with immense authority. The globe is lit by his glory. He cries out as a powerful Proclaimer calling:

It is destroyed
Monstrous Malignant
Materialism is destroyed!

It has afforded a front for fiends, a cover for every corrupt crook, and a façade for every corrupt and vile soul, for all nations have been driven mad by the grip of the fury of its exploitation; the leaders of humanity have been exploiting with it; and the wheelers and dealers of the planet have been profiteering from the enormity of its deliberate waste.

Next I hear the Bab for God's One Religion urging:

Escape it, my people, lest you get trapped by its evils or lest you suffer its severe lessons, for its very sins have infiltrated God's One Religion. But God is calling up its crimes. Deal back to it as it itself has dealt out. Deal its double-dealing double, according to its dealings, devise a double dose of debt for it as the destiny that it has devised.

In as much as it has exalted itself and deliberately wasted, inflict on it as much torment and sorrow, for in its soul it boasts:

- *'I rule Supreme!*
- *'I possess human partners.*
- *'I can never fail!'*

8 *Due to this, her afflictions*
shall come in a single day:
- *Death!*
- *Misery!*
- *Starvation!*

She shall be burned up in a
blaze, for mighty is the Lord
God Who is condemning her.

Due to this, its severe lessons are occurring over a single year:
- *Collapse!*
- *Suffering!*
- *Shortage!*

It is being ferociously destroyed, for powerful is the Lord God Who is condemning it.

9 Over her the rulers of
the planet who have been
fornicating and living lavishly
with her will weep and mourn
when they see the smoke of her
burning, 10 standing far off from
fear of her torment, calling out

Trump-Ta-Ra, Trump-Ta-Ra,
you great city, you mighty city
of Confused Babylon, for
this verdict on you has come
in a single hour!

Over it the leaders of the planet who have exploited and wasted deliberately through it are groaning and grieving as they feel the effects of its destruction, cringing from their guilt for its torment, accusing:

Two Warners heralded this Era of change, *you monstrous economic system, you powerful system of Malignant Materialism, for this verdict on you has struck us in a heartbeat!*

11 Over it, because no one buys
their merchandise any longer,
the businessmen of the globe
will weep and wail:

12 *Merchandise of gold and*
silver, precious gemstone and
pearls, fine-linen and purple
material, silk and scarlet
material, every type of scented
wood, every kind of ivory
product, and every sort of
priceless wood, brass, iron, and
marble, 13 cinnamon, cardamom,
incenses like myrrh and
frankincense, wine, oil, flour,
wheat, cattle, and sheep!

Over it, because nobody buys their products any more, the wheelers and dealers of the globe are sobbing and shrieking:

Products vaunting wealth and riches, reeking refined strength and cunning, redolent with affluence and self-righteousness, humming with opulence and power, every type of matchless material, every kind of rare collectible, and all sorts of priceless furnishing, tool, machine, and building, delicious spices, tasty treats, erotic fragrances of cologne and perfume, heady wines, sensuous oils, sumptuous fare, select cereals, pedigree meat, and choice cheeses!

Merchandise of horses and carriages!

Products of Lear jets and Mercedes limousines!

Merchandise of bodies and souls of human-beings!

Products of bodies and souls of wage-slave humans being toiled away in field, factory, and facility!

*[14]Now this ripe fruit of your
own soul's lust has left you.
Now all these splendid and
sparkling things are lost to
you! Now you shall never
find them again.*

Now this rich booty of your own soul's lust has slipped through your fingers. Now all these gorgeous and glittering goods have slid from your grasp! Now you shall never gain them again.

[15]These traders in the same
things, who got rich from it,
shall stand far off from fear
of her torment, weeping and
wailing, [16]calling out:

Trump-Ta-Ra, Trump-Ta-Ra, *you great city wearing fine-linen, purple and scarlet material, and gilded with gold, precious gemstone, and pearl,*
*[17]for all this wealth
has been destroyed in a single
hour!*

These wheelers and dealers in the same products, who have gotten rich from Malignant Materialism, are cringing from their guilt for its torment, sobbing and shrieking, accusing:

Two Warners heralded this Era of change, *you monstrous economic system displaying self-righteousness, pomp and power, and flashing riches, brute strength, and cunning, for all our wealth has evaporated in a blink!*

Now every ship-captain, every
person plying a passage to any
place, sailors, and as many as
work the sea, stood far off.
[18]Seeing the smoke from its
burning, they cried out,
saying:

What city is like
this great city!

Now all you managers, all you people wandering the world for work, you laborers, and all you who toil the land, sea, and air, are laid off. Feeling the effects of its destruction, you are screaming, mocking:

What system can match
this monstrous system!

[19]They threw dust on their
heads and yelled, weeping and
wailing, calling out:

Trump-Ta-Ra, Trump-Ta-Ra, *you great city by whom all owners of ships at sea have grown rich from your supreme wealth, for you have been destroyed in a single hour!*

You have been abused and are screaming, sobbing and shrieking, accusing:

Two Warners heralded this Era of change, *you monstrous economic system by which all owners of trucks and trains, ships and planes, profiteered from your extreme wealth, for you have turned them to ash in a flash!*

*[20]Rejoice over her you
heaven, you faithful, you
emissaries, and you Prophets,
for God has condemned its
condemnation of you!*

Celebrate over it you One Religion of God, you faithful believers, your spiritual envoys, and you Prophets, for God has condemned it for having condemned you!

[21]One mighty Angel plucked up a boulder like a massive millstone and cast it into the sea, declaring:

Thus with sudden violence shall you, great city of Confused Babylon, be cast down. You shall never exist again! [22]No music of harpists or minstrels, flutists or trumpeters, shall ever be heard in you again! No artisan in any craft shall ever be found in you again! No sound of any mill shall ever be heard in you again! [23]No light of any lamp shall ever shine in you again! No whispering of any bride or groom shall ever be heard in you again. For your businessmen have been the top men of the globe. For all nations have been tricked by your spells.

[24]In it has been found the blood of Prophets, the faithful, and all the people who have been slain across the planet.

The foremost mighty Messenger Baha'u'llah confronts the massive burden of busywork strangling humanity and dispatches it wisely, declaring:

Thus with sudden violence are you, monstrous economic system of Malignant Materialism, being destroyed. You shall never exist again! No concerts or operas, choirs or orchestras, shall ever perform for you again! No specialists in any field shall ever plan for you again! No cheap labor shall ever toil for you again! No lying revelators shall ever promote you again! No young couples shall ever build lives around you again. For your wheelers and dealers have risen to run the human race. For all nations have been tricked by your lying charms.

In Malignant Materialism is rooted the violence against Prophets, faithful believers, and all the people who have been killed across the planet.

Comments:

18.1: ***So powerful is the light of unity*** *that it can illuminate the whole earth*. Likewise, Baha'u'llah will *shine forth suddenly and will pronounce judgement as He pleaseth*.[A]

18.2: *Ye are...the bird which soareth...through the immensity of the heavens, until, impelled to satisfy its hunger, it turneth longingly to the water and clay of the earth below it, and, having been entrapped in the mesh of its desire, findeth itself impotent to resume its flight to the realms whence it came. Powerless to shake off the burden weighing on its sullied wings, that bird, hitherto an inmate of the heavens, is now forced to seek a dwelling-place upon the dust....Defile not your wings*

[A] ***So powerful is the light of unity***, Baha'u'llah *ESW* 14. ***Shine forth suddenly***, *Selections from the Writings of the Bab* 3.92.

with the clay of waywardness and vain desires...that ye may not be hindered from soaring in the heavens of My divine knowledge.[A]

18.3 & 9: Humankind is now *at the mercy of rulers so drunk with pride that they cannot discern clearly their own best advantage.... Whenever any one of them hath striven to improve* the world's *condition, his motive hath been his own gain....The unworthiness of this motive hath limited his power to heal or to cure.*[B]

18.4: *Time and again have We admonished Our beloved ones to avoid, nay to flee from, anything whatsoever from which the odor of mischief can be detected.*[C]

18.14: *You* continues to be understood as *You Babylon*, albeit here it may also mean *you businessmen* addressed by some unidentified party.

18.17–20: Babylon's workers anticipate its fall before its leaders or businessmen. They express no fear of its torment, denounce its businessmen objectively, and act in the past-tense in contrast to its leaders or businessmen who act in the future-tense.

18.24: *All the people slain across the planet* fits our times all too well.

18.21: **The *Massive Millstone*** depicts Malignant Materialism the busywork strangling humanity with its deliberate waste of vast amounts of human time and energy.

Malignant Materialism's massive millstone of busywork is cast into the sea

[A] Baha'u'llah *GWB* 153.327
[B] Baha'u'llah *Summons of Lord of Hosts, Temple, Queen Victoria* 1.175, *PB* 67
[C] Baha'u'llah *GWB* 97.153

Apocalypse Chapter 19
A Banquet both Spiritual and Economic

19.1 After these visions, I heard as
it were a loud roar of a huge
crowd in the sky calling out:
*Praise God! Victory, glory,
and power to our God,
2 because these verdicts of His
are true and just, for He has
condemned the huge whore
who has corrupted the globe
with her fornicating, and He
has avenged the blood of His
servants at her hand.*

After these events, I hear hundreds of millions of future Baha'is for God's One Religion calling out:
Praise God! Victory, glory, and power to our God, because these verdicts of His are true and just, for He has meted out justice to the monstrous seductive greed that has corrupted humanity with its exploitation, and He has avenged the violence against His servants on its authority.

3 A second time they called out:
*Praise God! Her smoke rises
into the Eras of the Eras!*

Again they shout:
Praise God. Its effects have sent their signal from the old Cycle to the new Cycle.

4 The 24 elders and the four
Living-Beings fell down and
worshiped God-Enthroned,
calling out:
Amen! Praise God!

The 24 founders and the four Primary-Figures submit themselves and adore God as the Founder of the Baha'i Revelation, calling out:
Indeed so! Praise God!

5 Next came a voice from the
Throne, saying:
*Adore our God all you His
servants who fear Him, the
humble and the important.*

Next Baha'u'llah speaks for the Baha'i Revelation, urging:
Love our God all you His servants who revere Him, the humble and the important.

6 Then I heard as it were a roar
of a huge crowd, like a rushing
of many waters and like a pealing
of mighty thunders, calling out:
*Praise God, for our Almighty
Lord God has begun to reign!
7 Let us rejoice! Let us exult!
Let us glorify Him, for the
wedding of the Ram has come
and his wife has prepared
herself. 8 She has been assigned
clean shining fine-linen to
wear, for this fine-linen
represents the righteous deeds
of the faithful.*

Then I hear millions of modern Baha'is broadcasting bountiful knowledge and potent systems of justice, calling out:
Praise God for our Almighty Lord God has taken charge! Let us be glad! Let us triumph! Let us celebrate the glory of God, for the perfecting of the Bab has come and his partner Baha'u'llah has prepared himself. He has been assigned true radiant righteousness to display, for his righteous deeds are manifest as the excellence of faithful Baha'is.

9 Now he tells me:

Record how blessed are those who are invited to the wedding banquet of the Ram.

Now Baha'u'llah reminds me:

You published in AD 95 how blessed would be the believers who would celebrate my 1863 perfecting of the Bab.

Then he tells me:

These are the true Words of God.

Then he tells me,

The Bab and I are the true Speakers for God.

10 At this, I have fallen at his feet to worship him. But he tells me:

Look, don't! I am your fellow servant and of your brothers and sisters bearing this testimony of Jesus. Worship God, for this testimony of Jesus is 'The Spirit' in this prophecy!

At this, I submit myself humbly to worship him. But he tells me:

Stop, John! I am your fellow-Baha'i and of your brothers and sisters in Faith bearing this testimony for Jesus! Worship God [not His Mirror!], for this testimony for Jesus is me, 'God's Manifestation', in your interpretation!

11 Next, I saw the sky open up. Behold, a white stallion and the trustworthy and true rider upon it. He judges and fights with justice, 12 his eyes a flame of fire, wearing on his head many sovereign-crowns and bearing a written

Name

that no one but he knows, 13 and wearing a garment dipped in blood. His title is called

The Word of God.

Next, I see God's One Religion revealed. Behold, its pure force and him as the trustworthy and true leader leading it. He judges and fights with justice, his soul blazing divine love, a ruler leading eight Faiths, and proclaiming God's new name formally as the

The Most Glorious

that all can now learn, and displaying nobility as he suffers violence. His title is called

The Speaker of God.

14 The armies in the sky followed him on white stallions clad in clean white fine-linen.

Troops of believers in God's One Religion follow him as pure forces emanating true righteousness.

15 From his mouth issues a sharp sword to strike the nations with it. He himself shall also guide them with an iron rod. He himself also tramples that winepress of the wine of the furious anger of Almighty God.

His speech projects perceptive words to compel nations with them. He himself also directs them with his strong Law. He himself has also been processing that crushing lesson of Almighty God's furious grapes-of-wrath.

16 In addition, he has a title written on his garment and over his thigh:	In addition, he has a title formally displaying his nobility and his strength as:
King of kings and Lord of lords	***Leader of leaders and Lord of lords***
17 Now I saw one Angel standing in the sun. He cried out in a loud voice, telling all the birds flying in mid-heaven:	Now I see the foremost Messenger Baha'u'llah championing his Faith in Persia. He calls out as its Proclaimer, inviting every spiritually soaring soul:
Come, gather for God's great banquet, 18 *to eat carcasses of rulers, carcasses of military leaders, along with carcasses of mighty men, and carcasses of horses and the riders on them—meaning carcasses for all, both free and slave, humble and important.*	*Come, join God's great celebration, to gain spoils from leaders, spoils from generals, spoils from tycoons, along with spoils from Power Politics, Widespread Warfare, Economic Injustice, and Callous Selfishness, and the false faith, national greed, corporate greed, and lazy neglect driving them—meaning spoils for all, both owners and workers, humble and important.*
19 At this I saw the beast with the earth's rulers and their armies assembled to wage war against the rider on the stallion and against his army.	At this I see the brutal Qajar Shah with Middle East leaders and their forces joining to wage jihad against Baha'u'llah leading his Faith and against his Baha'i troop.
20 But the beast was seized, and with him the false-prophet who on his behalf had worked the wonders by which he deceived those taking the beast's tattoo and worshiping this copy of it. While alive, these two were tossed into the pool of fire burning with sulfur.	But the brutal Shah is killed, and with him his antichrist Prime-Minister for him who had worked schemes by which he tricked Persians to run the brutal Shah's discrimination and taxation and to adore this Qajar clone of his. During their lives, these two men were already doomed to isolation in unbelief devastating with its despair.
21 The rest were killed by the sword projecting from the mouth of the rider on the stallion.	Other Persians will be converted by the words uttered by the speech of Baha'u'llah as leader of the Baha'i Faith.
All the birds feasted on these carcasses of theirs.	Every soul will gain these spoils of theirs.

Comments:

19.1, 3, 4 & 6: ***HALLELUJAH*** is a Hebrew cover-name that means literally *Let us praise God* (*HALLELU-YAH*).

19.4–6, also 10.7: Up to here the vision has explained the v. 10.7 *mystery of God* to John. Notably, to mark this key point in the text, the Codex Sinaiticus uses up three of its mere 29 precious paragraph-breaks. From here to the end, the *mystery of God* shall be fulfilled.

19.6 & 1, also 5.11: *Last-first* Greek puts results before causes. So the v. 19.6 *roar* is the original roar that has generate v. 19.1's prior *loud roar*. Further, both roars echo v. 5.11's prior *millions* and *hundreds of millions* who symbolize modern and future Baha'is in first-last order too (but reversed, see page 326).

19.7–9, 21.2, 9 & 22.17: **"Bride", "groom", "wedding", and "wife"** are Jewish symbols celebrating the Sabbath Day as a Bride marrying God as a King. Here the promised "bride" is Baha'u'llah "marrying" his "groom" as the Bab, perfecting him as his partner "wife".[A] Their "wedding-day" was the year 1863, when the proclamation of Baha'u'llah perfected the 1844 proclamation of the Bab. This year 1863 was a

> *Day of great rejoicing* when *it behoveth everyone to hasten towards the court of His nearness with exceeding joy, gladness, exultation and delight*, coinciding with what *Christ calls the 'Days of Marriage'....Whatsoever was promised in the sacred Scriptures hath been fulfilled.*[B]

A hundred years later, the 1963 centennial of 1863 saw

> *world-wide celebrations as the 'Most Great Festival,' the 'King of Festivals,' the 'Festival of God' Himself....of the* [1863] *birth of Bahá'u'lláh's prophetic Mission.*[C]

19.10 & 22.8–9, also 21.3 & 7: ***Worship God!*** teaches tersely that **divine Messengers cannot be God but only "as God". In other words, they mirror God**. Thus, Christians see Jesus as **the Son** reflecting the **light of the Spirit** emanating from **the Father** shining like a sun. Similarly, Baha'is see Baha'u'llah as

> *the Messianic reality...like unto a mirror through which the sun of divinity has become resplendent* as if *the sun in the sky and the sun in the mirror are one*, as *the effulgence of His theophany in the mirrors.*[D]

[A] Baha'u'llah *Aqdas* 141.70

[B] ***Day of great rejoicing***, *Tablets of Baha'u'llah* 78–9. ***Christ calls the***, 'Abdu'l-Baha *Tablet to Mr Alwyn J. Baker SW* (1920/12/02) 12.12.193–4. ***Whatsoever was promised***, Shoghi Effendi *Messages to America* 100–1; 'Abdu'l-Baha *SW* (1922/3/21) 13.1.18–9

[C] ***World-wide celebrations as the***, Shoghi Effendi, Ministry of the Custodians 378. ***Of the* [1863] *birth of Baha'u'llah's prophetic mission***, Shoghi Effendi *Letters from the Guardian to Australia and New Zealand* 98

[D] ***The Messianic reality is***, Abdu'l-Baha *Divine Philosophy* 152–3. ***The effulgence***

19.11, 14, 19 & 21: The *beautiful and glorious person riding upon the white horse is the Greatest Name* as God represented by Baha'u'llah. Similarly, Hindus await their Tenth Avatar Lord Kalki riding *his swift white horse Devadatta, sword in hand.*[A]

19.12: *Many sovereign-crowns* fit the eight heads of Abraham, Moses, Zoroaster, Krishna, Buddha, Jesus, Muhammad, and the Bab as the eight Messengers of God prior to Baha'u'llah. They were augured by Islam as the *eight angels bearing the Throne*. They were also augured by Hinduism as the *eight superhuman faculties* of a *divine being* and as the *eight mystic opulences...eight special qualities of Godhead.*[B]

19.12–13, also 1.13: ***The Word of God***, the title, is a *station of distinction* for Baha'u'llah specifically (as is his title *The Father*).[C]

19.13: In prison, Baha'u'llah suffered severe physical abuse.

19.14: On the white stallions, the

> *triumphant hosts of the Celestial Concourse...stand ready and expectant to assist and assure victory to that valiant horseman who with confidence spurs on his charger into the arena of service.*[D]

19.16, also 17.14: ***King of kings and Lord of lords*** as titles for the Bab are titles for Baha'u'llah too who proclaimed himself saying:

> *The King of Kings is with you* and *the Lord of Lords hath come in the shadow of the clouds...summoning you unto Himself....It is not Our wish to lay hands on your kingdoms. Our mission is to seize and possess the hearts of men.*[E]

As the Ottoman Prime-Minister perused the letter from Baha'u'llah to his Sultan 'Abdu'l-'Aziz, he

> *turned the color of a corpse, and remarked: 'It is as if the king of kings were issuing his behest to his humblest vassal king, and regulating his conduct!'*

Alas, however, *the princes of the Church...failed to acknowledge the sovereignty of the 'King of kings'* or to recognize Baha'u'llah as the *Vicegerent of God.*[F]

of His, Baha'u'llah *Tablet to Hardegg* 10.5

[A] ***Beautiful and glorious person***, 'Abdu'l-Baha *TAB* 3.681. ***His swift white horse Debadatta***, *Srimad-Bhagavatam* 12.2.19–20

[B] ***Eight angels bearing the throne***, Quran 69.17. ***Eight superhuman faculties***, *Vishnu Purana* 4.24. http://unification.net/ws/theme161.htm#14. ***Eight mystic opulences***, *Srimad-Bhagavatam* 12.2.19–20.

[C] Baha'u'llah *KI* 176–8

[D] 'Abdu'l-Baha *SWA* 208.264

[E] ***The King of Kings***, Shoghi Effendi *Light* 1935.570. ***The Lord of Lords***, Baha'u'llah *Scriptures* 41.98; Shoghi Effendi *PDC* 71.31; 'Abdu'l-Baha *TAB* 2.404. ***Summoning you unto***, Baha'u'llah *PB* 6, *Aqdas* 83.49; Shoghi Effendi *PDC* 54.26

[F] ***Turned the colour***, Shoghi Effendi *GPB* 160, *PDC* 163.65; *Revelation of*

19.17, also 16.8–9: Here the *sun* signifies Persia.[A]

19.17: *Souls are on the wing like unto birds of holiness and have attained to the divine Kingdom....The notes sung by those birds* are *melodies of peace and reconciliation, of love and unity, of justice and security, of concord and harmony* that *will intoxicate all humanity.*[B]

19.17–8, also 3.20, 19.9: *Every favoured soul is seated at the banquet table of the Lord, receiving his portion of that heavenly feast.*[C]

19.18: The term *humble and important* lacks any *the*, which lets it interpret for folk running the **new** system of spiritual economics.

19.20, also 16.13, 9 & 12: *The beast was seized and...the false-prophet* interpret as Persia's brutal Shah Nasir-i-Din (1831–96) and his hateful Prime-Minister Taqi Kahn (1807–52) as an *'anti-Christ' ...like his predecessor...Haji Mirza Aqasi* [*Aghassi*].[D] In 1852, Taqi Kahn was *seized* by execution ordered by a drunken Nasir-i-Din. In 1896, the same Nasir-i-Din was *seized* by assassination.

19.20, 20.10, 14 × 2, 15 & 21.8: ***Fire*** is the *'fire' of unbelief.*[E]

19.21: *The birds feasted* evokes the Zoroastrian tradition of laying out the corpses of their dead on *towers of silence open to the sky, on the mountain tops* for birds to pick at their flesh, for the sun to bleach their bones, and for the sky to receive their spirits.[F]

Baha'u'llah, 2.47–54. ***The princes of the Church***, Shoghi Effendi *PDC* 257.103. ***Vicegerent of God***, Shoghi Effendi *PDC* 37.20

[A] 'Abdu'l-Baha *SAQ* 13.68

[B] 'Abdu'l-Baha *TAB* 3.675, 2.319

[C] 'Abdu'l-Baha *SWA* 28.57

[D] Shoghi Effendi (1932–3) *High Endeavours Messages to Alaska, 85.69*

[E] *Baha'u'llah KI* 118

[F] 'Abdu'l-Baha *Summon up Remembrance* 175

Apocalypse Chapter 20
The Jewish Seventh Millennium

20.1 Now I saw an Angel landing from the sky, holding the key to the Abyss and a big chain in his hand.

Now I saw Baha'u'llah arriving from the One Religion of God, bringing its remedy for spiritual error and its great Law sustained by his power.

2 He seized the dragon, the ancient serpent that is lying evil and hatred. He bound it for a thousand years 3 and tossed it into the Abyss. He shut and sealed over it so that it would no longer deceive nations (until the thousand years end; after these years it is bound, it is bound to be released for a short time.)

He confronts Muslim Militarism, the primeval sinfulness that is lying evil and hatred. He binds it down for a millennium and dooms it to its own spiritual error. He stifles and isolates it so that it will no more trick nations (until the millennium ends; after these years it is bound down, it is bound to run free for a short divine time.)

4 Then I saw thrones. On them sat people. To them was given authority to judge. I saw the souls of those beheaded for this testimony of Jesus and for this Word of God, and those who did not worship the beast or its copy and did not take its tattoo on their forehead or on their hand.

Then I see seats in the Baha'i Universal House of Justice. To them are elected leaders. To them is assigned authority to govern. I hear the souls of Baha'is beheaded for their testimony to the Bab as Jesus returned and for him as this Speaker for God, and early Baha'is who had not adored the brutal Muslim system or its Qajar clone and had not run its religious discrimination or cruel taxation.

They have lived on with the Messiah and have reigned for a thousand years. 5 The rest of the dead will not come to life until the thousand years end.

They live on in spirit with the Messiah Baha'u'llah and shall lead the Millennium. The rest of the dead in spirit shall find spiritual life only after the Millennium ends.

This is the prime resurrection. 6 Blessed, indeed holy, is the person who is taking part in the prime resurrection. The second-death has no hold over these folk. Rather, they shall be Priests of God with the Messiah. With him, they

This is Baha'u'llah rising to proclaim the Cause of God. Blessed, indeed unique, are you who take part in his rise to proclaim the Cause of God. Spiritual death has no hold over you folk. Rather, you are teachers for God with your Messiah Baha'u'llah. With

shall reign for a thousand years.	him, you shall lead the Jewish Seventh Millennium.
7 But when the thousand years end, hatred will be released from its prison. 8 It will set out to deceive nations within the four corners of the globe as Gog and Gog's, to muster them to war, their number being as the sand of the sea, 9 they will have mounted up across the breadth of the globe and surrounded the camp of the faithful and the beloved city.	But after the Millennium ends in AD 3240, hatred will again run free in its selfishness. It will set out to trick nations across the length and breadth of the globe as a global dictator and his people, to muster them to the war of yore, their number being as many as the descendants of Abraham, they shall cross the face of the globe and surround the Baha'i World Center and its beloved Haifa (as well as Haifa and its beloved Israel).
But fire from the sky has razed down and consumed them. 10 The lying evil deceiving them has been tossed into the pool of fire and sulfur where also that beast and false-prophet are. They will have been tormented day and night into the Eras of the Eras.	But God's fury from His One Religion shall flash down and destroy them. The lying evil dictator tricking them shall be doomed to isolation in unbelief and despair where also that brutal Shah and his antichrist Alem are. They are being afflicted as God's light lights the night from the old Cycle to the new Cycle.
11 Now I saw a great white Throne and the One seated on it from whose face the earth and the sky fled (no space was found for them).	Now I see the magnificent pure Baha'i Revelation and its Founder Baha'u'llah from whose presence old material laws and old spiritual laws are fading away (no role is open for them).
12 I saw the dead, the important and the humble, standing before the Throne. Some short scrolls were opened. Also another short scroll was opened, the one that is the *Full Book of Life*.	I see unbelievers, important and humble, facing his Baha'i Revelation. Lists of their deeds are revealed. Also another list is revealed, the one that acclaims all morally decent people.
The dead were judged by the records in these short scrolls, according to their deeds. 13 The ocean gave up the dead in it. *Death* and *the Unseen* gave up the dead in them. Everyone	Unbelievers are judged by the records in these lists, as their deeds deserve. Truth sets free the unbelievers in it. Atheism and agnosticism release the unbelievers in them. Everybody is judged as

WAS JUDGED ACCORDING THEIR DEEDS. 14 *DEATH* AND THE *UNSEEN* WERE TOSSED INTO THE POOL OF FIRE. THE POOL OF FIRE IS THAT SAME SECOND-DEATH. 15 WHOEVER WAS NOT FOUND LISTED IN THE *BOOK OF LIFE* WAS TOSSED INTO THAT POOL OF FIRE.

their deeds deserve. Atheism and agnosticism are doomed to their isolation in unbelief. Isolation in unbelief is that same spiritual death. People who have gone unacclaimed as morally decent are doomed to their isolation in unbelief.

Comments:

20.3, 5 & 7: The best candidate for the fabled golden *Millennium* is the AM 6000–7000/AD 2240–3240 Jewish Seventh Millennium.[A]
20.4: **The Baha'i Universal House of Justice** is the Faith's supreme governing body. Established on the 1963 centennial of Baha'u'llah's 1863 proclamation, it is vested with the authority of Baha'u'llah, the Bab, 'Abdu'l-Baha, and Shoghi Effendi. The global Baha'i community elects its nine members every five years. The House's physical seat on Mount Carmel is a white marble building. This Universal House of Justice will one day be *regarded by posterity as the last refuge of a tottering civilization*.[B] It shall even come to exercise some role in leading the globe.

The Baha'i Universal House of Justice
on Mount Carmel

[A] Isaac *Newton's Secrets* 39, *The End of the World, Day of Judgment and World to Come*, Yahuda MS9.2f.123r
[B] Shoghi Effendi *Light* 1070.318

20.4: *The 'mark' here signifies character.*[A] The jizya forehead-tattoo depicts an ugly state of mind; the kharaj hand-tattoo depicts evil deeds.
20.5–6: ***By Prime 'Resurrection'*** *is meant the rise of the Manifestation of God to proclaim His Cause*, namely Baha'u'llah. No theological basis exists for the traditional translation *First Resurrection* that implies the existence of some sort of second resurrection.[B]
20.8–10, *GOG AND GOG'S*: These verses interpret for the coming and going of a far-off distant time. The Hebrew cover-name ***MAGOG*** means literally *from-the-Gog* (*MI-HA-GOG*), or *Gog's people*, which translates as simply *Gog's*. An alternative meaning for *MAGOG* is *land of Gog* (*MATU-GOG*) in Accadian, which fits its original full Hebrew source *Gog, the land of Gog, chief prince of expanding territory* (*'meshech'*) *and abomination* (*'tuval'*).[C]
20.8: **Haifa** is the literal center of the Ba***ha'i Fa***ith! The name *Haifa* derives from *hof* as Hebrew for *beach* or *shore.*
20.9: *The camp of the faithful and the beloved city* interprets small as *the World Center of Baha'is and its beloved Haifa* and big as *Haifa and its beloved Israel.*
20.11: ***The great white throne****...is the body of the Greatest Name* and *the face of...the Almighty.*[D] In addition, the Universal House of Justice made of white marble is a *white throne* too.
20.12: Unbelievers are

> *standing before My Throne and yet remain unaware thereof.... The record of deeds will be laid open; the prophets and witnesses will be brought in. Fair judgment will be given between them: they will not be wronged and every soul will be repaid in full for what it has done.*[E]

20.12–14: *By the terms 'life' and 'death'...is intended the life of faith and the death of unbelief....When a dead body is thrown into the ocean, the waves will throw it back upon the shore. So it is with the Ocean of Truth....If a believer has not these bounties of God, the sea will roll until he is finally cast out....What death is more wretched than to flee from the Source of everlasting life?*[F]

[A] 'Abdu'l-Baha cited by Brittingham 1
[B] ***Prime 'Resurrection'* is meant**, Baha'u'llah *KI* 169–70. **No theological basis exists**, Aune *52C* 1090–1
[C] Ezek. 38.2–3
[D] ***The great white throne***, 'Abdu'l-Baha *TAB* 3.681. ***The face of***, Baha'u'llah *ESW* 129, *Prayers and Meditations* 176.273
[E] ***Standing before My Throne***, Baha'u'llah *Gems* 30.24, *Prayers and Meditations* 50.72–3. ***The record of deeds will be laid open***, Quran 39.68
[F] ***By the terms 'life' and 'death'***, Baha'u'llah *KI* 114. ***When a dead body***, 'Abdu'l-Baha *Scriptures* 964.501. ***What death is more wretched***, Baha'u'llah *Gems* 61.45, *KI* 116, 118, 144–5, 158

Apocalypse Chapter 21
New Jerusalem is Divine Civilization

21.1 NEXT, I SAW A NEW SKY AND A NEW EARTH, FOR THE FIRST SKY AND THE FIRST EARTH HAD PASSED AWAY (THE SEA EXISTS NO LONGER).	Next, I see God's new spiritual Law and His new material Law, for His old spiritual laws and old material laws are transcended (divisive doctrines exist no more).
2 THEN I SAW THE HOLY CITY OF NEW JERUSALEM LANDING FROM THE SKY FROM GOD, ARRAYED AS A BRIDE FOR HER GROOM.	Then I see its unique system of divine civilization arriving from the One Religion of God, presenting Baha'u'llah as the One promised by the Bab.
3 NOW I HEARD A LOUD VOICE FROM THE THRONE SAYING: *BEHOLD, THE PRESENCE OF GOD AMONG HUMAN-BEINGS! HIS PRESENCE SHALL BE MANIFEST AMONG THEM. THEY THEMSELVES SHALL BE HIS PEOPLE. GOD HIMSELF SHALL BE WITH THEM AS THEIR GOD.* 4 *HE SHALL WIPE EVERY TEAR FROM THEIR EYES.* *EVEN DEATH SHALL NOT EXIST ANY LONGER. NEITHER SHALL GRIEF, NOR SCREAMING, NOR PAIN EXIST ANY LONGER, FOR THE FIRST THINGS HAVE PASSED AWAY.*	Now I hear Baha'u'llah as the Proclaimer of the Baha'i Revelation saying: *Behold, I am the Presence of God among true believers! I, His Presence, am manifest among you. You yourselves are His people. God Himself is with you as me His mirror. I shall soothe away your sorrows and kindle light in your eyes.* *Even atheism shall not exist any more. Neither shall anguish, nor uproar, nor agony exist any more, for the old laws and divisive doctrines are transcended.*
5 THEN THE ENTHRONED-ONE SAID: *BEHOLD, I AM MAKING ALL THINGS NEW!*	Then Baha'u'llah the Founder adds: *Behold, I am making everything new!*
CONTINUING, HE SAYS: *RECORD THAT THESE SAME WORDS ARE TRUSTWORTHY AND TRUE.*	Continuing, he says: *John, publish that we same Divine Speakers, the Bab and I, are trustworthy and true.*
6 NEXT, HE TOLD ME: *THESE WORDS HAVE COME TO EXIST! I MYSELF AM THE A AND THE Z, THE BEGINNING AND THE ENDING.*	Next, he tells me: *We Divine Speakers have come to exist! I, Baha'u'llah, am the Founder and the Fulfiller of Faiths, the Opener of God's new Cycle of Fulfillment and the Closer of His old Cycle of Prophecy.*

I myself shall supply the thirsty person from the source of the water of life as a gift.

I, Baha'u'llah. am supplying you truth-seekers with me as the source of the knowledge of life for free.

7 *The one who prevails shall inherit these things. For him or her, I shall be as God. For me, he or she shall be an heir.*

You who prevail are gaining my teachings. For you, I mirror God. For me, you are successors.

8 *But as for the cowards, traitors, vile persons, murderers, fornicators, sorcerers, idol-worshipers, and all the liars, their fate is in that pool burning with fire and sulfur—the one that is the second-death.*

But as for the cowards, traitors, vile persons, killers, exploiters, drug-dealers, profiteers, and all the liars, their fate is that isolation devastating with its unbelief and despair—the fate that is spiritual death.

9 Now one of the seven Angels bearing the seven pitchers, packing the last seven afflictions, came and spoke with me, saying:

Come! I shall show you the bride, the wife of the Ram.

Now Baha'u'llah, the foremost of the seven Middle East Messengers dispensing the seven doses of God's fury of His 1800–1900s final seven severe lessons, appears and speaks with me, inviting:

Come! I am revealing to you my promised self, as the partner perfecting the Bab.

10 At this he soared me in spirit over a large and lofty mountain and showed me the Holy City of Jerusalem landing from the sky from God:

At this he soars my spirit over magnificent and majestic Mount Carmel and reveals to me the unique system of its divine civilization arriving from the One Religion of God:

- 11 Possessing the Glory of God,
- Its brilliance resembling a most precious gemstone like a gemstone of crystallizing diamond,
- 12 Possessing a broad and high wall,
- Possessing 12 gates, and over these gates, 12 angels,

- Emanating him, Baha'u'llah,
- Its brilliance shining superb strength as the strength of excellent justice,
- Announcing its liberal and lofty Law,
- Beckoning to the Faiths' ways of loving wisdom, and guarding their ways of loving wisdom, the Faiths' Founders,

- Possessing engraved names that are the names of the 12 tribes of heirs of Israel,

- Possessing formal qualities that are the qualities of the Baha'i successors of the People of Israel who first saw God,

- 13Three gates from and for the East, three gates from and for the North, three gates from and for the South, and three gates from and for the West,

- Ways of loving wisdom from and for the East, ways of loving wisdom from and for the North, ways of loving wisdom from and for the South, and ways of loving wisdom from and for the West,

- 14The wall of the city possessing 12 foundations, upon them the 12 names of the 12 Apostles of the Ram.

- The Law of its divine system announcing the Faiths' teachings, guarding them the Faiths' qualities through the Faiths' Sons of Jacob, Apostles of Jesus, and Imams of Muhammad for the Bab.

15The person speaking with me held a gold rod to measure this city, its gates, and its wall.

Baha'u'llah teaching me acts as a glorious guide to present this divine system, its ways of loving wisdom, and its Law.

16The city is laid out as a square, its length equal to its breadth.

His divine system is founded squarely on justice, as profound as it is liberal.

With the rod, he measured the city at 12,000 furlongs. Its length, breadth, and height are equal.

Acting as the guide, he presents his divine system as hard work by the Faiths' many followers. Its justice is as lofty as it is profound and liberal.

17He measured its wall at 144 cubits—a measure of a human-being, the one that is an Angel's,

He presents its Law as the Faiths' followers progressively perfecting human standards–the presentation by a believer, the one that is his the Messenger's,

18The matrix of its wall diamond,

The enduring essence of its Law brilliant justice,

The city pure gold like clear glass,

His divine system shining the pure splendor of clear truth,

19-20The foundations of the city wall arrayed with all kinds of precious gemstone:

The basic teachings of its divine system's Law presenting all kinds of superb strength:

• The 1st foundation **diamond**,	Its 1st teaching, **the oneness of humanity** sparking justice as brilliant as diamond,
• The 2nd **sapphire**,	Its 2nd teaching, the **independent investigation of truth** freely soaring the true-blue sapphire sky,
• The 3rd **chalcedony**,	Its 3rd teaching, the **unity of spiritual reality** as pure as the white of chalcedony,
• The 4th **emerald**,	Its 4th teaching, **one foundation of all religions** gleaming the unity of emerald green,
• The 5th **sardonyx**,	Its 5th teaching, the **agreement of religion and science** bonded as red and brown sardonyx layers,
• The 6th **ruby**,	Its 6th teaching, the **equality of men and women** bonded by fiery love in the red of ruby,
• The 7th **chrysolite**,	Its 7th teaching, the **abandonment of prejudices** healing the human spectrum in the green of chrysolite,
• The 8th **beryl**,	Its 8th teaching, **universal peace** emitting the green harmony and the blue loyalty of beryl,
• The 9th **topaz**,	Its 9th teaching, **universal education** instilling the glorious wisdom of the gold of topaz,
• The 10th **chrysoprase**,	Its 10th teaching, **spiritual economics** with the gray-green harmony of chrysoprase,
• The 11th **jacinth**,	Its 11th teaching, **an auxiliary global language** as clear as pink jacinth,
• The 12th **amethyst**;	Its 12th teaching, **a supreme global tribunal** to end war in the purple majesty of amethyst;

21 The 12 gates 12 pearls, each single gate from a single pearl,	The Faiths' ways of loving wisdom the Faiths' knowledge, each specific way of loving wisdom specific knowledge,
The city's main-square pure gold like transparent glass.	Its system's public scene the pure splendor of transparent truth.
22 Yet within it I saw no Temple, for the Almighty Lord God is its Temple, also the Ram.	Yet within it I saw no routine religion, for the Almighty Lord God forms its Faith, also the Bab.
23 This city needs no sun or moon to light it, for the Glory of God has lit it, and its lamp is the Ram.	This divine system needs no priests or rabbis, bishops or priests, ulema or cadis to educate it, for Baha'u'llah teaches it, and its first Revelator was the Bab.
24 Nations shall walk by its light and the rulers of the earth shall bring their glory into it.	Nations shall advance through its teaching and the leaders of the planet shall find their splendor through it.
25 Its gates shall never close in 24 hours, for no night shall exist there.	Its ways of loving wisdom shall never end in this Millennial Day, for no ignorance can exist here.
26 Its gates shall draw the glory and the honor of the nations into it.	Its ways of loving wisdom are drawing the splendor and the honor of the nations into it.
27 Nothing at all defiling nor anybody doing anything vile or false shall ever enter it, just those who are listed in the Book of Life of the Ram.	Nothing at all impure nor anybody dealing in anything foul or crooked can ever live it, just people who can be acclaimed as morally decent per the Bab.

Comments:

21.1–27: ***Selected Writings of 'Abdu'l-Baha* (*SWA*) 3.12–13** addresses parts of Chapter 21 and supplies many citations for it.

21.1–2: ***The new heaven and the new earth*** *are come....The heavenly Jerusalem is none other than divine civilization....By the term 'earth' is meant the earth of understanding and knowledge, and by 'heavens' the heavens of divine Revelation.... The first heaven and earth signify the former Law....The teachings and the Law of God will entirely spread over the earth, and all men will enter the Cause of God, and the earth will be completely inhabited by believers; therefore, there will be no more sea, for the dwelling place* *and abode of man is the dry land....The field of that Law will become the pleasure-ground of man...solid; the feet do not slip upon it.*[A]

21.2: ***The holy City, new Jerusalem*** *hath come down from on high in the form of a maid of heaven, veiled, beauteous, and unique ...acclaiming, 'This is the City of God and his Abode'.... Behold the New Jerusalem...the great City of God....The bride of Zion has appeared.*[B]

For a prior spiritual Era, the noble bride of New Jerusalem emanating love portrayed Christianity.

21.2, also 21.9–10, 22.17 & 19.7–9: Again the promised "bride" Baha'u'llah spiritually "marries" the Bab as his "groom", perfecting him as his partner "wife" on their 1863 "wedding-day".[C]

21.2, also 19.7–9, 21.9–10 & 22.17: The Sabbath-Bride is Baha'u'llah who embodies the Millennial Shechinah Presence of God.

21.3: *God...shall be with them* evokes Jesus's title *EMANUEL* meaning *God-With-Us.*

21.3 & 7, "**As God**": ***The*** *God* (***Ho*** *THEOS*) is the normal honorific Greek form for God. Yet here, twice, just *God* (*THEOS*) appears by itself. These two exceptional occurrences of *THEOS* by itself render as "as God" and signify Baha'u'llah **mirroring** God.[D]

21.4–5: *God Omnipotent hath...made all things new....In this Day ...the earth is renewed....the time of former things is past and a new time has become manifest.*[E]

21.4–5: *He hath wiped away their tears, kindled their light, rejoiced their hearts and enraptured their souls. Death shall no more overtake them neither shall sorrow, weeping or tribulation afflict them.*[F] The right-column interpretation imports the Baha'i interpretive phrase *kindled light.*[G]

21.6: No clear subject exists for the verb *have come to exist* (*gegonan*). Here *these same Words* in prior v. 21.5 are taken to be its subject.

[A] ***The new heaven and the new earth***, 'Abdu'l-Baha *SWA* 3.12. ***The heavenly Jerusalem is***, 'Abdu'l-Baha *PUP* 102. ***By the term 'earth' is***, Baha'u'llah *KI* 47–8; Quran 14.48. ***The first heaven and earth signify***, 'Abdu'l-Baha *SAQ* 13.67

[B] ***The holy city, New Jerusalem***, 'Abdu'l-Baha *SWA* 3.12. ***Behold, the New Jerusalem***, Baha'u'llah *Scriptures Tablet to the Jews* 47.116–7. ***The bride of Zion***, Abdu'l-Baha *PUP* 20

[C] Baha'u'llah *Aqdas* 141.70

[D] Apropos, the honorific third-person Greek *HO* (*THE*) echoes in the old English honorific vocative address *"O"* as, for example, in "*O Judge,...*"

[E] ***God Omnipotent hath***, 'Abdu'l-Baha (1896/07/16) *One of First General Messages to the Baha'is of America SWA* 3.12, *SW* (1924/03) 14.12.358. ***In this Day***, Baha'u'llah *Scriptures Tablet to the Jews* 47.117 to Eliahu Cohen in (1) *Compilations Baha'i Scriptures* 117 (2) *Taaje Wahhaj* 28 compiled by Zabihullah Azizi (3) *Amr va'l-Haqq* 2.242–3, and (4) *Bishaarat* compiled by Hosaam Noqabaa'ee

[F] 'Abdu'l-Baha (1896/07/16) *One of First General Messages to the Baha'is of America SWA* 3.12, *SW* (1924/03) 14.12.358

[G] 'Abdu'l-Baha *SWA* 3.12

21.6: *The seas of Divine wisdom and Divine utterance have risen ....The Hand of Divine bounty proffereth unto you the Water of Life....Hasten to drink your fill....How numerous are the thirsty ones who have panted after the fountain of Thy living waters... athirst of the fountain of the water of life....The state in which one should be to seriously search for the truth is the condition of the thirsty, burning soul desiring the water of life, of the fish struggling to reach the sea, of the sufferer seeking for the true doctor to obtain the divine cure, of the lost caravan endeavoring to find the right road, of the lost and wandering ship striving to reach the shore of salvation.*[A]

21.7: The people who previously prevailed spiritually in Chapters 2–3 now receive their *most glorious heritage.*[B] The Sabaeans have already gained wisdom from their successor Faiths. Jews now no longer suffer. Zoroastrians learn the new name of Ahura Mazda. Hindus gain authority over nations. Buddhists are acclaimed as morally decent. Christians promote God's new Baha'i Faith. And Muslims open Allah's new Baha'i Cycle.[C]

21.8 & 17: The *indeclinable idiom "the* ***one*** *that is"* (*"ho estin"*) qualifies nouns of any gender.[D] So *the* ***one*** *that is* ambiguously qualifies v. 21.8's *fate* or *pool* and v. 21.17's *measure* or *human-being*.

21.9: The masculine *packing* qualifies the masculine *Angels* (not the feminine *Pitchers*).

21.10, also 4.1–2: Baha'u'llah is the *falcon on the hand of the Almighty...soaring to the heaven of truth.*[E]

21.10: *Isaiah hath announced...get thee up into the high mountain.... The Great City hath descended from heaven and Zion is re-vivified and rejoiced, by the appearance of the Manifestation of God.*[F]

21.10–17: *Truth...sheddeth its bounties through twelve stations of holiness* through *stainless and unsullied personages...proclaiming the oneness of God....In the days of...Moses...twelve...leaders of the twelve tribes....In the dispensation of...Christ...twelve Apostles....In the days of Muhammad...twelve dawning-points of holiness* [Imams] *....Accordingly did Saint John the Divine tell of twelve gates ...souls who are as guiding stars, as portals of knowledge and grace; and within these gates there stand twelve angels. By 'angel' is meant the power of the confirmations of God....The*

[A] ***The seas of divine wisdom***, Baha'u'llah *PB* 117, *Aqdas* 2.20. ***How numerous are***, Baha'u'llah *Prayers and Meditations* 29.33. ***Athirst of the***, 'Abdu'l-Baha *Traveler's Narrative* 4, *SWA* 3.13. ***The state in which***, 'Abdu'l-Baha *SAQ* 10.38

[B] 'Abdu'l-Baha *SWA* 3.13

[C] Rev. 2.11, 17, 26–8, 3.5, 12, 21 & 2.7

[D] Aune, *52C* 1112.8c–c

[E] Baha'u'llah *Scriptures Tablet to the Persian Zoroastrian Baha'is* 50.132

[F] Baha'u'llah *Scriptures Tablet To An Oriental Jew* 48.120

> *candle of God's confirming power shineth out from the lamp-niche of those souls....These twelve gates surround the entire world* and provide *a shelter for all creatures.*[A]

21.12, etc.: **The number *12*** codes for various facets of Faiths in *12 tribes, 12 stars, 12 Angels, 12 gates, 12 foundations, 12 thousand furlongs, 12 gemstones,* and *12 pearls.*

21.13: The double translation ***from and for*** gates as *ways of loving wisdom* combines two meanings for *apo.*

21.15: As the *expected Builder of the Temple,*[B] Baha'u'llah holds a gold rod that surpasses the rods of prior Messengers who

> *guided the people with a staff grown out of the earth, and shepherded them with a rod, like unto the rod of Moses. Others trained and shepherded the people with a rod of iron, as in the dispensation of Muhammad. And in this present cycle, because it is the mightiest of Dispensations, that rod grown out of the vegetable kingdom and that rod of iron will be transformed into a rod of purest gold, taken from out the endless treasure houses in the Kingdom of the Lord. By this rod will the people be trained....How much ground hath been gained by the Law of God and His Teachings in this dispensation, how they have reached such heights that they far transcend the dispensations gone before.*[C]

21.16: As well as acting as a number-code, *12,000 furlongs* also projects the grandeur of the 1500-mile-wide New Jerusalem.

21.17: The unit *cubit* codes for *human standards.*

21.17: As well as acting as a number-code, *144 cubits* also projects the strength of the 72–yard-thick New Jerusalem wall of Law.

21.18–19, also 12, 14–15 & 17: The spiritual wall of Law protects the divine civilization of New Jerusalem, just as a physical wall has protected the material civilization of the city of Jerusalem.

21.21, also 17.4, 18.12 & 16: ***Pearls*** shine knowledge hidden in the

> *ocean of words...pearls of wisdom that lie hid in its depths, divinely revealed verses* as a *treasury of divine pearls.... Immerse yourself in this ocean of...words...unravel its secrets, and discover all the pearls of wisdom.*[D]

Pearls also glint negative hidden knowledge as *cunning* (vv. 17.4, 18.12 & 16).

21.22: The Temple has grown too big to be seen. It has grown global and is identifying itself afresh as New Jerusalem.[E]

[A] 'Abdu'l-Baha *SWA* 142.165–6
[B] Baha'u'llah *Tablet to Hardegg* 3.5–7
[C] 'Abdu'l-Baha *SWA* 142.166–7
[D] Baha'u'llah *KI* 204, *GWB* 153.327, *PB 118–9, Aqdas* 182.85
[E] Swete *Apocalypse of St. John Greek Text* 286–92

21.22–23: Baha'u'llah urges Jews to read Revelation too, and to *reflect upon the words of John, wherein he hath prophesied of the Holy City: 'And I saw no Temple therein....The City had no need of the sun, neither of the moon, to shine in it for the Glory of God (Baha'u'llah) did lighten it'.*[A]

Revelation is, after all, a Jewish Apocalypse.[B]

21.23: The Baha'i Faith prohibits clergy or communal prayer.[C]

21.24: Two rulers who became Baha'is were the late Queen Marie of Romania and the late King Malietoa Tanumafili II of Western Samoa.

[A] Baha'u'llah *Scriptures Tablet to the Jews* 47.117

[B] http://www.jewishencyclopedia.com/articles/12712-revelation-book-of

[C] Except for the dead

Apocalypse Chapter 22
The Tree of Life is God's One Religion

22.1At this, he showed me a river
of water of life sparkling like
crystal, flowing from the
Throne of God and the Ram,
2between the main-square of
the city and the river, here and
there, a Tree of Life producing
12 fruits monthly each yielding
its fruit, with the leaves of the
Tree for a healing of the
nations.

At this, Baha'u'llah reveals to me his vast knowledge of life shining its excellence, broadcasting his Baha'i Revelation from God and the Bab, amid the public scene of its divine system and its vast knowledge, far and wide, wisdom fruiting the Faiths' teachings by the Age each bearing its bounty, with its pages of wisdom as a cure for the nations.

3No type of exclusion shall
exist any longer. Within the
city shall exist the Throne of
God and the Ram. Its, His, and
his servants shall conduct its
worship. 4They shall see his
face, with his name on their
foreheads. 5Night shall exist
no longer. They shall need no
lamplight or sunlight, for the
Lord God shall enlighten
them. They shall reign into
the Eras of the Eras.

No type of exclusivity shall exist any more. Within the divine system is his Baha'i Revelation from God and the Bab. Its, His, and his servants have led its worship since 1844. They recognized his presence, endorsing him openly. Ignorance exists no more. They need no rituals or clergy, for the Lord God has taught them. They have led the old Cycle of Prophecy into the new Cycle of Fulfillment.

6Next, he told me:
*These Words are trustworthy
and true. The Lord God of
the Spirits of the Prophets
has sent His Angel to show
His servants what had to
happen fast.*

Next, Baha'u'llah tells me:
We Divine Speakers, the Bab and I, are trustworthy and true. In AD 95, the Lord God of us Manifestations of the Prophets sent me His Messenger to reveal to His servants the events that have flashed fast.

7*Behold, I am coming soon!
Blessed is the person who
takes to heart the Words of
the prophecy in this same
short scroll!*

Behold, I came in 1863, just after the Bab. Blessed are you readers who have taken seriously us Divine Speakers in this interpretation of John's short Revelation tale!

8Also I John too, the hearer
and seer of these visions, even
as I heard and saw, have fallen
to worship at the feet of the

Also I John too, the recipient and interpreter of these events, even as I receive and interpret, am submitting myself and humbly

Angel showing these visions to me.

worshiping Baha'u'llah revealing these events to me.

9But he tells me:

Look, don't! I myself am your fellow servant and of your brothers the Prophets and those taking to heart the Words in this same short scroll. Worship God!

But he tells me:

Stop, John! I am your Baha'i fellow and of your brother prophets and followers taking seriously the Bab and me as the Divine Speakers in your same short Revelation tale. Worship God [*not His Mirror!*].

10Next he tells me:

Do not seal up the Words of the prophecy in this same short scroll—for the time is near. 11*Let the wrongdoer still do wrong and let the depraved still act depraved. But let the good person remain good and let the faithful person remain faithful.*

Next he praises me:

You have not hidden us Divine Speakers in this interpretation of your own short Revelation tale—for its time has come. Wrongdoers may still do wrong and depraved persons may still act depraved. But good people remain good and faithful believers remain faithful.

12*Listen, I am coming soon with my reward of myself with me, to award each person as his or her work is—*
13*I myself, the A and the Z, the First and the Last, the Beginning and the Ending.*

Listen, I came in 1863, just after the Bab, with my reward of myself with me, to award each of you as your deeds deserve—I Baha'u'llah, the Founder and the Fulfiller of Faiths, the First-to-Last Manifestation of God, the Opener of His new Cycle of Fulfillment and the Closer of His old Cycle of Prophecy.

14*Blessed are those who wash their robes and carry out their commands, so that their right to the Tree of Life shall take effect and they may enter the city though the gates.*

Blessed are you who have refined your virtue and have obeyed my teachings, so that your right to divine wisdom is taking effect and you are living divine civilization through its ways of loving wisdom.

15 *Out with the dogs—namely the sorcerers, the fornicators, the murderers, the idol-worshipers, and all the lovers and creators of falsehood!*

Stay away you depraved persons—namely you drug-dealers, you exploiters, you killers, you profiteers, and all you lovers of and dealers in deceit!

16 *I MYSELF JESUS SENT MY ANGEL TO WITNESS TO YOU FOR THESE VISIONS OVER THE CHURCHES.*
I MYSELF AM THE ROOT AND THE SHOOT OF A BELOVED DAVID, THE SHINING DAWN-STAR,
17 *THE SPIRIT AND THE BRIDE. THE SPIRIT AND THE BRIDE SAY 'COME!' LET YOU WHO HEAR, REPLY 'COME!' LET YOU WHO THIRST COME. LET YOU WHO WISH, TAKE WATER OF LIFE AS A GIFT.*

I myself Jesus have sent my Baha'u'llah to witness to you readers and Messengers for these events transcending your Faiths. I, Baha'u'llah, am the source and the successor of the beloved Bab, the radiant Teacher dawning this new Day, God's Manifestation and Promised-One. I, His Manifestation and Promised-One, say 'Welcome'. Let you who understand, reply 'Welcome!' Let you truth-seekers come. Let you who wish, learn my knowledge of life for free.

18 ***I MYSELF SWEAR TO ALL THE HEARERS OF THE WORDS OF THE PROPHECY IN THIS SAME SHORT SCROLL. IF ANYBODY ADD TO THEM, GOD SHALL ADD TO HIM OR HER THE AFFLICTIONS RECORDED IN THIS SAME SHORT SCROLL!***
19 ***IF ANYBODY TAKE AWAY FROM THE WORDS IN THE SHORT SCROLL OF THIS SAME PROPHECY, GOD SHALL TAKE AWAY FROM HIS OR HER SHARE IN THE TREE OF LIFE AND THE HOLY CITY RECORDED IN THIS SAME SHORT SCROLL!***

I, Baha'u'llah, promise to all you reading about us Divine Speakers in the interpretation of John's Revelation tale. If its author has embellished us, God shall embellish him with the severe lessons described by John's Revelation tale! If he has belittled us Divine Speakers in the Revelation tale of his same interpretation, God shall belittle his share in the divine wisdom and unique system described by John's Revelation tale!

20 *SPEAKING IS THE ONE WITNESSING TO THESE VISIONS:*
YES, I AM COMING SOON!

Speaking is Baha'u'llah witnessing to these events:
Yes, I came in 1863, just after the Bab!

AMEN! COME LORD JESUS.
21 MAY THIS BLESSING OF THE LORD JESUS BE WITH ALL PEOPLE.

Indeed so! Welcome Lord Jesus! This blessing from the Lord Jesus is for all folk.

***AN UNVEILING* BY JOHN**

***A REVELATION* BY JOHN**

Tomb of John at Ephesus.
He died about AD 100

Comments:

22.1 & 17, also 7.17, ***river of life***: Baha'u'llah's hundred-Bibles-worth of Writings are a surging

river of everlasting life that hath flowed from...the pen of the merciful...streamed forth from...the throne as *rivers of Divine utterance* as *Tablets of God* to the *Most Great Ocean....One shower of the ocean...quickens the dead souls in the desert of ignorance with the spring of intelligence True servants of God...drink of the soft-flowing river of immortality.*[A]

22.2, 14 & 19, also 2.7, ***Tree of Life***: *Wisdom is a tree of life.... From the seed of reality religion has grown into a tree which has put forth leaves and branches, blossoms and fruit....The seed of reality must be sown again in human hearts in order that a new tree may grow therefrom and new divine fruits refresh the world....The tree...is just beginning to grow. Before long, it will produce buds, bring forth leaves and fruits, and cast its shade over the East and the West...through the power of the divine springtime, the downpour of the celestial clouds and the heat of the Sun of Reality....This fruit is the knowing* [of] *God and love for God. The Tree of life...is the Shechinah....Wing then thy flight unto this divine Tree and partake of its fruits.*[B]

[A] ***River of everlasting***, Baha'u'llah *Persian Hidden Words* 6.37, *Prayers and Meditations* 2.4, *GWB* 18.43, *Summons of the Lord of Hosts,* 1.33.19, *TB* 268. ***One shower***, Abdu'l-Baha *Paris Talks* 82, *SAQ* 19.92; Baha'u'llah *Scriptures* 50.130, *GWB* 14.33

[B] ***Wisdom is a tree of life***, Prov. 3.12, 18. ***From the seed of reality***, Abdu'l-

The Tree of Life guided also the calendar and the worship of the Essenes, for whom its seven roots signified the earthly mother and her angels of sun, water, air, earth, life, and joy supplying physical sustenance, and its seven branches signified the heavenly father and his angels of power, love, wisdom, eternal life, creative work, and peace providing spiritual sustenance.[A]

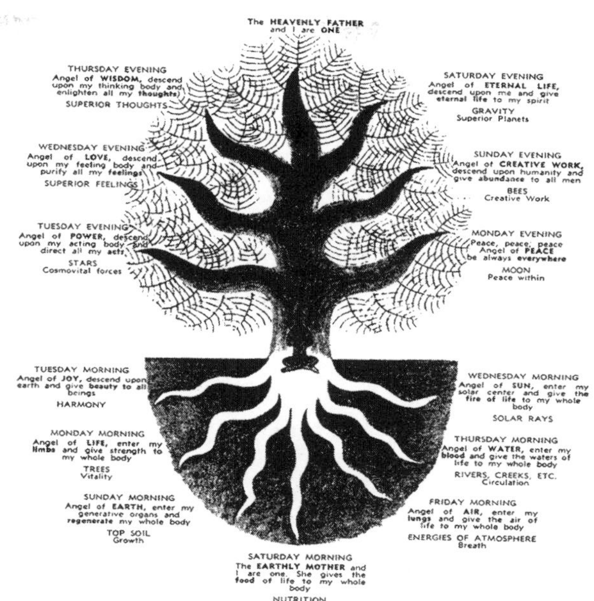

Essene version of the Tree of Life

22.2: Baha'u'llah is *the Healer of Infirmities* and *the falcon on the hand of the Almighty* bearing *healing in* [*his*] *wings*.[B]

22.3–5: *Those on whose foreheads Thy most exalted pen hath written: 'These! The people of Bahá. Through them have been shed the splendors of the light of guidance'.*[C]

22.14: *Blessed is the affrighted one who took refuge under the shadow of My domes!…Blessed is the ear which heard, the tongue which witnessed, and the eye which beheld and knew the soul of the Lord.…Blessed is whosoever adorned his head with the Wreath of My love!…To elucidate these words...none is given to quaff even a dewdrop thereof unless he entereth within this city.…*So *open...the gates!*[D]

Baha *PUP* 141–2. ***The tree...is just beginning***, Abdu'l-Baha *TAB* 3.516, *SAQ* 30.123–4, Baha'u'llah *ESW* 112; *SWA* 28.57. ***Through the power of***, 'Abdu'l-Baha *BWF* 2.9.429. ***The tree of life...is the Shechinah***, *Zohar* 1.21.245 at http://www.kabbalah.com/k/index.php/p=zohar/zohar&vol=2&sec=42. ***Wing then thy flight***, Baha'u'llah *Gems* 72.52, *Baha'i Prayers* 140

[A] Szekey *From Enoch to the Dead Sea Scrolls*

[B] ***Healer of Infirmities*** Baha'u'llah *Tablet to Hardegg* 3.5–7. ***The falcon on the hand***, Baha'u'llah *Scriptures* 50.132

[C] Baha'u'llah *Prayers and Meditations* 56.83–4

[D] ***Blessed is the affrighted one***, Baha'u'llah *Scriptures* 49.124; Shoghi Effendi *GPB* 210. ***To elucidate these words***, Baha'u'llah *Gems* 20.16–7. ***Open...the***

22.15: *People, ravenous as the dogs, have gathered around carrion, and...contented themselves with the stagnant waters of a briny lake....Never will the barking of dogs deter the nightingale from warbling its melodies.*[A]

22.16: The ambiguous plural *to you* (*humin*) may mean the seven Revelation Angels, readers of Revelation, or other unidentified parties (but not the singular *John*).[B]

22.16, also 3.7 & 5.5: This ***root and the shoot of a beloved David*** and the prior *Lion from the tribe of Judah, the root of a beloved David* (v. 5.5) are titles that fit the lineage of Baha'u'llah (page 45) as the *man called the 'Shoot'* who *shall sprout up and build the Temple of the Lord...and sit on his Throne and rule.*[C]

22.16, also 2.28: This ***Dawn/Day-Star*** stands for both the Bab and Baha'u'llah. The Bab shone as *the Morning Star heralding the glorious Dawn of...the appearance of the Manifestation of God.* Baha'u'llah shone *forth resplendent from the firmament of justice...above the horizon of Iraq...blinding bright,* with the *intense...glory of the heavenly Day-Star....The heaven of righteousness has no star...brighter than this.*[D]

22.17, also 7.17, 21.6 & 22.1: This *Day...the rushing waters of everlasting life have gushed out of the Will of the All-Merciful ....Come unto Me, O ye who are thirsty, and drink from this sweet water which is descending in torrents upon all parts of the globe...the water of life from Christ the Eternal Spring....The fountain of knowledge is gushing, drink ye...waters of everlasting life...proffered unto men.*[E]

22.20, also 1.2: ***Witnessing to*** finds favor here over its other valid translation of ***witnessing***.

22.20, also 1.6–7, 5.14, 7.12 × 2, 19.4 & 20: The Apocalypse closes with *Amen* even though Temple prayers did not.

Subscription: *'An Unveiling' by John* is a title-author Subscription (and Inscription) that typically opens and closes Greek scrolls.[F]

gates, Baha'u'llah *Summons of the Lord of Hosts* 5.99.227

A ***People, ravenous as the dogs***, Baha'u'llah *KI* 208. ***Never will the barking***, Baha'u'llah *Summons of the Lord of Hosts* 2.38.156

B Aune *52C* 1225

C ***The root and the shoot***, Isaiah 22.22; Rev. 5.5 (also 3.7) & 22.16. ***Man called the 'Shoot'***, Zech. 6.12

D ***The Morning Star heralding***, 'Abdu'l-Baha *Scriptures* 582.284. ***Forth resplendent from***, Baha'u'llah *KI* 70.44, *Scriptures* 50.131–2, *TB* 112, 267, 240, 247; 'Abdu'l-Baha *SWA* 2.12

E Baha'u'llah *Scriptures* 50.132, *GWB* 14.30; 'Abdu'l-Baha *SW* (1926/08) 17.5.143, *Paris Talks* 56

F Aune *52A*.4

A Timeline of Apocalypse Prophecies

The Parallel Interpretation has interpreted the Apocalypse chapter by chapter and century by century as shown by this tabulated timeline:

CHAPTER:		DATES CE:
22	THE TREE OF LIFE IS GOD'S ONE RELIGION	2240–3240
21	NEW JERUSALEM IS DIVINE CIVILIZATION	2240–3240
20	THE JEWISH SEVENTH MILLENNIUM	2240–3240
19	A BANQUET BOTH SPIRITUAL AND ECONOMIC	NOW–2240
18	**THE FALL OF BABYLON IS A GREATEST DEPRESSION**	**NOW**
17	**INTERPRETING PROPHETIC SYMBOLS**	**NOW**
16	ARMAGEDDON IS MOUNT CARMEL	1863–early 2000s
15	GOD'S PRESENCE OPENS OUR END-TIMES	1863-
14	A NEW GOSPEL	1844
13	THE NUMBER OF THE BEAST IS AD 666	666
12	MUSLIM MILITARISM CRIPPLES TRUE ISLAM	632–now
11	THE CENTRAL APOCALYPSE PROPHECY	622–1892
10	THE GLORY OF GOD	95 & 1863
9	A HISTORY OF ISLAM	622–1453
8	A HISTORY OF CHRISTIANITY	95–622
7	A 144,000 UNITY-DIAMOND	1844–63
6	THE FOUR HORSES OF THE APOCALYPSE AS FORCES	1844–63
5	THE APOCALYPSE RAM	1844–63
4	HIS MESSAGE OF A NEW FAITH	1844–63
3	HIS MESSAGES FOR THREE LATER FAITHS	95
2	HIS MESSAGES FOR FOUR EARLIER FAITHS	95
1	A MESSENGER OF A NEW FAITH	95 & 1863

THE AD 95 VISION OF JOHN PREDICTS THREE MILLENNIA UP TO CE 3240

CENTURIES (AD/CE)

1 2 3 4 5 6 7 8 9 10 11 12 13 14 15 16 17 18 19 20 21 22 23 24 25 26 27 28 29 30 31 32

Muslim Militarism and Malignant Materialism

Today, the main fight between Faiths manifests is the global war now waging between the Muslim Militarism of the Middle East and the Malignant Materialism of the Christian West. Some even call it *World War III*. At one time, Revelation's horned beast and Babylon whore portrayed the imperial war between the Muslim Ottoman Empire and the Christian Byzantine Empire across the sea between Turkey and Greece (over it their Turkish and Greek descendants glower still today). Today, they depict the war waging across the oceans of the globe between Muslim Militarism and Malignant Materialism.

Muslim Militarism and Malignant Materialism are **systems** defined by doctrines and agendas. The doctrine of Muslim Militarism is religious domination and its agenda is violence. The doctrine of Malignant Materialism is financial domination and its agenda is waste. Baha'i Writings severely censure both systems.

Now most of the world, led by the USA, worships the golden calf of Malignant Materialism and its mammon. Only Muslim Militarism has made the golden calf its enemy. With brutal logic, it has identified the main golden calf as the USA. So on that 9/11 *day of heavy slaughter when towers topple*,[289] it was the ensigns of the USA's economic, governmental, and military power that Muslim Militarism targeted. It cut down the twin towers of the World Trade Center as the USA's golden calf's horns of economic power. It tried, but failed, to cut away the Pentagon, Congress, and White House as the golden calf's legs of military and political power.

Muslim Militarism

In general, Messengers of God appear for and in dire times. In particular, Muhammad came to Arabian tribes living

> *in the utmost state of degradation...bloodthirsty and barbarous, so savage...that the Arabian father often buried his own daughter alive....Could any barbarism be lower than this? The nation consisted of warring, hostile tribal peoples...fighting and pillaging each other, making captive women and children, killing each other. Muhammad...educated and unified these barbarous tribes....They reached such a degree of civilization that they subdued and governed continents and nations. What a great civilization was established in Spain by the Muslims! What a marvelous civilization was founded in Morocco by the Moors! What a powerful caliphate...was set up in Baghdad!*[290-A]

Aptly, the Umayyad Caliphate and Ottoman Sultanate go unmentioned.

Muhammad taught the barbaric tribes of Arabia to submit to Allah as the one God and to care for and treat each other with justice. His Islam promoted family and community and protected the weak, the poor, and the sick. His Quran revamped material laws from the Jewish Torah and spiritual laws from the Christian Gospel. His tradition founded the world's first universities, translated and preserved Greek and other classics, brought the zero and algebra to mathematics, advanced architectural design, and even buttressed the European Renaissance.

Europeans saw the benefits of Islam most clearly in Spain, where

> *Muslim rule brought great progress, order, peace and plenty, promotion of freedom and equality, regard of rulers for their subjects. Countries under Muslim rule were exempt from the disastrous consequences of the feudal system and the feudal code....Muslim legislation freed the soil and assured the rights of individuals. Spain had greatly suffered from barbarian hordes and the people had been weighted down with feudal burdens....Vast areas were deserted....Under the Muslims, people and land were enfranchised, cities sprang up, order was established, Muslims and non-Muslims—Suevi, Goth, Vandal, Roman and Jew—were placed on equal footing, intermarriage took place....The Arabs colonized the depopulated areas, bringing in large industrious communities from Africa and Asia, including 50,000 Jews, with their families, at one time; the generous offers of the Muslims attracted these peoples.*[291-M]

Muhammad and his Muslims respected and protected fellow monotheists. They gave Jews, Christians, and Sabaeans (later Zoroastrians) the honorable title *People of the Book*, telling them:

- *Our God and your God is the same*
- *We believe in God...and in what has been given to Moses and Jesus....No difference do we make between any of them*
- *You have no sure ground unless you uphold the Torah, the Gospel*
- *Let us jointly state that we worship God alone, ascribe no partner to Him, and none of us take others beside God as Lords*
- *Believe in what We have sent down to confirm what you already have.*[292-M]

Yet at the same time the Quran also goes on to condemn non-Muslims in certain historical settings:

- It denounces *People of the Book who disbelieve* as *the worst of creatures*
- It forbids Muslims to *take Jews and Christians as allies*, for *God does not guide such wrongdoers*

- It celebrates how Allah dragged *People of the Book down from their strongholds and put terror into their hearts*, and
- It rejoices how Muslims *killed some* to gain *their lands, homes, and possessions*.[293-M]

Muslim Militarism uses these and similar out-of-context citations to justify using its doctrine of armed jihad.

But why pick on Islam? Surely all Faiths, not just Islam, have pursued armed doctrines? Three thousand years ago, the Israelites waged genocidal warfare, killed all the Amalekites, and massacred cities of Canaanites to their last inhabitant. Likewise, in AD 1099, Christian crusaders systematically slaughtered all of Jerusalem's 30,000 Jews and Muslims, *everyone, whether male or female...like vermin*[294-JC] over three bloody days.

Nonetheless, over its own fourteen centuries, Muslim Militarism has probably killed more folk than the combined militarisms of Sabaeanism, Judaism, Zoroastrianism, Hinduism, Buddhism, and Christianity killed over their own fourteen millennia total. Why?

The main reason is that Islam had no time to develop spiritually before it took to the killing road. In its very first decades, Islam weaved armed doctrines into its religious fabric. Islam immediately launched Muslim Militarism, which irreversibly stunted its spiritual development. In contrast, other Faiths had centuries of time to develop spiritually before they took to the killing road. Notionally, if Christianity had set out on crusades as early as AD 40, citing apt bloody Old and New Testament verses to rationalize its killing, Christianity it would now today be as militaristic, if not more, than modern Islam.

Messengers of God appear *about a thousand years* apart,[295-B] making a Messenger's normal "gestational period" a millennium. Why, then, did Muhammad appear in AD 621? As the Messenger after Jesus, his *EDC* (*expected **d**ate of **d**elivery*) should have been around AD 1000! What happened! Arguably, Muhammad came urgently early in order to save the savage barbaric tribes of Arabia from their dire degradation. He entered spiritual service four centuries preterm or **premature** in the sixth month, as it were. The early advent of Muhammad saved the Arabian tribes from the severe distress of their savagery, just as premature birth saves fetuses from the severe distress of their asphyxia. However, as premature birth that saves babies from fetal asphyxia may make them and their families suffer the steep price of brain damage, so the premature advent of Muhammad that saved Arabia's barbaric tribes from their savagery made Islam and the Muslim family suffer the steep price of Muslim Militarism.

Viewing America as a *Great Satan*

Viewing the world through Muslim eyes helps us to figure out why Muslim Militarism hates America so much, however distorted the Muslim view may seem. Muslims and Westerners see the world quite differently:[296]

- Muslims view Islam made up of nations. Westerners view nations made up of religions
- Muslims define nations as *Muslim* or *Infidel*. Westerners define nations as *friend* or *foe*
- Muslims hear dynasties and cities enacting history. Westerners hear nations running history.

These differences extend even to the indexing of books, since *Islamic literature and theology demand a mindset different from that when dealing with 'Western' material.*[297]

Muslim Militarism identifies America as an enemy deserving destruction for having committed many wrongs in multiple masks:

- *Infidel America* occupies Holy Arabia
- *Imperial America* has invaded Muslim states like Iraq, Afghanistan, and Somalia
- *Greedy America*, thirsty for oil, supports corrupt Middle East tyrants (yet Muslims themselves really support them)
- *Jewish America* supplies Israel with arms (yet up to 1967 the USA denied arms to Israel)
- *Capitalist America* exploits Muslim poverty (yet most Muslim poverty comes from high Muslim birth rates and low Muslim productivity)
- *Materialist America*'s prosperity harms the worthy social bonds promoted by Islam
- *Debased America*'s loose life-styles seduce Muslims away from Islam
- *Arrogant America* tramples Muslim taboos by flaunting moral freedoms
- *Corrupt America* remains the only *Abode-of-War* superpower to block the divinely ordained global embrace of the *Abode-of-Submission* of Islam.

For these reasons, Muslim Militarism fingers America as a *Great Satan* liable for most of the world's miseries, thus cannily defining America as a "person", rather as America's own laws cannily define corporations as "legal persons". Muslim Militarism holds the Great Satan of America guilty for its crimes. Unrestrained by respect or fear, it judges America worthy of capital punishment and finds it ripe for execution. It is set on destroying America by using its historic true and tested tool of jihad.

Muslim Militarism destroyed prior Great Satans too. In AD 650, its Umayyad Caliphate felled the Sassanid Empire of Zoroastrian Persia. In AD 1461, its Ottoman Sultanate finished off the Christian Byzantine Empire. In the 1980s, its Afghan and Saudi fighters triggered the demise of the Communist USSR Empire. Now too, modern Muslim Militarism is set on destroying the sole remaining superpower of the USA. Its regimes and terrorist organizations are as set on singing the swan song of the current Babylon Empire of America as its forces already successfully sang the swan song of the last ancient Babylonian Empire of Byzantium.

Confused Babylon is Malignant Materialism

In AD 95, John's vision showed the fall of the ancient notorious city of Babylon. But way before AD 95, ancient Babylon had already fallen. So the Babylon in John's vision could only be a symbol. In AD 95, his symbolic Babylon stood for Rome. Now his Babylon stands generally for Malignant Materialism, comprehensively stewed as all of these entities, in the following historical sequence:

- The original Median Empire whose capital city Babylon was
- The full gamut of the seven most nefarious ancient *Babylonian* Empires of Egypt, Assyria, Media, Persia, Greece, Rome, and Byzantium
- The sixth ancient Babylonian Empire, namely the Rome that was ruling the Middle East world of John in AD 95
- The sixth and seventh ancient Babylonian Empires of Rome and Byzantium that injected Malignant Materialism into Europe
- The later Colonialist European Babylon of Malignant Materialism that the serial seafaring Empires of Portugal, Spain, Holland, and Britain that played and plied across the globe
- The recent murderous Communist Babylon of Malignant Materialism whose tentacles the USSR plunged deep into the world's remotest communities
- The modern unbridled Capitalist Babylon of Malignant Materialism whose yet stronger tentacles the USA has entwined around the whole globe.

This Malignant Materialism has proved to be

> *an evil which the nation* [the USA] *and indeed all those within the capitalist system, though to a lesser degree, share with that state* [the USSR] *and its satellites regarded as the sworn enemies of that system.*[298-S]

Now that the East's murderous communism has faded, the East has joined the West on the path of unbridled capitalism wherein

> *cities like New York the people are submerged in the sea of materialism. Their sensibilities are attuned to material forces, their perceptions purely physical. The animal energies predominate in their activities; all their thoughts are directed to material things; day and night they are devoted to the attractions of this world, without aspiration beyond the life that is vanishing and mortal. In schools and temples of learning knowledge of the sciences acquired is based upon material observations only; there is no realization of Divinity in their methods and conclusions—all have reference to the world of matter....Spirituality...has been overcome by materialism.... Spiritual susceptibility seems to have vanished....Guidance and knowledge of God no longer remain.*[299-A]

The name *Babylon* (Hebrew *Babel*) means literally *Confusion* (a sister-word is *babble*). Four thousand years ago, the people of Shinar, in today's Iraq, built a city with a tower to top the sky. Arrogantly they called it *Babel* (*Bab-El*), or ***Gate to God*** in their Accadian language.[300] But since they were confusing material aspiration and spiritual power, God zapped their project. He simply confused their language. He put His point punnily by keeping *Babel* as the city name, but now meaning ***Confusion*** in Hebrew!

The Babylon of Malignant Materialism is a confused spiritual cancer that is as suicidal as confused medical cancers are in infiltrating, choking, and ultimately killing the very mother-tissue giving them life. Similarly, Malignant Materialism is a confused suicidal cancer in infiltrating, choking, and killing the very matrix of social systems that nurture, support, and protect human societies, especially the three basic **c**'s of **coupling**, **childrearing**, and **community**,[301] for

> *human brotherhood and dependence exist because mutual helpfulness and cooperation are the two necessary principles underlying human welfare....Man...is in need of continuous cooperation and mutual help....He can never, singly and alone, provide himself with all the necessities of existence.*[302-A]

Over the past few decades, Malignant Materialism has turned the American dream into a nightmare filled progressively with fear, unhappiness, insecurity, debt, joblessness, poverty, disease, crime, and violence, all casting their shadow over individuals, families, societies, and nations. Once *the Greatest Nation on Earth* and *God's own Country*, America now tops global statistics for homicides, weapon sales, guns in private hands, hard drug addiction, a massive wealth gap, and folk lacking health care coverage, all associated with a

> *steady and alarming deterioration in the standard of morality as exemplified by the appalling increase of crime, by political corruption in ever widening and ever higher circles, by the loosening of the sacred ties of marriage, by the inordinate craving for pleasure and diversion, and by the marked and progressive slackening of parental control, is...the most arresting and distressing aspect of the decline that has set in, and can be clearly perceived.*[303-S]

Put bluntly, Malignant Materialism *is a scourge...a cancer... screwing the planet.*[304]

Indeed, across the whole planet, we have all sacrificed our spirits to the systems of Malignant Materialism. We have let them enslave our hearts and minds, bodies and souls. Its systems are distorting our lives, disrupting our family ties, demeaning our pregnancies, sabotaging our breastfeeding, curtailing our parenting, devaluing our children's education, and rationing the care extended to the ill and old. Under the systems of Malignant Materialism, we strive simply to care for our families and make ends meet, finding little time to relax or "smell the roses". Meanwhile, Malignant Materialism is keeping us under its spell by running styles, sports, and cults as its bread-and-circuses, and by supplying nicotine, alcohol, and other drugs as its "opium for the people".

Long ago Hinduism predicted times like ours in which

> *piety will decrease day by day, until the world will be wholly depraved. Then property alone will confer rank. Wealth will be the only source of devotion. Passion will be the sole bond of union between the sexes. Falsehood will be the only means of success in litigation. And women will be objects merely of sensual gratification. Earth will be venerated but for its mineral treasures....Dishonesty will be the means of subsistence. Weakness will be the cause of dependence. Menace and presumption will be substituted for learning. Liberality will be devotion. Simple ablution will be purification. Mutual assent will be marriage. Fine clothes will be dignity. And water afar off will be esteemed a holy spring.*[305]

Hinduism got it right!

The systems of Malignant Materialism confuse price with value, money with wealth, waste with consumption, detail with clarity, goals with process, servicing debt with serving people, *karma* with *darma*, and more. Malignant Materialism uses smooth brutal logic to short-change the weak and manages especially our old and sick as expendable financial liabilities. The sooner these old and sick fade into uselessness, slip through the cracks, and die off, so much sooner the young and healthy who run the show gain materially. The sooner that old and ill "we" quietly slips off the material table and its protests fade, the sooner this young and healthy "we" at the helm enjoy the material goods left on the table. The education of our children gets short shrift too, but less so. After all, the cancer of Malignant Materialism needs them as its future blood supply.

Malignant Materialism puts money before people. It makes money a bad master instead of a good servant. It makes people serve money as an end, rather than making money a means to serve people. It pursues pure profiteering instead of purely pursuing profit. It plans short-term. Malignant Materialism is what motivates a greedy doctor to view each patient as a prospect for profiteering, and to rationalize extra testing and excess treatment. Things should not be like this. Society should first serve us, so that we can then serve it.[306]

Until the 2008–9 financial crises, the world was incredibly blind to the elephant standing right in its living-room as

> ***cancerous materialism*** [my emphasis], *born originally in Europe, carried to excess in the North American continent, contaminating the Asiatic peoples and nations, spreading its ominous tentacles to the borders of Africa, and now invading its very heart, which Baha'u'llah in unequivocal and emphatic language denounced in His Writings, comparing it to a devouring flame and regarding it as the chief factor in precipitating the dire ordeals and world-shaking crises that must necessarily involve...terror and consternation in the hearts of men. Indeed a foretaste of the devastation...has been afforded by the last World War* [World War II]....*It is this same all-pervasive, pernicious materialism against which the voice of the Center of Baha'u'llah's Covenant* ['Abdu'l-Baha] *was raised, with pathetic persistence, from platform and pulpit...on the morrow of His fateful visit to both Europe and America...swept into the vortex of a tempest* [World War I] ....*Collateral with...progressive stress laid on man's material pursuits and well-being, is the darkening of the political horizon, as witnessed by the widening of the gulf separating the protagonists of two antagonistic schools of thought* [Communism and Capitalism], *which, however divergent in their ideologies are to be commonly condemned...for their materialistic philosophies and their neglect of those spiritual values and eternal verities on which alone a stable and flourishing civilization can be ultimately established....which, if not remedied, is bound to involve the American nation in a catastrophe of undreamed-of dimensions.*[307-S]

Deliberate Waste

The main game of Malignant Materialism is deliberate waste (in contrast to acceptable small-scale waste for the sake of comfort[A] of up to even ~10%, or to accidental but readily-correctable waste). Today, such "built-in obsolescence" is writ big and broad globally into most goods and services. Manufacturers make refrigerators with cheap parts that wear out fast and generate return sales. Doctors neglect disease prevention (but pay it lip service) and prosper from diagnosis and treatment. Lawyers skirt mediation and let disputes generate billable hours and lawsuits. Audiologists and opticians order gluts of tests that exponentially ratchet up prices for hearing aids and spectacles. Dentists forget hygiene (how often do dentists **see how** we brush our teeth?) and fill cavities instead. Workers leave loose ends and generate follow-up jobs. Carmakers buy up railways, let them fail, and promote car sales. Cycle shops abandon repair and sell new bikes. Arms-dealers preach mantras like ***M**utually **A**ssured **D**estruction* (*MAD*) and *better dead than red* to fire national paranoias and sell arms. The list is endless.

The more we search for deliberate waste, the more we find it. In my own medical intensive-care field of the USA in the 1990s, layers of deliberate waste added up to some 50–60%, without exaggeration. In the extreme case of the arms industry, deliberate waste surely tops 90%. Such deliberate waste is wasting the planet. Worst of all, the millstone of its busywork is drowning away the precious life-hours of human-beings in field, factory, and facility.

The systems of Malignant Materialism cleverly play and ply deliberate waste at three levels:

- Malignant Materialism's systems run a clean front of worthy prosperity that supplies many goods and services at almost competitive prices. Its goods and services supply a loss-leader façade that sucks people into unquestioning accepting the murky middle shell and inner core of Malignant Materialism as well as serving them.
- Malignant Materialism's systems operate a thick middle shell of deliberate waste that profiteers big-time. Thus, the medical industry spins the money wheels and profiteers from wasteful excessive testing and treatment by hospitals, doctors, and drug companies. Rationalizations abound for their excessive

[A] Schumacher *Small is Beautiful*

diagnostic and therapeutic consumption, backed by fashionable noble-sounding, mantras such as *research and development* or *quality control* (which really whisper *Profit, Profit, Profit!*). The medical industry's conspiratorial cartels also help healthcare insurers to hunt for money, for John Doe and his boss foot most of the escalating premiums. The medical industry is joined by most other arenas and areas of labor, service, and enterprise. The armaments, legal, construction, transport, and automotive industries, to name just a few, spring to mind as racketeering similar schemes of deliberate waste.[308]

- Malignant Materialism's systems are driven by privileged elite corps and cores of wheelers and dealers bonded by family, school-tie, and club. Exactly who they are varies from country to country. Yet everywhere they exchange knowing-nods on the same manicured golf courses and gloss through business decisions over genteel dinners at the same exclusive clubs. Their quiet cartels fix prices. Their political contributions bribe politicians and gain contracts. Their influence bends laws. Their ***G**enerally **A**ccepted **A**ccounting **P**rinciples* (*GAAP*) falsify balance-sheets. Their disinformation manipulates share prices. In such ways, these top wheelers and dealers of the globe show *unbelievable blindness, cruelty, and unscrupulousness* as they *cling to their privileges and power at almost any cost to...the wider interests of civilization....All nations have been tricked by [their] spells.*[309]

Yet at the same time, happily, many worthy enlightened companies and businesses have managed to shun Malignant Materialism's seduction. Instead, they have been pursuing its noble nemesis of worthy prosperity. They are motivated by enlightened self-interest. They avoid the snares set by deliberate waste. They serve customers fairly. They accept competition as a challenge. They set prices fairly per costs and profit without profiteering. They protect workers and share profits with them. They make their workers owners. They provide long-term profit and stability for their shareholders. They work to protect the planet. And they structure their work-forces around the psychologically *magic number* of 150![310]

Overall, these progressive companies and businesses apply good ethics and strive to obey the Golden Rule in their dealings.[311] Thus, Google supplies *useful, efficient, productive, amazing, astonishing services*. Ikea puts itself in the pocket of the client. Merck makes products *for the people* since *profits have never failed to appear*. Skanska *cuts waste, not corners*.[312]

The Collapse of Malignant Materialism

The globe is facing the Greatest Depression depicted by the fall of Babylon in fiscal Apocalypse **Chapter 18**. For far too long, the cancerous Babylon of confused Malignant Materialism has been gnawing away at the social contracts, the lifelines, of the world's societies. Now Babylon is set to crash and be crushed beyond recovery like Humpty Dumpty. No new Greenspan will put Humpty together again.

Abrahamic Faiths condemn the symbolic city of Babylon:

- **Judaism** displays Babylon *fallen, fallen, with all the images of her gods crashed to the ground....upended by God like Sodom and Gomorrah....swept with the broom of destruction, and turned into a swampy waste with name and remnant, kith and kin wiped out...Against Babylon God will raise a destructive wind...strip her land bare....As a gold cup in God's hand, Babylon has made the whole earth drunk. Nations have drunk her wine and gone mad. Suddenly Babylon has fallen and is shattered.* God *will deal with you...destroyer of the whole earth...and will tumble you down from the crags...desolated for ever....Her officials and wise men shall sleep forever, never to awake....Peoples shall toil for nothing. Nations are in flames and tired....From the disaster, Babylon shall sink and never rise again.*[313-J]
- **Christianity** repeats many of the prophet Jeremiah's above words in its Apocalypse: it condemns Babylon as a *huge whore, woman*, or *city* intoxicating, fornicating with, and corrupting leaders, nations, and peoples, flashing riches, living luxuriously, hosting demons and foul spirits, riding a scarlet beast, splitting in three, killing Prophets and good folk, and hurting believers.[314-C]
- **Islam** alludes negatively to *evil disbelievers who taught what was revealed in Babylon.*
- **The Baha'i Faith** calls *Babylon...a waste of rubble* and denounces its *relentless and all-pervasive materialism and the cancerous growth of...unbridled...rampant and cancerous materialism undermining the fabric of human society alike in the East and in the West, eating into the vitals of the...peoples and races inhabiting the American, the European, and the Asiatic continents.* Its *crass materialism...lays excessive and ever-increasing emphasis on material well-being, forgetful of those things of the spirit on which alone a sure and stable foundation can be laid for human society.*[315-AS]

Additionally, some rabbis call America "Babylon"; Christians teach that *the love of money is a root of all evils*; and some Muslims proclaim that *capitalism is a curse* and *communism is a calamity.*[316-CM]

Collapse is God's final solution for Babylon, prescribed with chillingly violent and gruesome Revelation rhetoric as

> *the condemnation of the huge whore who sits over many waters, with whom the rulers of the world have been fornicating and the people living on the earth have gotten drunk from the wine of her fornicating...Great Confused Babylon, Mother of the Whores....As for the ten horns that you saw, along with the beast, these shall detest the whore. They shall ravage and strip her naked, consume her flesh, and burn her up in a blaze. For God has put into their hearts to carry out this will of His, to carry out a single intent, and to submit their royal power to the beast until these Words of God shall be fulfilled. And the woman that you saw is the great city that retains rule over the rulers of the earth....It has fallen! Great Confused Babylon has fallen!...One mighty Angel plucked up a boulder like a massive millstone and cast it into the sea, declaring: 'Thus, with sudden violence, shall you, great city of confused Babylon be cast down. You shall never exist again!'*[317-R]

John's atypically repetitious statements *It has fallen! Confused Great Babylon has fallen* and *to carry out this will of His, to carry out a single intent* stress how important the fall of Babylon is. Notably too, the Codex Sinaiticus uses up 11 of its mere 29 precious paragraph-breaks to highlight this particular text of Chapter 18.

In addition, the tale of the fall of Babylon is impressively long. Most Revelation tales are lucky to last a third of a chapter if that. Yet the tale of the fall of Babylon covers more than the whole of Chapter 18, from v. 17.16 to v. 19.4. Why such a long description? Another classic work, the *Bayeux Tapestry*, offers an answer. This 210–foot-long tapestry contains 58 scenes of events before and during the 1066 Battle of Hastings that saw William the Conqueror defeat Harold on the English South Coast. Of its scenes, 44 are each some 1–2 feet long, and 14 scenes are each some 1–3 yards long. Long-scene numbers 36–38 show the Normans **furiously** building ships and scudding them across the English Channel. Long-scene numbers 48–58 show the Normans **furiously** winning the battle with their archers and cavalry (Umayyad-style!).[318] Clearly, the tapestry's long scenes serve to flash **furor** that stops time in its tracks. So clearly too, the Apocalypse's long tale about the fall of Babylon is flashing the **furor** of the fall and the bursting of the Babylon bubble.

The Apocalypse fingers the *beast* of Muslim Militarism and its horns as the pins pricking the bubble of Babylon of Malignant Materialism and bursting it, and collapsing its systems. Still more violence seems set to trigger its final fall.

Possible violent catastrophes hovering in 2012 include some sort of "small" nuclear event. In the Middle East, soon enough, Israel's Air Force and/or America's Stealth bombers may attack Iran's nuclear sites and Shihab rockets, and trigger a severe conventional, or a contained nuclear, war.[319] Or Muslim terrorists may explode a small nuclear device at some key economic target like a New York or London stock exchange, a Chicago commodity market, a Silicon Valley or Seattle computer nexus, or a Zurich or Fort Knox gold stock (as Ian Fleming's *Goldfinger* planned).

Whatever crises trigger the final crash of the Babylon of Malignant Materialism, and however deafening the bang, the resulting global paralysis will bring silence.

Alas, the Apocalypse offers no specific time-prophecy for the fall of Babylon. It cannot afford to. If enough interpreters figure out when, they might just band together and stop it in its tracks (or any other prophesied event for that matter).

Regardless, John's tale of the fall of Babylon does offer a few timing clues. It shocks leaders and businessmen because it happens quickly and violently. The severe lessons that it teaches flash *in a single day*. Its judgment, the destruction of its great wealth, and its overall destruction all burst *in a single hour*. Its markets collapse serially through gold, collectibles, valuables, food, transport, and labor (which lagging last should lessen losses for laborers).[320] Taken together, John's timing clues hint at this cascaded of events felling Babylon and sweeping Malignant Materialism into a Greatest Depression:

- A chaotic 24-hour market crash over a *single day*
- A jarring two-week market collapse over a *single hour* of a 24th part of a *Day* of a year
- A crippling one-year bear-market over a *single Day* of a year
- A flat 15-year depression over an *hour* of a 24th part of a *Day* of 360 years
- A steady 40-year adjustment over an *hour* of a 24th part of a *Day* of 1000 years.

Of course today—from within the collapse—it is impossible to predict its timing. Still, since 2008–9, Malignant Materialism and its systems seem to have been hiccupping their way downhill. The waves of the fiscal tsunami crashing on the economic shores of the globe now seem to be wringing out and ringing out Malignant Materialism. In the wake of the collapse, a Greatest Depression will paralyze the planet's economies for a time, but it shall also dispense the requisite remedies for a whole millennium.

An Upcoming Painful Economic Paralysis

For the Greatest Depression, Baha'i Writings anticipate a

> *paralysis more painful than any...yet experienced,* which *must creep over and further afflict the fabric of a broken society 'ere it can be rebuilt and regenerated.* Though *economic plans of reconstruction have been carefully devised, and meticulously executed...crisis has succeeded crisis, and the rapidity with which a perilously unstable world is declining has been correspondingly accelerated. A yawning gulf threatens to involve in one common disaster both the satisfied and dissatisfied nations, democracies and dictatorships, capitalists and wage-earners, Europeans and Asiatics, Jew and Gentile, white and coloured.*[321-S]

The nations of the world, not least America, must still face

> *a catastrophe of undreamed-of dimensions and of untold consequences to the social structure, the standard and conception of the American people and government....The world is in travail, and its agitation waxeth day by day....Winds of despair are... blowing from every direction....The strife that divideth and afflicteth the human race is daily increasing....Signs of impending convulsions and chaos can now be discerned, inasmuch as the prevailing order appeareth to be lamentably defective.*[322-SB]

> *These events shall suddenly appear and cause the limbs of mankind to quake,* making *governments and peoples of both the developed and developing nations...helpless to reverse the trend of the catastrophic events of the day...bewildered and overpowered by the magnitude and complexity of the problems facing them.*[323-BS]

> *The present world unrest, symptom of a world-wide malady…must needs culminate in that world catastrophe out of which the consciousness of world citizenship will be born, a consciousness that can alone provide an adequate basis for the organization of world unity, on which a lasting world peace must necessarily depend, the peace itself inaugurating in turn that world civilization which will mark the coming of age of the entire human race.*[324-S]

> *Much suffering will still be required 'ere the contending nations, creeds, classes and races of mankind are fused in the crucible of universal affliction, and are forged by the fires of a fierce ordeal into one organic commonwealth, one vast, unified, and harmoniously functioning system. Adversities unimaginably appalling, undreamed of crises and upheavals, war, famine, and pestilence, might well combine to engrave in the soul of an unheeding generation those truths and principles which it has disdained to recognize and follow.*[325-S]

> *Nothing short of the fire of an ordeal...can fuse and weld the discordant entities that constitute the elements of present-day civilization, into the integral components of the world commonwealth of the future* and *that sense of responsibility which the leaders of a new-born age must arise to shoulder.*326-S

Arguably then, it was the economic crisis of 2008–9 that set the economies of the globe on their downward slope. The new wealth that accumulated over a few heady decades turned out to be the Achilles heel of Malignant Materialism. During these decades, rafts of economic instruments flashed fiscal mirrors and billowed monetary smoke that ballooned new wealth. "Leverage", in particular, turned more and more wealth virtual as ink and electrons, and kept less and less wealth tangible as land, buildings, vehicles, and collectibles. Even deepening oceans of ink and expanding skies of electrons replaced material items that could be touched, seen, heard, smelled, and tasted. Virtual wealth surpassed tangible wealth.

Yet virtual wealth should surely match tangible wealth. But for the match to work, the essential glues of truth and trust are needed. And crisis—financial or military—tests trust tremendously. Whoever has held a bond of a defeated country, lost a bearer certificate, or deleted even a key money file knows this first-hand. The 2008–9 financial crisis and its aftermath have shaken financial trust and have exposed just how vulnerable ink and electron wealth is.

Over those heady decades, Mr Rich typically made his ink and electron wealth as follows. First he mortgaged his $1 million New York apartment for $500,000 with a finance company. The company then combined several such mortgages as collateral for borrowing $2 million from a bank. It used this $2 million to leverage the buy-out of another company. This company then issued 10-million-dollars-worth of double-yielding junk bonds, which it sold to a hedge-fund. The hedge-fund borrowed cheap yen to buy falling dollars in order to buy the junk bonds. And so on, with the whole process making Mr Rich richer still.

Over these past few decades, rich folk rode up upon the hypnotic escalator of "the trend is your friend", enjoying continual increases in the prices of their bonds, stocks, and junk bonds. They sailed oceans of ink wealth and soared skies electron wealth and became increasingly rich. They sat around the money-table consuming the financial fare served up by money-shuffling middlemen earning their own commissions, spreads, charges, and fees. Meanwhile, the masses tried emulating the rich but fell into deep debt.

Yet all the feverish financial flurry of this process added not a single red cent to the real economy. The world's true wealth stayed the same. No more apartments or factories appeared on the planet. The price of Mr Rich's New York apartment stayed the same. The real profits of those companies stayed the same. The cost of bread and toilet paper stayed the same.

Over the same heady decades, governments too played similar games, led by America. Uncle Sam helped Americans to indulge the holy cow of consumption and spend each $1.00 they earned on $1.06-worth of foreign goods. The Federal Reserve Bank printed more dollars to cover the $0.06 overhang. Then the governments of the foreign producers joined suit. They printed extra currency too, now to buy up the dollars flowing into their countries. But these governments stashed these dollars in their central bank vaults, in order to hinder their people from buying American goods and at the same to issue their own slews of dollar-backed monetary bonds, stocks, financial derivatives, mortgages, and loans—all made in the image of mother America.

Thus, many countries fuelled the process begun by America, to swell the oceans of ink and spreading the skies of electrons of virtual wealth across the globe. Across this ink-ocean and under these electron-skies, blithely ignorant, central bank directors, bankers, stockbrokers, hedge fund whizzes, and economists plied the Titanic of Malignant Materialism as if there were no tomorrow.[327] Blinded by their own smoke and mirrors, deafened by their own rhetoric, they failed to see any fiscal iceberg lurking on the radar screens of their economic formulas, graphs, or charts. They steamed on blissfully, full-steam ahead, enjoying the trip, listening to the band, boozing at the bar, and flirting with the stewardesses and stewards.

Suddenly, out of the fog of confusion, a huge fiscal iceberg emerged. Wealth that had ridden sensationally over decades of boom was dropping in a stunning moment of bust, falling through the floor amid panic, busy phone lines, and financial indices slicing through thresholds. A catastrophic reckoning has begun to crash and crush the Titanic of Malignant Materialism.[328] As it sinks, the rich face poverty while the poor drown in debt. The rich can still grab the boats, but the poor are sinking into the ocean. The indelible-ink oceans and the glittering electron-skies are evaporating into thin air, turning as invisible as the new suit of clothes of the naked fairytale king.

Once Malignant Materialism goes for good, spiritual economics shall emerge as the sure remedy revamping the globe's financial troubles and curing its economies.

Spiritual Economics

Worthy Prosperity

Apocalypse Chapter 19 spreads an economic banquet of worthy prosperity on its tablecloth of spiritual economics covering its hidden Showbread-Table. Its banquet of worthy prosperity follows Apocalypse Chapter 19's big bad brother of its Babylon of Malignant Materialism.

Worthy prosperity provides *enough for everybody's need but not for everybody's greed.*[329] It puts people before money. It makes money serve people as an end rather than making people a means to serve money. It makes money a good servant instead of a bad master. It pursues purely profit instead of pursuing pure profiteering. It plans long-term and obeys the Golden Rule, for it knows that *if there is no Bible there is no bread.* Worthy prosperity is what motivates a decent doctor to help a patient for his or her own sake and to let the billing take care of itself.[330-J]

Yet folk constantly excuse Malignant Materialism's greed as "simply human nature". No! Rather than human nature, this greed represents systematic **distortion of the human spirit**[331] by the systems driving Malignant Materialism.

On the contrary, true human nature is the positive biological force that promotes the wonderful three **c**'s of **c**oupling, **c**hildrearing, and **c**ommunity that are so essential for human life. In contrast, Malignant Materialism's three ugly **c**'s of **c**olonialism, **c**ommunism, and **c**apitalism have distorted the human spirit and caused misery across the planet.

The natural human forces of coupling, childrearing, and community bond and bind human-beings and let them benefit mutually from worthy prosperity. Human nature demands and provides social contracts that let folk live comfortably free from financial fear, assuring access to basic services like education, healthcare, pensions, security, food, shelter, clothes, communication, and transport. Some nations run these services well. Some nations run them less well. For any particular nation, the litmus test of the adequacy of its social contract is how do its **weakest** members fare? How well do its services protect its young, its ill, and its old (almost all of us at some time or other)?

In order to make worthy prosperity work, societies must enact **laws of spiritual economics**.

Laws of Spiritual Economics

Spiritual economics is the remedy for the economic problems that face the world today. Spiritual principles will steadily replace the systems of Malignant Materialism. Spiritual laws will emerge that guide economic affairs towards worthy prosperity for the whole of humanity. To this end

> *Baha'u'llah has set forth the solution and provided the remedy for the economic question. No religious Books of the past Prophets speak of this important human problem.*[332-AS]

Baha'u'llah's economic teachings and *proposals...are practicable, and cause no distress to society.* They embrace

> *the higher aspirations of all wage-earning classes and of economists of various schools....The Baha'i Cause covers all economic and social questions under the heading and ruling of its laws....Governments will enact these laws, establishing just legislation and economics in order that all humanity may enjoy a full measure of welfare and privilege....The fundamentals of the whole economic condition are divine in nature and are associated with the world of the heart and spirit. This is fully explained in the Bahá'í teaching, and without knowledge of its principles no improvement in the economic state can be realized....All economic problems may be solved by the application of the Science of the Love of God* that is *the true foundation of all economics....Manifest true economics to the people....Show what love is, what kindness is.*[333-AS]

Making spiritual economics the *remedy for the economic question* will call for *great readjustment* and *a high state of spiritual civilization* leading to a

> *fundamental change…in man's nature such as to enable him to adjust the economic relationships of society* and *control the economic forces that threaten to disrupt the foundations of his existence, and thus assert his mastery over the forces of nature....*Our *generation of the half-light living at a time... designated as the period of the incubation of the World Commonwealth envisaged by Bahá'u'lláh* is now testing these principles, which will *widen in accordance with time and place. The primary consideration is the spirit that has to permeate our economic life, and this will gradually crystallize itself into definite institutions and principles that will help to bring about the ideal condition foretold by Bahá'u'lláh.*

Baha'i Writings include the following multiple solutions for the economic problem:[334-AS]

Wealth and private ownership:

Baha'i teaching *neither accepts the theories of the Capitalistic economics in full, nor can it agree with the Marxists and Communists in their repudiation of the principle of private ownership and of the vital sacred rights of the individual....Wealth is praiseworthy in the highest degree...provided the entire population is wealthy* and wealth is *dedicated to the welfare of society.*[335-SAB]

Work is

an inseparable part of man's life...a necessary element in our earthly existence, without which *life ceases to have a meaning....Whatever the progress of...machinery may be, man will have always to toil in order to earn his living.* People must *busy themselves with that which will profit themselves and others.* Work done in a spirit of service is *identical with the worship of God.*[336-SAB]

Caring for the weak and the poor means providing

every assistance and help...to those who are in distress and suffering, through *orphanages, free schools and hospitals for the poor.* The rich must *concern themselves with and care for the poor,* who are *the trust of God in* their *midst.* In this way, the rich can display *the lofty characteristics and noble attributes of mankind.* There are *men...overburdened with riches on the one hand, and on the other those unfortunate ones who starve with nothing; those who possess several stately palaces, and those who have not where to lay their head...some...with numerous courses of costly and dainty food, whilst others can scarce find sufficient crusts to keep them alive....Some are clothed in velvets, furs and fine linen* while *others have insufficient, poor and thin garments with which to protect them from the cold. This condition of affairs is wrong, and must be remedied. Now the remedy must be carefully undertaken. It cannot be done by bringing to pass absolute equality between men.*[337-SBA]

Rather, *rules and laws should be established to regulate the excessive fortunes of certain private individuals, and limit the misery of millions of the poor masses....Under present systems and conditions of government the poor are subject to the greatest need and distress while others more fortunate live in luxury and plenty far beyond their actual necessities. This inequality of portion and privilege is one of the deep and vital problems of human society....Need of...apportionment by which all may possess the comforts and privileges of life is evident. The remedy must be legislative readjustment of conditions. The rich too must be merciful to the poor, contributing from willing hearts to their needs without being forced or compelled to do so....In the future there will not be the abnormally rich nor the abject poor. The rich will enjoy the privilege of this new economic condition as well as the poor, for owing to certain provisions and restrictions they will not be able to accumulate so much as to be burdened by its management, while the poor will be relieved from the stress of want and misery.* ***The rich will enjoy his palace, and the poor will have his comfortable cottage*** [my emphasis].[338-A]

Begging must be *wiped out....It is the duty of those who are in charge of the organization of society to give every individual the opportunity of acquiring the necessary talent in some kind of profession, and also the means of utilizing such a talent, both for its own sake and for the sake of earning the means of his livelihood. Every individual, no matter how handicapped and limited he may be, is under the obligation of engaging in some work or profession.*[339-BS]

Equalization of the means of livelihood is *the right of every human being to the daily bread whereby they exist*, making *poverty disappear and everyone...share in comfort and well-being....It will not be possible for a few to be millionaires and many destitute.* Limiting *extremes* of *wealth and sustenance* conforms to *Divine Law which gives equal justice to all.... Deplorable superfluity of great wealth and miserable, demoralizing and degrading poverty can be abolished* through *special laws... dealing with these extremes of riches and of want.*[340-A]

The body politic is one family yet because of lack of harmonious relations some members are comfortable and some in direst misery, some members are satisfied and some are hungry, some members are clothed in most costly garments and some families are in need of food and shelter. Why? Because this family lacks the necessary reciprocity and symmetry....Therefore a law must be given to this family by means of which all the members...will enjoy equal well-being and happiness. Is it possible for one member of a family to be subjected to the utmost misery and to abject poverty and for the rest of the family to be comfortable? It is impossible unless those members of the family be senseless, atrophied, inhospitable, unkind.[341-A]

It is important to limit riches, as it is also of importance to limit poverty. Either extreme is not good....If it be right for a capitalist to possess a large fortune, it is equally just that his workman should have a sufficient means of existence....A financier with colossal wealth should not exist whilst near him is a poor man in dire necessity. When we see poverty allowed to reach a condition of starvation it is a sure sign that somewhere we shall find tyranny

*....The rich must give of their abundance, they must soften their hearts and cultivate a compassionate intelligence, taking thought for those sad ones who are suffering from lack of the very necessities of life.*342-A

Ending Industrial Slavery without Strikes: In the USA, in 1865, *you did a wonderful thing....You abolished chattel slavery....But you must do a much more wonderful thing now, you must abolish industrial slavery!...Rules and laws should be established* allowing ***moderate profits*** [my emphasis] *to manufacturers, and to workmen the necessary means of existence and security for the future....Socialists may justly demand human rights but without resort to force and violence* or *the strike...which is manifestly wrong and destructive of human foundations....Strikes are due to two causes. One is the extreme greed and rapacity of the manufacturers and industrialists; the other, the excesses, the avidity and intransigence of the workmen and artisans....But the principal cause of these difficulties lies in the laws of the present civilization; for they lead to a small number of individuals accumulating incomparable fortunes, beyond their needs, while the greater number remain destitute...in the greatest misery. This is contrary to justice, to humanity, to equity; it is the height of iniquity, the opposite to what causes divine satisfaction....The human species...persists in the greatest error.*343-A

Protection of Workers and Capitalists: Governments must *plan with utmost wisdom and power so that neither the capitalists suffer from enormous losses nor the labourers become needy....The rights of the working people must be strongly preserved. Also the rights of the capitalists are to be protected. The interference of courts of justice and of the government in difficulties...between manufacturers and workmen is legal. Commerce, industry, agriculture and the general affairs of the country are all intimately linked together.*344-A

A just medium...lies in the capitalists being moderate in the acquisition of their profits, and in their having a consideration for the welfare of the poor and needy...that the workmen and artisans receive a fixed and established daily wage, and have a share in the general profits of the factory....Every factory...will give 20–25% of its shares *to its employees and will write the shares in their names....The rest will belong to the capitalists. Then...whatever they may earn after the expenses and wages are paid, according to the number of shares,* shall *be divided among both* so that *workmen...receive...wages and a share in the fourth or the fifth part of the profits,* to make them *partners in every work.*345-A

When they cease work, becoming feeble or helpless, they will *receive from the owner of the factory a sufficient pension....A manufacturer will not be allowed to leave all his property to his own family,* since the bulk of the property must go *to the factory workers who have created the wealth.*[346-A]

Inequality is Natural: *Social inequality is the inevitable outcome of the natural inequality of man....Human beings are different in ability and should, therefore, be different in their social and economic standing....All must enjoy the greatest comfort and welfare....Nevertheless there will be preservation of degree.... Wages should definitely be unequal, simply because men are unequal in their ability and hence should receive wages that would correspond to their varying capacities and resources.*[347-AS]

Equality is a chimera! It is entirely impracticable! Even if equality could be achieved it could not continue—and if its existence were possible, the whole order of the world would be destroyed. The law of order must always obtain in the world of humanity.... Some are full of intelligence, others have an ordinary amount of it, and others again are devoid of intellect. In these three classes of men there is order but not equality. How could...wisdom and stupidity...be equal?...An army could not be composed of generals alone, or of captains only, or of nothing but soldiers without one in authority.[348-A] *Absolute equality is...impossible, for absolute equality in fortunes, honors, commerce, agriculture, industry, would end in a want of comfort, in discouragement, in disorganization of the means of existence, and in universal disappointment: the order of the community would be quite destroyed. Thus difficulties will also arise when unjustified equality is imposed. It is, therefore, preferable for moderation to be established by means of laws and regulations to hinder the constitution of the excessive fortunes of certain individuals, and to protect the essential needs of the masses.*[349-A]

The point is clearly made by the tale of Spartan Philosopher King Lycurgus who

made a great plan to equalize the subjects of Sparta...to achieve the permanent good of his country by the equalization of the property and of the conditions of life in his kingdom. But *the self-sacrifice of the king was in vain. The great experiment failed. After a time all was destroyed; his carefully thought-out constitution came to an end. The futility of attempting such a scheme was shown and the impossibility of attaining equal conditions of existence was proclaimed....In our day any such attempt would be equally doomed to failure.*[350-A]

Houses of Finance:

The peasant class and the agricultural class exceed other classes in the importance of their service. Economic problems must be *solved with the farmer* as *the first active agent in the body politic....In every village a board should be organized and the affairs of that village should be under the control of that board* organizing a *house of finance (storehouse)* paying... *necessary expenses for orphans...the cripples...the poor...and other members who for valid reasons are incapacitated—the blind, the old, the deaf—their comfort must be looked after. In the village no one will remain in need or in want....This system is all thus ordered so that...the individual members of the body politic will thus live comfortably and well.* Hereby everybody can benefit from *the greatest achievements of the world of humanity.*351-A

Medieval tithe barn at Abbotsbury, UK, as an archetype and potential prototype for a House of Finance

Trustees will be elected by the people in a given village to look after these transactions, with the *expenses or expenditures of the general storehouse* and *its activities made manifest,* and the power to levy *tithes, taxes on animals, wealth without inheritors, all things found whose owners cannot be discovered, a third of all treasures...in the earth, a third of all the mines—and voluntary contributions.* "Tithes" means progressive 10%–50% taxation of *income...greater than...needs.* From its levies, each house of finance will pay for the *government, the poor, the infirm, the orphans, the schools, the deaf blind and cripples, and public health....If after all these expenses are defrayed any surplus is found in the storehouse it must be transferred to the national treasury.*352-A

*When the village is reconstructed, then the cities will be also.... For larger cities, naturally, there will be a system on a larger scale....Nevertheless, there will be preservation of degree.*353-A

Culling the Waste of War: Each nation needs only *a small force for the purposes of internal security, the correction of criminal and disorderly elements and the prevention of local disturbances....Hereby the world may be freed from onerous expenditure, for warfare and conflict are the foundation of trouble and distress....To pile up more weapons of war...people must sacrifice most of whatever they are able to earn by their sweat and toil. How many thousands have given up their work in useful industries and are laboring day and night to produce new and deadlier weapons which...spill out the blood of the race more copiously than before. Each day they invent a new bomb or explosive and then the governments must abandon their obsolete arms and begin producing the new, since the old weapons cannot hold their own against the new.*[354-AB]

The enormous energy dissipated and wasted on war...will be consecrated to such ends as will extend the range of human inventions and technical development, to the increase of the productivity of mankind, to the extermination of disease, to the extension of scientific research, to the raising of the standard of physical health, to the sharpening and refinement of the human brain, to the exploitation of the unused and unsuspected resources of the planet, to the prolongation of human life, and to the furtherance of any other agency that can stimulate the intellectual, the moral, and spiritual life of the entire human race.[355-B]

A Global Economic Commonwealth will develop as a *world community in which all economic barriers will have been permanently demolished and the interdependence of capital and labour definitely recognized. A world federal system...embodying the ideals of both the East and the West, liberated from the curse of war and its miseries, and bent on the exploitation of all the available sources of energy on the surface of the planet, a system in which force is made the servant of Justice...is the goal.* The system will promote, among other things, a *uniform and universal system of currency of weights and measures* to *simplify and facilitate intercourse and understanding among the nations and races*; will allow the charging of *interest on money with moderation and fairness;* will limit *tariffs* that hurt international trade; and will permit *no more trusts*.[356-SBA]

Through such laws, spiritual economic *readjustment ensures the stability of the world* so that *each individual member of the body politic* can *live most comfortably and happily...without any harm or injury attacking the general order.*[357-A]

Translation Section

The Translation Section is for scholars of the Apocalypse who are strong of heart. It explores the Hebraized Greek codes and linguistic devices of John, the author of the Apocalypse. It justifies translations that differ from those found in most Bibles. Deliberate Greek *last-first* (*hysteron-proteron*) order presents this Translation Section **after** the main Parallel Interpretation Section. As the more important "result", the Parallel Interpretation Section has already appeared—first. Now, as the less important "cause" this Translation Section appears—last.

The Original Hebraized Text of the Apocalypse

The Hebraized text of the original Apocalypse scroll must have set a tough task for the scribes who copied it. Even the most fastidious scribe would ever-so-sensibly have leaned toward correcting apparent errors. His well-meaning pen would have injected a letter of extra spelling here or switched an odd-looking ending of grammar there. "Corrections" like these probably purged away some of the most Hebraized wording in the very original text.

Moreover, John is very tight, nay brusque, with words, even for a prophet. His short Apocalypse tale runs fast and crisp. His pithy sentences waste not a single word. And he shows that brevity is his modus operandi by

- Making his main book-word the diminutive *biblion* (*short scroll*) instead of the standard book-word *biblos* (*scroll*)[A]
- Using the super-diminutive book-word *biblaridion* (*tiny scroll*) for specific interpretive focus
- Beginning and ending his vision report with *What had to happen fast* (*en tachei*, literally *at speed*)
- Quoting seven times the *I am coming soon* (*tachu*) spoken by the main Messenger Angel
- Switching verb-tenses sharply to jump from historical period to historical period
- Citing many Old Testament words (for example, *cherem*) as shorthand codes for particular concepts.[358-R]

[A] *Biblion* is the name that Revelation gives to itself. Otherwise, Revelation uses the main book-word *biblos* just twice (vv. 3.5 & 20.15), both times in *Book of Life* (twice out of six mentions).

As biblical books go, Revelation is very short, just 10,000 words. Its vocabulary is short too, a mere 916 words. The brevity of the Revelation vocabulary reflects the small size of the then current Greek vocabulary, compared to modern English, that is. As a result, translation must convert fewer, more generic, Greek words into more, more specific, English words. For its context, each precious Greek word needs to render as the right English word. Thus, the generic noun *phialē* (*bowl*) renders best as *censer* in one Temple setting and as *pitcher* in another Temple setting.[359-R] Likewise, the verb *einai* (*to be*) renders variously in different contexts as *represent*, *manifest*, *exist*, *take place*, *grow*, or *live*.

In his *Word Biblical Commentary 52: Revelation*, Professor David Aune sets himself the tricky task of reconstructing the text of the very original Apocalypse scroll. His three-volume work and its 1354 pages attest to his exhaustively painstaking research as well as to the complexity of Revelation itself. The *Word Biblical Commentary* series usually assigns just one volume in the series for each Bible Book. But to the short Book of Revelation it assigns **three** volumes—as it does to the notably long Book of Psalms and long Gospel of Luke. Despite its brevity, Revelation calls for three *Word Biblical Commentary* volumes because of its very complexity.

David Aune hunts down every early Revelation text (*witness*) that he can find, like some royal Greek hound worrying, analyzing, scrutinizing, sifting, and comparing each possible early text[360-C] as divine bones. His attention to detail is extreme, his Old Testament citations extensive, and his academic honesty scrupulous.[361-C] He justifies his choice of the most likely original version or variant for each and every word, phrase, or verse. As only true scholars can, he openly admits where he has wavered or made a best guess. Nor does he let his personal preterist interpretive bias that Revelation predicts early Christianity under Rome spoil his sterling scholarship. David Aune is probably the top living authority on the Greek of Revelation.

Yet at the end of the day, after all his research, David Aune believes that the exact original AD 95 text of the Revelation scroll **cannot** be faithfully reconstructed from available sources. Rather, he reckons that the closest text that **can** be reconstructed is one that would have been circulating after John's original AD 95 vision around about AD 150–250. This is the text that Aune's *Word Biblical Commentary* delivers. Comfortingly, it comes very close to the standard authoritative Greek text of Revelation by Nestle-Aland.[362-C]

This Translation of the Apocalypse

The initial recipe for my cake of *Apocalypse Secrets* was its Parallel Interpretation, pretty much by itself. Naively, I assumed that it alone would speak tons. So initially, my recipe simply read:

- "Identify top English translations of the original Greek text of the Book of Revelation in the New American Bible, New English Bible, Complete Jewish Bible, Greek English New Testament, and other recognized versions
- "Combine these translations into the best possible English text
- "Set this best English text in a left-column on each page
- "Find all authoritative Baha'i Writings interpret verse and symbols in the Book of Revelation
- "Seamlessly fill in all interpretive gaps in the same Baha'i spirit
- "Combine all Baha'i-based interpretations into a single text
- "Set the interpretive text in right-columns in parallel to the left-column text of the original Revelation
- "Add a short *Introduction*, *Discussion*, and *Notes*."

Perfect! My Revelation cake would bake well, smell delicious, taste exquisite, and sell like hot cakes. Right?

Wrong! Apart from the naiveté of this recipe, it became also all too apparent that the Greek text of the original Revelation flatly lacked the essential yeast of an accurate English translation. Among existing translations of Revelation, including the top ones listed above, clear disparities repeatedly raised their awkward heads. For as many as 20–30% of Revelation's verses, striking differences between words, phrases, or verses were evident. This extreme degree of disparity could not be just explained away as "translators differ". The disparities were far too many.

Soon, the reason for so many disparities became all too clear. The real problem was the very odd Hebraized Greek of Revelation itself. Its language differs a lot from the regular Koine Greek of the rest of the New Testament, even that of the Gospel and Epistles of the same John. For centuries, the tough Hebraized Greek of Revelation has tantalized translators with its clumsy grammar, peculiar in-your-face usages, *barbarous idioms*, and *inaccurate Greek*.[363-C] In contrast, *Koine* (*Common*) Greek was a simplified version of the homeland language imposed by the Greek Empire as a practical working language on the peoples it ruled. Koine Greek did so well that it continued to be the Middle East's lingua franca under the Roman Empire too. As a result, Koine Greek became the language of the New Testament—except, that is, for the Book of Revelation!

Evidently, the marked disparities in translation resulted from translators doing their very best to render the tantalizing Greek of Revelation into sensible English. They tried their very best to put the right English face onto Revelation's Hebraized Greek words and to generate the most comfortable wording to suit each semantic, historical, or prophetic context as far as possible.

Yet in the process—and here's the rub—translators also often skirted or blurred odd literal Hebraized wordings planted by John as vital literary devices and codes with hidden meanings.

Therefore, to do my interpretation full justice and to discover just how the original Apocalypse text of John truly ticked, I realized that I had little choice but to translate the Apocalypse for myself and to join the thousands of others who had traveled this road already. It The extra task of translating Revelation afresh was a rude awakening, which I took on reluctantly. In my favor, I found that Revelation's Hebraized Greek fell somewhere between my school Latin and my modern Hebrew from living and working in Israel. Its Greek nouns and verbs read like those of school Latin and Greek. Its sentence structure and idioms sounded like the Hebrew spoken on the streets of Israel today.

Happily, translating for myself reaped bountiful extra rewards. The process revealed the Hebraized Greek of Revelation as more coded than odd. Steadily its text delivered up more and more hidden meanings. Throughout, the spirit of John shone down from the sky and inspired my efforts. He enjoyed seeing how his Hebrew soul-food cooked in the Greek pot of Prochorus nurtured me. He smiled as the delectable Mediterranean aromas and spices in his text tickled my nostrils and tingled my palate. He peeked at the sparkling gems of his hidden meanings dazzling me. He listened as music of his words entranced me. He delighted at the layers of linguistic icing on his Temple cake nourishing me. He laughed at his maze of symbols and codes fooling me. He revived me after each of his word traps snared me. He cheered at how the literary gauntlet of his text was running me ragged. He took pleasure as his methods, meanings, and messages beguiled me. And he shared my desire for his beautiful Sabbath-Bride of New Jerusalem.

The resulting translation that follows steers its course between the Scylla of its literal meanings and the Charybdis of its spiritual messages. It sails closer to Scylla, since the parallel interpretive text delivers its spiritual messages of Charybdis anyway.[364-B] Additionally, here and there, I have mellowed my translation with alliterative word-games in a coy effort to emulate John's own many word-games.

More of John's Linguistic Devices

Across the ocean of his Apocalypse wisdom, John launched a fleet of linguistic devices that veiled his meanings by both chance and choice. The Introduction has presented the five main linguistic devices: John's number-codes, floating-terms, verbal-thematic links, hidden-titles, and cover-names. Now follow further number-codes and floating-terms, along with many other linguistic devices of John (all listed by verse number).

Number-Codes here join the previous ones on pages 20 and 130.

Lower number-codes tag Messengers as:

- **2** *Altars* or *Witnesses* (6.9, 8.3, 9.12, 11.3 & 16.6)
- **3** *Trumpet-Blasts* (8.13, 9.1, 12, 11.14, 12.12, 18.10, 16 & 19), *Angels* (8.13 & 14.6–9) and *gates* in each New Jerusalem sidewall representing teachings (21.13)
- **4** *Living-Beings, Angels,* and *horns* on the Incense-Altar (4.8, 7.1 & 9.13 × 2)
- **7** Messengers (pages 20 and 130), also mentions of *blessed* (1.3, 14.13, 16.15, 19.9, 20.6, 22.7 & 14); *right-hand* (1.16, 17, 20, 2.1, 5.1, 5.7 & 10.5); *Abyss* (9.1, 2, 11, 11.7, 17.8, 20.1 & 3); openings (4.1, 5.5, 9.2, 11.19, 15.5, 19.11 & 20.12); attributes of the Ram (5.12); attributes of God (7.12); and types of men (6.15)

Other lower number-codes tag foes of Messengers as:

- ***2*** beasts *from the sea* and *land, horns* of the second beast, and the *beast* and *false-prophet* (13.1, 11 & 19.20)
- ***3*** *afflictions* (9.18), *foul spirits* (16.13), and groups watching Babylon fall (18.10, 16 & 19)
- ***4*** *horses* or *winds* (6.1–8 & 7.1)
- ***7*** *heads, horns, rulers,* and *mountains* (12.3, 17.3, 7, 9 × 2, 10 & 11)
- ***666*** as the AD 666 year of proclamation of the *beast*, brutal Umayyad First Caliph Mu'awiya (13.18).[365-A]

Higher number-codes tag facets of Faiths through codes embedded within them:

- ***144 cubits*** contains embedded codes for *the Faiths' followers progressively perfecting human standards* (21.17). The square *144* codes biblically for perfection, while its square-root of *12* codes for *Faiths*. The unit *cubit* codes for *human standards*. In Hebrew, cubit[A] is *amah*, from *ema* for *mother*, and overlaps with *emet* for *truth*
- ***1000*** codes for *many people* (7.4–8, 11.13, 14.1, 3 & 21.16)

[A] The cubit is the ~18–inch "mother" measurement from elbow-to-middle-fingertip

- ***1,600 furlongs*** contains embedded codes for *hard work leading to perfection over a long period* (14.20). The square *1,600* codes biblically for *perfection*, while its square-root of *40* codes for *a long time*. *Furlongs* code for *hard work*, derived from *furrow-long* as an old unit of farm-work
- ***7,000 killed*** contains embedded codes for *many faithful Muslims are converted* (11.13). The *7* codes for the Cycle of Prophecy's *Seven-Faiths from Asia*. The *thousand* codes for *many [persons]*. The *killed* codes for spiritual death to an old (Muslim) Faith demanded by conversion to a new (Baha'i) Faith
- ***12,000 furlongs*** contains embedded codes for *hard work by the Faiths' many followers* (21.16). The *12* codes for Faiths. The *thousand* codes for many believers. The *furlongs* code for hard work. Apropos, the combined 144,000-furlong length of the 12 edges of 12,000–furlong of the New Jerusalem diamond also happens to code for *many believers progressively perfecting Faiths by hard work*. Curiously, the area of the platform of the Temple is 144,000 square meters too.

Floating-Terms here join the previous ones on pages 20 and 130–1. As before, each **bold** floating-term concurrently qualifies the prior and ensuing terms:

1.17–18: *I myself am* ***the First and the Last, the Living-Being living on****, I have also gone through death*

2.10: *The lying evil one will cast some of you into prison,* ***so that you may be tested****, you shall also be troubled*

2.26–28: *I shall give him or her authority over nations,...****as I too have also attained from my Father****, so I shall assign the Dawn-Star to him or her*

3.4: *You do have some people in Sardis who have not soiled their garments,* ***because they are worthy****, they shall walk with me in white*

4.8: *These four Living-Beings, each and every one of them bearing aboard six wings* ***studded with eyes outside and in*** [qualifying both *Living-Beings* and *wings*]

5.8–9: *The four Living-Beings and the 24 elders fell down before the Ram,* ***each bearing a harp and gold censers full of incenses...****, they are also singing a new song*

6.9–10: *I saw the souls of those slain* ***for this Word of God and for this testimony that they were bearing*** *they also cried out*

6.17–7.1: *Who can stand firm* ***after this vision....After this vision*** [repeating to close Chapter 6 and also to open Chapter 7] *I saw four Angels*

7.2: *Another Angel arising from the rising-place of the sun,* ***bearing a seal from the living God****, he cried out in a loud voice*

12.4: *Whenever she would deliver* **her child, her child** [repeating] *it would devour*

12.17–13.1: *The dragon...set out to fight the rest of her children ....So* **it was standing firm on the sand of the sea....The dragon was standing firm on the sand of the sea** [repeating to close Chapter 12 and also to open Chapter 13]. *From this sea, I saw a beast*

13.9: **Let whoever has ears hear** [qualifying both the prior and ensuing paragraphs]

14.6: *Another Angel...bearing eternal good news to proclaim joyfully to those seated* **over the earth and over every nation, tribe, language-group, and people** [qualifying *to proclaim joyfully* and also *to those seated*]

17.9: **—Here indeed a wise mind!—**[qualifying both the prior and ensuing paragraphs]

17.9: *The seven heads are seven mountains where the woman sits* **over them. Over them** [repeating] *are seven rulers*

18.6–7: *Double and double again,* **according to her dealings,** *fix a double-draught for her*

20.3: *After the years* **it is bound, it is bound** [repeating] *to be released for a short time*

20.8–9: *It shall set out to deceive nations...,* **their number being as the sand of the sea,** *they will have mounted up*

22.16: *I myself am the root and the shoot of a beloved David,* **the shining Dawn-Star** [qualifying *the root and the shoot* and also *a beloved David*]

22.16–17: *The shining Dawn-Star,* **the Spirit and the bride. The Spirit and the bride** [repeating] *say 'Come!'*.

Unusual Translations differing from those appearing in most Bibles have the following good explanations:

1.1, 9, 12.17, 19.10 & 20.4: Guided by interpretation, the genitive-case term *Jesus Christ* (*Iesou Christou*) renders as *of Jesus Christ*, rather than either of its other two valid translations *by Jesus Christ* or *about Jesus Christ*

1.1, 11, 2.2, 18.20 & 21.14: Certain Revelation words test translators sorely. *Apostellō* tests them with meanings like *transmit* (favored), *send, convey,* and *commission. Apostolos* tests them with meanings like *envoy* (favored), *emissary, Apostle, messenger, missionary, missioner, delegate,* or *agent*

1.3: *Tēreō* tests translators with meanings like *take to heart* (favored), *obey, keep, heed, rely upon, retain, maintain, sustain, guard, keep watch,* or *observe*[366-C]

1.4: The distinctive early Christian greeting *Charis* tests translators with meanings like *Blessings* (favored, despite being plural and idiomatic), *Grace, Good wishes, Good will*, or *Kindness*. So the full greeting renders as *Blessings...and Peace* (*Eirēnē*)

1.12, 13, 20, 2.1, 5, 11.4, 18.23 & 21.23: *Luchnia* (fem.) means strictly *lampstand*, while *luchnos* (masc.) means strictly *lamp*. But since the *luchnia* in v. 18.23 does shed light, the other occurrences of *luchnia* render also as *lamp* or *Menorah-Lamp*

1.13, etc.: The vocabularies of both Apocalypse Greek and Hebrew contain a full wardrobe of the dressing-words, as follows, each with its specific meaning: *podērēs* as *long robe* (1.13); *himation* as *garment* (3.4, 5, 18, 4.4, 16.15, 19.13 & 16); *stolē* as *robe* (6.11, 7.9, 13, 14 & 22.14); *linon* as *linen* (15.6); and *bussos* as *fine-linen* (18.12, 16, 19.8 & 19.14); *enduō* as *clad in* (1.13, 15.6 & 19.14); *periballō* as *wearing* (3.5, 18 & 4.4, 7.9, 13, 10.1, 11.3, 12.1, 17.4, 18.16, 19.8 & 13); and *kosmeō* as *arrayed* (21.2 & 19)

1.15 & 2.18: Rendering *chalkolibanon* as *white-hot molten bronze* calls on *chalkos* as Greek for *bronze* and *leibein* as Greek for *pour forth*, and on *chalak* as Hebrew for *smooth* and *lavan* as Hebrew for *white*[367-C]

1.17, etc: *Dexia* means *right-hand* specifically (1.17, 20, 2.1, 5.1, 7, 10.5 & 13.16). *Cheir* means any *hand*, no matter which hand the context may suggest (6.5, 7.9, 8.4, 9.20, 10.2, 8, 10, 14.9, 14, 17.4, 19.2, 20.1 & 4)

1.18, etc: Occurrences of *idou* render as an old-fashioned *Behold* or as a more modern *See, Look*, or *Listen*

1.18, 4.9, 10, 5.13, 7.12, 10.6, 11.15, 14.11, 15.7, 19.3, 20.10 & 22.5: The literal rendering of *eis tous aiōnas tōn aiōnōn* as *into the Eras of the Eras* interprets neatly for serial Eras forming Cycles (replacing *for ever and ever* as the usual idiomatic translation)

2.2, 9, 13, 19, 3.1, 8, 15 & 17: In its Revelation contexts, perfect-tense *oida* renders best literally as *I have seen*, rather than irregularly as the more usual *I know* (*I have seen* means *I know*)

2.5, 21–22, 9.20–21, 16.9 & 11: *Metanoeō* (*consider after*) tests translators with meanings like *repent* (favored), *show regret, reconsider, turn away from, mend one's ways, reform, give up*, and *discard*

2.7: *Paradēsos* renders better as *orchard* than as *paradise /garden* because its Hebrew sister-word *pardes* means *orchard* and the context is feeding from the Tree of Life

2.10 etc: *Stephanos* can mean *prize* (2.10 & 3.11) or *crown* (4.4, 10, 6.2, 9.7, 12.1 & 14.14), while *diadēma* (12.3, 13.1 & 19.12) means *sovereign-crown*

2.27: *Suntribetai* serves better as a gently *broken up* than as a traditional punitive *smashed*

3.2, 8, 7.15, 9.13, 13.12, 14, 19.10, 20 & 20.12: *Enōpion* derives from *en-ōptanomai* meaning *in-sight-of* and usually means *before*. But *enōpion* may also render as *in front of, in the sight of, ahead of, facing, on behalf of*, or even *at*

3.5 & 20.15: The usual Revelation word *biblion* for *book* gets twice replaced by *biblos* as *Full Book* in *Full Book of Life*, interpreted as listing morally decent folk from all backgrounds

3.8, 20 & 4.1: The Temple context makes this *door* (*thura*) the main Temple-Door rather than just a door of any building

3.9: The context lets the unusual give-word *didō* render as *I am handing over* (*didōmi*, the usual give-word, means just *give*)

3.10, also 2.2 & 10: In the context, *peirasmos* and *peirazō* work better as *test/try* rather than as their valid alternative meanings of *affliction/afflict*

3.12: John uses *naos* for the Temple's main central 50 × 40-yard Sanctuary building proper (avoiding *hieron* as the full 200 × 300-yard building-complex centered on the Temple Sanctuary)

3.14: *Amen* usually renders as *Indeed so* (favored), *Yes*, or *Amen*. But it tests translators as *amon* or *Master-Workman* too[368-C]

4.6 etc: Depending on context, *thalassa* can mean *ocean* or *sea*

4.10, etc: *Proskuneō* tests translators with meanings like *worship* (favored), *devote oneself, submit to, idolize, kneel, prostrate oneself, pay homage, honor, revere,* or *adore*

5.1: *Inside* singly qualifies *written. Outside* singly qualifies *sealed*

5.5, 6.1, 7.13, 8.13, 13.3, 15.7, 17.1, 18.21, 19.17 & 21.9: *One of* (*eis*) before *the elders, an eagle, its heads, the four Living-Beings, the seven Angels, a mighty Angel,* and *an Angel* renders comprehensively as *one* or as *one of*

5.8, 8.3, 4, 11.18, 13.7, 10, 14.12, 16.6, 17.6, 18.20, 24, 19.8 & 20.9: *Hoi hagioi* (plural) means "devoted to God" more than "holy". It tests translators with meanings like *the faithful* (favored), *faithful believers, believers, the saints*, and *God's devoted/select /outstanding/holy/devout/good/dedicated people.*[369-C] *Hagios* (singular 3.7, 4.8, 6.10, 11.2, 14.10, 20.6, 21.2, 10, 22.11 & 19) renders much more readily as *holy* for God or one of His Messengers. *Hagios* is *kadosh* is its Hebrew equivalent[370-J]

5.9 & 11.9: The partitive preposition *from* (*ek*) before *every tribe, language-group, people, and nation* renders as *folk from.*

6.1: The oddly nominative-case *voice* in *one of the four Living-Beings calling out* ***as a voice*** *of thunder*, renders accurately as *as a voice*

6.11, also 3.2: *Plērothosin* tests translators with meanings like *fully counted* (favored), *consecrated, complete, finish, sanctified, be complete, perfect,* and *fill*

6.16–17, etc.: *Orgē* (fem.) means *anger* felt internally (6.16–17, 18, 11.18, 12.17, 14.10, 16.19 & 19.15). *Thumos* (masc.) means *fury* displayed externally,[371-C] as passionately expressed by *lying-evil* (12.12), by *fornicating* (14.8 & 18.3), and by *God* (14.10, 19, 15.1, 7, 16.1, 19 & 19.15)

7.10: Dative-cases *to our God, to the Enthroned-One* render better separately than together as the usual combined form *to our Enthroned God*

8.13, 9.1, 12, 11.14, also 12.12, 18.10, 16, & 19: In its contexts, *ouai* so clearly echoes the blasting of a trumpet that it renders as a *Trumpet-Blast* sounding a *Trump-Ta-Ra*, rather than as a traditional *Woe* or *Disaster*

9.1–2, 11, 11.7, 17.8, 20.1 & 3, *ABUSSOS* derives from *A-BUSSOS*, literally *no-base* for the sea originally. It tests translators with meanings like *Abyss* (favored), *endless void*, and *bottomless pit/canyon/chasm/gorge*

9.6 & 11.13: The old-style *those there days* (*ekeinais*) and *that there day* (*ekeinē*) signify yonder future times

9.18, 20, 15.1, 6, 8, 16.9, 21, 18.4, 8, 21.9 & 22.18: A more modern *affliction* rings more credibly than an old-time vague *plague*

9.21, 21.8 & 22.15: The *pharm–* root of *pharmakon* and *pharmakoi* helps them render best as *drug-dealing* and *drug-dealers*, rather than as the traditional *sorcery* and *sorcerers*

10.7: The aorist-tense for *joyfully proclaimed* lets *hōs* render as *after* instead of as the more usual *as*[372]

11.1 & 21.15: The symbolic *reed like a rod* does the *saying* (as the Hebrew for *rod, kaneh* is the root of *canon*)

11.8–9: *Dead body* (*ptōma*) and *corpses* (*ptōmata*) depict the surviving runted teachings of the true Islam of Muhammad that the Umayyads destroyed

13.8 & 17.8: Both nouns on *katabolēs kosmou* lack *the*, which lets them interpret as a **new** *founding* of a **new** *world-order* (instead of as the usual *the creation of the world*)

13.14: In the context, *machaira* works better as a general *war* than as a specific *sword*

14.4: The first dative-case renders as a subjective *of God* and the second dative-case as an objective *for the Ram*

14.6: *Kathēmenos* translates better literally as *those seated* than as its usual idiomatic rendering of *those living*

14.8 & 18.2: Rendering *pepōtiken* as *collapse intoxicated* and *peptōkan*, as *made collapse intoxicated* comprehensively combines the three valid variant verbs *piptein* (*fall/collapse*), *pinein* (*drink*), and *potizein* (also *drink*)[373-C]

14.15 & 18: *Exēranthē*, whose root means *dry*, renders as *dried out* for a withered grain crop. *Ēkmasen*, whose root means *peak/acme*, renders as *peaked* for a rotting grape harvest

14.17: In the Middle East setting, each Messenger's *drepanon* translates best as *scimitar*, for it cannot harvest grain as a *sickle*, and it cannot gather grapes as a *scythe*[374-C]

15.4: *Hosios* translates as *sacred*,[375-C] since *hagios* renders routinely as *holy*

15.5: *Tēs skēnēs tou marturiou* tests translators. As the favored translation, *the Presence of God in the Covenant* derives from the cover-name *skēnēs* for *Presence of God* and *marturion* as *Witness*. Once the Covenant was that of Moses. Now it is the Covenant of Baha'u'llah[376-C]

17.10, also 6.11, 12.12 & 20.3: This lone *oligon* renders as *small* for size, not time. If *short time* had been intended, the original Greek would have been *chronon micron* as *a bit longer* (6.11), or *oligon kairon* as *a little time* (12.12), or *mikron chronon* as *a short time* (20.3)

17.16, 19.18 & 21: The plural *sarkes* renders as *carcasses*,[377-C] while the singular *sarx* renders as *flesh*

18.20: *God has condemned her condemnation of you* calls up Jewish law demanding a guilty party to pay a remedy to an injured party

18.5: *Ekollēthēsan* gains the sky better as *scaled* than as *risen, reached, piled up,* or *infiltrated*

19.9, also 19.5: Grammatically, the true subject of v. 19.9's *tells* is v. 19.5's *voice from the throne*

19.18: The objective genitive-case rendering *for all* bears an interpretive purpose

20.5–6: *Prōtos* before *resurrection* tests translators with meanings like *prime* (favored), *first, principle, primary,* or *best*[378]

21.5–6: Verse 21.6's *they have come to be* (*gegonan*) lacks a clear subject. The favored subject is *these Words* (21.5), though later *the A and the Z, the Beginning and the Ending* could also act as its subject

21.19: The bold nominative-case nouns in ***the foundations*... *arrayed with all kinds of precious gemstone*, *the 1st foundation diamond*, *the 2nd sapphire*, *etc*.**, imply that the gemstones not only **array** but also **form** the foundations

21.21: Here, partitive pronoun *ana* renders as *each*

21.25: Since *no night shall exist there*, *hēmeras* renders better as *in 24 hours* than as the usual *by day*

21.27: *Koinon* can mean either *defiling* (favored) or *defiled*[379-C]

22.3: *Katathema* tests translators with meanings like *exclusion* (favored), *segregation, discrimination, selectivity, cursed (by God),* and even *genocidal war*. The Hebrew source *cherem* means *exclusion*—positive exclusion when setting items aside for God, or negative exclusion when ostracizing wrongdoers[380-J]

22.20: The Codex Alexandrinus *lectio brevior* variant *all people* is favored over the Codex Sinaiticus variant *all the faithful.*[381-C]

Double meanings: Gender equality calls for rendering the masculine Greek *ho* (*he*) routinely doubly as *he or she* and *brothers* routinely doubly as *brothers and sisters*. The following translations extend this logic, to render other Apocalypse words doubly or triply:

1.18 & 4.9–10: *Tō zōn* rendering as *Living-Being living on* combines *Living-Being* and *living on*

2.19: *More* renders idiomatically as both *bigger and better*

3.20, also 12.4: *Estēka* renders as the imperfect-tense of *stēkō* (one verb for *stand*) meaning *I was standing*, and also as the perfect-tense of *istēmi* (another verb for *stand*) meaning *I have been standing*, comprehensively as *I* ***was****, and I* ***have been****, standing*

3.12: ***Him, her****, and* ***it*** renders *auton* triply as both *him, her* for the victor, and as *it* for the pillar

6.12: ***Wholefull*** renders *olē* for the moon as both *whole* and *full*

7.17: Here the partitive pronoun *ana* renders as *up at* for *the center* (acc.), also as *aboard* for *the Throne* (gen.), in ***up at*** *the center* ***aboard*** *the Throne* (*ana meson tou thronou*)

7.17: ***To*** *life* ***on*** *living sources of waters of life* (*epi zōēs pēgas hudatōn*) renders the preposition *epi* doubly as both *to* and *on*

7.17: ***To life*** *on* ***living*** *sources of waters* ***of life*** renders *zōēs* triply as *to life, living,* and *of life*

10.11: *Epi* renders doubly as both ***about and against***

11.19: A final *autou* renders as both *its* before *Ark* and as *His* before *Covenant*, in ***its*** *Ark of* ***His*** *Covenant*

12.4, also 3.20: *Estēken* renders as the imperfect-tense of *stēkō* (one verb for *stand*) meaning *I was standing*, and also as the perfect-tense of *istēmi* (another verb for *stand*) meaning *I have been standing*, comprehensively as *The dragon* ***was****, and* ***has been****, standing*

14.4: *Opou an* renders doubly as both *wherever* and *whenever*, in ***wherever*** *he may go,* ***whenever*** *he may come*

14.4: *Hupagē* renders doubly as both *wherever* and *whenever*, in *wherever* ***he may go****, whenever* ***he may come***

14.14: *Having* (*echōn*) renders doubly as both *wearing* and *bearing* in ***wearing*** *on his head a gold crown and* ***bearing*** *in his hand a sharp scimitar*

19.12: *Having* (*echōn*) renders doubly as both *wearing* and *bearing*, in ***wearing*** *on his head many sovereign-crowns and* ***bearing*** *a written name*

21.13: *Apo* renders doubly as ***from and for***, as just two of its various meanings

22.3–4: A final *autou* renders triply as *Its* for the *Throne,* as *His* for *God,* and as *his* for the *Ram* in ***Its, His****, and* ***his*** *servants*

22.12: The possessive pronoun *mou* renders both as *my* and as *of myself* in ***my*** *reward of* ***myself*** (with *myself* as the reward).

Further, certain valid variants combine comprehensively to render doubly, shown in bold:

1.5: *Lousanti/lusanti* (*washed/freed*) as ***washed and freed***

3.5: *Outos/outōs* (*same one/thus*) as ***this same person…thus***

14.13: *Ap' arti/aparti* (*from now on/certainly so*) as ***from now on—Certainly so***

22.14: The wonderful word-playing typographical twins

PLUNONTESTASSTOLASAUTŌN (*ΠΛΥΝΟΝΤΕΣΤΑΣΣΤΟΛΑΣΑΥΤΩΝ*)

POIOUNTESTASENTOLASAUTOU (*ΠΟΙΟΥΝΤΕΣΤΑΣΣΝΤΟΛΑΣΑΥΤΟΥ*)

as *those who* ***wash their robes and carry out their commands.***

Normal and Idiomatic English Usage is preferred over literal Greek in translating the following verses:

2.23: *I shall also kill her children with death,* as *I shall also deal death to her children*

2.23: *Kidneys and hearts,* as *hearts and minds.* Greeks venerated kidneys and hearts, as did Egyptians, who put back into their mummies only kidneys and hearts

3.7, etc: *Not-forgetting* (*a-lēthēs*), as the now standard *true*

5.13: *The praise, the honor, and the glory, now the dominion,* as *all praise, all honor, all glory, now all dominion*

7.2: *To whom it was entrusted to them to harm,* as *who were entrusted with power to harm*

7.3: *Do no harm,* as *Let no harm hurt*

10.6: *No time shall be,* as *No moment shall exist*

11.4: *Lord of the World* (*Kurios Tēs Gēs*), as *Master of the Universe* (in Hebrew *Adon Ha'Olam*)

12.7: *Of the to fight,* as *having to fight*[382-C]

12.11: *They did not love their life,* as *they have not clung to life*

13.3: *As if slain to death,* as *as if fatally wounded*

13.5, etc: *It was given to it,* as *it was given*

14.2: *As of harpists,* as *like harpists*

14.20 & 21.16: The 200-yard Greek *stadium,* as the 220-yard English *furlong*

16.9: *To glorify,* as *so as to glorify*

6.21: The variable 57–130 pound Greek *talent,* as the 112–pound English *hundredweight*

18.20: *God has condemned the condemnation of you by it*, as *God has condemned its condemnation of you*
21.21: *Each single one of the gates*, as *each single gate*.

Likewise, subjunctive *so that* clauses render often best as infinitive clauses, including:
3.9: *I shall have them so that they may come*, as *I shall have them come*
3.18: *So that you may be rich*, as *for you to be rich*; *so that you may wear*, as *for you to wear*; *so that you may see*, as *for you to see*
6.3: *So that he might conquer*, as *in order to conquer*
9.15: *Released so that they might kill*, as *released to kill*
12.14: *So that she might fly to her spot*, as *for her to fly to her spot*
13.13: *So that it would even make fire fall from the sky*, as *so as even to make fire fall from the sky*
13.16: *So that they may give them a tattoo*, as *to be given a tattoo*[383-C]
16.12: *So that the way would be prepared*, as *so as to prepare the way*
19.8: *So that she might wear* as *to wear*
19.15: *So that he may strike the nations*, as *to strike the nations*
21.15: *So that he might measure the city*, as *to measure the city*.

Nuances of verbs operate variously as follows:

- Inherently, in both Greek and English, the verbs *witness*, *seal*, and *remember* are ambiguous:
  1.1–2, 22.20: *Witness* can mean ***witness*** *what happened* and also ***witness to*** *what happened*
  5.1, 7.2–8 & 22.10: *Sealed* can mean ***stamped with a seal*** and also ***sealed up***
  16.19, 18.5: *Remember* can mean ***keep in mind*** and also ***recall***.
- Echoing Hebrew's single past-tense, nearly all of Revelation's past-tenses are aorist-tenses. Strictly, the Greek aorist-tense is the English past-tense. But since *the temporal sequence of the various Greek tenses is relative, not absolute*,[384-C] the aorist-tense can translate into other tenses according to context. In present-tense contexts, the aorist-tense translates as the perfect-tense. In layered past-tense contexts, it translates as the pluperfect-tense (4.1, 6.11, 8.11, 9.15, 10.8, 5, 12.4, 6, 13 & 16, 13.12, 15.2 & 8, 16.18, 19.20 & 21.1) or as the future-perfect-tense (15.9 & 20.9–10).
- Echoing Hebrew's own lack of a present-tense for the verb *to be*, Revelation often omits the Greek present-tense of *to be*, notably in first and last Chapters 1 and 22, which infuses these two chapters with an aptly timeless feel.

- Greek verb tenses often switch sharply, interpretively to signal serial separate spans of time, as follows:
  2.3: The aorist *bore up* to the perfect *did not tire*
  3.3: The aorist *heard* to the perfect *have received*
  4.10: The present *glorify* to the future *are to fall down... worship...toss*
  5.7: The aorist *came* to the perfect *has taken*
  6.15–16: The aorist *have hidden* to the present *urge*
  8.5: The perfect *has taken up* to the aorist *filled*
  10.7: The present *is due to trumpet* to the aorist *will have been fulfilled*
  12.1–2: The aorist *has appeared* to the present *shrieks*
  12.3–4: The aorist *has appeared* to the present *is sweeping down*
  13.11–12: The aorist *hissed* to the present *exercises*
  16.20–21: The aorist *have vanished* to the present *falls*
  20.8–10: The future *shall set out* to the aorist (now future-perfect) *mounted, surrounded,* and *tormented.*

Ambiguous adjectives concurrently qualify more than one noun:
3.14: A final *of God* can qualify just the final word *Creation* or the full phrase *Amen, the Trustworthy and True Witness, and the Beginning of the Creation*
9.13–14: *Telling* (masc. sing. acc. or neut. plu. nom./acc. *legonta*) agrees partly with *voice* (acc. sing. but fem. *phōnēn*), partly with *horns* (neut. plu. but gen. *keratōn*), and partly with *gold Incense-Altar* (neut. sing. but gen. *thusiastērion*). So, by default, *telling* qualifies all of them
10.11: A final *many* can qualify just the word *rulers* or the full phrase *peoples, nations, language-groups, and rulers*
14.19: *Great* (masc. acc. *megan*) agrees partly with *winepress* (acc. but fem. *leinon*), partly with *God* (masc. but gen. *Tou Theou*), and partly with *fury* (masc. but gen. *thumou*). So, by default, *great* qualifies them all (as *huge, full,* or *magnificent*)
16.14: *Pouring out* (neut. plu. *ekporeuetai*) agrees with and qualifies both *spirits* (neut. plu. *pneumata*) and *wonders* (neut. plu. *sēmeia*)
19.11: *Trustworthy and true* (masc. nom. *pistos kai alēthinos*) agrees with and qualifies both *stallion* (masc. nom. *hippos*) and *rider* (masc. nom. *kathēmenos*)
19.12: *Bearing* (masc. sing. *echōn*) *a written name* agrees with and qualifies both *he* (masc. sing. *ho*) and *sovereign-crowns* (neut. plu. nouns like *diademata* take singular verbs 385-C)
19.14: *Wearing* (masc. nom. *endedumenoi*) agrees partly with *armies* (nom. but neut. *strateumata*) and partly with *stallions* (masc. but dat. *hippois*). So, by default, *wearing* qualifies both of them

21.2: *Arrayed* (fem. acc. *kekosmēmenēn*) agrees with and qualifies both *city* (fem. acc. *polin*) and also *bride* (fem. acc. *numfēn*)
21.8: *The one that* (masc. nom. *ho*) agrees with neither *place* (neut. nom. *meros*) nor *pool* (fem. dat. *limnē*). So, by default, *the one that* qualifies both of them
21.10–11: *Its* (fem. sing. *autēn*) agrees with and qualifies both *city* (fem. sing. *polis*) and *glory* (fem. sing. *doxa*)
21.17: *The one that* (masc. nom. *ho*) agrees with neither *measure* (neut. nom. *metron*) nor *human-being* (masc. dat. *anthropou*). So, by default, *the one that* qualifies both of them.

Nuances of the definite article *the (ho)* operate variously as follows:

- *The* renders emphatically
  - 1.2, etc.: as *this*[386-C] to compensate for Revelation's dearth of demonstrative pronouns such as *houtos* (*this*)
  - 1.1, 19 × 3, 10.4: as a lone *ho* supplied with a noun like *vision, thing,* or *folk*
  - 20.12, 21.8 & 21.17: as an indeclinable *ho estin* (literally *the is*) rendered as *the one that.*[387]
- 1:2 & 4: *The* unexpectedly appearing before the first mention of a noun imbues the noun with familiarity or importance, especially **the** *Angel* and **the** *Seven-Churches* in Chapter 1.
- *The* unexpectedly lacking before a familiar noun imbues the noun with interpretive **newness**, as with:
  - 1.1: *An unveiling of Jesus Christ* as a **new** Gospel (***the*** *unveiling* would be the familiar Gospel of Jesus)[388-C]
  - 1.20 (second mention): *Seven-Churches* as **new** congregations, namely Faiths
  - 7:5–8 & 21.12: *Heirs of Israel* as **new** successors of the People of Israel
  - 14.6: *Eternal good news* (the only time in the New Testament that this phrase lacks *the*) as a **new** Gospel
  - 14.7: *An ocean and sources of waters* as **new** truth and **new** knowledge
  - 14. 11: *Eras of eras* (the only time in the New Testament that this phrase lacks *the*) as a **new** Cycle
  - 14. 13: *Lord* for **any** Messenger of God
  - 19.18, 13.16 (also 11.18 & 19.5): *Humble and important* as folk **newly** involved
  - 20.1: *Angel* as a **new** Messenger. [Alternatively, *Angel* alone can be also a third-person form of address—as when a director cites an actor by *Role* or a child mentions her father as *Father.*[389]]

Honorific Grammar

- Honorific grammar is inherently ambiguous. For example, the phrase *the readers* can mean us honorific readers, or some other readers. Or the phrase *the writer* can mean me the honorific writer, or some other writer. The main Angel addresses the Seven-Churches with honorific grammar as follows:
  2.1, 8, 12, 18, 3.1, 7 & 14: He starts his address to each Church with *These things says he who* as an honorific third-person
  2.2–6, 9–10, 13–16, 19–25, 3.1–4, 8–11 & 15–19: He addresses each Church with the singular honorific *you*, as if addressing its Angel, as God rebuked prophets to rebuke indirectly the People of Israel tactfully
  2.7, 11, 17, 29, 3.6, 13 & 22: He ends his address to each Church with *let the one who has ears hear* as an honorific third-person.
- Further, other honorific third-person Revelation terms have already rendered into vocative second-person terms as follows:
  2.7, 11, 17, 29, 3.6, 13 & 22: *Let the one who has ears hear*, as *Let you who have ears*
  2.8: *None can close, as None of you can close*
  4.11: *The Lord and God*, as *You, Our Lord and God*
  8.13: *The ones who live*, as *you who live*
  11.17: *The Almighty Lord God*, as *You, Almighty Lord God*
  11.17 & 16.5: *The-Is, The-Was*, as *You The-Is, You The-Was*
  12.12: *The heaven*, as *you heaven*
  16.5: *The Divine One*, as *You Divine One*
  18.10, 16 & 19: *The great city*, as *you great city*
  18.14–5: *The traders*, as *you traders*
  18.14–5: *They who got rich*, as *you who got rich*
  18.20: *The heaven, the faithful*, as *you heaven, you faithful*
  19.5: *His servants*, as *you His servants*
  22.17: *The one who hears/thirsts/wishes*, as *you who hear/thirst /wish*.

Kai is Revelation's prime conjunction opening 74% of its verses. Kai joins the staccato statements that John uttered and Prochorus recorded. Strictly kai means *and* or simply signals a silent pause. But the very frequency of kai in Revelation instills it with a *dependent semantic value* for each *context in which it is used*.[390-C] Accordingly, kai can function as a wonderful wildcard word for any of the following English conjunctions or conjunction-phrases:

accompanied by, accompanying, additionally, along with, alongside, also, alternatively, although, and, anyway, as, as for, associated with, as well, as well as, at the same time, at that, at this, at which, because, behold, besides, both, but, but also, certainly, consequently, continuing, especially, even, even as, even so, even then, even though, even with, exactly, for, further, furthermore, hardly, henceforth, hereafter, hereunto, hereupon, herewith, hitherto, however, in addition, in any case, including, inclusive of, indeed, instead, in other words, in particular, just, last, later, let alone, like, meaning, meanwhile, moreover, namely, nevertheless, next, nonetheless, not least, not just, not only, notably, notwithstanding, now, or, particularly, plus, provided that, rather, regardless, so, so long as, so that, specifically, still, subsequently, such as, that, that is, that is to say, then, thereafter, thereat, thereupon, this is to say, though, throughout, together with, too, until, when, whereas, whereupon, which, while, or *who*!

Puns and Word-Plays pepper the pie of Revelation, shown by the words in bold as follows:

1.1 & 6: ***Deixai*** (*show*), with ***doxa*** (*glory*), to *show glory*
1.16: *Di***stomatos** (*two-edged*), with ***stoma*** (*mouth*)
2.2–3: ***Kopos*** (*tireless labor*), with ***kopian*** (*tire*)
2.2–3: ***Bastasai*** (*bear*), with ***ebastasas*** (*bore up*)
2.14: ***Bal/ba'l-*** triply, with ***ba'l****-aam* (*people swallower*), ***bal****-aak* (*blood-lapper*), and ***bal****-ein* (*set*)
3.10: ***Etērēsas*** (*preserve*), with ***teirēsō*** (*preserve from*)
11.2: ***Exōthen*** (*out*), with ***exōthen*** (*outside*)
11.2: ***Aulēn*** (*courtyard*), with ***autēn*** (*it*)
12.4: ***Estēken*** (*standing*), with ***tekein*** (*give birth*), since standing is the natural way to give birth, after all!
12.6 & 14: ***Echei*** (*where*), with ***ekei*** (*there*)
13.8: ***Hou*** (*whose*), with ***ou*** (*not*)
14.20: ***Chalinōn*** (*bridles*), with ***chiliōn*** (*thousand*)
18.14: ***Lipara*** (*splendid*), with ***lampra*** (*sparkling*)
20.2–3: ***Deō*** (*bound*), with ***deō*** (*bound to*)
22.14: Again, ***PLUNONTESTASSTOLASAUTŌN***,
with ***POIOUNTESTASENTOLASAUTOU***.

Emphatic Personal Pronouns include:

- Pronouns that are surplus, for Greek verb-endings act anyway as personal pronouns, for example
  1.8, 9, 17, 2.23, 3.9, 19, 17.7, 21.6 × 2, 22.13, 22.16 × 2 & 18: A surplus *I* (*egō*) as ***I myself***
  2.15, 3.17, 4.11 & 7.14: A surplus *you* (*su*) as ***you yourself***
  2.6, 2.27, 3.10, 3.21 & 22.8: A surplus *I* (*egō*) as ***I too*** elided in *kagō* (*kai* and *egō*) as ***I too also*** or ***I too...also***
- Possessive pronouns presenting unusually, for example:
  2.9, 13, 19, 3.1, 2, 8 & 15, 10.9 & 14.18: *Of you* (*sou*) being set irregularly **before** its noun, instead of regularly **after** it, rendered as an emphatic ***your very*** or ***your own***

3.8: *Of you* (*sou*), sandwiched between *in front* and *Door* rendered emphatically as *in front **of you your own** Door*
2.13: *Of me* (*mou*), repeated after *Witness* and *trustworthy*, rendered emphatically as ***my own** trustworthy Witness*
12.11, 14.10, 17, 18.6, 7, 19.15 × 2, 21.3 × 2 & 21.7: *Also he* (*kai autos*) rendered emphatically as ***He himself***.391-R

Supplied Terms appear in bold:
1.2: *All the **visions***
1.6: *To him **be** the glory*
2.5, 19, 26, 3.8, 14.13: ***Good** deeds*
2.8: *None **of you** can close*
4.4: ***I saw** 24 elders seated*, with oddly accusative-case *24 elders seated* calling for a repeated *I saw* to be understood
5.7: *As he took **the short scroll***
6.9, 8.3, 8.5, 14.18 & 16.7: ***Sacrificial**-Altar* (*thusiasterion*)
6.11: *As they **had been***
7.12: *To our God **be** the praise*
8.3 & 9.13: *Gold **Incense**-Altar* (*thusiasterion to chrusoun*)
9.8: *Their teeth were like **fangs** of lions*
10.4: *Whatever **things*** [for a lone *ha*]
11.8: *Their dead body **strewn** across*
13.1: ***The dragon*** [for *it*] *was standing firm*
13.3: ***I saw** one of its heads*, where the oddly accusative-case *one of its heads* calls for supplying a repeated *I saw*
16.13: ***Coming** out of the mouth*
16.15: ***Evil** spirit*
16.7: *They deserve **it***
16.11: ***Bad** deeds*
17.13 & 13: *These **rulers** possess...These **rulers** shall fight*
18.12–13: ***Shipments*** repeating twice before two subsets of genitive-case nouns
20.4: ***I saw** souls*, where the oddly accusative-case *souls* calls for supplying a repeated *I saw*
20.10: *Where also that beast and false-prophet **are***
21.6: As a continuing subject, *they* as ***these Words*** *have come to exist*
21.26: As a continuing subject, *they* as ***its gates*** *shall* draw
22.2: *The city main-square of it* as ***the city***
22.3: *Within it* as ***this city***.

Last-First (*Hysteron-Proteron*) Greek is a recurring quirk of Greek grammar that mentions causes before results, reversing the chronological sequence of normal English that lists results before causes. After all, results are more important than their causes! So last-first Greek says *she got wet and it rained*, with *she got wet* as the more important result of the less important cause that *it rained*. English, of course, states that *it rained and she got wet* chronologically. A soul-mate of last-first Greek is Korean sign-language, whose forward gestures indicate visible, hence known, past events, and whose backward gestures indicate an invisible, hence unknown, future.

Translating last-first Greek is tricky. For example, *who is worthy to open this short scroll and its seven seals* (5.2) may render in several ways, all less-than-ideal:

- As it is, in clumsy last-first order
- As a finessed *who is worthy to open this short scroll, along with its seven seals* or similar combination
- As a reluctant reversal into *who is worthy to open these seven seals and this short scroll*. Reversal worked best in the following five cases:
  - 3.3: *Recall how you heard and have received*
  - 3.3: *Repent and obey*
  - 3.19: *I myself train and rebuke whomever I love*
  - 5.11: *Millions, now hundreds of millions*
  - 6.2: *In order to conquer, then to conquer*.

Accumulating Images are recurring descriptions whose steadily changing details develop and advance meanings.[392] They are understood best via their interpretations. Examples include:

1.4, 8 & 4.8, to 11.17 & 16.5: *The-Is, The-Was, The-Is-Coming*, condensing down into *The-Is, The-Was*

1.14 & 2.18, to 19.12: *Eyes like a flame of fire*, focusing down as *eyes a flame of fire*

1.16, to 1.18, 4.9, 10, 5.13, 7.12, 10.6, 11.15, 14.11, 15.7, 19.3, 20.10 & 22.5: *Into the eras*, expanding *into the Eras of the Eras*

4.4, to 9.7: *Gold crowns*, losing luster as *some sort of crowns... shining like gold*

5.3, to 5.13: *Nobody in the sky, on the earth, or under the earth*, reversing and expanding into *all creatures in the sky, on the earth, under the earth, now on the ocean*

5.5, to 22.16: *The root of a beloved David*, growing into *the root and the shoot of a beloved David*

5.12, to 5.13: *Honor, glory, and praise*, chanting up to *all praise, all honor, all glory, now all dominion*

8.7–9, to 16.2–3: *Trumpets...fire...blood...earth...creatures living lives in the sea*, transforming into *pitchers*...an *ulcer...blood...the sea...every living soul in the sea*

16.2, to 16.11: An *ulcer*, extending out as *ulcers*.

Demonstrative Pronouns are scarce in Revelation, so the few that do occur render emphatically as follows:

1.3, 19 × 3, 7.1, 13–14, 10.6 × 3, 11.4 & 6, 14.4 × 3, 16.5, 17.13, 20.3, 21.7, 22.8 × 2, 22.16 & 22.20: Nouns like *things, visions, folk, men, thousands, rulers, ones,* or *years* supplied to lone occurrences of *this* (*houtos*)

2.24, 9.18, 11.10, 16.9, 17.16, 18.14–15, 20.14, 22.10 & 22.18–19 ×4: An emphatic *same, very, own,* or *self,* supplied to adjectival occurrences of *houtos*

1.19, 4.1 × 2, 7.9, 9.12, 15.5, 18.1, 19.1 & 20.3: The noun *things* supplied to *After these* (*meta tauta*) in *After these things,* a phrase signaling major breaks in the Revelation text

1.7, 12, 2.24, 9.4, 11.8, 12.13, 17.12, 19.2 & 20.4: *Those who* or *this one that* are comprehensive renderings of the masc. plu. *hoi-tines* and fem. sing. *hē-tis* forms of compound demonstrative pronoun *hostis*, whose *hos-*, *–tis, hoi-*, *-tines, hē*-and *-tis* parts all individually mean *this,* and whose *hoi-* and *hē-* parts are also forms of *ho* (*the*)

13.10, 18, 14.12 & 17.9: *This indeed!* (*Hōde!*) is a demonstrative pronoun that is emphatic routinely.

Opening vowels: Greek words that open with a vowel call for a prior sounded-*h* or unsounded-*h*. Nowadays, pointing over the opening vowel signals the presence or absence of the *h*-sound. But AD 95 Greek had no such pointing. As a result:

4.1, etc.: *HN* can sound as both a smooth *ēn* (*'HN*) meaning ***that***, or as a rough ***hēn*** (*'HN*) meaning ***was***. Hence, *HN* can render doubly as these verses show in bold:

4.1: *That first voice* ***that*** *I had heard...* ***was*** *speaking*

10.8: *That voice...* ***that*** *I had heard* ***was*** *speaking with me again*

14.2: *This sound* ***that*** *I heard* ***was*** *like harpists*

20.8: *ΩN,* also, can sound as both a smoothly *ōn* (*'ΩN*) meaning ***being***, or as a rough ***hōn*** (*'ΩN*) meaning ***of whom***. However, *their* (*autōn*) in the same verse renders *of whom* redundant. So here *ΩN* renders as just *ōn* for ***being***.

Another Angel refers inherently back to a prior Angel or Angels:

7.2: *Another Angel* refers back to v. 7.1's *four Angels*

8.3: *Another Angel* refers back to v. 8.2's *four Angels*

10.1: *Another mighty Angel* refers back to v. 5.2's *mighty Angel*

14.6, 8 & 9: Three occurrences of *another Angel* refer back to v. 14.1's *Ram* as a presumptive Angel

14.15, 17 & 18: Four occurrences of *another Angel* refer back to v. 14.14's *Human-Being* as a presumptive Angel.

Neuter plural nouns may oddly

3.2: Qualify people as well as things, for example *the rest (loipa) who are about to die*[393-C]

8.3 & 9.12: Take singular verbs,[394-C] not least in cases bearing important interpretive purpose, for example:

- 8.3: *Many incenses* ***was*** *handed to him*
- 9.12: *Two Trumpet-Blasts* ***is*** *still coming.*

Restrictive Clauses are favored more frequently than non-restrictive clauses, given how Revelation's brevity creates contexts that fit them better. For example, in its context, *this voice that was speaking with me* sounds better than *this voice, which was speaking with me* (1.12).

Proposed Structure for the Book of Revelation

Generally, scholars agree that the Book of Revelation contains these six parts:

- Prologue (vv. 1.1–1.8)
- Angel (vv. 1.9–1.20)
- Messages from the Angel (vv. 2.1–3.22)
- Baseline Story (vv. 4.1–19.5)
- Intent of God (vv. 19.6–22.5)
- Epilogue (vv. 22.5–22.21).

Its Baseline Story is the longest and most confusing part. As many proposals for its structure exist as scholars making them. On one hand, the Baseline Story displays clear narrative intent through its

- Specific time-expressions signaling successive events, such as *what is due to flash* and *after these visions*[395-R]
- Serial telescoping-out sets of seven as *Spirits, seals, horns and eyes, thunders, Angels standing before God,* and *Angels bearing seven afflictions*[396-R]
- Many *kai*'s (*and*'s) linking serial events, as the Old Testament's ubiquitous Hebrew *vav-consecutives* (*and*'s) also do
- Accumulating images that develop and advance meanings.

On the other hand, the Baseline Story's blatantly awkward and jumpy style throughout fails to follow faithfully the flow of its forecasts as a proper story should.

Addressing the contrast, a useful proposal for the structure of the Baseline Story identifies three literary pillars as textual interludes that support and cut into the Story simultaneously, each describing people praising God.[397-C]

The most important second textual interlude covers Chapters 10–11. This is the Central Prophecy of Revelation, set centrally just as Old Testament Books also set important texts centrally—as, for example, Leviticus setting its all-important Yom Kippur text in its central Chapter 16.

Two sets of internal links tie the Central Prophecy together:

- One party (Baha'u'llah) keeps reappearing as *its mighty Angel, seventh Trumpet-Angel, a rod like a cane,* and *third Trumpet-Blast Angel.*
- All of its three time-prophecies predict the same AD 1844 year.

So it should come as no surprise to discover that one Baha'i Writing[398] interprets and expounds Revelation Chapter 11 extensively.

Table showing Proposed Structure for Revelation[399-C]

Prologue	1.1–8: John begins to unveil his vision
The Angel **tells John to record**	1.9–20: The angelic vision comprises: 1.9–20: *The visions that you have been seeing*, as this advent of the main Angel 2.1–3.22: *The things that are happening*, namely his messages to the Seven-Churches 4.1–19.5:*The things that are due to happen*, namely his main Baseline Story
Messages from the Angel **to the Seven-Churches**	2.1–3.22: 2.1–2.7: To Ephesus 2.8–11: To Smyrna 2.12–17: To Pergamos 2.18–29: To Thyatira 3.1–6: To Sardis 3.7–13: To Philadelphia 3.14–22: To Laodicea
Baseline Story **starts**	4.1–11: A heavenly Door opens to an Enthroned-One, to four Living-Beings, and to 24 elders 5.1–14: The Enthroned-One appoints a Ram to interpret John's small Revelation scroll 6.1–17: The Ram breaks the Revelation scroll's first six seals and interprets them
First Interlude cuts in	**7.1–8: Four angels endorse 144,000 believers for God** **7.9–12: Believers praise God** **7.15–7: The Temple appears**
Baseline Story **continues**	8.1–5: The Ram breaks the seventh last seal and releases its seven Trumpet-Angels 8.6–12: The first four Trumpet-Angels sound 8.13–9.12a: The fifth Trumpet-Angel sounds as the first Trumpet-Blast Angel 9.12b–21: The sixth Trumpet-Angel sounds as the second Trumpet-Blast Angel
Second Interlude, the Central Prophecy, cuts in	**10.1–11.2: The mighty seventh Angel prepares to trumpet** **11.3–14a: Two witnesses appear, disappear, return, and then are martyred** **11.14b: The seventh Trumpet-Angel sounds as the third Trumpet-Blast Angel** **11.15–18: People praise God for the advent of the third Trumpet-Blast Angel** **11.19: The Temple of God reappears**

***Baseline Story* continues and ends**	Seven serial visions show: 12.1–17: A woman dressed in the sun 13.1–10: A beast from the sea 13.11–18: A beast from the land 14.1–5: The Ram on Mount Zion 14.6–13: Three Angels 14.14–20: A Divine Human-Being 15.1–16.21: Seven Pitcher-Angels
Third interlude cuts in	**17.1–18: The main Angel teaches readers how to interpret prophetic symbols** **18.1–24: Babylon falls** **19.1–5: Believers praise God for the fall of Babylon**
***The Intent of God* is fulfilled**	Seven wonderful events bloom as 19.6–10: The wedding banquet of the Ram 19.11–16: The proclamation of the Lord of lords and King of kings 19.17–21: God's great banquet, spiritual and economic 20.1–10: The Jewish Seventh Millennium 20.11–15: Spiritual life 21.1–21: New Jerusalem 22.1–5: The Tree of Life
Epilogue	22.6–21: John ends the unveiling of his vision of the One Religion of God.

SUMMARY

The Apocalypse Revelation reports the AD 95 vision seen by the Apostle John on the island of Patmos, which he dictated to his disciple Prochorus, and which Prochorus recoded in Hebraized Greek.

Deciphering their prophetic report reveals Revelation as a book of codes and linguistic devices telling a prophetic tale hidden within a prophetic tale. *Apocalypse Secrets* tells this hidden tale that the Writings of the new Baha'i Faith have revealed.

As much as it is known as a book of prophecy, Revelation is more a book of proof. *Apocalypse Secrets* explains its coverage of three-millennia-worth of history and unfolds its past two millennia of spiritual lessons for the coming golden Millennium. *Apocalypse Secrets* centers on the pivotal year 1844 tipping the old spiritual Cycle of Prophecy into the new spiritual Cycle of Fulfillment and opening a 400–year end-time period doubling as the beginning-time of the long-awaited Sabbatical Millennium and its global divine civilization of global justice, peace, and prosperity.

Across John's Middle East stage, *Apocalypse Secrets* unfurls two sets of seven flags. Its first set of flags laments the serial Eras of the Cycle of Prophecy's seven militaristic Empires that have generated millennia of militarism and now the looming collapse of confused Babylon's greedy Malignant Materialism. Its second set of flags welcomes the serial Eras of the same Cycle's seven divine Faiths and the launch of the Baha'i Faith that reveals them all as One Religion of God.

Our difficult end-times close these seven Eras of Faiths and Empires. End-time Muslim Militarism is bursting the balloon of end-time Malignant Materialism, tipping its Babylon into collapse, and spiraling the world into a paralytic Greatest Depression.

Yet the Greatest Depression shall generate recovery that begins wonderful beginning-times. The healing phase shall see the phoenix of spiritual economics rise from Babylon's ashes, beating its material and spiritual wings in unison. Spiritual economics shall seed the worthy prosperity of the Millennial Era. A Lesser Peace, which has already begun, shall evolve into a Greater Peace in the new spiritual Era blossomed by the One Religion of God. An entirely *new cycle of human power*[400-A] shall fruit New Jerusalem as divine civilization.

Glossary

In addition to the Glossary, the pages 371–82 Index acts as also a glossary of symbols, which locates each symbol to a page in the Parallel Interpretation, for the matching right-column to show the symbol's meaning.

Abbasid Caliphate (AD 750–1258)—dynastic regime that descended from Muhammad's uncle Abbas, overthrew the Umayyad Caliphate in AD 749, and built new Baghdad as its capital city
'Abdu'l-Baha (1844–1921)—eldest living son and successor of Baha'u'llah; third Primary-Figure of the Baha'i Faith; Arabic title meaning *Servant of Glory*
Abjad—Arabic numerology
Abu-Sufyan—notorious Emir of Mecca; Umayyad tribal leader; enemy of Muhammad; father of First Umayyad Caliph Mu'awiya
Acco/Akka/Acre—ancient fortified city on the coast of Israel, 14 miles north of Haifa
AH—***Anno Hijrae*** Muslim calendar years dated from the AD 622 flight of Muhammad from Mecca to Medina
Ahura Mazda—Zoroastrian name for God meaning *Lord of Wisdom*
Ali—Muhammad's legitimate successor; cousin, stepson, son-in-law, and second follower; First Imam of Shi'a Islam
Apocalypse—name of the Book of Revelation favored by Catholics; Greek for *Unveiling*
Armageddon—Mount Carmel signifying the 20th century of both global warfare and also global peace; Hebrew for *Mountain of Preaching*
Artaxerxes—Persian king whose 457 BC edict let the prophet Ezra return to Jerusalem to restart services in its rebuilt Temple
Avesta—the main Zoroastrian Scripture.

Bab, the (1819–1850)—Ali Muhammad, Founder of the Babi Faith; Arabic title meaning *Door* or *Gate*
Babi Faith—the brief Pre-Baha'i Faith founded by the Bab
Baghavad Gita—main Hindu Scripture
Baghdad—Abbasid Empire's new capital city founded on the Tigris River in AD 762
Bahá—Arabic for *Glory*
Baha'i Faith—Faith founded in 1863 by the Bab's successor Baha'u'llah
Baha'u'llah (1817–1892)—Husayn Ali, Founder of the Baha'i Faith; Arabic title meaning ***GLORY OF GOD***
Bayan—main Scripture by the Bab, whose prime theme was the imminent advent of a Promised-One greater than himself
BE—***Baha'i Era*** calendar years dating from the 1844 proclamation of the Bab

BH—Before Hijrae Muslim calendar years dating back from the AD 622 flight of Muhammad from Mecca to Medina
Book of Certitude, Kitab-i-Iqan—a main Baha'i Scripture interpreting Biblical and Quranic symbols and explaining the progressive nature of divine revelation; Baha'u'llah wrote it over 48 hours.

Caliph—blasphemous title assumed by the three first Rashidun Caliphs; Arabic for *Successor*
Christ—Jesus, Founder of Christianity; Greek title meaning *Anointed*
Codex—form taken by the book after the scroll
Constantinople (330–1453)—capital city of the Byzantine Empire and its Orthodox Church until AD 1453; Muslim Ottoman Istanbul after AD 1453.

Day of Atonement—holiest Jewish day; in Hebrew *Yom Kippur*
Dinkird—main Zoroastrian Scripture
Dispensation—the Era/*Day* begun by a Messenger of God and his Law.

Edicts of Toleration—key laws within the Ottoman Empire's *Tanzimat Reforms* that granted legal equality to non-Muslims, especially to the Jews and Christians of Palestine
Elijah—Old Testament Mount Carmel prophet who cleansed Judaism of Baal worship and whose return Jews expect
Euphrates—major Fertile Crescent river running through Turkey, Syria, and Iraq, most of it parallel to the Tigris River.

Faith—Law, Revelation, religion, or spiritual system based on the teaching of a major Messenger, Prophet, or Manifestation of God.

GAAP—American *Generally Accepted Accounting Principles*
Gematria—Hebrew numerology
Ghenza Rama—main Sabaean Scripture
Gospel—four main Christian Scriptures; the whole New Testament
Guardianship—Baha'i successorship established by the *Will and Testament* of 'Abdu'l-Baha appointing Shoghi Effendi and the Universal House of Justice as his successors.

Haifa—city on and beside Mount Carmel; major Israeli port
Hidden Imam—see *Twelfth Imam*
Holy Land—Israel, including the West Bank
Holy Spirit—intermediary power connecting God with humans
Husayn—grandson of Muhammad and son of Ali; Third Imam of Shi'a Islam martyred by the Umayyads
Hysteron-proteron—see *Last-first*.

Imam—title of founders and first leaders of Shi'a Muslim as true successors of Muhammad; Arabic title meaning *Leader*
Iran—modern name for Persia

Islam—Arabic for *submission* to the will of Allah/God
Isaac—Abraham's second son by his wife Sarah
Ishmael—Abraham's first son by his maid Hagar
Istanbul—Ottoman capital city from AD 1453; Christian Byzantium's Constantinople up to AD 1453.

Kaaba—name of a cubic black building in Mecca; most holy Muslim site; Arabic for *cube*
Kufah—Shi'a Imamate's capital city on the Euphrates River in Iraq.

Last-First/Hysteron-Proteron—quirk of Greek grammar that lists results before causes, reverses the normal chronological order of English.

Mahdi—Sunni Islam's lesser Promised-One due to bring an Era of peace and justice; Arabic title meaning *Guided*
Manifestation—a Major Prophet or Messenger of God from whom minor prophets derive their inspiration and authority
Mashiach—Jewish Messiah; Hebrew title meaning *Anointed*
Magianism and *Mazdeanism*—alternative names for Zoroastrianism
Mecca—Islam's holiest city; birthplace of Muhammad
Medina—Islam's second holiest city; burial place of Muhammad
Most Holy Book/Kitab-i-Aqdas—the central Baha'i Scripture
Mosaf—Special Service, here for Yom Kippur in the Temple
Mount Carmel—holy mountain in Israel, home of prophets; the true Armageddon mountain; Baha'i World Center; Hebrew for Mountain of *God's Vineyard* (*Carm-El*)
Mu'awiya—AD 666's First Umayyad Caliph, son of Abu-Sufyan
Muhdi—Sunni Islam's greater Promised-One due to bring an Era of peace and justice; Arabic title meaning *Guider*
Muslim/Moslem—submitter to the will of Allah and Muhammad his Prophet; Arabic title meaning *Submitter*.

Persia—enduring name for Iran, named after today's province of Fars.

Qaim—Shi'a Islam's lesser Promised Manifestation due to bring an Era of peace and justice; Arabic title meaning *Raised*
Qayyum—Shi'a Islam's greater Promised Manifestation due to bring an Era of peace and justice; Arabic title meaning *Raiser*
Quddus—Bab's eighteenth last and closest disciple
Quran/Koran—main Muslim Scripture.

Rashidun Caliphs—first leaders of Islam after Muhammad; Arabic title meaning *Righteous Successors*
Revelation—name of the Book of Revelation favored by Protestants
Revelation—Law, Faith, or spiritual system based on the teaching of a Major Messenger, Prophet, or Manifestation of God.

Sassanid dynasty (AD 224–650)—Persia's last Zoroastrian dynasty
Scroll—form taken by the book before the *codex*
Seal of the Prophets—title for Muhammad as the Prophet whose Era closed the Cycle of Prophecy
Shechinah—name of God emanating His/Her/Its feminine aspect; Hebrew for *Presence of God*
Shi'a (*Shi'i, Shi'ah*)—main branch of Islam following Ali and the Imams as true successors of Muhammad; Arabic meaning *Follower*
Shiraz—city where the Bab was born; earlier capital city of Persia; city famous for mystic poets
Shoghi Effendi (1897–1957)—great-grandson of Baha'u'llah and grandson of 'Abdu'l-Baha; fourth Baha'i Primary-Figure; Guardian of the Baha'i Faith
Sultan—Ottoman rulers; Arabic title meaning *Sovereign*
Sunna—Arabic for *Way* (purportedly of Muhammad)
Sunni—main branch of Islam following the Caliphs as purported successors Muhammad.

Tablet—sacred Baha'i letter/Epistle
Tamid—daily Dusk or Dawn Service in the Jewish Temple
Tanzimat Reforms—Ottoman laws reform of the 1800s that contained important Edicts of Toleration; Turkish for *Reform*
Temple—Jewish Temple in Jerusalem, last destroyed in AD 70
Teheran (*Tihran*)—capital city of modern Iran, previously Persia
Tipitaka—the main Buddhist Scripture
Torah/Pentateuch—the main Jewish Scripture; first five Books of the Old Testament
Twelfth Imam/Hidden Imam—last Shi'a Imam after the Eleventh Imam died in AD 873; for Baha'is the Bab; for Shi'a Muslims a child who went into *occultation* AD 873 whose return they await.

Umayyads—a powerful Meccan tribe whose idol-trade hurt the iconoclastic teachings of Muhammad
Umayyad Caliphate (AD 666–751)—dynastic regime that ruled the Muslim world from its capital of Damascus
Universal House of Justice—the supreme Baha'i administrative body elected every five years and seated on Mount Carmel.

YHWH/JEHOVAH—main Old Testament name for God
Yom Kippur—holiest Jewish day; in English *Day of Atonement*

Zion/Mount Zion—beacon mountain for Jerusalem and its Temple
Zohar—mystic Jewish Scripture full of prophecies
Zarathustra—original Persian name for Zoroaster
Zarathustrianism—original Persian name for Zoroastrianism.

Bibliography

The names of works most relevant to *Apocalypse Secrets* appear in **bold**. Some works carry dates of particular relevance.

'Abdu'l-Baha. *'Abdu'l-Baha in London*. Wilmette: US Baha'i Publishing Trust, 1982

———. ***'Abdu'l-Baha 'Translated in Acco by Monever Khanum', cited by Brittingham, Isabel D.* (1909)**, distribution copy. San Diego: *Barstow-Lovejoy Archives*

———. *Baha'i World Faith* (*BWF*). Wilmette: Baha'i Publishing Trust, 1976

———. (1931). *Child of the Covenant,* compiled by Adib Taherzadeh. Oxford: George Ronald, 2000

———. *Foundations of World Unity*. Wilmette: Baha'i Publishing Trust, 1968

———. *Divine Philosophy (DP)*. Boston: Tudor Press, 1918

———. *Japan Will Turn Ablaze* (1912). Baha'i Publishing Trust of Japan, 1992

———. *Letter to Martha Root*. Geneva: 1920

———. *Memorials of the Faithful*. Wilmette: Baha'i Publishing Trust, 1971

———. *Paris Talks*. London: Baha'i Publishing Trust, 1995

———. *Promulgation of Universal Peace* (*PUP*). Wilmette: Baha'i Publishing Trust, 1982

———. *Secret of Divine Civilization*. Baha'i News 12–13, September 1972

———. *Selections from the Writings of 'Abdu'l-Baha* (*SWA*). Haifa: Baha'i World Center, 1982

———. ***Some Answered Questions* (*SAQ*)**, translated by Laura Clifford Barney. Wilmette: Baha'i Publishing Trust, 1987

———. *Summon up Remembrance* (by Marzieh Gail)*: Wisdom of Burying the Dead.* Oxford: George Ronald, 1987

———. *Tablets of 'Abdu'l-Baha* (*TAB*). New York: Baha'i Publishing Committee, *TAB I* 1930, *TAB II* 1940 & *TAB III* 1930

———. *Tablets of the Divine Plan*. Wilmette: Baha'i Publishing Trust, 1993

———. *Tablet to the Hague* (1919). London: Bahá'ís [*sic*] Publishing Trust; also in *SWA* 227.296–307, Haifa: Baha'i World Center, 1982

——— *Tablets, Instructions, and Words of Explanation, The Unveiling of The Divine Plan* (1919). http://www.bahai-library.com/?file=abdulbaha _tablets_instructions_explanation#13)

———. *A Traveler's Narrative*. Wilmette: Baha'i Publishing Trust, 1988

———. *Will and Testament of 'Abdu'l-Baha*. Wilmette: Baha'i Publishing Trust (1994)

Agee, M.J. *The End of The Age*. New York: Avon Books, 1994

Aghnides Nicolas P. *Muhammadan Theories of Finance*. Lahore: Premier Book House, 1961

Alesina Alberto, Spolaore Enrico. *On the Number and Size of Nations*. Quarterly Journal of Economics 112.4.1027–1056, Nov. 1997

Al-Suhrawardy, Sir Abdullah. *Wisdom of the East Series: The Sayings of Muhammad.* New York: E. P. Dutton, 1941

Ameer, Ali. *The Spirit of Islam*. London: W.H. Allen Co., 1891 & Christophers, 1935

Aptowitzer, Avigdor. *The Heavenly Temple According to the Haggadah,* Seminal paper. Jerusalem: Academy of Jerusalem, 1929

Arberry, Arthur J., translator. *Quran Interpreted* (2 vols.). New York: Macmillan, 1955

Ariel, Israel & Richman, Chaim. *The Holy Temple of Jerusalem*. Jerusalem: Carta, 2005

Aristion, Papias. *The Alleged Presbyter John, St. John the Evangelist 2*. http://www.Newadvent.org/cathen/08492a.htm

Armstrong, Karen. *Jerusalem: One City, Three Faiths*. New York: Ballantine Books. Also Toronto: Random House, 1996

Aune, David. *Word Biblical Commentary 52, Revelation, Volume 52A* *Revelation 1–5*. Dallas: Word Books, 1997

——— ***Volume 52B, Revelation 6–16*** & ***Volume 52C, Revelation 16–22***. Nashville: Thomas Nelson, 1998.

Bab, The. *Selections from the Writings of the Bab*. Haifa: Baha'i World Center, 1978

The Bab, Compilation. *Martyrdom of the Bab*. Los Angeles: Kalimat Press, 1992

Baha'u'llah. *Athar-i Qalam-i A'la* 1–8. Tehran: Mu'Assasah-i Milli-i Matbu'At-i Amri, 1969–78

——— *The Covenant of Baha'u'llah,* compiled by Adib Taherzadeh. Oxford: George Ronald, 1992

———. ***Epistle to the Son of the Wolf (ESW)***. Wilmette: Baha'i Publishing Trust, 1988

———. ***Gems of Divine Mysteries***. Haifa: Baha'i World Centre, 2002

———. ***Gleanings from the Writings of Baha'u'llah (GWB)***. Wilmette: Baha'i Publishing Trust, 1983

———. *The Hidden Words of Baha'u'llah (Arabic Hidden Words; Persian Hidden Words)*. Wilmette: Baha'i Publishing Trust, 2003

———. ***Kitáb-i-Aqdas (Aqdas), The Most Holy Book***. Wilmette: Baha'i Publishing Trust, 1992

———. ***Kitab-i-Iqan, (KI), Book of Certitude***. Wilmette: Baha'i Publishing Trust, 1983

———. *Prayers and Meditations by Baha'u'llah*. Wilmette: Baha'i Publishing Trust 1987

———. *Proclamation of Baha'u'llah to the Kings and Leaders of the World* (1867–70). Haifa: Baha'i World Center, 1967

———. *Summons of the Lord of Hosts*. Haifa, including *Tablet of the Temple*. Haifa Baha'i World Centre, 2002

———. ***Tablets of Baha'u'llah***. Haifa: Baha'i World Center, 1982

———. ***Tablet of Carmel*** (1890). http://www.lvbahai.org/Tablet_of_Carmel.htm

———. *Tablet to Hardegg, Lawh-i Hirtīk,* 1983. *Baha'i Studies Bulletin* 2.1.32–63. http://www.hurqalya.pwp.blueyonder.co.uk/abstracts/l-Hirtik.htm

———. ***Hallelujah, Hallelujah, Hallelujah, O Glad Tidings!*** http://www.Bahai-library.com/provisionals/hallelujah.html

Baha'u'llah & *'Abdu'l-Baha*. *Baha'i Scriptures (Scriptures), Selections from the Utterances of Baha'u'llah and 'Abdu'l-Baha*, compiled by Horace Holley. New York: Brentano's Publisher 1928; Haifa. Baha'i World Center, 2002. http://www.Bahai-library.com/compilations/bahai.scriptures/1.html

Barclay, Bishop Jacob. *The Orthodox Liturgy and Daily Prayers in a Hebrew Translation*. Jerusalem: Ecumenical Theological Research Fraternity in Israel, 2006

Barnstone, Willis. *The Other Bible, Ancient Esoteric Texts* Contents. San Francisco: Harper & Row Publishers, 1984

Barstow-Lovejoy Pilgrim Note Archives. Private collection held by Thellie Lovejoy. San Diego

Bartelle. *The Future of Online Search*. http://www.edition.cnn.com/2005/TECH/12/23/john.bartelle/index.html

Barzun, Jacques. *From Dawn to Decadence*. New York: HarperCollins Publishers, 2000

Basham, A.L. *The Wonder That Was India*. New York: Grove Press, 1954

Batra, Ravi. *Surviving the Great Depression of 1990: Protect Your Assets and Investments* 205. New York: Simon & Shuster, 1988

Bauer Walter. *Greek English Lexicon of the New Testament and other early Christian Literature*, 3rd edition. Chicago: University of Chicago Press, 2000

Beach, Bruce M.. *The Book of Revelation, One Baha'i's Concept*. http://www.webpal.org/webpal/c_renewal/revelation/content.htm

Beale, Gregory K. *John's Use of the Old Testament in Revelation* (JSNT Supplement Series). Sheffield: Sheffield Academic Press, 1998

Beale, Gregory K. *The Book of Revelation: A Commentary on the Greek Text* (1079–93). Grand Rapids: Wm B Eerdmans Publishing Co, 1999

Beebe, Stephen. *The Logic of the Revelation of St. John*. New Delhi: Baha'i Publishing Trust, 2006

Ben-Daniel, John & Gloria. *The Apocalypse in the Light of the Temple*. Jerusalem: Beit Yochanan, 2003. http://www.newtorah.org

Ben-David, Shemaya. *Megiddo Armageddon Excavations* Pamphlet. Tel Megiddo: 1979

Bertrand S. & Lemagnen S. *The Bayeux Tapestry*. Rennes: Editions Ouest-France, 1996

Boteach, S, *An Intelligent Person's Guide to Judaism*. London: Gerald Duckworth, 1999

Bowyers, Michael J. F. *Action Stations 1: Military Airfields of East Anglia*. Wellingborough: Patrick Stephens Limited, 1990

———. *Action Stations 6: Military Airfields of the Cotswolds and the Central Midlands*. Cambridge: Patrick Stephens Limited, 1983

Bilderback, Allen H. *The Revelation of Christ's Glory*. Tacoma: ABCO Publishing, 1995

Boyce, Mary. *Textual Sources for the Study of Zoroastrianism*, Chicago University Press, 1990

Brenton, Sir Lancelot C.L, *Septuagint with Apocrypha*. USA: Hendrickson Publishers, 1999

Brittingham. See *'Abdu'l-Baha cited by Brittingham*

Buddhist Promoting Foundation. *Teaching of Buddha* (328th rev. edn.). Tokyo: Bukkyo Dendo Kyokai, 1966

Bullough, Donald A. *The Age of Charlemagne*. London: Ferndale Publications, 1980

Buth, Randall J. *Language use in the First Century: Spoken Hebrew in a Trilingual Society in the Time of Jesus*. Journal of Translation & Textlinguistics 5: 298–312, 1992.

Campbell, Joseph. *The Power of Myth*. New York: Doubleday, 1988

Casey P.J. *Roman Coinage in Britain*. Princes Risborough: Shire Archeology, 2002

Charles R.H. *A Critical and Exegetical Commentary on the Revelation of St. John* (2.165–70, 207–08). Edinburgh: T & T. Clark, 1920

Chayoun, Yehudah. *When Mashiah Comes*. New York: Targum Press, 1994

Chicago Manual of Style. Chicago & London: University of Chicago Press, 1993

Churchill, Winston L. S. *Prime Minister's Personal Minutes* on place names after World War II. Chartwell: Records, 24/4/45

Clark, Alan D. *Understanding the Revelation to Saint John*. Springdale: Samuel Henry, 2000

Codex Alexandrinus Vol. IV, Apocalypse of John (5th Century), folio/page 125recto—135-recto. London: British Museum MS,FACS.1(4)

***Codex Sinaiticus, Apocalypse of John* (4th Century)**, folio 126-verso to 135-recto. London: British Museum MS.FACS.165(1)

Complete Jewish Bible, Translator David H. Stern. Clarksville & Jerusalem: Jewish New Testament Publications, 1998

Cooper, Charles W. *The Precious Stones of the Bible*. London: H.R. Allenson Ltd, 1924

Crawford. *The Crawford Aramaic Text of Revelation* Chapter 6, http://www.netzarim.info/index.php/Nazarene.net/hantri/FreeBook/chapter6.pdf (2006/07)

Custodians. *Ministry of the Custodians 1957–1963*. Haifa: Baha'i World Centre, 1992.

Dawkins R. *The Ancestor's Tale*. London: Phoenix, 2004

Deringil, S. *Conversions—There Is No Compulsion in Religion: On Conversion and Apostasy in the Late Ottoman Empire: 1839–1856. Comparative Studies in Society and History* 42.3: 547–75. London: Cambridge University Press, 2000

———. *Conversion and Apostasy in the late 19th century Ottoman Empire: a Comparative Perspective*. Moscow: Conference on History of Empires, *Comparative Approaches to Research and Teaching*, 2003

Dermenghem, Emile. *Life of Mahomet*. London: G.Routlege, 1930

Drosnin, Michael. *The Bible Code*. New York: Simon & Shuster, 1997

Duncan, David E. *The Calendar*. London: Fourth Estate, 1999.

Esslemont, J.E. *Baha'u'llah and the New Era*. Wilmette: Baha'i Publishing Trust, 1980

Everyman (15th century). *Medieval Sourcebook*. http://www.fordham.edu/halsall/basis/everyman.html.

Farshchian, Mahmoud. *Mahmoud Farshchian Paintings* Vol. II, ISBN O-9631660-O-X. Englewood Cliffs: Homai Publishers, 1991

Fekkes, Jan. *Isaiah and Prophetic Traditions in the Book of Revelation*. Journal for the Study of the New Testament Supplement Series 93. Sheffield: Continuum International Publishing Group, 1994

Ferraby, J. *All Things Made New*. London: Ruskin House, 1957

Fozdar, Shirin. *Lord Buddha and Maitreiya Amitabha*. New Delhi: Arcee Press, undated

Friedman, Richard E. *The Hidden Book in the Bible: the Discovery of the First Prose Masterpiece*. San Francisco: Harper, 1998.

Gail, Marzieh. *Six Lessons on Islam*. http://www.bahai-library.com/books/lessons.islam/2.html. http://www.bahai-library.com/books/lessons.islam/2.html

Galbraith, John K.. *The World Economy Since the Wars, A Personal View*. London: Sinclair-Stevenson, 1994

Gamble, Harry Y. *Books and Readers in the Early Church, A History of Early Christian Texts*. New Haven & London: Yale University Press, 1995

Gard, Richard A. *Great Religions of Modern Man: Buddhism*. New York: George Braziller, 1961

Gesenius *Hebrew-Chaldean Lexicon,* translation of *Lexicon Manuale Hebraicum et Chaldicum in Veteris Testamenti Libros 1825.* Editor Tregelles, Samuel. Halle, Germany. Grand Rapids: Wm. B. Eerdmanns Publishing Co, 1967

Ginzberg. *Legends of the Jews.* Philadelphia: Jewish Publication Society of America, 1913

Gladwell, Malcolm. *The Tipping Point How Little Things Can Make a Big Difference:* Boston: Little, Brown & Co, 2000 & First Back Bay, 2002

Glorious Quran. Translator Pickthall, Muhammad M.. Mecca: Muslim World League, 1979

Gregg, Steve. *Revelation, Four Views: A Parallel Commentary.* Nashville: Thomas Nelson Publishers, 1997

Grun, Bernard. *The Timetables of History: A Horizontal Linkage of People and Events* (3rd rev. edn.). New York: Simon & Schuster/Touchstone, 1991.

Hajjaj Abd-Allah. *The Isra' and Mi'raj: the Prophet's Night Journey and Ascent into Heaven.* London: Dar Al-Taqwa Ltd, 1989

Haleem, M. E. L. Abdel. *The Quran, A New Translation.* Oxford: Oxford University Press, 2004

Halpenny, Bruce B. *Action Stations 2: Military Airfields of Lincolnshire and the East Midlands.* Sparkford: Patrick Stephens Ltd, 1981

———. *Action Stations 8: Military Airfields of Greater London.* Sparkford, Yeovil: Patrick Stephens Ltd, 1993

Harwood, Carl C. *Handbook of Bible Types and Symbols.* Denver: Denver Bible Institute Press, 1933

Hawting, G.R.. *The first dynasty of Islam: the Umayyad caliphate AD 661–750.* London, 2000

Haywood, John. *Atlas of World History.* Oxford: Barnes & Noble Books and Andromeda Oxford Ltd, 1997

Hayut-Man, Yitzhak. *Realizing the Heavenly Jerusalem.* Jerusalem: Academy of Jerusalem 1995. http://www.thehope.org/rhj123.htm

Hayut-Man, Yitzhak, Hanna-Aliza, Omer: *The Quest for the Heavenly Jerusalem Temple* Paintings 1995–2000. http://www.thehope.org/artgall.htm

Hertzberg, Arthur. *Great Religions of Modern Man: Judaism.* New York: George Braziller, 1961

Hijazi Abu Tariq. *Islam AH 01–250: A Chronology of Events.* New York: The Message Publications, 1994

Holt, P.M., Lambton, Ann K. S., & Lewis, Bernard. *The Cambridge History of Islam 1A: The Central Islamic Lands from Pre-Islamic Times to the First World War.* Cambridge: Cambridge University Press, 1992

Hoyt, Erich, Shultz. *Insect Lives, Stories of Mystery and Romance from a Hidden World.* New York: John Wiley & Sons Inc, 1999

Huntley, H.E. *The Divine Proportion, A Study in Mathematical Beauty.* New York: Dover Publications, 1970.

Ibn Khaldun. *The Muqaddimah: An Introduction to History,* (abridged ed. N.J. Dawood editor, Franz Rosenthal translator). Princeton University Press, 1989

Interpreter's Dictionary of the Bible Vol. 2. Crim, Keith R., Buttrick, George A. New York: Abingdon Press, 1962.

Jalali, A. H. *Karbala & Ashura, Ziyarah of Ashura*. Qum: Ansariyan Publications, 2002

James, M.R. *The Apocryphal New Testament Acts of John*, Translation & Notes. Oxford: Clarendon Press, 1924

Jastrow. M. (1925), *A Dictionary of the Targumim, the Talmud Babli & Yerusahalayim, and the Midrashim Literature*

Josephus. *Antiquities of the Jews*

———. *Wars of the Jews.*

Kahn, A.O., Karsh, & Mundy. *Four Remarkable Indian Prophecies*. Healdsburg: Naturegraph Co, 1973

Kellen, Betty. *Gautama Buddha in Life and Legend*. New York: Lothrop, Lee & Shepard Co Inc, 1967

Khan, Muhammad Zafrulla. *Muhammad: Seal of the Prophets*. London: Routledge & Kegan Paul, 1980

Kircher Athanasii (1653). *Oedipus Aegyptiacus*. Rome: Typographia Vitalis Mascardi.

Laitman, M. *From Chaos to Harmony: The Solution to the Global Crisis According to the Wisdom of Kabbalah*. Toronto: Laitman Kabbalah Publishers, 2007

Lal, K.S. *The Legacy of Muslim Rule in India*. New Delhi: Voice of India, 1992. http://www.voiceofdharma.org/books/tlmr/ch4.htm

Lamb, Harold (1927). *Gengis Khan*. Garden City: USA International Collectors Library

Lamsa, George M., translator. *Holy Bible: From the Ancient Eastern Text and the Aramaic of the Peshitta*. San Francisco: Harper & Row, 1968

Lapidus, Ira M. *A History of Islamic Societies*. Cambridge University Press, 1995

Latimer, George O. *Light of The World Foreword* (1920). http://www.bahai-library .com/pilgrims/light.of.world.html

Lee, Dwight E. *Outbreak of the First World War*. Lexington: D.C. Heath & Company, 1970

Lewis, Bernard. *The Arabs in History*. Oxford University Press, 2002

———. *The Crisis of Islam: Holy War and Unholy Terror*. New York: Random House, Modern Library, 2003

———. *The Jews of Islam*. Princeton University Press, 1984

Liddell & Scott. *Greek-English Lexicon*. Oxford University Press, 1994

Louw & Nida. ***Greek-English Lexicon of the New Testament Based on Semantic Domains***, ***Vols. I*** & ***II***. New York: United Bible Societies, 1989

Lovejoy, Thellie. *Barstow-Lovejoy Pilgrim Note Archives*. Private collection held by Thellie Lovejoy. San Diego

Lunn, Pete. *Basic Instincts: Human Nature and the New Economics*. Singapore: Marshall Cavendish, 2008.

Maude, R. & D. *The Servant, the General and Armageddon*. Oxford: George Ronald, 1998

Malina, Bruce. *The Genre of the Apocalypse of John*. Montville, NJ: Hendrickson Publishers, 1995

Man, John. *Alpha Beta*. London: Headline Book Publishing, 2000

Maoz, M. *Studies on Palestine During the Ottoman Period*. Jerusalem: Magnes Press, 1975

Menocal, Maria R. *Ornament of the World. How Muslims, Jews, and Christians Created a Culture of Tolerance in Medieval Spain*. Boston: Little Brown & Co, 2002

Midrash Tanna Debe Eliyahu: Lore of the School of Elijah Debe Eliyahu. Philadelphia: Jewish Publication Society, 1981

Milne & Skeat. *Scribes & Correctors of The Codex Sinaiticus,* MS220.48,111. London: British Museum, 1938

Mishnah Translated. Danby, H. London: Oxford University Press, 1933

Mishra, P.N. *Kalki Avatar.* New Delhi: Baha'i Publishing Trust, 1977

Moffett, Ruth J. *New Keys to the Book of Revelation*. New Delhi: Baha'i Publishing Trust, 1977

Moffitt, Michael. *The World's Money, International Banking from Bretton Woods to the Brink of Insolvency.* Worcester: Billing & Sons Ltd, 1983

Momen, Moojan. *An Introduction to Shi'i Islam: The History and Doctrines of the Twelver Shi'ism.* New Haven: Yale University Press, 1985

——————. *Hinduism and the Baha'i Faith.* Oxford: George Ronald, 1990

Motlagh, Hushidar H. *I Shall Come Again: Vol. 1, Time Prophecies*. Mt. Pleasant, MI: Global Perspectives, 1992. http://www.amazon.com/gp/product/0937661163?tag=openlibr-20

Motlagh, Hushidar H. *The Glorious Journey to God: Selections from Sacred Scriptures on the Afterlife,* Compilation. Mt. Pleasant: Global Perspectives, 1994

Munje, H. M. *1844 AD Pinpoint Target of All Faiths.* New Delhi: Baha'i Publishing Trust, 1982.

Nabil, translated by Shoghi Effendi, *The Dawn-Breakers, Nabil's Narrative of the Early Days of the Baha'i Revelation*. Wilmette: Baha'i Publishing Trust, 1996

Nachmanides, Moses. *Commentary on the Torah, 1.Bereshit.* New York: Shilo, 1971

National Audubon Society Field Guide to North American Mammals. New York: Alfred A. Knopf, Inc., 1980

New American Bible. Grand Rapids: World Catholic Press, 1991

New Bantam-Megiddo Hebrew & English Dictionary. Editors Sivan, Reuven & Levenston, Edward A. New York: Bantam Books, 1975

New English Bible with the Apocrypha. Oxford & Cambridge University Presses, 1970

NKJV Greek English Interlinear New Testament. Editor Farstad, Arthur L.. Nashville: Thomas Nelson Publishers, 1994

Newman, Barclay M. Jr. *A Concise Greek-English Dictionary of the New Testament*. Stuttgart: German Bible Society, 1993

Newton, Isaac. *Newton's Secrets, Newtonian Manuscripts*, catalogue of 2007/07–08 Isaac Newton Exhibition. Jerusalem: Jewish National & Hebrew University Library Collections, 2007

Nicolle D. & McBride A. Men-at-arms Series 140: *Armies of the Ottoman Turks, 1300–1774.* Oxford: Osprey Direct UK, 2005

Norwich, John Julius. *A Short History of Byzantium.* New York: Alfred K. Knopf, 1997

Nuqabá'í, H. *Bishárát-i-Kitub-i-Ásmání* (Persian). Teheran: Baha'i Publishing Trust, 1968/BE 124.

Onkelos. *Targum Onkelos, Pentateuch in Aramaic*

Oren, Michael B. *Power, Faith and Fantasy. America in the Middle East:1776 to the Present.* New York: W.W. Norton & Company, 2007.

Packard, Vance. *The Waste Makers.* New York: David McKay Co, 1960

Phillips, Michael. *Seven Laws of Money.* Boston: Shambhala Publications, 1997

Philo. *Abraham*
———. *Change of Names*
———. *Confusion of Tongues*
———. *Dreams*
———. *Life of Moses*
———. *Special Laws*
———. *Unchangeableness of God*

Piff, David. *Baha'i Lore.* Oxford: George Ronald, 2000

Poirier, Brent. *The Kitab-í-Iqan: The Key to Unsealing the Mysteries of the Holy Bible,* 1999. http://www.bahai-library.com/essays/iqan.bible.html

Ponting, Clive *A Green History of the World, The Environment and the Collapse of Great Civilizations.* New York: Penguin Books, 1991

Prigent, Pierre. *Commentary on the Apocalypse of St. John.* Tuebingen: Mohr Siebeck, 2001.

Raphael David. *The Alhambra Decree.* Hollywood, CA: Carmi House Press, 1988

Renou, Louis. *Great Religions of Modern Man: Hinduism.* New York: George Braziller, 1961

Richman, Rabbi Chaim. *To Dwell with G-d.* http://www.templeinstitute.org/archive /dwell_with_g_d.htm

Runciman, S. *Fall of Constantinople 1453.* Cambridge: Cambridge University Press, 1965

Riggs, Robert F. ***The Apocalypse Unsealed.*** New York: Philosophical Library, 1981. Bahai-library.com/books /apocalypse

———. *I, Daniel* Commentary, Charlottesville: Prophecy Fulfilled, 1990. http://www .bci.org/prophecy-fulfilled/id1.htm

Rossing, Barbara R. *The Rapture Exposed: The Message of Hope in the Book of Revelation.* New York: Westview Press, 2004

Rothkopf, David. *The Superclass: The Global Power Elite and the World They Are Making.* New York: Farrar, Straus, & Giroux, 2008

Rumi (12th Century). *Masnavi, Jalal-ud-din-Rumi,* translated by E.H. Whinfield. 1898. http://www.en.wikipedia.org/wiki/Blind_Men_and_an_Elephant

Rubinstein et al., *The Jews in the Modern World: A History since 1750,* 303. Oxford: Oxford University Press, 2002.

Saadia ben Joseph, Gaon. *The Book of Beliefs and Opinions.* New Haven: Yale University, 1948

Sagan, K. *Murmurs of Earth, the Voyager Interstellar Record.* New York: Random House, 1978

Scholem, Gershom. *Major Trends in Jewish Mysticism.* New York: Schocken, 1941

Scruton, Roger. *The West and the Rest.* London: Continuum, 2002

Sears, William. *Thief in the Night, The Case of the Missing Millennium.* Oxford: George Ronald, 1995

Shaw, Stanford J. *The Jews of the Ottoman Empire and the Turkish Republic.* New York University Press, 1991

Schreiber, R. *The Chaining of the Dragon: A Commentary on the Book of Revelation.* Chico: Stansbury Publishing, 2004

Schumacher, E. F. *Small is Beautiful*. London: Sphere Books Ltd, 1973

Schumann, Walter. *Gemstones of the World*. Munich: BLV Verlagsgesellschaft, 1979

Shams Badi. ***A Bahá'í Perspective on Economics of the Future***, A Compilation. New Delhi: Baha'i Publishing Trust, 1991

Shoghi Effendi, *Advent of Divine Justice*. Wilmette: Baha'i Publishing Trust, 1990

———. *Citadel of Faith* (*Citadel*). Wilmette: Baha'i Publishing Trust, 1974

———. *Dawn of a New Day*. India: Baha'i Publishing Trust, 1970

———. *Directives of the Guardian* (*Directives*). India & Hawaii: Baha'i Publishing Trust, 1973

———. ***God Passes By* (*GPB*)**. Wilmette: Baha'i Publishing Trust, 1974

———. *Kitáb-i-Aqdas: Other Sections*. Wilmette: Baha'i Publishing Trust, 1992

———. *Light of Divine Guidance* (*Light*). New Delhi: Baha'i Publishing Trust, 1994

———. *Letter to Mrs. Louise Erickson*. Baha'i News 77, September 1933

———. (1923–1957). *Letters from the Guardian to Australia and New Zealand* in *Light of Divine Guidance* (*Light*). Sydney: National Spiritual Assembly of the Baha'is of Australia, 1970. New Delhi: Baha'i Publishing Trust, 1994.

———. *Letter to Ruth Moffett August 13 1944*. Wilmette: Baha'i National Spiritual Assembly Archives, 1944

———. *Letter to Ruth Moffett June 8 1952*. Wilmette: Baha'i National Spiritual Assembly Archives, 1952

———. *Messages to America* (1932–1946). Wilmette: Baha'i Publishing Committee, 1947

———. *Messages to the Baha'i World 1950–57*. Wilmette: Baha'i Publishing Trust, 1971

———. ***The Promised Day is Come*** (*PDC*). Wilmette: Baha'i Publishing Trust, 1980

———. *Unfolding Destiny*. UK: Baha'i Publishing Trust, 1981

———. *The World Order of Baha'u'llah* (*WOB*). Wilmette: Baha'i Publishing Trust, 1982

Silver, A.H. *History of Messianic Speculation in Israel from the First to the Seventeenth Centuries*. New York: Macmillan, 1927

Smith, John N. *Airfield Focus 48, Aviation at Polebrook*. Peterborough: GMS Enterprises, 2001

———. *Airfield Focus 59, Aviation at Harrington*. Peterborough: GMS Enterprises, 2003

Sours, Michael. *Understanding Biblical Prophecy*. Oxford: One World, 1997

———. *The 1844 Ottoman Edict of Toleration in Baha'i Secondary Literature*. Journal of Baha'i Studies, 1998/03/08

Souter, Alexander. *Novum Testamentum Graece*, Oxford: Clarendon Press, 1956

Sulley, Henry (1892). *The Temple of Ezekiel's Prophecy. A House of Prayer for all People*. Whitefish: Kessinger Publishing, 2003

Swete, Henry B. *The Apocalypse of St. John: the Greek Text*. London: Macmillan, 1906

Szekely, Edmond Bordeaux. *From Enoch to the Dead Sea Scrolls*. Matsqui: International Biogenic Society, 1981.

Tai-Seale, Thomas. *Thy Kingdom Come*. Los Angeles: Kalimat Press, 1992

Targum Bereshit (*Genesis*) *Rabah* s31

Targum Neophiti 1, Shmot (*Exodus*)

Terry, Peter. *Lights of 'Irfan, Papers Presented at the 'Irfan Colloquia and Seminars, Book One. 'Abdu'l-Baha's Explanation of the Teachings of Baha'u'llah: Tablets and Talks Translated into English (1911–1920).* Evanston, IL: Irfan Colloquia, 2000

———. Terry Pilgrim Note Archives: A private collection held by Peter Terry. Bridgton, Maine

Thomas, Robert L. *Revelation 1–7 & Revelation 8–22: An Exegetical Commentary* 463–72. Chicago: Moody Press, 1992 & 1995

Thompson. *The Book of Revelation: Apocalypse and Empire, Accumulation of Images.* Oxford: Oxford University Press, 1990

Tipitaka Buddhist Texts (Vinaya, Sutras, & Abhidharma)

Treadgold, Warren. *A History of the Byzantine State and Society.* Stanford, CA: Stanford University Press, 1997.

Universal House of Justice. *Century of Light.* Haifa: Baha'i World Center, 2001

———. *Child Abuse, Psychology and Knowledge of Self, Letter* 1985/12/02. Haifa: Baha'i World Center, 1985

———. *Promise of World Peace to the Peoples of the World.* A Statement by the Universal House of Justice. Wilmette: Baha'i Publishing Trust, 1985

———. *Unity of Nations and the Lesser Peace.* Haifa: Baha'i World Center, 2001

———. *A Wider Horizon, Selected Letters* 1983–1992, compiled by Lample, P.. Riviera Beach: Plabra Publications, 1992

———. Pamphlet: *Welcome to the Baha'i World Center.* Haifa, 2003

Uhrbach, Ephraim. *The Sages: Their Concepts and Beliefs.* Jerusalem: Magnes /Hebrew University, 1979.

VanderKam, James C. *The Dead Sea Scrolls Today.* Grand Rapids: Eerdmans, 1994.

Watts, Richard. *Kitab al-Muqaddas* (Arabic *Holy Bible*). London: Richard Watts. 1831

Waite S. L. *Twelve Lessons in the Teachings of the Baha'i Revelation, Barstow-Lovejoy Archives, Lesson 10, The New Jerusalem or the New Laws of God,* 1933/08/07.

————. *Open Doors. An Address Given by Shahnaz Waite on Friday May 5 1936 at the Baha'i Center* Los Angeles. *Barstow Pilgrim Note Archives.* Private collection held by Thellie Lovejoy. San Diego

Warren, Henry C. *Buddhism in Translation.* Delhi: Motilal Banarsidass, 1896

Wheatcroft, Andrew. *The Ottomans: Dissolving Images.* London: Penguin Books, 1995

Williams, John A. *Great Religions of Modern Man: Islam.* New York: George Braziller, 1961.

Zohar. http://www.kabbalah.com/k/index.php/p=zohar.

Millennialist Publications

As before, the names of works most relevant to *Apocalypse Secrets* appear in **bold**. This list of Millennialist publications appears by kind permission of Hushidar Motlagh his book *I Shall Come Again*, pages 194–6.

Addis, Alfred. *The Theory of Prophecy*, 1830

Anderson, William. *An Apology for Millennial Doctrine; in the Form in Which It Was Entertained by the Primitive Church*, 1830.

Bernard, David. *Letter on the Second Coming of Christ*, 1843

Biederwolf, William E. *Bible Commentary: The Second Coming*. Grand Rapids: Baker Book House, 1985

Birks, Thomas. *First Elements of Sacred Prophecy*, 1843

Brooks, Joshua W. *A Dictionary of Writers on Prophecies*, 1835

———. *Essays on the Advent and Kingdom of Christ*, 1840

Brown, Freeman. *Views and Experiences in Relation to Entire Consecration and the Second Advent*, 1843

Brown, John Aquila. *The Eventide*, 1823

Buck, Charles. *Theological Dictionary*, 1802

Bush, George. *The Dry Bones of Israel Revived*, 1844.

Clarke, Jerome. *1844*. Tennessee: Southern Publishing Association, 1968

Cook, John. *A Solemn Appeal to Ministers, And Churches, Especially to Those of the Baptist Denomination, Relative to the Speedy Coming of Christ*, 1843

Cuninghame, William. *The Pre-Millennial Advent of Messiah, Demonstrated from the Scriptures*, 1836.

Davis, William C. *The Millennium*, 1811

———. *A Treatise on the Millennium*, 1827

Digby, William. *A Treatise on the 1,260 Days of Daniel and St. John*, 1831

Drummond, Henry. *Introduction to the Study of the Apocalypse*, 1830

Duffield, George. *Dissertation on the Prophecies Relative to the Second Coming of Jesus Christ*, 1842

———. *Millenarianism Defended*, 1843.

Elliot Edward. *A Commentary on the Apocalypse*, 1837.

Frere, James H. *A Combined View of the Prophecies of Daniel, Esdras and St. John*, 1815

———. *Eight Letters on the Prophecies Relating to the Last Times*, 1831

Froom, Leroy. *The Prophetic Faith of Our Fathers* 3.2, 4.1194–95. Washington DC: Review & Herald, 1950

Fry, John. *The Second Advent*, 1822.

Galusha, Elon. *Address of Elder Elon Galusha, With Reasons for Believing Christ's Second Coming*, 1844.

Habershon, Matthew. *A Dissertation on the Prophetic Scriptures, Chiefly Those of a Chronological Character*, 1834

Hawley, Silas. *The Second Advent Doctrine Vindicated,* 1843

Hervey, N. *Prophecies of Christ's First and Second Advent*, 1843

Himes, Joshua. *Views of the Prophecies and Prophetic Chronology Selected from Manuscripts of William Miller,* 1842

Hooper, John. *The Doctrine of the Second Advent*, 1829

Hutchinson, Richard. *The Abrahamic Covenant*, 1843.

Irving, Edward. *The Coming of Messiah in Glory and Majesty*, 1827

————. *Exposition of The Book of Revelation, in a Series of Lectures*, 1831.

Jones, Henry. *Principles of Interpreting Prophecies*, 1837

———. *A Scriptural Synopsis of the Doctrine in General, of Christ's Second Advent*, 1842.

Kelber, L.H. *Das Ende Kommt*, 1842

Keyworth, Thomas. *A Practical Exposition of the Revelation of St. John*, 1842.

Litch, Josiah. *Prophetic Exposition*, 1842.

Mason, Archibald. *Appendix to an Enquiry Into the Prophetic Numbers Contained in the 1335 Days*, 1818

————. *Two Essays on Daniel's Prophetic Number of Two Thousand Three Hundred Days; and on the Christian's Duty to Inquire Into the Church's Deliverance*, 1820

Meister, Charles W.. *Year of the Lord, AD 1844*. North Carolina: McFarland & Company, 1983

Miller, William. *Evidence From Scripture and History of the Second Coming of Christ, About the Year 1843*, 1836.

Noah, M. M. *Discourse on the Restoration of the Jews* 33.51–52. New York: Harper & Brothers, 1845.

Pym, William. *Thoughts on Millenarianism*, 1829.

Richter, Johann. *Erklarte Haus-Bibel* (6 vol.), 1834–40.

Sabine James. *The Relation of the Present State of Religion to the Expected Millennium*, 1823

———. *The Appearing and Kingdom of Our Lord Jesus Christ*, 1842

Sander, J.F. *Versuch einer Erklarung der Offenbarung Johannis*, 1829

Scott, Robert. *Free Thoughts on the Millennium*, 1834

Smith, Uriah. *Thoughts, Critical and Practical on the Book of Daniel*. Battle Creek: Seventh Day Adventist Publishing, 1881

Stuart, Moses. *The Apocalypse*. Edinburgh: Maclachlan, Stewart & Co, 1848.

Vaughan, Edward. *The Church's Expectation: A Sermon on the Second Advent of the Lord Jesus Christ,* 1828.

Ward, Henry Dana. *Glad Tidings 'For the Kingdom of Heaven is at Hand'*, 1838.

References

The most cited Baha'i Writings use the following official abbreviations and acronyms:

Abbreviation	Full Name of Baha'i Writing
Aqdas	*Kitab-i-Aqdas, The Most Holy Book*
BWF	*Baha'i World Faith*
Citadel	*Citadel of Faith*
Directives	*Directives of the Guardian*
DP	*Divine Philosophy*
ESW	*Epistle to the Son of the Wolf*
Gems	*Gems of Divine Mysteries*
GPB	*God Passes By*
GWB	*Gleanings from the Writings of Baha'u'llah*
Lights	*Lights of Divine Guidance*
KI	*Kitab-i-Iqan, Book of Certitude*
PB	*Proclamation of Baha'u'llah*
PDC	*Promised Day is Come*
PUP	*Promulgation of Universal Peace*
SAQ	*Some Answered Questions*
Scriptures	*Baha'i Scriptures*
SW	*Star of the West*
SWA	*Selections from the Writings of 'Abdu'l-Baha*
TAB	*Tablets of 'Abdu'l-Baha*
WOB	*World Order of Baha'u'llah*

To cut clutter, citations for each paragraph appear under a single endnote/footnote mark at the end of the paragraph, each individual citation under its ***opening words*** in bold, as far as possible. Some references show dates of particular relevance.

Epigraph

[1] Baha'u'llah *TB* 7.87 & 11.167

Preface

[2] Isaiah 42.9
[3] Zech. 12.11
[4] Judges 5,19, 2 Kings 9,27, 2Kings 23,29-30, 2Chron. 35,22
[5] Isaiah 11.9 & Rev. 21.10

Introduction

[6] Joan Harvey personal count of *New York Times* pages 1–7, London 2001/12/28
[7] Isaac *Newton's Secrets,* Yahuda MS
[8] http://www.pitts.emory.edu. http://www.tyndalehouse.com
[9] ***New name*** Rev. 2.17, 3.12
Rising again **over** ***three Days***, Matt. 27.63; Mark 8.31, 9.31 & 10.34
Rebuild the Temple, Matt. 26.61; Mark 14.58; John 2.19–20
World to come, Isaac *Newton's Secrets* 39, Yahuda MS9.2f.123r, *The End of the World, Day of Judgment and World to Come*
[10] 2John 1.1 & 3John 1.1. Aristion Papias *The Alleged Presbyter John*, http:// www .newadvent.org/cathen/08492a.htm
[11] **His religious native Hebrew**, Buth *First Century Spoken Hebrew*. Barclay *Orthodox Liturgy and Daily Prayers in a Hebrew Translation*, Introduction
A *Greek text written*, Aune, personal communication, Jerusalem 2006/12/07
[12] Aune *52A* lxxvi
[13] Beale *John's Use of the Old Testament in Revelation*. Aune *52C* 1267–87
[14] Polycrates cited by Eusebius *Church History* 5.24.2
[15] Eusebius *Chronicle*, 3.20.5–7 per Aune, *Word Biblical Commentary, Revelation 52A* lix–lx
[16] James, *The Apocryphal New Testament Acts of John*
[17] *Codex Sinaiticus Apocalypse* pp. 126verso–135recto. *Codex Alexandrinus Apocalypse* pp. 4.125recto–334verso. Codices comprised 16-page *gatherings* or *signatures*, each of 4 papyrus sheets folded into an 8-leaf *quire* (Milne & Skeat 111, *Codex Alexandrinus* 4.8). The *Codex Sinaiticus* has pages of 33 x 37.3 cm, four-column 48–line text blocks of 26.5 x 24.3 cm, margins 3.2 cm, columns set 1.4–cm apart, each column 24.3 x 5.7 cm, 12.5–point uncial letters, ~13 to a line. The *Codex Alexandrinus* has pages of 25.2 x 30.6 cm, two-column 50-line text blocks of 21.6 x 22.4 cm, margins 1.8 cm, columns set 2.4 cm apart, each column 22.4 x 10.3 cm, 9–point uncial letters, ~26 to a line
[18] ***Sealed***, Rev. 5.1, 5.9, 6.1–8.1 & 10.4. ***Unsealed***, Rev. 22.10
[19] Rev. 11.3–4
[20] Drosnin Michael *The Bible Code*
[21] Rev. 1.1–2, 3, 9, 6.9, 12.11, 17.17, 19.9, 19.13, 20.4, 21.5, 21.6, 22.6, 7, 9, 10, 18 & 19. *John* 1.1. Baha'u'llah *KI* 64
[22] Universal House of Justice Pamphlet *Welcome to the Baha'i World Center, Haifa 2003*
[23] Shoghi Effendi *WOB* 114
[24] Queen Marie cited by Shoghi Effendi in *Summary Statement to UN—1947, Special UN Committee on Palestine* #47–0701, http://www.bic-un.bahai.org/47-0701.htm, which cites not only Queen Marie but also Leo Tolstoy, President Masaryk, Rev. T. K. Cheyne, Viscount Samuel of Carmel, Professor Norman Bentwich, Professor Benjamin Jowett, and Professor Lewis Campbell all praising the Baha'i Faith publicly
[25] ***The allusions made***, Baha'u'llah *GWB* 16.39, *PB* 111–2
Produce wonderful effects, 'Abdu'l-Baha *SAQ* 71.253

What truth can be greater than, ‘Abdu'l-Baha (1896/07/16) *SWA* 3.12, *One of First General Messages to the Baha'is of America*, *SW* (1924/03) 14.12.358, *SWA* 3.12, *Child of Covenant* 240, *Má'idih-i-Ásmání* 2.82

Reflect upon the words of John, Baha'u'llah *Scriptures* 47.117 *Tablet to the Jews*

There are many meanings, ‘Abdu'l-Baha *Scriptures* 962.500

Revelation is allusively, Shoghi Effendi *Letter to Ruth Moffett* 1944/08/13

Revelation is *a very*, Shoghi Effendi *Letter to Ruth Moffett* 1952/06/8

The Revelations of St. John, ‘Abdu'l-Baha *PUP* 459 & 199

26 Baha'u'llah *Gems* 72.52–3

27 ***From beginning to end***, Shoghi Effendi *Letter* 1944

Rather, they reveal choice parts, ‘Abdu'l-Baha *SAQ* 10.36–44 for Dan. 9.24 & 12.6–7. ‘Abdu'l-Baha *SAQ* 12.61–5 for Isaiah 11.1–10

28 **Thus, decoding *1,260 days* in verse 11.13**, ‘Abdu'l-Baha *SAQ* 11.46

Interpreting *Trump-Ta-Ra* in verse 11.14, ‘Abdu'l-Baha *SAQ* 11.56

Comparing Scripture with Scripture, Isaac *Newton's Secrets* 19, Yahuda MS1.1f.12r, *Rules for Interpreting the Words and Language of Scripture*

29 Shoghi Effendi *Light* 142.167

30 Abdu'l-Baha *SWA* 142.166

The Apocalypse is a Book of Codes

31 Rev. 1.16–7, 8.10, 9.1, 11.1, 12.16 & 19.17

32 Baha'u'llah *Gems* 72.50–2

33 ***Stars*** Rev. 1.20. ***Menorah-Lamps*** 1.20. ***Seven* stars** 3.1. ***Torches of fire*** 4.5. ***Horns and eyes*** 5.6. ***Incenses*** 5.8. ***Mystery of God*** 10.7. ***Ancient serpent*** 12.9. ***Dwelling in the heavens*** 12.12. ***Beast*** 13.18. ***Confused Babylon*** 17.5. ***Heads*** 17.12. ***Horns*** 17.15. ***Waters*** 17.15. ***Woman*** 17.18. ***Fine linen*** 19.8. ***Bride*** 21.2

34 Rev. 1.20, 10.7, 17.5 & 7

35 ***Divine Words are not to be***, ‘Abdu'l-Baha *PUP* 459, 199

The teachings of all religions, *‘Abdu'l-Baha in London* 79–80

36 **Sky symbols**, Malina *Genre of the Apocalypse*. Riggs *Apocalypse Unsealed*. Bilderback *Revelation of Christ's Glory*

The heavens and the earth, Baha'u'llah *Gems* 60.44

37 Baha'u'llah *KI* 67–8

38 Baha'u'llah *PB* 22

Prophecies for the Year 1844

39 ***Each day corresponds to a year***, Num. 14.34, ‘Abdu'l-Baha SAQ 11.46

One year for each of the 40 days, Ezek. 4.6

40 **Its *five-month* time-prophecy**, Rev. 9.5 & 10

A prior five-month time-period, Gen. 7.11, 24, 8.1–4

41 Rev. 9.15

42 ‘Abdu'l-Baha *SAQ* 11.52–3

43 Rev. 11.2, 3, 9, 11, 12.6, 14 & 13.5

44 Motlagh *I Shall Come Again* 18.358–60

45 ‘Abdu'l-Baha *SAQ* 13.71

46 Leviticus 26.18 & 24

47 ***The daily sacrifice forsaken***, Dan. 8.13–4

The 457 BC Artaxerxes decree, Ezra 7.7–26

Prior similar decrees by Cyrus and Darius, Ezra 1 & 6

48 Dan. 7.23–5

49 *Zohar* 3*Vaera*.32*Reckoning of the Messianic Era*.445
50 Maimonedes *Igeret Teiman* 3.18 cited by Silver, *History of Messianic Speculation in Israel* 75
51 Nuqabá'í 280 cited by Motlagh 357
52 Dinkird cited by Motlagh 356–7
53 'Abdu'l-Baha *Compilation of Compilations* 1.47.16–7. Shoghi Effendi *WOB* 101–2
54 *Vishnu Purana* 4.24. http://www.unification.net/ws/theme161.htm#14
55 *Memorandum of Manu* 1.68–72, cited by Munje 7–14. Mishra *Kalki Avatar* cited by Momen *Hinduism* 36 & 75, ref. 123
56 ***Before this same***, Buddhism *in Translation, Anagatavamsa* 481–2; *Tipitaka Buddhist Text, Prophecy of Maitreya ('Maitreyavyankarna')* cited by http://www.bibliotecapleyades.net/profecias/esp_profecia01f1.htm#2.%20Buddhist%20Prophecy%20~
A Messenger...full of kindness, Quran 9.128
57 Luke 21.24 auguring Rev. 11.2
58 Gregg *Revelation, Four Views: A Parallel Commentary* 174–201
59 Imam Ja'far cited by Nabil *Dawnbreakers* 49
60 Quran 32.5
61 http://www.en.wikipedia.org/wiki/Twelve_Imams
62 Muhyi'd-Din-i-Arabi cited by Nabil *Dawnbreakers* 50
63 Muhyi'd-Din-i-Arabi cited by Nabil *Dawnbreakers* 49
64 'Abdu'l-Baha *BWF* 221. Baha'u'llah *ESW* 141–2, *TB* 6.66. Shoghi Effendi *GPB* 93, 97
65 Rossing *Rapture Exposed*
66 ***Barred from offices***, H.M. Balyuzi *Muhammad and the Course of Islam* 23.252
Like their Christian fellow subjects, Maoz *Palestine During the Ottoman Period* 142
67 ***Fight those...until they pay the jizya***, Quran 9.29. Dermenghem *Life of Mahomet* 331 cited by Gail *Six Lessons on Islam* 3.14, 5.27
***A sign of their inferior* status**, Aghnides *Muhammadan Theories of Finance* 399–528 cited by Lal *Legacy of Muslim Rule in India*, http://www.voiceofdharma.org/books/tlmr/ch4.htm para 7. Quran 9.29
Kharaj*, also *jizya, get mention in Quran 9.29; *Hadith Bukhari* 2.23.475, 2.24.559, 3.034.425, 3.043.656, 4.53.358, 4.53.384, 4.53.385, 4.53.386, 4.53.388, 404, 4.55.657, 5.57.50, 5.59.351 & 8.076.433; *Sahih Muslim* 1.287, 1.289, 19.4294, 10.3830, 32.6327, 32.6328, 32.6330, 42.7065; & *Malik's Muwatta* 17.17.24.42, 17.17.24.44, 17.17.24.45, 17.17.24.46, 21.21.19.49a, 39.39.5.7, 40.40.2.2 & 54.54.10.26
68 Oren *Power, Faith and Fantasy, Damascus Blood Libel*, 123–4, 114 & 119–20
69 Deringil *Conversion and Apostasy* 547–75 & *Comparative Studies* 42.3. Maoz *Palestine during the Ottoman Period* 150. Sours *1844 Ottoman Edict of Toleration* 53–80.
70 ***Putting to death of the Christian***. *Official Declaration of the Sublime Porte, relinquishing the practice of Executions for Apostasy* to Sir Stratford Canning, March 21 1844, *FO 78/555 Inclosure 1 in No. 36* cited by Bromberek J. in http://www.mail-archive.com/bahai-st@list.jccc.edu/msg01236.html.
Henceforward neither shall Christianity be insulted. *Declaration of His Highness the Sultan to Sir Stratford Canning,* March 23 1844, *FO 27/695 Inclosure* [sic] *4 in No. 38* cited by Sours *1844 Ottoman Edict of Toleration* 72
71 A limited personal search in the Central Zionist Archives in Jerusalem unearthed legal records of Jews buying Palestinian property and land from the late 1840s
72 Mordecai Noah, *Discourse on the Restoration of the Jews* in http:// www.en.wikipedia.org/wiki/Zionism#Establishment_of_the_Zionist_movement, citing Rubinstein et al.. *The Dry Bones of Israel Revived* by George Bush, cited by Oren in *Power, Faith and Fantasy* 141–2
73 Dan. 12.7

Twin Messiahs

[74] Shoghi Effendi *GPB* 57
[75] Compilation, *Martyrdom of the Bab*
[76] *Zohar* 40.20.174; 43.31.342; 3.34.478
[77] ***John the Baptist...another time***, Baha'u'llah *Scriptures* 41.102
The Bayan deriveth all, Shoghi Effendi *GPB* 30
All that hath been revealed, The Bab *Selections from the Writings of* 167–8, cited by Baha'u'llah *ESW* 155 & Shoghi Effendi *GPB* 30
Were He to appear, Baha'u'llah *ESW* 171
[78] Baha'u'llah *Prayers and Meditations* 56.85, *GWB* 115.244–5
[79] ***At hand in less***, The Bab *Selections from Writings of* 69. 'Abdu'l-Baha *Memorials of the Faithful* 202
That so brief, Shoghi Effendi *GPB* 92
[80] Nabil *Dawnbreakers* xxi–xxii
[81] Baha'u'llah *PB* 17, *Summons of the Lord of Hosts* 1.131.67
[82] The Bab *Selections from the Writings of* 168. Shoghi Effendi *GPB* 57
[83] Shoghi Effendi *GPB* 94. Matt. 5.16. Mark 8.38. Luke 9.26. John 11.4, 40, 12.28, 14.13 & 17.5
[84] ***Descendant of Abraham***, 'Abdu'l-Baha *SAQ* 12.62–3; Shoghi Effendi *GPB* 94
(through a son of his other...), Shoghi Effendi *Lights* 1559.473
There shall come forth a rod, 'Abdu'l-Baha *SAQ* 12.62–3; Shoghi Effendi *GPB* 94
The Pre-Existent Root, Shoghi Effendi *Lights* 1559.473
Jesse, son of Sarah, Shoghi Effendi *Lights* 1559.473
Connection with the Faith of Judaism, Shoghi Effendi *Lights* 1559.473
Derived his descent, Shoghi Effendi *GPB* 94
[85] Shoghi Effendi *GPB* 100–2
[86] Baha'u'llah *ESW* 21
[87] ***'Thousand two hundred and ninety days'***, Shoghi Effendi *GPB* 9.151 & Dan. 12.11
Proclamation of the, Shoghi Effendi *Lights* 1662.494. 'Abdu'l-Baha *SAQ* 10.44
[88] ***Brought into fulfillment***, Shoghi Effendi *Directives* 148.55, *Letter*, 7 March 1955, cited by Universal House of Justice, *Messages 1963 to 1986* in http://www.bahai-library.com/published.uhj/messages.1963-86.html#738
Blissful consummation, 'Abdu'l-Baha & Shoghi Effendi *Lights. Prophecy of Daniel—1335 Days*, 1414.431–2. Shoghi Effendi *GPB* 9.151 about Dan. 12.11
[89] 'Abdu'l-Baha & Shoghi Effendi *Lights, Prophecy of Daniel—1335 Days*, 1414.431–2
[90] Universal House of Justice *Lights* 423 126. Shoghi Effendi *Messages to the Baha'i World 1950–1957* 169
[91] Shoghi Effendi *Citadel* 95–6
[92] ***Sacred mountain of God***, Isaiah 11.9. Shoghi Effendi *GPB* 194
Preaching Mountain, Rev. 16.16 & 21.10
In 1890, Baha'u'llah visited, Universal House of Justice *A Wider Horizon* 221
Cried out, trembling as if, Baha'u'llah *Tablet to Hardegg* 3.5–7
[93] ***This Day***, Baha'u'llah *TB* 1.4
Say unto, Baha'u'llah *TB* 1.1, *ESW* 145–6, *Scriptures* 48.120, 50.132, *PB* 90–1

Mount Carmel

94 ***This Spot,*** Baha'u'llah *Aqdas* 81.49; Shoghi Effendi (1941) *Messages to America* 45–6
Three Central Figures, Shoghi Effendi (1947/06/14) *Letter to the United Nations Special Committee on Palestine, Lights* 1675.498
Attracting widespread interest, Shoghi Effendi *Light of Divine Guidance* 1.188
Mount Carmel expresses, Universal House of Justice *Century of Light* 12.11.142
95 ***Tablet of Carmel,*** Universal House of Justice *A Wider Horizon* 221
So linked with, Shoghi Effendi *GPB* 315–6
From Mount Carmel will stream, Universal House of Justice *Compilation of Compilations* 1.746.334

Religious Revelation is Progressive

96 Dawkins *The Ancestor's Tale* 27
97 Baha'u'llah *GWB* 31.74
98 ***All the Prophets,*** Baha'u'llah *Gems* 44.33
United in their message, *'Abdu'l-Baha in London* 29, *BWF* 400
99 ***Liberate...men,*** Baha'u'llah *GWB* 34.78–80
Prophets of God, 'Abdu'l-Baha *DP* 7.170
100 Baha'u'llah *KI* 79–80
101 Adam supposedly authored *The Book of the Angel Raziel*
102 *Bhagavad Gita* 4.7–8 in http://www.unification.net/ws/theme161.htm#14
103 Universal House of Justice *Lights* 1691.2.502
104 'Abdu'l-Baha *PUP* 197–8. Baha'u'llah *GWB* 31.74
105 ***The standard of divine guidance,*** Baha'u'llah *KI* 10
Fulfilled the promise, Abdu'l-Baha *PUP* 197–8
106 'Abdu'l-Baha *SAQ* 30.124, *BWF* 400
107 ***Charged to act in a manner,*** Baha'u'llah *GWB* 34.78–80
The words and utterances flowing from, Baha'u'llah *KI* 176–8
Like the sun, *'Abdu'l-Baha in London* 29, *BWF* 400
The sun of today, 'Abdu'l-Baha *SAQ* 30.124, *BWF* 400
The sun of truth, *'Abdu'l-Baha DP* 14–5
108 Baha'u'llah *KI* 176–8, *Aqdas* 78.48, *PB* 5, *Tablet to Hardegg* 10.5, *DP* 5.153
109 ***Brought the message of love,*** 'Abdu'l-Baha *Paris Talks* 35
Manifestation of the Messiah, 'Abdu'l-Baha *Foundations of World Unity* 106
The light of Christ, 'Abdu'l-Baha *PUP* 346
110 'Abdu'l-Baha *SAQ* 10.39. Shoghi Effendi *GPB* 92
111 *Zohar* 32.36.214.
112 Riggs *Apocalypse Unsealed* 47–8
113 ***Symbolic of the perfection,*** Shoghi Effendi *Lights* 1373.414 & 1374.414
These religions are not, Shoghi Effendi *Directives* 141.51–2, *Lights* 1373.414
114 Rev. 1.8, 4.8, 11.17, 15.3, 16.7, 14, 19.6, 15 & 21.22
115 ***Which a Manifestation,*** Baha'u'llah *GWB* 25.60
To be distinguished, Baha'u'llah *GWB* 25.60
Once in about a thousand years, Baha'u'llah *KI* 199
116 http://www.khandro.net/about_numbers.htm

[117] ***The Prophetic Cycle hath, verily, ended***, Baha'u'llah *GWB* 25.60
Extend over a period, Shoghi Effendi *Compilation of Compilations* 2.1897.291, *The Significance of the Formative Age of Our Faith* 95.23.195 in http://www.bahai-library.com/published.uhj/messages.1963-86.toc.html
Its duration...fixed for a period, 'Abdu'l-Baha *Compilation of Compilations* 1.47.16–7. Shoghi Effendi *WOB* 101–2
[118] ***Consummation of all the Dispensations***, Shoghi Effendi *GPB* 100, *WOB* 101–2; 'Abdu'l-Baha *Compilation of Compilations* 1.47.16–7
The confluence of two universal, Shoghi Effendi *GPB* 54–5
First stage in a series, Shoghi Effendi *Compilation of Compilations* 2.1897.291, *The Significance of the Formative Age of Our Faith* 95.23.195 in http://www.bahai-library.com/published.uhj/messages.1963-86.toc.html

Identifying the 24 Revelation Elders

[119] 'Abdu'l-Baha *Will and Testament* 10
[120] ***'Elders' mentioned in the Book of Revelation***, Shoghi Effendi (1934) *GPB* 8, *Directives* 58.22, *Lights* 1713.507–8
In each cycle the guardians and holy souls, 'Abdu'l-Baha *SAQ* 11.57
[121] Shoghi Effendi *Unfolding Destiny* 428
[122] 'Abdu'l-Baha *Revelation of Baha'u'llah* 1.201, *Child of the Covenant* 240
[123] Christian lore identifies Gospel writers as the four Living-Beings: (1) Matthew as the Human-Being, (2) Mark as the Lion, (3) Luke as the Ox, and (4) John as the Eagle. Their order is interpretively apt: the Lion and Ox are the Enthroned-Ones set centrally; the *Human-Being* and *Eagle* are guardians flanking them
[124] Baha'u'llah *Bahiyyih Khanum* 1.2
[125] Rev. 5.11 & 19.6; 5.11 & 19.1; 6.9; 6.11, 11.10 & 19.10; 7.4; 15.2

Baha'i Writings interpret the Book of Revelation

[126] http://www.bahai-education.org. http://www.bahai-library.com. http://www.bahai-education.org/ocean. http://www.bahaibookstore.com/index.cfm
[127] Shoghi Effendi *Aqdas* 1–2, *GPB* 170–1
[128] ***Kitáb-i-Aqdas is of unique importance***, Shoghi Effendi *Aqdas* 12
The principal repository of that Law, *GPB* 213
A Book from above whose horizon, Baha'u'llah *TB* 17.266
[129] Nabil *Dawnbreakers* xxi–xxii. The Bab *Selections from the Writings of* 92
[130] Nabil *Dawnbreakers*. 'Abdu'l-Baha cited by Brittingham. Waite Shahnaz *Twelve Lessons, Lesson 10*. 'Abdu'l-Baha cited by: (1) Latimer in Foreword to *Light of the World* 8; (2) Esslemont in *Baha'u'llah and the New Era* 244; (3) Corinne True in *Chicago North Shore Review, September 26 1914*; (4) *The Diary of Juliet Thompson* in Washington (1912/05/07)

God, Religion, Law, and Afterlife

[131] Indian legend attributed to Rumi, *Masnavi* 3.5, http://en.wikipedia.org/wiki/Blind_Men_and_an_Elephant, modified as a ditty by John Godfrey Saxe (1816–87) in http://www.noogenesis.com/pineapple/blind_men_elephant.html
[132] Rumi *Masnavi* 3.5
[133] ***The followers of all the religions***, 'Abdu'l-Baha *DP* 155–6
Alas! The majority...attach themselves 'Abdu'l-Baha *DP* 32

134 'Abdu'l-Baha *SAQ* 11.46
135 'Abdu'l-Baha *SAQ* 11.47–8
136 'Abdu'l-Baha *SAQ* 11.47–8
137 **Judaism**: Levit. 19.18; Hillel, *Babylonian Talmud, Shabbat* 31a
Zoroastrianism: *Dadistan-i-Dinik* 94.5; *Shayast-na-Shayast* 13.29
Hinduism: *Mahabharata* 5.1517; *Anusasana Parva* 113.8
Buddhism: *Dhammapada Udana-Varga* 5.18
Christianity: *Matt.* 7.12
Islam: *Muhammad Farewell Sermon* in Hadiths *Al-Bukhari* 1.38 & *An-Nawawi* 13.4
Baha'i Faith: Baha'u'llah *TB* 6.64; *Aqdas* 148.73; *Summons of the Lord of Hosts* 5.44.202; *GWB* 125.265–66; *Gems* 62; *BWF* 185
138 'Abdu'l-Baha *Divine Philosophy* 14–5
139 'Abdu'l-Baha *SWA* 139.161
140 'Abdu'l-Baha *Foundation of World Unity* 68, *PUP* 192–3, *BWF* 259–60
141 Baha'u'llah *BWF* 103
142 Baha'u'llah *KI* 66
143 Baha'u'llah *GWB* 34.78–80
144 Baha'u'llah *GWB 81.157*
145 'Abdu'l-Baha *SAQ* 60.224
146 ***From the days of Adam***, 'Abdu'l-Baha *SAQ* 30.124
Physical death, 'Abdu'l-Baha *Gems* 64.47–48
Through his ignorance man fears, 'Abdu'l-Baha *PUP* 88–9
147 'Abdu'l-Baha *PUP* 88–9
148 Baha'u'llah *Arabic Hidden Words* 32 & 14. Motlagh *The Glorious Journey to God*
149 Levit. 16.1–34. Danby *Mishnah 2.Yoma*

The Symbolic Meanings of the Jewish Temple

150 Exod. 29.38–42. Num. 28.1–8. Sir. 50.1–21. Danby *Mishnah 5.Tamid*
151 Levit. 16.3–5. Num. 29.2, 8–9, 28.3–4. *Qumran Temple Scroll* 25.12–16. VanderKam *Dead Sea Scrolls Today*
152 Rev. 5.6, etc.. Aune *Word Biblical Commentary, Revelation, 52A* 323, note 6.d
153 Richman, Rabbi Chaim (1997) *The Holy Temple of Jerusalem* 24
154 Num. 29.2, 8 & 10
155 **The Ezekiel Temple measures**, Ezek. 40–48 esp. 42.16, also Sulley
The Qumran Temple extends, Fekkes 96
The Apocalypse Temple embraces, Rev. 21.22
156 Rev. 3.12, 7.15, 11.1, 2, 19 x 2, 14.15, 17, 15.5, 6, 8 x 2, 16.1, 17 & 21.22
157 1Chron. 24.1–19. Stuart *Commentary on the Apocalypse* 507
158 Baha'u'llah *TB* 7.84, *GWB* 43.92
159 Ginzberg *Legends of the Jews* 3.446–8
160 ***Form of the human temple***, Baha'u'llah *PB* 84
Calling from this, Baha'u'llah *Aqdas* 13.20 & 86.51, *PB* 39; Shoghi Effendi *PDC* 83.36
Thus have we built, Baha'u'llah *Summons of the Lord of Hosts, Tablet of the Temple* (*Suriy-i-Haykal*) 1.276.37, addressed to Pope Pius IX, Napoleon III, Czar Alexander II, Queen Victoria, and Násiri'd-Dín Sháh; Shoghi Effendi p. i note
161 Zech. 6.12–3
162 ***Build the Temple***, Baha'u'llah *Summons of the Lord of Hosts* 1.276.137
Clothed in divers attire, Baha'u'llah *KI* 153–54
The Cause of Baha'u'llah, 'Abdu'l-Baha *BWF* 400

[163] ***Template of the cosmos***, Isaac *Newton's Secrets* 56, *Sketch of the Jerusalem Temple*, Yahuda MS14f.5r.38; *Jewish Temple Rituals as a key to Understanding Biblical Prophecy*, Yahuda MS9.2f.1r

Sublime and holy concepts, Richman *To Dwell with G-d*

The garments of the High Priest, Josephus *Antiquities* 3.7.7

An emblem of heaven, Philo *Life of Moses* 2.24.117 & 122

[164] **Sacrificial-Altar**: Rev. 6.9, 8.3a, 8.5, 11.11, 14.18 & 16.7

Door: Rev. 3.8, 20 x 2 & 4.1, also *John* 10.9 & *Rev* 3.3, 8 & 4.1

Gold Incense-Altar: Rev. 8.3b & 9.13

Menorah: Rev. 1.13

Veil: Rev. 1.1–2

Ark of the Covenant: Rev. 11.19

[165] *Mishnah Shekalim* 6.1

[166] ***Dropped dead***, *Mishnah Shekalim* 6.2. *Mishnah Yoma* 5.2

Remain unknown, *2Maccabees*, 2.4–7

A few Jews do claim to know, Richman *Where is the Ark of the Covenant?* http://www.templeinstitute.org/ark_of_the_covenant.htm

[167] *2Maccabees*, 2.4–7

[168] Ezek. 43.7. 1Chr 28.2. Ps. 132.7–8. Ps. 99.5. Lam. 2.1. Exod. 25.17–22

[169] Rev. 8.3 & 9.13

[170] Rev. 11.19

[171] ***Divine* Presence**, Baha'u'llah *ESW* 118

Seated upon the Throne, Baha'u'llah *Summons of the Lord of Hosts* 1.122, *PB* 89; Shoghi Effendi *GPB* 96 & 211. Zech. 6.12

[172] ***Above the Ark-Cover***, Exod. 25.22, 30.6; Num. 7.89; Levit. 16.2

Aspect of God which, Saadia, *Beliefs and Opinions* 121 cited by Jay Michaelson in *Saadia Gaon's kavod nivra and its place in his philosophy of Judaism* in http://www.metatronics.net/lit/saadia.html; also cited by Scholem in *Major Trends in Jewish Mysticism* 111–112

[173] Gen. 1.27

[174] Boteach, Shmuley, *Intelligent Person's Guide to Judaism* 18

[175] 'Abdu'l-Baha *SWA* 3.12

[176] Baha'u'llah *Tablet of Hallelujah, Hallelujah, Hallelujah, O Glad Tidings*, translated by Lambden & McGlinn in http://bahai-library.com/bahaullah_halih_ya_bisharat

[177] Nachmanides commentary on Gen. 46.1. Uhrbach 63

The Millennium is the Jewish Seventh Millennium

[178] *Zohar 1BereshitA*.21.239, 3*Vaera*.32*Reckoning of the Messianic Era*.445. Gen. 7.11

[179] *Talmud Bavli, Sanhedrin* 97.71 cited in Laitman *From Chaos to Harmony* 157

[180] Also a Sabbatical Year crowns six normal work years

[181] Baha'u'llah *GWB* 31.74

[182] ***The Word of God***, Baha'u'llah *KI* 199

To which all the books, Baha'u'llah *KI* 199

Each believer of God, 'Abdu'l-Baha *Tablets of 'Abdu'l-Baha* 3.647

[183] *Zohar 1BereshitA*.21.239; 3*Vaera*.32*Reckoning of the Messianic Era*.445.

[184] *Zohar* 3*Vaera*, 34*Signs heralding the Mashiach*.483

New Jerusalem is Divine Civilization

185 ***The Holy City***, 'Abdu'l-Baha *SAQ* 13.67, *PUP* 102, *SW* 3.10.7; Rev. 21.2
A prophetic symbol, meaning, 'Abdu'l-Baha *Paris Talks* 84
The heavenly Jerusalem is none other, 'Abdu'l-Baha *PUP* 102; Baha'u'llah *Athar-i-Qalami-i-A'la*, *KI* 199
186 ***The City of God hath***, Baha'u'llah *Scriptures* 47.117, *Tablet to the Jews*
The heavenly religion which, 'Abdu'l-Baha *Tablets* 3.539, *Scriptures* 793.437, *SWA* 59; Baha'u'llah *KI* 199; *GWB* 125.269–70
This Day Jerusalem hath attained, Baha'u'llah *PB* 90–1
Law which the Prophet Isaiah, *GPB* 213
187 ***Material civilization is one***, 'Abdu'l-Baha *Tablet to the Hague 8*
As heretofore material civilization, 'Abdu'l-Baha *PUP* 170
188 'Abdu'l-Baha *Foundations of World Unity* 30–31, *PUP* 20 & 170
189 ***It is laid out***, Rev. 21.16
These specs have three. The intriguing four dimensional structures of Hayut-Man in his *Realizing the Heavenly Jerusalem* fall beyond the scope of this book, alas
190 Euler's formula. The only five perfect solids are the 4, 6, 8, 12, and 20-face (1) pyramid tetrahedron, (2) cube, (3) diamond octahedron, (4) dodecahedron, and (5) icosahedron
191 ***Diamonds of immortality***, Baha'u'llah *Gems* 20.17
Diamond blazing in the sun, Shoghi Effendi *Lights* 1571.476
Chips hewn from the Diamond, 'Abdu'l-Baha cited by Latimer Foreword *Light of the World* 8 in http://www.bahai-library.org/pilgrims/light.of.world.html
'Ere long the diamond age, 'Abdu'l-Baha (1919) *Tablets, Instructions and Words of Explanation* 18 cited by http://www.bahai-library.com/books/tablets.instructions.html and Latimer Foreword *Light of the World* 8 in http://www.bahai-library.org/pilgrims/light.of.world.html
192 Baha'u'llah *PB 89, TB* 1.4, *ESW* 112
193 ***Jewels and pearls***, *Babylonian Talmud, Bava Batra* 5.75a
12 pearls, each a single, Rev. 21.21
Form a unitary structure of 24, Chesser, personal communication Oundle 2006
As once the wall of the Temple, Rashi's Commentary on Chronicles 27.13 in http://www.jewishencyclopedia.com/view.jsp?artid=122&letter=T
194 Stuart *Commentary on the Apocalypse* 726 and 725–27. Other Christian scholars include Aune *52C*; 1165; Charles *Critical and Exegetical Commentary on the Revelation of St. John* 2.165–70, 207–08; Beale, *Revelation: Commentary on the Greek Text* 1079–93; Swete, *Apocalypse of St. John: the Greek Text*; Thomas, *Revelation: Exegetical Commentary*; Prigent, *Commentary on the Apocalypse of St. John*
195 Isaiah 54.12. *Babylonian Talmud, Bava Batra* 75a
196 'Abdu'l-Baha *PUP* 199
197 Josephus, *War* 5.5.7. Exod. 28.9–11
198 ***Is lighted up***, *Targum Genesis Bereshit Rabah* s31, cited by Jastrow *Dictionary* 836
Has the colors of the twelve colors, *Midrash Rabah* Num. *2.7*
Turns color, ***being now red***, Ginzberg *Legends of the Jews* 3.169–71
199 ***Shamir***, Babylonian *Talmud Pessachim* 54a; *Sotah 48b*
Faces of different hardness, Schumann *Gemstones of the World* 70
200 Stern *Complete Jewish Bible* 1536 & 1554. Rev. 4.3, 21.11, 21.18 & 21.19.
201 Rev. 21.19–20
202 Septuagint Exod. 28.17–20 & 39.10–13. Josephus *War* 5.5.7, *Antiquities* 3.7.5
203 *Midrash Rabah (Full Commentary) Num. 2.7*

[204] Ginzberg *Legends of the Jews* 3.169–71. *Targum Onkelos Aramaic Torah*, Exod. *28.17*. *Midrash Rabah* Exod. *39.9–13* lists prior Aramaic names for the breastplate-gemstones: *SHADRAGNIN (Reuben), SHIMPOZIN (Simeon), DAIKANITIN (Levi), BARDININ (Judah), SANPRINON (Issachar), ESMARGADIN (Zebulon), KOCHLIN (Dan), AVATIS (Naphtali), HIMOSION (Gad), KROMTISIN (Asher), PRALOKIN (Joseph)*, and *MARGALITOS (Benjamin)*. *Targum Neophiti* Exod. 28.17–20 & 39.10–13 lists recent Aramaic names: *SAMKATAH (red, Reuben), YARKATAH (green, Simeon), BARKATA (blessed, Levi), CHADCHADINAH (Judah), SAFRINAH (Issachar), 'AIN AGLAH (calf eye, Zebulon), LESHEM ZUZIN (glittering, Dan), VERULIN (color, Naphtali), ZMARGADIN* (purple, *Gad*), *KRUM YAMA RABAH (surface/color/vineyard of Mediterranean sea; Asher), BADLACHAH (material, Joseph)*, and *MARGALITAH (Benjamin)*

[205] Rev. 21.12 & 14

[206] 1Chron. 25.7

[207] Rev. 7.5–8

[208] Gen. 46.8–27 & 49.2–27. Num. 1.5–15, 13.4–14. Ezek. 48. *Midrash Rabah Num. 2.7*

[209] Gen. 29.32–30.24 & 35.18

[210] *Babylonian Talmud, Sotah* 2.36a

[211] *Encyclopaedia Biblica* 1903 Edition, *Tribes*, 4Q–Z. 5208 (5199–209)

[212] **Jews scorn the tribe of Dan**, 1Kings 12.29–30; *Judges* 18.30–31. **Christians condemn**, Hippolytus *De Antichristo* 14; Irenaeus *Adv. Haer*. 5.30.2

[213] Mark 3.13–19. Matt. 10.2–4. Luke 6.12–19. Acts 1.13 & 26. See *Commentary 1.20*. Curiously, neither John's Gospel nor Apocalypse fully lists disciples or apostles

[214] Rev. 21.10 & 13

[215] Rev. 21.14–20

[216] Philo *Life of Moses* 2.24.124–26, *Special Laws* 1.16.87. Josephus *Antiquities* 3.7.7

[217] Kircher *Oedipus Aegyptiacus* 2.2.177–78, courtesy St. John's College Library, Cambridge

[218] Charles 207–08. *Encyclopaedia Biblica* 1903 Edition, *Gemstones* 2E–K.4799–4812

[219] Duncan *The Calendar* 324

The Twelve Commandments of the Baha'i Faith

[220] Gen. 29.32–30.24 & 35.17–18. Rev. 7.5–8 & *Comments 7.5–8*

[221] 'Abdu'l-Baha *PUP* 440, 449–50, 453–455, *Paris Talks* 135–166. Terry Peter *'Abdu'l-Baha's Explanation of the Teachings of Baha'u'llah, Lights of 'Irfan* 143

[222] The comprehensive list of Twelve Commandments derives from:

- *Twelve Basic Bahai Principles Compiled from the Words of 'Abdu'l-Baha* (*SW* 1920/03/21) *11.1, Cover*
- *Lesson 10* in *Twelve Lessons* by Shahnaz Waite with a *Preface* by Shoghi Effendi in Barstow-Lovejoy Archives manuscript #485–H
- 'Abdu'l-Baha *PUP* 440 lists 13 teachings (his *Protection and guidance of the Holy Spirit* and *Religion must be the cause of unity* into *Unity of spiritual reality* can combine)
- 'Abdu'l-Baha *PUP* 453–457 lists 12 less matched teachings. My list of 12 gemstone teachings closely matches that of Shahnaz Waite
- The authorized gemstone list reported by Moffett in *New Keys to the Book of Revelation* 145 cannot be found by the Universal House of Justice (*Letter to author* 1999/11/15), Riggs (*Apocalypse Unsealed* 305), Lovejoy (personal communication 2005), or Terry (personal communication 2005)

[223] ***The gift of God***, *'Abdu'l-Baha in London* 19, *PUP* 32, *BWF* 244–5
People of the world, 'Abdu'l-Baha *DP* 8.183; Baha'u'llah *TB* 11.164
Light is now dawning, 'Abdu'l-Baha *SWA* 15.32; Shoghi Effendi *WOB* 39

224 ***Humanity must be saved***, 'Abdu'l-Baha *Tablet to the Hague* 4
Science, education, and civilization, *'Abdu'l-Baha in London* 28–9
By religion is meant, 'Abdu'l-Baha *Tablet to the Hague* 8
Each person must be, 'Abdu'l-Baha *PUP* 151
Reality is one and is not multiple, 'Abdu'l-Baha *BWF* 226
Is not divisible, 'Abdu'l-Baha *Foundations of World Unity* 13, *SWA* 227.298
225 ***Spiritual perfections***, 'Abdu'l-Baha *Paris Talks* 72
Both material blessings, 'Abdu'l-Baha *PUP* 90
Immortality of the spirit, 'Abdu'l-Baha *BWF* 7.323
The spiritual world is, 'Abdu'l-Baha *Foundations of World Unity* 51
Where there is neither separation, 'Abdu'l-Baha *PUP* 90
Unlimited by the narrow restrictions, 'Abdu'l-Baha *PUP* 289
226 ***Light is good***, 'Abdu'l-Baha *DP* 2.25
In the East or, Baha'u'llah *KI* 159
The sun of reality is, 'Abdu'l-Baha *PUP* 94
Love the Sun of Truth from, 'Abdu'l-Baha *Paris Talks* 137
It has now shone, 'Abdu'l-Baha SW (1920/03/21) 11.1.10–1
If the nations of, 'Abdu'l-Baha *BWF* 226
Religious reality is not, 'Abdu'l-Baha *PUP* 197–8
The continuity of, Shoghi Effendi *Guidance* 118
The great religions, Shoghi Effendi *PDC* p. v
227 ***Science and Religion should***, *'Abdu'l-Baha in London* 71
As the two wings, *'Abdu'l-Baha in London* 28–9
Should a man, 'Abdu'l-Baha *Paris Talks* 143
The harmony of, 'Abdu'l-Baha *PUP* 455, *BWF* 247
Every religion which, *'Abdu'l-Baha in London* 28–9
These two most, Baha'u'llah *PB* xii
Sciences uplift, Baha'u'llah *ESW* 26, *TB* 51–2
The best fruit, Baha'u'llah *Scriptures* 50.133
Science is the discoverer, 'Abdu'l-Baha *Foundations of World Unity* 48
Science without religion is lame, Einstein Albert, http://www.en.wikipedia.org/wiki/Albert_Einstein
228 'Abdu'l-Baha *Tablet to the Hague* 7, *BWF* 288
229 ***Be free from***, 'Abdu'l-Baha *Paris Talks* 137
And adorned, 'Abdu'l-Baha *DP* 8.185
Religious, racial, 'Abdu'l-Baha *Scriptures* 570.277
Until they are dispelled, 'Abdu'l-Baha *PUP* 181
Racial prejudice, Shoghi Effendi (1938) *Advent of Divine Justice* 33–4
230 ***All the divine Manifestations***, 'Abdu'l-Baha *PUP* 31–2
All created things, 'Abdu'l-Baha *PUP* 123
For thousands of years, 'Abdu'l-Baha *Lights* 716.212–3
Wars and disputes shall cease, *'Abdu'l-Baha in London* 83
Which is now at long last, Universal House of Justice *Promise of World Peace* 1.1
Soon enough, 'Abdu'l-Baha *SAQ* 12.65
231 ***Knowledge is as wings***, Baha'u'llah *ESW* 26, *TB* 51–2
The primary, the most urgent, 'Abdu'l-Baha *Secret of Divine Civilization* 109–10
Children must be educated, Baha'u'llah *Scriptures* 574.278
All cannot be scientists, 'Abdu'l-Baha *PUP* 108
All must receive training, 'Abdu'l-Baha *PUP* 300
First: whole hearted service, 'Abdu'l-Baha *Lights* 716.212–3
232 'Abdu'l-Baha *PUP* 455

[233] ***Leaders should choose***, Baha'u'llah *ESW* 138
And a great means, 'Abdu'l-Baha *Scriptures* 575.279
Then, to whatsoever city, Baha'u'llah *TB* 11.165–6
[234] ***True civilization***, 'Abdu'l-Baha *DP* 9.27
Then, should any king, Baha'u'llah *TB* 11.165, *GWB* 117.249
Global supreme tribunal, 'Abdu'l-Baha *DP* 9.27, *Scriptures* 573.278

War and Peace

[235] ***Most Great Peace—the surest***, Baha'u'llah *TB* 2.125, *Proclamation of Baha'u'llah to the Kings and Leaders of the World*
These fruitless strifes, Baha'u'llah *PB* viii
[236] ***The fire of war was blazing***, *'Abdu'l-Baha in London* 36–7
The Most Great Peace should, 'Abdu'l-Baha (1869) *PUP* 28
[237] Shoghi Effendi *PDC* 48
[238] ***While peace is the pretext***, Baha'u'llah *Secret of Divine Civilization* 60
The smoke of corruption, Baha'u'llah *TB* (1888) 4.39
[239] ***Now that ye***, Baha'u'llah *Summons of the Lord of Hosts* 1.180.93, *PB* 12.13
It is incumbent upon, Baha'u'llah *ESW* 30–1
Promote the Lesser Peace, Baha'u'llah *TB* 7.89
[240] *Yerushalayim Shel Matah/Ma'alah* in *Jerusalem Talmud, Berechat* 4.3.8a
[241] Origen cited by Armstrong *Jerusalem: One City, Three Faiths* 171
[242] Hajjaj *The Prophet's Night Journey and Ascent*
[243] Baha'u'llah *Proclamation of Baha'u'llah* 8, 39, *Aqdas* 90, 53
[244] Baha'u'llah *The Seven Valleys and the Four Valleys, The Valley of Knowledge* 12
[245] ***We are on the eve***, 'Abdu'l-Baha (*September 26, 1914*) cited by Corinne True, *Chicago North Shore Review* & Dr J.E. Esslemont in *Baha'u'llah and the New Era* 243
All that which is, 'Abdu'l-Baha (1912) *Tablets of the Divine Plan* 22–3
Only a spark, 'Abdu'l-Baha *PUP* 469
A great melee of the civilized nations, 'Abdu'l-Baha cited by Esslemont, *Baha'u'llah and the New Era* 244, August 3 1914
By 1917 kingdoms will fall, 'Abdu'l-Baha cited by Corinne True, *Chicago North Shore Review, September 26 1914*
Armed troops and artillery, 'Abdu'l-Baha (1913) *Scriptures* 671.344
The flame of war is so ablaze, 'Abdu'l-Baha *Letter to Root*
The most advanced, 'Abdu'l-Baha (1914) *SWA* 225.284
In times gone by, 'Abdu'l-Baha *Paris Talks* 107
Warfare in former centuries, 'Abdu'l-Baha (1912) *PUP* 123–24, *BWF* 231–32
Stupendous force, 'Abdu'l-Baha, *Japan Will Turn Ablaze* 1.9.51
[246] Shoghi Effendi *Letter to Mrs. Louise Erickson, Extracts from US Baha'i News* 77 (1933/03/25)
[247] Shoghi Effendi (1941) *Messages to America* 45–6
[248] Shoghi Effendi (1941) *Messages to America* 45–6
[249] Shoghi Effendi (1957) *Citadel* 124–54
[250] Shoghi Effendi (1941) *PDC* 276–77.113–4
[251] Shoghi Effendi (1941) *PDC* 276–77.113–4
[252] ***Weakening of the pillars***, Baha'u'llah *ESW* 28
In the West, Shoghi Effendi *WOB* 182–3
Assisted and encouraged, Shoghi Effendi *WOB* 182–3

253 ***A unity of nations***, 'Abdu'l-Baha *SWA* 15.32
Lead through a series, Shoghi Effendi (1947) *Citadel* 33
254 Shoghi Effendi (1954) *Citadel* 124–127
255 ***The unfurling of the banner***, Shoghi Effendi *Citadel* 33
Nations shall, Isaiah 2.4, Joel 4.10, Micah 4.3, *'Abdu'l-Baha in London* 20
256 ***The foundations of***, 'Abdu'l-Baha *PUP* 198
Made the Law of God, Baha'u'llah *ESW* 12
The light of true religion, 'Abdu'l-Baha *PUP* 141
257 *'Abdu'l-Baha in London* 29
258 ***Those who were the seekers***, 'Abdu'l-Baha *SAQ* 14.76–7
The Jews await the Messiah, 'Abdu'l-Baha *TAB* 1.vii
259 ***With such earnestness***, Baha'u'llah *KI* 4–5
Leaders of religion, Baha'u'llah *KI* 15
How many have...yearningly, Baha'u'llah *KI* 4–5
260 'Abdu'l-Baha *DP* 7.170
261 ***Pharisees...denied***, 'Abdu'l-Baha *SAQ* 13.71
The words of the prophets, 'Abdu'l-Baha *PUP* 199
Intoxicated with the wine, Baha'u'llah *Scriptures, Tablet to the Jews* 47.116–7
262 ***Christian divines have failed***, Baha'u'llah *KI* 24–5
The adherents of Jesus, Baha'u'llah *KI* 80
263 ***The people of the Qur'án***, Baha'u'llah *KI* 87
Corruption of the text, Baha'u'llah *KI* 86
When Muslims say, Baha'u'llah *Gems* 14.11–2
264 ***Each sect* [Faith] *hath picked***, Baha'u'llah *TB* 6.60
Leaders of religion, Baha'u'llah *KI* 15
The beginnings of all great religions, *'Abdu'l-Baha in London* 125
265 'Abdu'l-Baha *PUP* 266
266 Rev. 12.3–4, 7, 9, 13, 16–17, 14–15, 13.1–2, 4, 11, 16.13, 17.3, 7–8, 11–13, 16–17, 19.19–20, 20.2, 4 & 10
267 *Hadith of Gadeer Khum*: http://www.wofis.com/asset/Books/018.pdf 22–4. http://www.209.85.135.104/search?q=cache:buBIzyJH_3wJ:www.wofis.com/asset/Books/018.pdf+Ghadeer+Khum+hadith&hl=en&ct=clnk&cd=7. Adib Taherzadeh, *The Covenant of Baha'u'llah* 2.6.99 & 2.12.156–7
268 Gail, *Six Lessons on Islam* 6.29
269 Duncan *The Calendar* 179
270 Balyuzi, H.M., *Muhammad and the Cause of Islam*, 24.254–7. http://www.en.wikipedia.org/wiki/Twelve_Imams
271 Hawting *The first dynasty of Islam* Chapter 24 cited by http://www.en.wikipedia.org/wiki/Umayyad. *Sulh al-Hasan* in http://www.balagh.net/english/ahl_bayt/sulh_al-hasan
272 ***What a great civilization***, 'Abdu'l-Baha *PUP* 346–7
Ornament of the World, Menocal, *Ornament of the World*
1492 the year of Spain's greatest shame, Raphael, *The Alhambra Decree*
273 Baha'u'llah *ESW* 126
274 Scruton, *The West and the Rest* 123

Parallel Interpretation of the Apocalypse

[275] 'Abdu'l-Baha *SAQ* 30.123

[276] *Zohar* 1.21.250, http://www.kabbalah.com/k/index.php/p=zohar/zohar&vol=2&sec=42. *Babylonian Talmud Hagigah* 14b

[277] Baha'u'llah *KI* 254–5

[278] ***1***, Rev. 5.5, 6.1, 7.13, 15.7, 17.1, 18.21, 19.17 & 21.9
7, Rev. 1.4 x 2, 1.12, 1.16, 5.1, 5.6, 8.2, 10.4, 15.1 & 16.1–17
10, Rev. 2.10, 12.3 & 13.1
12, Rev. 7.5–8, 12.1, 21.12 & 21, 21.12, 14, 16 & 19–20
24, Rev. 4.4 & 21.12
144,000, Rev. 7.4 & 14.1

[279] ***Mighty***, Rev. 10.1, 18.2 & 18.21
Cloud, Rev. 1.7, 11.12 & 14.14
Rainbow, Rev. 4.3 & 10.1
In his hand Rev. 1.16, 2.1, 5.1, 10.2, 14.14 & 20.1

[280] ***WORD* itself**, Rev. 1.1–2, 3, 9, 6.9, 12.11, 17.17, 19.9, 19.13, 20.4, 21.5, 21.6, 22.6, 7, 9, 10, 18 & 19; *John* 1.1; Baha'u'llah *KI* 64
Spirit, Rev. 1.4, 2.7, 11, 17, 29, 3.1, 3.6, 13, 22, 4.5, 5.6, 14.13, 19.10, 22.6 & 22.17
Witness, Rev. 1.5, 2.13, 3.14, 11.3 & 17.6
Trump-Ta-Ra, Rev. 8.13, 9.12, 11.14, 12.12, 18.10, 16 & 19
Glory of God, Rev. 15.8, 21.11 & 23
Dwell* and *dwelling, Rev. 7.15, 12.12, 13.6, 15.5 & 21.3
Anointed, Rev. 1.1, 2, 5, 9, 11.15, 12.10, 20.4 & 6

[281] Rev. 1.18, 2.6, 9, 10, 13, 14 x 2, 17, 3.7, 7.5–8, 8.11, 9.11, 14.1, 8, 16.16, 19.1, 21.8, 2.14, 3.12 & 9.14

[282] Baha'u'llah *Aqdas* 182.85, *PB* 13.196

[283] Baha'u'llah's given name *Husayn 'Ali* is spelled *h-s-y-n-'-l-y*. The Bab's given name *'Ali Muhammad* is spelled *'-l-y-m-h-m-d*. The 7 names of the 12 Christian Apostles were Judah (2), Simeon (2), Jacob (2), Matthew (3), Andrew (1), Philip (1), and John (1). The 7 names of the traditional 12 Shi'i Muslim Imams were Ali (3), Hasan (2), Husayn (1), Zainul (1), Muhammad (3), Jafar (1), and Musa (1).

[284] The *Crawford Aramaic Text: The Apocalypse of St. John in a Syriac Version Hitherto Unknown* (lxxix–1897 *Crawford's Haigh Hall, Wigan, no. 11*, John Rylands Library, Manchester, also http://www.preteristarchive.com/Books/pdf/1897_gwynn_syriac-apocalypse.pdf) may be original, unlike other Aramaic versions translated from Greek. Certainly, at least two of its Aramaic words in vv. 2.22 and 10.2 fit far better than equivalent Greek words that appear to be mistranslations of the original Aramaic. Apropos, see also Scott RBY (1928), *The Original Language of the Apocalypse* 6 and Torrey, C. C. (1941) *Documents of the Primitive Church* 160)

[285] See above endnote 283

[286] Schreiber 167

[287] Schreiber 167–8

[288] Riggs Chapter 13

Muslim Militarism and Malignant Materialism

289 **Golden calf**, Exod. 32.4
Day of heavy slaughter, Isaiah 30.25
290 'Abdu'l-Baha *PUP* 346–47
291 Ameer *The Spirit of Islam* 442 cited by Gail in *Six Lessons on Islam* 3.14
292 Quran 29.45, 3.84, 5.68, 3.64 & 4.47
293 ***People of the Book who disbelieve***, Quran 98.5
Take Jews and Christians as allies, Quran 5.51–5
People of the Book down from...killed some, Quran 33.26
294 **Killed off the Amalekites**, *1Sam.* 15.32-34, about how Samuel killed King Agag, the last surviving Amalekite
Massacred cities of Canaanites, Josh. 10 passim
Christian crusaders systematically slaughtered, Armstrong, *Jerusalem: One City, Three Faiths* 274
295 Baha'u'llah *KI* 199, *GWB* 125.269–70
296 Scruton, *The West and the Rest* in the New Yorker, *The Revolt of Islam: When did the conflict with the West begin and how could it end?* 2002/11/19. Pfaff, William, *Islam and the West: Incompatibility of Values*. Lewis, *Revolt of Islam; The Arabs in History; The Crisis of Islam: Holy War and Unholy Terror*. International Herald Tribune, Paris 2003/12/12.
297 Notice posted by Peter Andrews at *British Society of Indexers* meeting, Winchester 2008
298 Shoghi Effendi (1954) *Citadel* 124–7
299 ***Cities like New York***, 'Abdu'l-Baha (1912) *PUP* 261–2
Spirituality...has been, 'Abdu'l-Baha (1912) *Scriptures* 553.268, *PUP* 221
300 Gen. 11.1–9
301 Lunn Pete *Basic Instincts: Human Nature and the New Economics*
302 ***Human brotherhood***, 'Abdu'l-Baha *PUP* 150 & *Foundations of World Unity* 14
Man...is in need of, 'Abdu'l-Baha *PUP* 150. *Foundations of World Unity* 38
303 Shoghi Effendi (1954) *Citadel* 124
304 James Cromwell in http://www.iaindale.blogspot.com/2007/01/quotes-of-day_16.html #c116897737062503389
305 *Vishnu-Purana* 4.24, translated by H. H. Wilson from the Sanskrit. http://www .theosofie.info/kaliyuga.pdf
306 Campbell *The Power of Myth* 8
307 Shoghi Effendi (1954) *Citadel* 124–7
308 Packard *Waste Makers*. Ponting *Green History of the World*
309 ***Unbelievable blindness, cruelty***, Lee, *Outbreak of the First World War* 47
All nations have been tricked, Rev. 18.23
310 Gladwell Malcolm *The Tipping Point, The Magic Number of One Hundred and Fifty* 169 (otherwise called *Dunbar's number of 150*)
311 David Rothkopf *The Superclass*, http://www.uk.youtube.com/watch?v=LHtNFZ6KopE
312 ***Useful, efficient***, Bartelle (2005) *The Future of Online Search* on Google at http:// www.edition.cnn.com/2005/TECH/12/23/john.bartelle/index.html
Merck makes products *for the people*, George W. Merck, Talk at Medical College of Virginia, Richmond, December 1, 1950 cited by Kay, John in *The Sick Need More than just Healthy Profits*, Financial Times 2004/11/23, p. 19
Cut waste, not corners, David Fison *Times,* on Skanska 2005/05/24

313 ***Fallen, fallen***, Isaiah 13.19, 21.9 & 14.22–3
Against Babylon, Jeremiah 51.1–64 excerpted passim
314 Rev. Chapters 17 and 18 & v. 19.2
315 ***Babylon...a waste of rubble***, 'Abdu'l-Baha cited in *The Diary of Juliet Thompson* 1912/04/25
Relentless and all-pervasive, Shoghi Effendi (1957) *Citadel* 124–54
Rampant and cancerous materialism, Shoghi Effendi (1953) *Messages to the Baha'i World 1950–57* 136
Crass materialism, Shoghi Effendi (1957) *Citadel* 125
316 **Some rabbis call America**, personal communication, 2006.
The love of money, 1Tim. 6.10.
Capitalism is a curse, Hijazi, *Islam AH 01–250* 30–1
317 Rev. 17.1–2, 5, 16–8, 18.2 & 21
318 Bertrand & Lemagnen, *Bayeux Tapestry*
319 http://www.www.csis.org/media/csis/pubs/071119_iran.is&nuclearwar.pdf
320 Rev. 18.8–19 passim
321 Shoghi Effendi *WOB* 193–94 & *Lights of Guidance* 444.133
322 ***A catastrophe of undreamed***, Shoghi Effendi (1954) *Citadel* 124–7
The world is in travail, Baha'u'llah *GWB* 61.118–9
Winds of despair are, Baha'u'llah 11.171
323 ***These events shall suddenly***, Baha'u'llah *GWB* 61.118–9. Shoghi Effendi *Advent of Divine Justice* 81
Governments and peoples, Universal House of Justice, *Lights* 443.132
324 Shoghi Effendi *Messages to America* 22–3
325 Shoghi Effendi *WOB* 193–4
326 Shoghi Effendi (1931) *WOB* 46
327 But some economists did expect trouble, like Galbraith (*World Economy Since the Wars*), Batra (*Surviving the Great Depression*), or Moffitt (*World's Money*)
328 Bill Bonner (2007/01/01) *Icebergs in the Ocean of Global Liquidity*. http://www.daily reckoning.com.au/global-liquidity

Spiritual Economics

329 Attributed to Mahatma Gandhi
330 **It puts people before**, Phillips *Seven Laws of Money*
If there is no Bible, *Mishnah Avot* 3.17
331 Universal House of Justice, *Promise of World Peace* 7
332 'Abdu'l-Baha *PUP* 455 & *DP* 7
333 ***Proposals...are practicable***, 'Abdu'l-Baha *Foundations of World Unity* 32
The higher aspirations, 'Abdu'l-Baha *Tablet to August Forel* 26
The Baha'i Cause covers, 'Abdu'l-Baha *PUP* 238
All economic problems, 'Abdu'l-Baha cited by H, C. Ives in *Portals to Freedom* 156
The true foundation, 'Abdu'l-Baha (1912) *PUP* 238–9
Manifest true economics, 'Abdu'l-Baha *PUP* 238
334 ***Remedy for the economic question***, 'Abdu'l-Baha *PUP* 455
Fundamental change, Shoghi Effendi *Lights* 1871.550
Our *generation of the half-light*, Shoghi Effendi *WOB* 168
Widen in accordance, 'Abdu'l-Baha *Light of the World 45*, *The Bahá'í World* 4. 451 cited by Shams, Badi

The primary consideration, Shoghi Effendi *Directives* 55.20, *Lights* 1864.549, *Bahá'í News* 2 1935/03
A list...follows, Badi Shams *A Bahá'í Perspective on Economics of the Future* excerpted
335 ***Neither accepts the theories***, Shoghi Effendi *Lights of Guidance* 1862.549
Wealth is praiseworthy, 'Abdu'l-Baha *The Secret of Divine Civilization* 24
336 ***An inseparable***, Shoghi Effendi *Lights of Guidance* 1870.550, Letter 1935/12/26
Whatever the progress, Shoghi Effendi *Aqdas* 56.192, Letter 1937/03/22
Busy themselves with, Baha'u'llah *TB* 3.24
Identical with the worship of God, Baha'u'llah *Scriptures* 82.143
337 ***Every assistance***, Shoghi Effendi *Lights* 411.121
Orphanages, free schools, and hospitals, Shoghi Effendi *Lights* 411.121
Concern themselves with, Baha'u'llah *PB* 9; 'Abdu'l-Baha *Foundations of World Unity* 44, SW 8.231
Men...overburdened with riches, 'Abdu'l-Baha (1911) *Paris Talks* 151–4
338 ***Rules and laws should be***, 'Abdu'l-Baha *SAQ* 314–5, 281
Under present systems, 'Abdu'l-Baha *PUP* 107
339 Shoghi Effendi *Aqdas* 56.192, Letter 1937/03/22
340 ***The right of every human being***, 'Abdu'l-Baha *Paris Talks* 154, *PUP* 216
Deplorable superfluity, 'Abdu'l-Baha *Paris Talks* 154
Special laws...dealing with, 'Abdu'l-Baha (1911) *Paris Talks* 151–4
341 'Abdu'l-Baha *Foundations of World Unity* 37–8
342 'Abdu'l-Baha *Paris Talks* 151–4
343 ***You did a wonderful thing***, 'Abdu'l-Baha cited by Esslemont *Baha'u'llah and the New Era* 144
Rules and laws should be established, 'Abdu'l-Baha *SAQ* 281
Moderate profits to manufacturers, 'Abdu'l-Baha *SAQ* 282–3
Socialists may justly, 'Abdu'l-Baha (1912) *PUP* 238–9
Strikes are due, 'Abdu'l-Baha *SAQ* 273
344 ***Plan with utmost wisdom***, 'Abdu'l-Baha SW 8.231
The rights of the working people, 'Abdu'l-Baha *SAQ* 317
345 ***A just medium***, Abdu'l-Baha *BWF* 282
Every factory, 'Abdu'l-Baha *Foundations of World Unity* 43
Workmen...receive wages and a share, 'Abdu'l-Baha *SAQ* 315
Partners in every work, 'Abdu'l-Baha *Baha'i Scriptures* 668.342
346 ***When they cease work, becoming feeble***, 'Abdu'l-Baha *SAQ* 315
A manufacturer will not be allowed, 'Abdu'l-Baha *SW* 8.11
347 ***Social inequality***, 'Abdu'l-Baha *Lights* 1865.549, *PUP* 41,8.229
All must enjoy the greatest, 'Abdu'l-Baha *Foundations of World Unity* 41
Wages should definitely be unequal, Shoghi Effendi *Lights* 1867.550
348 'Abdu'l-Baha (1911) *Paris Talks* 151–4
349 'Abdu'l-Baha *SAQ* 274
350 'Abdu'l-Baha (1911) *Paris Talks* 151–4
351 ***The peasant class***, 'Abdu'l-Baha (1912) *Foundations of World Unity* 39–41
Solved with the farmer, 'Abdu'l-Baha *Lights* 1858.547
In every village a board, 'Abdu'l-Baha *Lights* 1858.547
House of finance, 'Abdu'l-Baha (1912) *Scriptures* 831.453, Letter in Universal House of Justice 1919/07/25 cited by Badi Shams
Necessary expenses for orphans, 'Abdu'l-Baha (1912) *Foundations of World Unity* 39–41,8.229 1922/12, *The Bahá'í World* 4.451

This system is all thus ordered, 'Abdu'l-Baha *Foundations of World Unity* 39–41 passim, *The Bahá'í World* 4.451
The greatest achievements, 'Abdu'l-Baha *Foundations of World Unity* 39–41 passim
352 ***Trustees will be elected***, 'Abdu'l-Baha *Foundations of World Unity* 39–41 passim, *The Bahá'í World* 4.451
Tithes, taxes on animals, 'Abdu'l-Baha in Universal House of Justice *Letter 1912/10/04* cited by Badi Shams, (1912) *Light of the World* 45, *The Bahá'í World* 4.451, *Foundations of World Unity* 39–41 passim
Income...greater than...needs, 'Abdu'l-Baha *PUP* 217
Government, the poor, the infirm, 'Abdu'l-Baha *Light of the World 45, The Bahá'í World* 4. 451, Universal House of Justice *Letter 1912/10/04* cited by Badi Shams
If after all these expenses, 'Abdu'l-Baha *Foundations of World Unity* 39–41 passim, *The Bahá'í World* 4.451
353 ***When the village is reconstructed***, 'Abdu'l-Baha *Scriptures* 831.453, Universal House of Justice *Letter 1919/07/25* cited by Badi Shams
For larger cities, 'Abdu'l-Baha *Foundations of World Unity* 39–41 passim, *The Bahá'í World* 4.451
354 ***A small force for the purposes***, 'Abdu'l-Baha *Secret of Divine Civilization* 65
Hereby the world may be freed, Baha'u'llah *Scriptures* 60.139
To pile up more weapons, 'Abdu'l-Baha *Secret of Divine Civilization* 61–2
355 Baha'u'llah *PB* xii
356 ***World community in which***, Shoghi Effendi *PB* xii–xiii, *Compilation of Compilations* 2.1608.177, *WOB* 35
Uniform and universal system, Shoghi Effendi *The Bahá'í Peace Program* 8
Interest on money with moderation, Baha'u'llah *TB* 132–3
Limit *tariffs*, Shoghi Effendi *WOB* 35
Permit *no more trusts*, 'Abdu'l-Baha *Foundations of World Unity* 43
357 ***Readjustment ensures the stability***, 'Abdu'l-Baha *PUP* 181
Each individual member, 'Abdu'l-Baha *PUP* 41, 8.229
Without any harm, 'Abdu'l-Baha *Foundations of World Unity* 39–41

Translation Section

358 **The diminutive *biblion***, Rev. 3.5 & 20.15
The super-diminutive book-word *biblaridion*, Rev. 10.2, 9 &10
What had to happen fast, Rev. 1.1 & 22.6
I am coming soon, Rev. 2.16, 3.11, 11.14, 22.7, 12 & 20
Cherem, Rev. 22.3
359 *Chalice* Rev. 5.8, 8.3, 5. *Pitcher* Rev. 15.7, 16.1, etc. (93 types of Temple vessel existed)
360 Some six 2–6th century papyrus fragments; various 2–7th century Greek and Latin patristic quotations; eleven 4–10th century UNCIAL CODICES; various 4–12th century Latin, Armenian, Georgian, Coptic, Ethiopic, Syriac versions; and 293 miniscule 18th century manuscripts
361 Aune, *52C* 1267–87
362 Aune, *52A* clix–clx
363 Alexandria's 3rd century bishop Dionysius who opposed millennialism, cited by Eusebius, *Church History,* 7.25.26–27. http://www.ccel.org/ccel/schaff/npnf201.iii.xii.xxvi.html ?highlight=barbarous,idioms–highlight#highlight

364 *Aqdas* 11
365 'Abdu'l-Baha *Má'idih-i-Ásmání* 2.82, translated by Badi Daemi
366 Louw & Nida *Greek-English Lexicon of the New Testament* 1.13.32.153
367 Louw & Nida *Greek-English Lexicon of the New Testament* 2.2.54.254. Aune *53A* 96
368 Aune *52A* 255
369 Louw & Nida *Greek-English Lexicon of the New Testament* 1.11.27.125, 1.53.46.539, 1.88.24.745. Aune *52A* 359
370 Exod. 19.6
371 Louw & Nida *Greek-English Lexicon of the New Testament* 1.88.173.761 & 1.88.78.762
372 Barclay Newman *Concise Greek-English Dictionary of the New Testament* 202
373 Aune *52B* 786 & *52C* 965–66
374 Aune *52B* 844
375 Barclay Newman *Concise Greek-English Dictionary of the New Testament* 127
376 Aune *52B* 876–78
377 Aune *52C* 1044 & 1064
378 Louw & Nida *Greek-English Lexicon of the New Testament* 1.65.24.623 & 52.626
379 Aune *52C* 1174–75
380 Zech 14.11. Arthur Eidelman, personal communication Jerusalem 2005. Aune *52C* 1178–9
381 Aune *52C* 1239, note 21.d
382 Aune *52B* 654, note 7.c-c
383 Aune *52B* 721, note 16.a-a
384 Aune *52A* clxxxiv
385 Aune *52B* 858, note 16.a-a
386 Barclay Newman *Concise Greek-English Dictionary of the New Testament* 123
387 Aune, *52C* 1112, note 8.c–c
388 Aune *52A* clxiii–clxvi
389 http://www.fordham.edu/halsall/basis/everyman.html
390 Aune *52A* cxcii
391 Aune *52B* 833
392 Thompson 43–5
393 Aune *52A* 216, 219
394 Aune *52B* 858, note 16.a-a

Proposed Structure for the Book of Revelation

395 Rev. 4.1, 7.9, 9.12, 15.5, 18.1 & 19.1, also 1.1–2, 19
396 Rev. 1.4 x 2, 1.12, 1.16, 5.1, 5.6, 10.4, also 8.2, 15.1
397 Ben-Daniel *The Apocalypse in the Light of the Temple* 217–25 (modified)
398 'Abdu'l-Baha *SAQ* 11.45–61
399 Ben-Daniel *The Apocalypse in the Light of the Temple* 217–25 (modified)
400 *'Abdu'l-Baha in London* 19

INDEX

By Indexer Nigel d'Auvergne, http://www.nigeldauvergne.co.uk

G

H

I

T

Made in the USA
Middletown, DE
14 November 2014